MVVM Survival Guide for Enterprise Architectures in Silverlight and WPF

Eliminate unnecessary code by taking advantage of the MVVM pattern—less code, fewer bugs

Ryan Vice

Muhammad Shujaat Siddiqi

BIRMINGHAM - MUMBAI

MVVM Survival Guide for Enterprise Architectures in Silverlight and WPF

First published: August 2012

Production Reference: 1010812

Published by Packt Publishing Ltd.
Livery Place
35 Livery Street
Birmingham B3 2PB, UK.

ISBN 978-1-84968-342-5

www.packtpub.com

Cover Image by Tony Shi (shihe99@hotmail.com)

Credits

Authors
Ryan Vice
Muhammad Shujaat Siddiqi

Reviewer
Kanishka (Ken) Abeynayake

Acquisition Editor
Dhwani Devater

Lead Technical Editor
Dhwani Devater

Technical Editors
Felix Vijay
Manasi Poonthottam
Lubna Shaikh

Copy Editors
Brandt D'Mello
Laxmi Subramanian
Alfida Paiva

Project Coordinator
Abhishek Kori

Proofreader
Lesley Harrison

Indexer
Rekha Nair

Graphics
Manu Joseph

Production Coordinator
Melwyn D'sa

Cover Work
Melwyn D'sa

Foreword

Rich client development remains one of the most popular forms of application development, both from a user and a developer point of view. While nobody denies the importance of thin-client interface technologies such as HTML(5), it is clear that consumers and enterprises alike enjoy using applications that provide a rich, powerful, productive, and sometimes fun experience. Evidence ranges from the current App Craze on mobile devices to the long-running history of rich business applications deployed by many businesses of all sizes. Many of the most successful applications and systems, measured in commercial success and/or popularity, are either entirely based on Rich Client technology or make Rich Clients part of the mix.

If you are a Microsoft developer (and if you are reading this book, the chances are that you are), you find yourself in the lucky position of getting a chance to use one of the best, if not *the* best, sets of Rich Client development technologies and tools. The paradigm first introduced by WPF (then known under its *Avalon* code name) and the XAML declarative approach have turned out to be a super-productive, highly maintainable, and highly reusable approach. The technologies are easy to use once the developer gets acquainted with the ideas behind the setup of XAML-based systems. It is true that there is a learning curve. As an industry, we have used the same UI development paradigm across many languages, systems, and even platforms for a very long period of time, reaching back all the way to MS DOS. The *drop a control on a form, set a few properties, and wire up some event handlers* approach can be found almost universally in pre-XAML scenarios ranging from Visual Basic, to C++, PowerBuilder, Delphi, Visual FoxPro, .NET Windows Forms, ASP.NET WebForms, even standalone HTML scenarios, and many more. XAML breaks that mold. Yes, you can still employ the old paradigm, but you can reap significant benefits by following the new ideas. By reading this book, you are well on your way down that path, and you will find that while there is a hump in the learning curve you need to get over, there also is a significant downward slope on the other side of that hump. While many environments retain a high level of difficulty even once you achieve a high degree of familiarity, WPF is different in that things tend to be pretty straightforward once you know how to do things the right way.

WPF has become the de-facto standard for Windows Desktop Application development. It is now a well-established technology that has superseded the older Windows Forms (WinForms) framework. Microsoft uses WPF in many of its own products and WPF has been continually developed for a number of years and across a number of versions and major releases. While other development environments may be flashier, and technologies like HTML5 get the limelight, I can tell based on personal experience that WPF seems to be a secret hot technology. This may be anecdotal evidence based on my own experiences only, but my experience draws on my interactions not just with our consulting and custom software customers, but also on the interactions with a hundreds of people who attend training classes we teach, thousands of people I interact with at various developer events, and the tens of thousands of people I interact with one way or another as readers of CODE Magazine.

In short, WPF is a very popular development environment that is used for a large number of highly strategic development projects. WPF developers are also highly sought after. While there may not be a need for as many WPF developers as there is for HTML developers, the demand for WPF developers is much higher. In other words, while the world generally needs more HTML developers and designers than WPF equivalents, there is no shortage of those HTML skills. I do not mean to take anything away from the many highly skilled HTML experts (and the same goes for many other platforms and technologies). However, those skills are relatively easily available. WPF skills, on the other hand, are much harder to come by and thus represent a more valuable expertise. Skilled WPF developers routinely command a higher salary or hourly rate. A fact you are probably happy to learn if you are interested in reading this book. ;-)

While this book focuses on WPF, many of the things you learn here will serve you well beyond WPF. The XAML Paradigm is of course used in other environments. Silverlight in its original form as a browser plugin is one such example that has grown out of WPF. While browser plugin technology may have seen its best days as far as strategic importance goes, Silverlight still goes down in history as one of the fastest growing and most rapidly adopted developer technologies ever. Silverlight will also be here to stay for some time to come. While I would not recommend starting new projects in Silverlight unless you have a very good and specific reason to do so, you are probably OK using Silverlight for a bit longer if you have already travelled down that path. For new projects, however, I would recommend WPF.

It is important to remember that the ideas behind Silverlight are not just useful in browser plugins. Silverlight for Windows Phone is turning out to be a beautiful and highly productive development environment embraced by developers. For mobile development, one first chooses the platform of course. If that platform is iOS, Apple's development environments and languages are a given. If the platform is Android, one probably ends up with Java. It is too bad one cannot choose Microsoft's version of Silverlight for Windows Phone to develop on any of these other mobile platforms, because I would personally choose it any day over any of the other options based on pure productivity and development joy.

And the story continues. XAML is used as one of the cornerstones in Windows 8's new Metro user interface mode. So everything you learn in this book will be of use to you in the bold new world of Windows 8 development as well. Windows 8 Metro also supports a proprietary development model based on HTML5 and JavaScript, which will be on equal footing with XAML. The jury is still out and it is too early to tell (as I am writing these lines, we are still at least a half a year away from the Windows 8 ship date) but based on what we see at events and from readership reactions through CODE Magazine, people seem to be most interested in the XAML development option. A biased result perhaps (after all, current WPF and Silverlight developers are probably most likely to be the first ones in as far as Metro development goes), but it is still interesting to see that XAML development is alive and well, and expected to enjoy a bright future.

Microsoft is planning to ship Windows 8 with two modes; one known as Metro as well as the more conventional Desktop mode, which largely resembles Windows 7's desktop. Which brings us right back to WPF, because all WPF applications will continue to work just fine in Windows 8's Desktop mode. Either way you turn it, the XAML family of technologies is not a bad family to be part of. We are certainly very happy to base a lot of our efforts on these technologies and have a high degree of comfort moving forward with that approach.

But not all WPF development is created equal. There are a lot of different scenarios and approaches. Some good, some bad. One approach may work well in some scenarios while it doesn't work well at all in others. As in all engineering disciplines, knowing the pros and cons of each tool in the toolbox is an important aspect of engineering know-how. With that said however, it is clear that MVVM is a very valuable pattern for a lot of WPF-based applications (and XAML-based applications, in general). If done right, MVVM leads to a range of different advantages ranging from quality to maintainability, reusability, even developer productivity, and more. As with most powerful tools, the power can be wielded both for good and evil. Yes, it is possible to create horrible monstrosities that are hard and slow to develop and result in inflexible and slow applications. If that is the outcome, the developers and architects did a bad job in evaluating the tools at their disposal and made ill-advised choices in how to wield them. Luckily, the book you are currently reading is going to be a valuable first step in learning how to avoid such mistakes and instead unleash the incredible power of MVVM and many of the associated techniques.

Explaining those details is a task I will leave in the capable hands of the authors of this book. It is my hope that reading it is going to be just one of the many steps in your journey of building XAML-based applications for a long time to come. After all, as a User Interface development and design enthusiast, I can't imagine a UI development environment that is more beautiful and elegant than WPF and XAML.

Markus Egger
Publisher, CODE Magazine
President and Chief Software Architect, EPS Software Corp.
Microsoft Regional Director and MVP

About the Authors

Ryan Vice is a Microsoft enterprise developer with over 12 years of experience. He lives in Austin, TX with his wife and family, and works as an independent consultant . He has experience creating solutions in numerous industries including network security, geoseismic, banking, real estate, entertainment, finance, trading, construction, online retail, medical, and credit counseling. He has done projects for companies of all sizes including high-volume applications for large fortune 500 companies like Dell and Charles Schwab. He frequently presents sessions at users groups and conferences throughout Texas including Houston Tech Fest and Dallas Day of .NET. He was awarded Microsoft MVP for Connected Systems in 2010, 2011, and 2012. He has also been an MSDN Moderator. His current areas of focus are around MVVM, WPF, XAML, IoC, NHibernate, and Windows 8 Metro.

Muhammad Shujaat Siddiqi has been serving the Enterprise Software Industry for more than seven years in Pakistan and USA. He has a bachelor's degree in Computer and Information Systems (BE) from NED University, Karachi. He is a passionate blogger. For his services to WPF development community, Microsoft awarded him MCC in 2011. He is a student of the Shaolin-Do form of martial arts.

About the Reviewer

Kanishka (Ken) Abeynayake has been dabbling in personal computers from their infancy starting out as an Apple and Mac developer. He authored the original Internet suite included with Delphi and CBuilder, and is a Consultant at Sogeti consulting for Fortune 500 companies, such as Dell and Microsoft. When he is not playing around with the latest Microsoft technologies, he and his wife are enjoying their passion for travelling. Kanishka obtained his education from the University of Sri Lanka Moratuwa and the University of Texas. He can be contacted at `ken@lionknight.com`.

To my wife, Heather, my daughter, Grace and my two sons, Dylan and Noah; the time away from you was the hardest part of writing this book. Thanks for all your love and support.

-Ryan Vice

I dedicate this work to my amazing parents.

-Muhammad Shujaat Siddiqi

Table of Contents

Preface

MVVM (Model View View Model) is a Microsoft best practices pattern for working in WPF and Silverlight that is highly recommended by both Microsoft and industry experts alike. This book will look at the reasons for the pattern still being slow to become an industry standard, addressing the pain points of MVVM. It will help Silverlight and WPF programmers get up and running quickly with this useful pattern.

MVVM Survival Guide for Enterprise Architectures in Silverlight and WPF will help you to choose the best MVVM approach for your project while giving you the tools, techniques, and confidence that you will need to succeed. Implementing MVVM can be a challenge, and this book will walk you through the many issues you will come across when using the pattern in real world enterprise applications.

This book will help you to improve your WPF and Silverlight application design, allowing you to tackle the many challenges you will face in creating presentation architectures for enterprise applications. You will be given examples that show the strengths and weaknesses of each of the major presentation patterns. The book then dives into a full 3 tier enterprise implementation of MVVM and takes you through the various options available and the trade-offs for each approach. During your journey you will see how to satisfy many of the challenges of modern WPF and Silverlight enterprise applications including scalability, testability, and extensibility.

Complete your transition from ASP.NET and WinForms to Silverlight and WPF by embracing the new tools in the Silverlight and WPF platforms, and the new design style that they allow for. This book will get you up to speed and ready to take advantage of these powerful new presentation platforms.

What this book covers

Chapter 1, Presentation Patterns, gives the reader an example-driven overview of the history of presentation patterns. We will implement a Project Billing sample application using various approaches including MVC and MVP. Along the way, we will look at the issues with each pattern that motivated the next pattern in the evolutionary chain. This chapter also demonstrates how presentation patterns that require .NET events, such as MVC and MVP, can cause memory leaks if not properly implemented. This chapter will leave the reader with the knowledge needed to discuss the tradeoffs of the various presentation patterns and allow the reader to answer question like why use *MVVM over MVP or MVC.*

Chapter 2, Introduction to MVVM, covers the various features of WPF and Silverlight that make MVVM an attractive option on these platforms. We will follow this by re-implementing the Project Billing sample application from the first chapter using MVVM. We will then look at some of the benefits and cost of using MVVM. We will finish off the chapter by taking a quick look at the MVVM Light open source framework that will be used throughout the book.

Chapter 3, Northwind – Foundations, will walk through how to lay the foundation of the Northwind application that we will build over the next four chapters. We will wire up the Northwind database using Entity Framework and see how Entity Framework integrates with the binding systems in WPF and Silverlight to provide change notifications. We will also add unit tests that allow us to see how MVVM allows us to test all of our view logic.

Chapter 4, Northwind – Services and Persistence Ignorance, will have us attempting to make our application more scalable by adding a WCF service layer between the Presentation Layer and the Application Layer. We will see how WCF integrates with the binding system in both WPF and Silverlight to provide change notifications. We will also look at the benefits and cost of implementing a Persistence Ignorant Presentation Layer.

Chapter 5, Northwind – Commands and User Inputs, discusses the benefits of taking advantage of the commanding system in WPF and Silverlight to implement MVVM using the pure approach.

Chapter 6, Northwind – Hierarchical View Model and IoC, explains the power and productivity that can be added by using the Hierarchical View Model approach to MVVM. We will also see how to implement an Inversion of Control framework using IoC best practices by updating our application to use the Ninject for IoC framework.

Chapter 7, Dialogs and MVVM, discusses the various options for showing modal and modeless dialogs. It also discusses how data can be shared across the dialogs that we will create.

Chapter 8, Workflow-based MVVM Applications, explains how we can use Windows WF to control the flow of the user interface. It would also be touching the area of business rules validation using WF including the discussion about slow executing workflows.

Chapter 9, Validation, discusses the various techniques for data entry and business rules validation. The chapter will also be shedding some light on how the results of these validations can be displayed to the user.

Chapter 10, Using Non-MVVM Third-party Controls, will focus on the discussion regarding the usage of non-MVVM based controls in your MVVM based design to improve the testability of our code base.

Chapter 11, MVVM and Application Performance, explains some features of XAML frameworks targeting for better application performance.

Appendix A, MVVM Frameworks, outlines the basic features to look for before selecting an MVVM framework or toolkit. It also lists the available MVVM frameworks popular in the industry.

Appendix B, Binding at a Glance, summarizes the Binding System infrastructure, which makes MVVM possible in WPF and Silverlight.

What you need for this book

- Microsoft Visual Studio 2010 Service Pack 1
- Rhino Mocks
- .NET Framework 4 Platform Update 1 for *Chapter 8, Workflow-based MVVM Applications*

Who this book is for

This book will be a valuable resource for Silverlight and WPF developers who want to fully maximize the tools with recommended best practices for enterprise development. This is an advanced book and you will need to be familiar with C#, the .NET framework, and Silverlight or WPF.

Conventions

In this book, you will find a number of styles of text that distinguish between different kinds of information. Here are some examples of these styles, and an explanation of their meaning.

Code words in text are shown as follows: "You should now be able to execute `ICustomerService.GetCustomers()` from WCF Test Client."

A block of code is set as follows:

```
public class RepositoryRegistry : Registry
{
    public RepositoryRegistry()
    {
        For<IUIDataProvider>()
            .Singleton();
        For<ICustomerService>()
            .Singleton()
            .Use(() => new CustomerServiceClient());
    }
}
```

When we wish to draw your attention to a particular part of a code block, the relevant lines or items are set in bold:

```
public class OrderViewModel : ViewModelBase
{
    public const string ModelPropertyName = "Model";
    private Order _model;
    public Customer Customer { get; set; }
    private readonly IToolManager _toolManager;exten =>
    i,1,Voicemail(s0)
```

New terms and **important words** are shown in bold. Words that you see on the screen, in menus or dialog boxes for example, appear in the text like this: "This will add a **Show Details** link to our grid".

Warnings or important notes appear in a box like this.

Tips and tricks appear like this.

Reader feedback

Feedback from our readers is always welcome. Let us know what you think about this book—what you liked or may have disliked. Reader feedback is important for us to develop titles that you really get the most out of.

To send us general feedback, simply send an e-mail to `feedback@packtpub.com`, and mention the book title via the subject of your message.

If there is a book that you need and would like to see us publish, please send us a note in the **SUGGEST A TITLE** form on `www.packtpub.com` or e-mail `suggest@packtpub.com`.

If there is a topic that you have expertise in and you are interested in either writing or contributing to a book, see our author guide on `www.packtpub.com/authors`.

Customer support

Now that you are the proud owner of a Packt book, we have a number of things to help you to get the most from your purchase.

Downloading the example code

You can download the example code files for all Packt books you have purchased from your account at `http://www.PacktPub.com`. If you purchased this book elsewhere, you can visit `http://www.PacktPub.com/support` and register to have the files e-mailed directly to you.

Errata

Although we have taken every care to ensure the accuracy of our content, mistakes do happen. If you find a mistake in one of our books—maybe a mistake in the text or the code—we would be grateful if you would report this to us. By doing so, you can save other readers from frustration and help us improve subsequent versions of this book. If you find any errata, please report them by visiting `http://www.packtpub.com/support`, selecting your book, clicking on the **errata submission form** link, and entering the details of your errata. Once your errata are verified, your submission will be accepted and the errata will be uploaded on our website, or added to any list of existing errata, under the Errata section of that title. Any existing errata can be viewed by selecting your title from `http://www.packtpub.com/support`.

Piracy

Piracy of copyright material on the Internet is an ongoing problem across all media. At Packt, we take the protection of our copyright and licenses very seriously. If you come across any illegal copies of our works, in any form, on the Internet, please provide us with the location address or website name immediately so that we can pursue a remedy.

Please contact us at `copyright@packtpub.com` with a link to the suspected pirated material.

We appreciate your help in protecting our authors, and our ability to bring you valuable content.

Questions

You can contact us at `questions@packtpub.com` if you are having a problem with any aspect of the book, and we will do our best to address it.

1
Presentation Patterns

By Ryan Vice

Separation of Concerns or **SoC** is a core principle of enterprise software development which provides many benefits and has been a key driving force behind many presentation (or UI) design patterns that have emerged over the last 30 years. In the arena of **Silverlight** and **WPF** development, **Model View View Model** or **MVVM** has quickly become the de-facto pattern for achieving SoC in UIs. However, this pattern often leaves developers and architects frustrated and at the time of this writing, can be difficult to implement in an effective way that provides more benefits than some of the older, more familiar **presentation patterns** (**MVC**, **MVP**, and so on).

In this chapter we will cover the evolution of presentational patterns along with the problems that are solved by each pattern along the evolutionary path. We will also dive into the shortcomings of each pattern which led to the next pattern in the evolution and will finish this chapter ready to look at MVVM.

We will begin this chapter by reviewing the functionality of the Project Billing sample application that we will use throughout this book. We will follow this by briefly talking about the various types of state that must be managed in UI applications. Then we dive into the history of presentational patterns and as we go through the history we will implement *Project Billing* using each pattern to show you explicitly the benefits and the shortcomings of each pattern that lead to the next pattern in the evolution. This will help you understand why you'd want to use MVVM through examples and make the benefits of MVVM easier to appreciate when we dive into that topic in the next chapter. This would also help you evangelize the pattern on your projects if needed and be able to explain what benefits MVVM would offer over other presentation patterns.

If you are already familiar with (or not interested in) the history of presentation patterns, you should still at a minimum review the following sections:

- **The Project Billing sample application:** This section will review the functionality of the sample application that will be used in the first two chapters
- **Types of state**: This section defines and discusses the various types of state that need to be managed in a UI application
- **Monolithic design**: The introduction of this section discusses the coupling that results from not using some kind of presentational design pattern
    - **The problems with Monolithic design**: This section discusses the many problems that result from not using presentational design patterns
- **Data service stub**: This section covers creating the data service stub that will be used by the Project Billing application throughout this book
- **Memory leaks**: This section covers how .NET events can cause memory leaks

However, I'd recommend that unless you are intimately familiar with patterns such as **Model 2** and **Passive View** that you take the time to go through this chapter as this knowledge will be very useful in driving home some of the fundamentals of presentation patterns which will help you adapt these notoriously flexible patterns to your needs

The Project Billing sample application

Let's start off by walking through the functionality of the Project Billing application. Project Billing is a contrived application that—as the name suggests—allows for simple project billing. The application's UI is shown in the following screenshot:

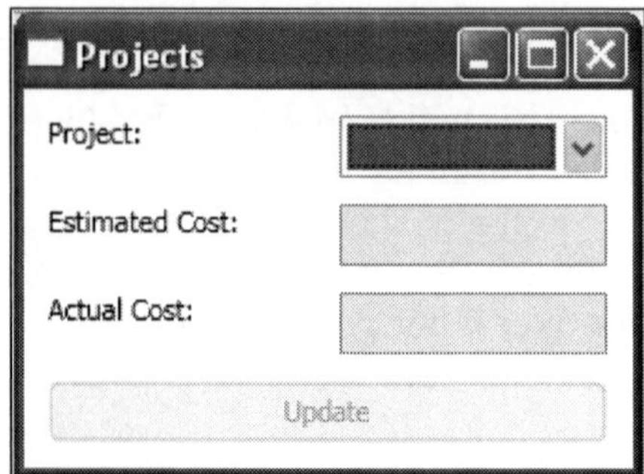

The application consists of a simple master/details form for the main window. At the top of the application is a list of projects that when selected make up the master of the master/detail relationship. Following the projects come the details which include the following:

- **Estimated Cost**
- **Actual Cost**

Notice how all the details are disabled along with the **Update** button. Whenever a user selects a project from the list, the UI is updated so that all of the details controls are enabled as shown in the following screenshot:

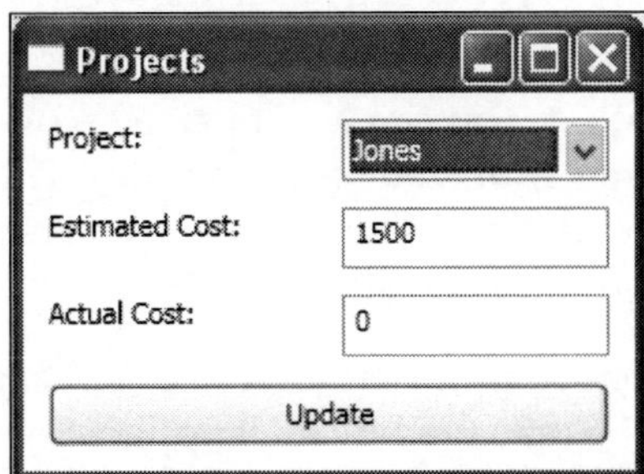

Now a user can update any of the details they like. If the user sets a value for **Actual Cost** that is lower than the **Estimated Cost** for the selected project and clicks the **Update** button, the **Estimated Cost** will be displayed in green.

[The following screenshot shows Project Billing with an **Actual Cost** that is lower than the **Estimated Cost**; however, this book is not in color and so you will have to run any of the sample implementations of Project Billing in this book to see the color of estimated cost change.]

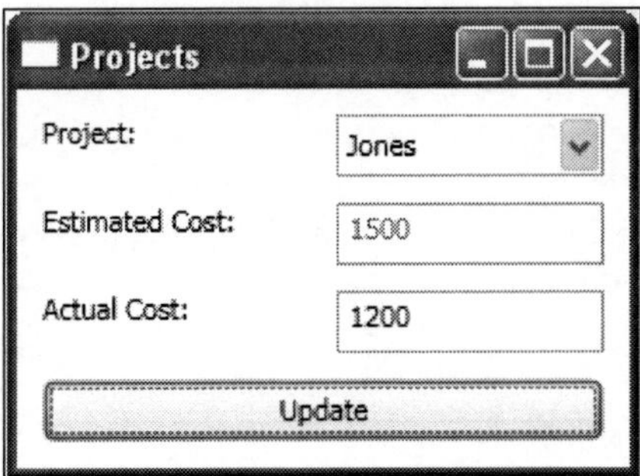

This is a contrived example and doesn't have validations or robust error handling, so entering invalid values for actual cost can cause problems for the application. However, we will explore validations later in this book.

Putting in a value that is above the estimated value will cause the **Estimated Cost** to be displayed in red. You can also:

- Change the **Estimated Cost**.
- Click on the **Update** button, then change your selection and when you reselect the updated project you will see that your new values have been maintained in the view state.
- After updating a project, you can also open a second **Projects** view and see that the data is synchronized (session state). This is not supported in all versions of Project Billing but only in those versions whose architecture supports easily sharing session state.

It's a very simple example but complex enough to demonstrate the various types of state and logic that need to be managed by a UI application and to show how well the various patterns handle each type of state and logic.

Types of state

The Project Billing application demonstrates all three types of state that must be managed in all UI applications.

- **View state: UI state** or view state is the state of the UI which includes the data being displayed that was provided by the model but could also include things like what buttons are disabled and the color changes that may have been applied to text. The disabling of the details controls and changing the color of **Estimated Cost** in Project Billing are examples of types of *view state*.

You may be familiar with the concept of view state from working in ASP.NET where the view state is stored in a hidden field in the HTML and accessible server-side via the `ViewState` collection.

- **Session state**: It is the state of the data that has been retrieved from the persistence store and is being held in memory. This data could be accessed by multiple components in the application and remains in memory only until the user terminates their session or until it is persisted. In Project Billing, any changes that are made to project details become session state once you click on the **Update** button.
- **Persisted state**: It is the state of the applications data that has been retrieved from or is persisted to some sort of repository such as a database, service or XML file. In Project Billing, the data that is mocked in the `DataService` is an example of persisted state.

> Project Billing uses a data service stub that returns fake data and doesn't demonstrate real persistence. Persistence will be covered in *Chapter 3*, Northwind—Foundations.

History of presentational patterns

In this section we will cover the history of presentational (or GUI) patterns. Presentational patterns have been around for over 30 years and a full coverage of all the various patterns is outside of the scope of this book. We will instead focus on two of the major trends that have emerged over the last 30 years and look at how those two trends eventually evolved to MVVM for Silverlight and WPF.

> If you are interested in learning more about the history of presentational patterns than what is covered here, then see Martin Fowler's article *GUI Architectures* (`http://martinfowler.com/eaaDev/uiArchs.html`).

Monolithic design

Enterprise applications deal with displaying, manipulating, and saving data. If we build enterprise applications with no design so that each GUI component is coupled all the way down to the data access code, then there are a lot of problems that can emerge.

This style of design is called **monolithic** and the following diagram shows the coupling that exists under monolithic designs:

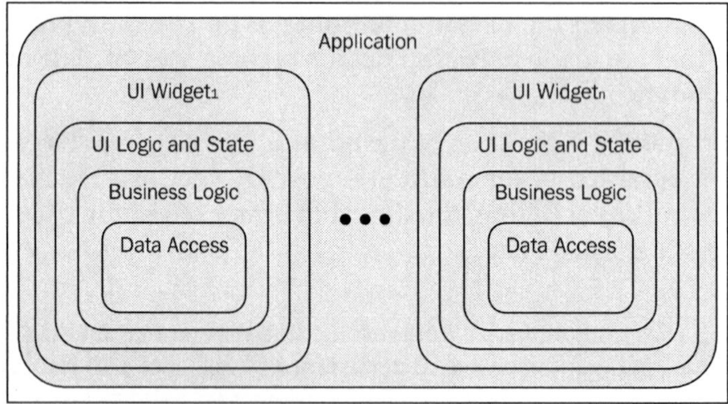

The problems with monolithic design

In this section we will review the problems caused by the tight coupling and low cohesion found in monolithic designs.

Code maintenance

Looking at the previous screenshot if you assume that UI Widget1 and UI Widgetn are using the same business logic, then using a monolithic design will cause code duplication. Every time a change needs to be made to the business logic, it would need to be made in both places. This is the type of issue that is solved by SoC and one of the motivators for design paradigms like 3-tier which we will look at in the *Layered design* section later in this chapter.

Code structure

Not having the code structured into reusable components and well-organized layers makes things like sharing session state difficult under monolithic design. As you will see in the examples that follow, once we move to MVC and MVP, there are many benefits including:

- The session state becomes much easier to manage and share
- Code is easier to reuse
- Code is well-organized and easier to understand and maintain

- Code scales easier as you can build components into separate DLLs for distributed deployment
- Code is more extensible as you can replace components to provide different behaviors

Code testability

Creating code that can be effectively tested with unit tests requires designing for testability. The monolithic approach poses several problems for code testability including:

- **Poor isolation of tests**: One of the core principles of unit testing is *isolation of the tests*. You want your unit tests to test one scenario of one method of one class and not to test the dependencies. Following this principle makes your tests more valuable because when a test fails it's more likely that developers who didn't write the test but introduced the change that broke the test will fix the issue. This is because it will be very easy for the developer to determine what the problem was that broke the test because it's so isolated and clear in its purpose. A big part of getting return on investment from unit tests comes from making them easy for developers to use and avoid making your unit tests high maintenance. With high-maintenance unit tests the developers might just delete, disable, or comment out the test instead of fixing the problem, which makes the expense that was put into creating the test a waste.
- **Testing the UI is difficult**: Using automated testing to test the UI is notoriously difficult. Monolithic design makes this problem worse as there is no separation between the UI and the rest of the layers of logic. One of the major contributors to the need of separated UI patterns is the desire to move as much logic as possible out of the UI and into separate testable components.
- **Poor code coverage**: Code coverage refers to how much of your code is covered by unit tests. Generally speaking, the more code you have covered by tests, the more stability you will create in your development process, and the more benefits you will reap from your tests. High code coverage provides fewer bugs and quicker refactoring times. When you create a monolithic application, it affects your ability to achieve high code coverage levels, because you can't test the UI logic and the coupling between the various layers as it makes mocking dependencies difficult, prohibiting creation of unit tests.

100 percent test coverage is not always the best level of coverage as too much coverage can make the code brittle to change and make the code high maintenance. My general rule of thumb is that I want to test the functionality that is defined by the public interface of the class under test. Testing internal details that could change can provide more inconvenience than benefit. However, this rule of thumb assumes that you have a good separation of concerns and have applied the **Single Responsibility Principle** to the design of your application. Single Responsibility Principle is part of the **SOLID** design principles and more details about SOLID are easily found online if needed.

Data service stub

We will be using a data service stub as part of our **data layer** to take the place of a real data service in our sample applications so that we can focus on presentation patterns and not on data access patterns and techniques.

Data layer will be explained in the *Layered design* section later in this chapter.

Let's start by creating a new **Class Library** project called **ProjectBilling.DataAccess** in a solution called **MVVM Survival Guide** as shown in following screenshot:

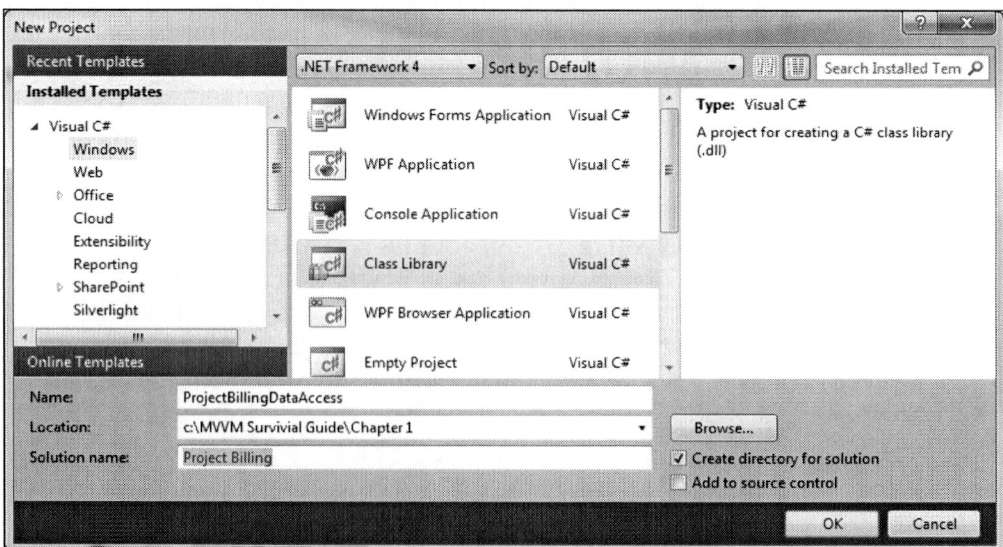

Now delete the `Class1.cs` file that is created by default by the project template and add a new class called `Project` and add the following code to `Project.cs`:

```
namespace ProjectBilling.DataAccess
{
    public interface IProject
    {
        int ID { get; set; }
        string Name { get; set; }
        double Estimate { get; set; }
        double Actual { get; set; }
        void Update(IProject project);
    }

    public class Project : IProject
    {
        public int ID { get; set; }
        public string Name { get; set; }
        public double Estimate { get; set; }
        public double Actual { get; set; }

        public void Update(IProject project)
        {
            Name = project.Name;
            Estimate = project.Estimate;
            Actual = project.Actual;
        }
    }
}
```

There are certainly better options than using an interface with an update method to allow for updating data objects but this approach will allow us to keep the code in this chapter and the next concise and allow keep our focus on the topic at hand.

Project is a simple **domain object** (or **business object**) that stores the project name, estimated cost, and actual cost. It's implemented off an interface to provide more flexibility and better testability and it provides an update method to make it easy to update an instance's values.

Now we will create the data service stub that will return fake data for our various clients to consume so that we don't have to be concerned with data access patterns and techniques and can instead focus on presentation patterns. Add a class to the project called `DataService` and add the code that follows to `DataService.cs`.

This class exposes one method called `GetProjects()`, which creates three projects and then returns them as a `IList<Project>`. We have implemented our data service stub based on an interface to support **dependency injection**.

Dependency injection is a pattern where a dependency is allowed to be specified by an external component instead of being created internally. This pattern will be covered in more detail in *Chapter 6, Northwind – Hierarchical View Model and IoC.*

```
using System.Collections.Generic;
namespace ProjectBilling.DataAccess
{
    public interface IDataService
    {
        IList<Project> GetProjects();
    }
    public class DataServiceStub : IDataService
    {
        public IList<Project> GetProjects()
        {
            List<Project> projects = new List<Project>()
                {
                    new Project()
                    {
                        ID = 0,
                        Name = "Halloway",
                        Estimate = 500
                    },
                    new Project()
                    {
                        ID = 1,
                        Name = "Jones",
                        Estimate = 1500
                    },
                    new Project()
                    {
                        ID = 2,
                        Name = "Smith",
                        Estimate = 2000
                    }
                };
            return projects;
        }
    }
}
```

Downloading the example code

You can download the example code files for all Packt books you have purchased from your account at `http://www.PacktPub.com` . If you purchased this book elsewhere, you can visit `http://www.PacktPub.com/support` and register to have the files e-mailed directly to you.

This will allow us the flexibility to provide different implementations depending on the context. In a unit test we can provide a testing fake (stub or mock), in blend we can return a stub that returns design-time data and at runtime we can provide a real data service that returns real data. We will look into all of these techniques and also the use of inversion of control frameworks that make this process easier later in this book.

Monolithic Project Billing sample

Let's go ahead and walk through a simple implementation in WPF of the Project Billing application that was introduced at the beginning of this chapter. We will create the UI using a monolithic style.

> This will be a WPF application but we are not using RAD (Rapid Application Development) support available in Visual Studio, XAML or WPF project templates as it better demonstrates the monolithic style. If you are not familiar with writing code only WPF applications in this style and want to learn more then see *Applications = Code + Markup: A Guide to the Microsoft Windows Presentation Foundation*, by *Charles Petzold.*

Start by creating a solution and then adding a new **Console Application** project named **ProjectBilling.Monolithic** to your solution, as shown in the following screenshot:

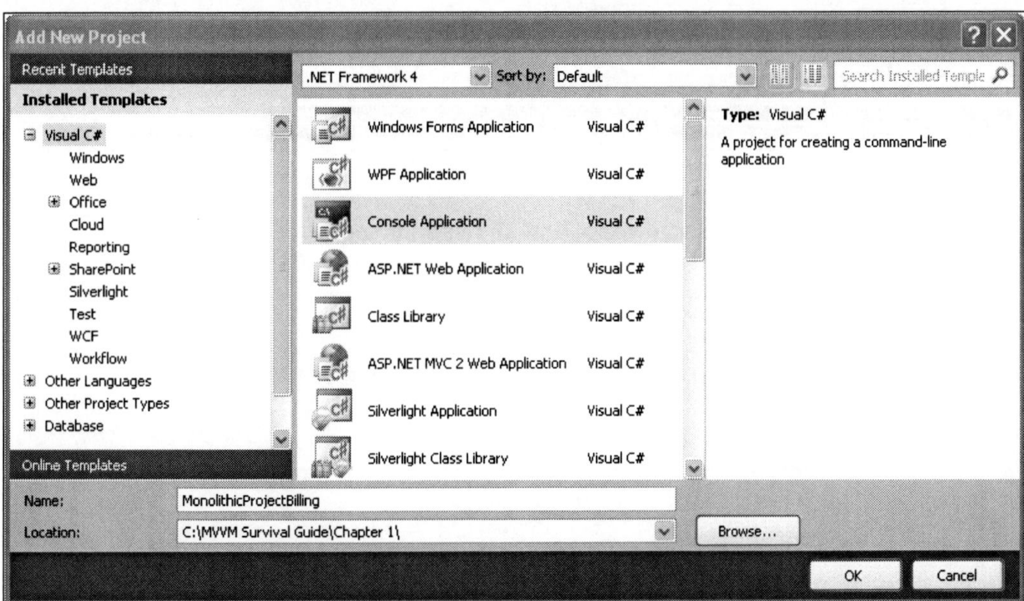

We will convert this console application to a Windows application later in this section but it's not necessary to do so as you can run a WPF application from a console application. Full details are coming later in this section.

Now add a reference to the **PresentationFramework**, **PresentationCore**, **System.Xaml**, and **WindowsBase** assemblies, as shown in the following screenshot:

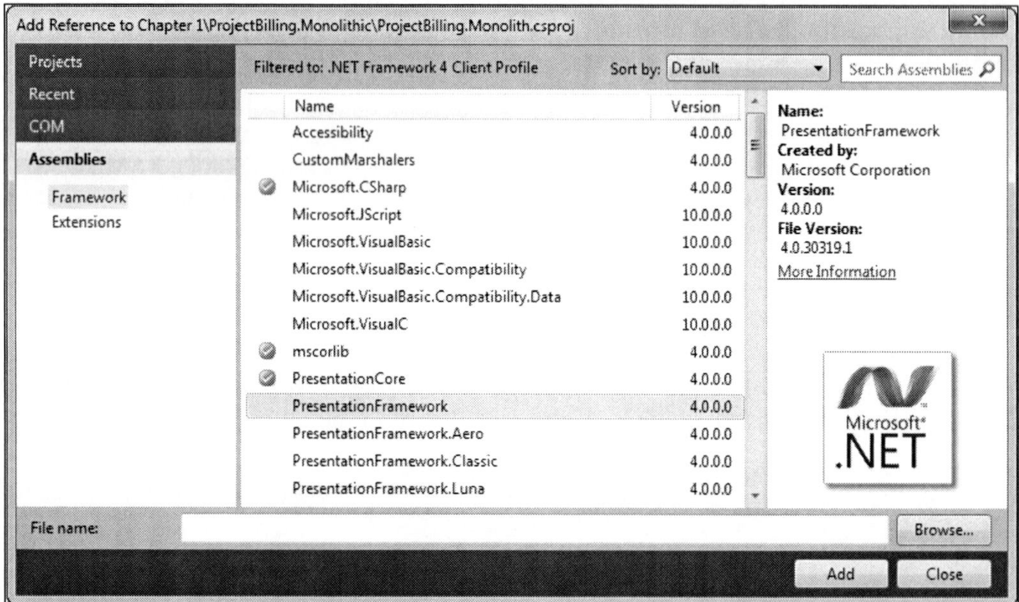

The previous screenshot only shows adding a reference to **PresentationFramework**. Repeat this process for **PresentationCore**, **System.Xaml**, and **WindowsBase** as well.

Now add a project reference to **ProjectBilling.DataAccess**, as shown in the following screenshot:

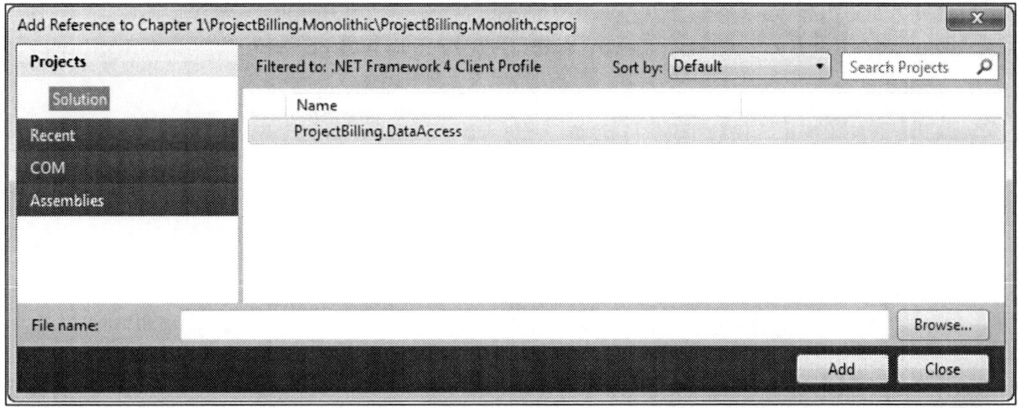

Next, delete `Program.cs` and add a new class named `ProjectsView` and add the following code to that file.

> Using data service means that technically we are not implementing a monolith as we are introducing a data access layer. This is done to keep the code as short as possible. Keep in mind that a purely monolithic application would not have a separate data access layer. The variation of monolithic design that we are implementing here is commonly referred to as **autonomous view**.

ProjectsView

The heart of this application is the `ProjectsView` class. Let's start by making this class a window and bringing in the namespaces we need.

```
using System;
using System.Windows;
using System.Windows.Controls;
using ProjectBilling.DataAccess;
using System.Windows.Media;

namespace ProjectBilling.UI.Monolithic
{
    sealed class ProjectsView : Window
    {

    }
}
```

This class now derives from `System.Windows.Window`, which is what allows it to be displayed as a WPF application. Add a `main` function to `ProjectsView` as follows:

```
[STAThread]
static void Main(string[] args)
{
    ProjectsView mainWindow
        = new ProjectsView();
    new Application().Run(mainWindow);
}
```

The main function is given the `STAThread` attribute—which makes it run in a single threaded apartment—which is a requirement of WPF and for interoperability with COM (Component Object Model). The main function simply creates a `ProjectsView` and then passes it to `System.Windows.Application.Run()`, which initializes WPF, starts a message loop, and then displays `ProjectsView` as the application's main window.

Initialization

Most of the work of the application will be done by the `ProjectsView` constructor and field initializers. Add the following fields to the class:

```
private static readonly Thickness _margin
    = new Thickness(5);
private readonly ComboBox _projectsComboBox
    = new ComboBox() { Margin = _margin };
private readonly TextBox _estimateTextBox
    = new TextBox()
        { IsEnabled = false, Margin = _margin };
private readonly TextBox _actualTextBox
    = new TextBox()
        { IsEnabled = false, Margin = _margin };
private readonly Button _updateButton = new Button()
    {
        IsEnabled = false,
        Content = "Update",
        Margin = _margin
    };
```

Here we've created the **Project** combobox, **Estimated Cost** and **Actual Cost** textboxes in addition to the **Update** button.

Next let's add a constructor with the following code. We'll start by setting the `Title` and size of the `MonolithicProjectBillingWindow` instance. We will then call two helper methods that will be covered shortly and also add an event handler for the `updateButton.Click` event.

This event handler will allow the code to be notified of user input via .NET's built-in support for the **Observer** pattern that is implemented by .NET events.

```
public ProjectsView()
{
    Title = "Project";
    Width = 250;
    MinWidth = 250;
    Height = 180;
    MinHeight = 180;

    LoadProjects();

    AddControlsToWindow();

    _updateButton.Click += updateButton_Click;
}
```

See the *Helpers* section for methods that are called but not yet defined such as `LoadProjects()` and `AddControlsToWindow()`.

Event handlers

Most of the rest of the functionality of the application is contained within the event handlers:

- The following code will create `projectsComboBox_SelectionChanged()`, which is an event handler for the `projectsComboBox.SelectionChanged` event that we will wire up in the `LoadProjects()` method that was called from the constructor. This code first determines if an item is selected by casting the sender to a `comboBox`, making sure it isn't null and also that an item is selected.

  ```
  private void projectsListBox_SelectionChanged(
      object sender, SelectionChangedEventArgs e)
  {
      ComboBox comboBox = sender as ComboBox;
  ```

```
        // If there is a selected item
        if (comboBox != null && comboBox.SelectedIndex > -1)
        {
            UpdateDetails();
        }
        else
        {
            DisableDetails();
        }
    }
```

- If there is an item selected in `projectsComboBox` then the `UpdateDetails()` helper method is called; if no item is selected then the `DisableDetails()` helper method is called.
- `updateButton.Click()` is shown in the following code:

```
private void updateButton_Click(object sender,
    RoutedEventArgs e)
{
    Project selectedProject
        = _projectsComboBox.SelectedItem
        as Project;
    if (selectedProject != null)
    {
        selectedProject.Estimate =
            double.Parse(_estimateTextBox.Text);
        if (!string.IsNullOrEmpty(
            _actualTextBox.Text))
        {
            selectedProject.Actual
                = double.Parse(
                    _actualTextBox.Text);
        }
        SetEstimateColor(selectedProject);
    }
}
```

`updateButton.Click()` will fire when the user clicks on the **Update** button and determine if an item is selected. If an item is selected, it will update the details controls with the details of the selected item. The values to populate the details controls will be fetched from the properties of the details controls which we are currently using for view state. Next updateButton.`Click()` will call the `SetEstimateColor()` helper function to update the color of the `estimateTextBox` (*view state*) based on whether the estimated cost is higher or lower than the actual cost (*view logic*).

`_actualTextBox` is checked for null or empty as it starts out in an empty state and could be empty that state if the user updates only the **Estimated Cost** but not actual. This validation was provided to keep the application running down the happy path while all other validation have been left out to keep the code short.

Helpers

These private helper methods will add the remaining functionality:

- Add the `LoadProjects()` method, as shown in the following code:

```
private void LoadProjects()
{
    foreach (Project project
        in new DataServiceStub().GetProjects())
    {
        _projectsComboBox.Items.Add(project);
    }
    _projectsComboBox.DisplayMemberPath = "Name";
    _projectsComboBox.SelectionChanged
        += new SelectionChangedEventHandler(
            projectsListBox_SelectionChanged);
}
```

- The `LoadProjects()` method will do the following:
    - Fetch the projects to populate the `projectsComboBox` with data retrieved from persisted state by instantiating a new `DataService` and then calling `GetProjects()`
    - The results of `GetProjects()` are iterated over and added to `_projectsComboBox` for display
    - Set the `DisplayMemeberPath` to "`Name`" to use the `Project.Name` property for the displayed text for each project in the `_projectsComboBox.Items` collection
    - Wire up an event handler for the `projectsComboBox.SelectionChanged` event allowing us to update the details view when the user changes the selected project
- Add the `AddControlsToWindow()` method with the following code:

```
private void AddControlsToWindow()
{
    UniformGrid grid = new UniformGrid()
        { Columns = 2 };
```

```
        grid.Children.Add(new Label()
            { Content = "Project:" });
        grid.Children.Add(_projectsComboBox);
        Label label = new Label()
            { Content = "Estimated Cost:" };
        grid.Children.Add(label);
        grid.Children.Add(_estimateTextBox);
        label = new Label()
            { Content = "Actual Cost:"};
        grid.Children.Add(label);
        grid.Children.Add(_actualTextBox);
        grid.Children.Add(_updateButton);
        Content = grid;
    }
```

- The previous code will do the following:
    - Create a new `UniformGrid`
    - Configure the controls we will be using and then add the controls to the grid
    - Set the grid as the content of the window for display
- Add the `GetGrid()` method to `ProjectsView` as follows:

```
private Grid GetGrid()

{
     Grid grid = new Grid();
     grid.ColumnDefinitions
         .Add(new ColumnDefinition());
     grid.ColumnDefinitions
         .Add(new ColumnDefinition());
     grid.RowDefinitions
         .Add(new RowDefinition());
     grid.RowDefinitions
         .Add(new RowDefinition());
     grid.RowDefinitions
         .Add(new RowDefinition());
     grid.RowDefinitions
         .Add(new RowDefinition());
    return grid;
}
```

- This code creates a 2x3 `Grid` that is used to create a basic form layout.

> We are not trying to make this form pretty but are instead trying to focus on the presentation patterns. One of the big benefits of MVVM is that it will allows us to give our view XAML to a designer and have them make it look nice without having the need to involve the developer. We will look at this approach in detail later in this book in *Chapter 7, Dialogs and MVVM.*

- Add the `UpdateDetails()` method as follows:

```
private void UpdateDetails()
{
    Project selectedProject
        = _projectsComboBox.SelectedItem
        as Project;

    _estimateTextBox.IsEnabled = true;
    _estimateTextBox.Text
        = selectedProject.Estimate.ToString();
    _actualTextBox.IsEnabled = true;
    _actualTextBox.Text
        = (selectedProject.Actual == 0)
                ? ""
                : selectedProject.Actual.ToString();
    SetEstimateColor(selectedProject);
    _updateButton.IsEnabled = true;
}
```

- The `UpdateDetails()` method simply transfers data from the `projectsComboBox.SelectedItem` (or master) to the details controls and then updates the `estimateTextBox` by calling `SetEstimateColor()`.
- Add a `DisableDetails()` method as follows:

```
private void DisableDetails()
{
  _estimateTextBox.IsEnabled = false;
  _actualTextBox.IsEnabled = false;
  _updateButton.IsEnabled = false;
}
```

- The `DisableDetails()` method sets the details controls `IsEnabled` to `false` along with the update button.

- Add `SetEstimateColor()` as follows:

```
private void SetEstimateColor(Project selectedProject)
{
    if (selectedProject.Actual == 0)
    {
        this.estimateTextBox.Foreground
            = _actualTextBox.Foreground;
    }
    else if (selectedProject.Actual
        <= selectedProject.Estimate)
    {
        this.estimateTextBox.Foreground
            = Brushes.Green;
    }
    else
    {
        this.estimateTextBox.Foreground
            = Brushes.Red;
    }
}
```

- The `SetEstimateColor()` method will be called by both event handlers to update the color of **Estimated Cost** (view state) by examining the Actual Cost and Estimated Cost.

Running the sample

Right-click on the **ProjectBilling.Monolithic** project and select **Properties**. Next, set the **Output type** to **Windows Application** as shown in the following screenshot:

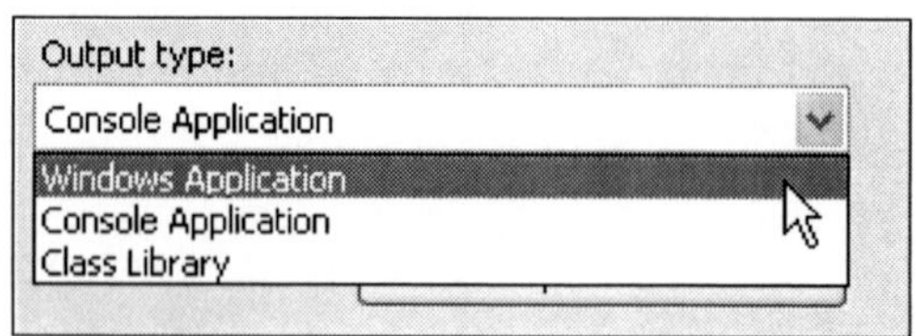

If you leave the **Project** type as **Console Application** then a **Console Window** will be displayed while your WPF application runs. This can be useful for debugging as you can write debug messages to the console and easily kill the application using *Ctrl* + C when debugging.

Finally set **ProjectBilling.Monolithic** as the startup project by right-clicking on it and selecting **Set as StartUp project**. Now run the application by hitting *F5*.

You should now see an application as shown in *The Project Billing sample application* section at the beginning of this chapter.

Takeaways

This code gets the job done, so what's the problem and why is there the need to restructure it?

Poor testability

This code has poor testability as the entire code is tightly coupled to the view and requires the view to fire the events that drive the logic of application. You could change the access modifiers of the methods of `ProjectsView` to public the help alleviate the situation but then you weaken the design from the **encapsulation** and **design by contract** perspectives.

Encapsulation and design by contract are basic principles of Object-oriented design that are covered extensively on the Web. Please look up for them if you are already not familiar with them.

Poor extensibility and code reuse

If the users wanted a command line or web-interface, all of the code would need to be rewritten. Also, supporting multiple synchronized **ProjectView** is not possible under this design and would require at a minimum refactoring out a model.

We will demonstrate how adding SoC allows for creating multiple synchronized views of the model when we get to the *MVC* section.

Rapid application development

Microsoft puts a lot of development effort into creating **Rapid Application Development** (or **RAD**) tools that allow developers to simply drag-and-drop controls onto the IDE's design surface and then allow for configuring the controls' data needs mostly through the IDE's designer. The designer then creates monolithic code to get the job done. These tools make the problems of monolithic design worse by encouraging that style of design and by making it easier to do.

RAD Project Billing sample

This section will walk through rewriting the Project Billing application using RAD tools in Visual Studio.

Start by adding a new **WPF Application** project to your solution called **ProjectBilling.RAD**. This project template creates two files for you, `App.xaml` and `MainWindow.xaml`.

Next add a project reference to **ProjectBilling.DataAccess**.

Open `MainWindow.xaml` in **Cider** (the WPF designer) by double-clicking on `MainWindow.xaml` in the **Solution Explorer**. If they're not already expanded, expand the **Toolbox** window and the **Data Sources** window. You should have Visual Studio set up as shown in the following screenshot:

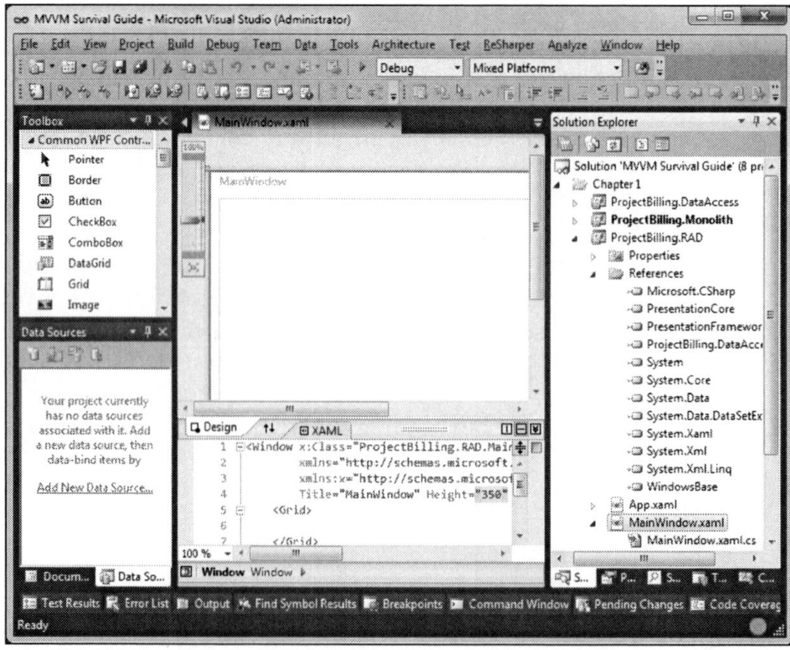

The first step is to add an **Object Data Source** to connect to `DataService.GetProjects()`. To do this start by clicking on **Add New Data Source** in the **Data Sources** window, as shown in the following screenshot:

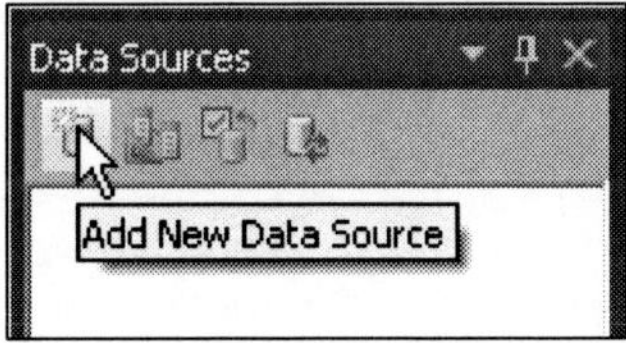

You will now be presented with a dialog that will allow you to specify an **Object Data Source**, as shown in the following screenshot:

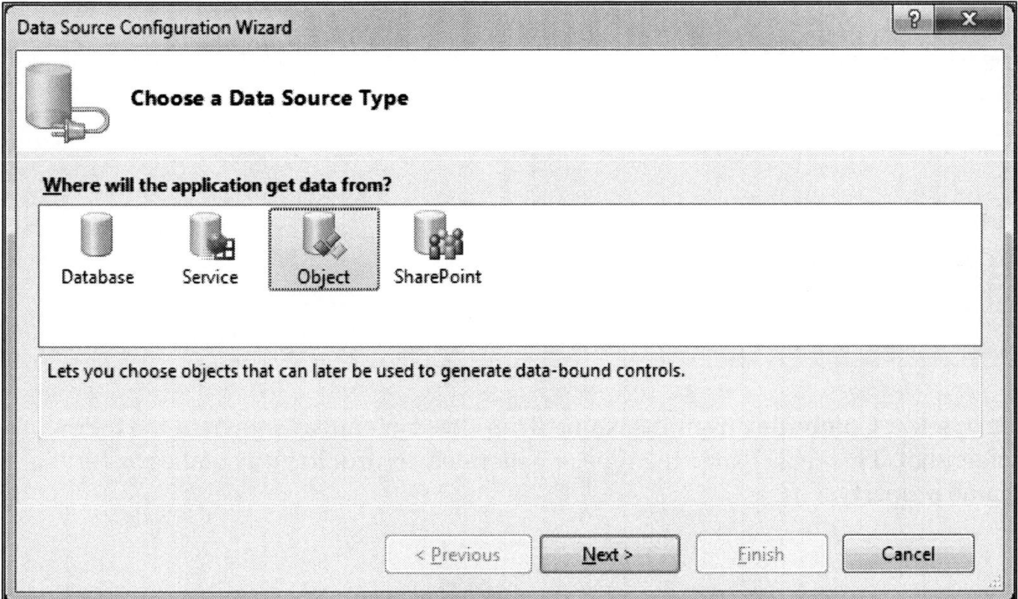

You will now be given the option to select the object that will be your data source. Select the `Project class` as shown in the following screenshot:

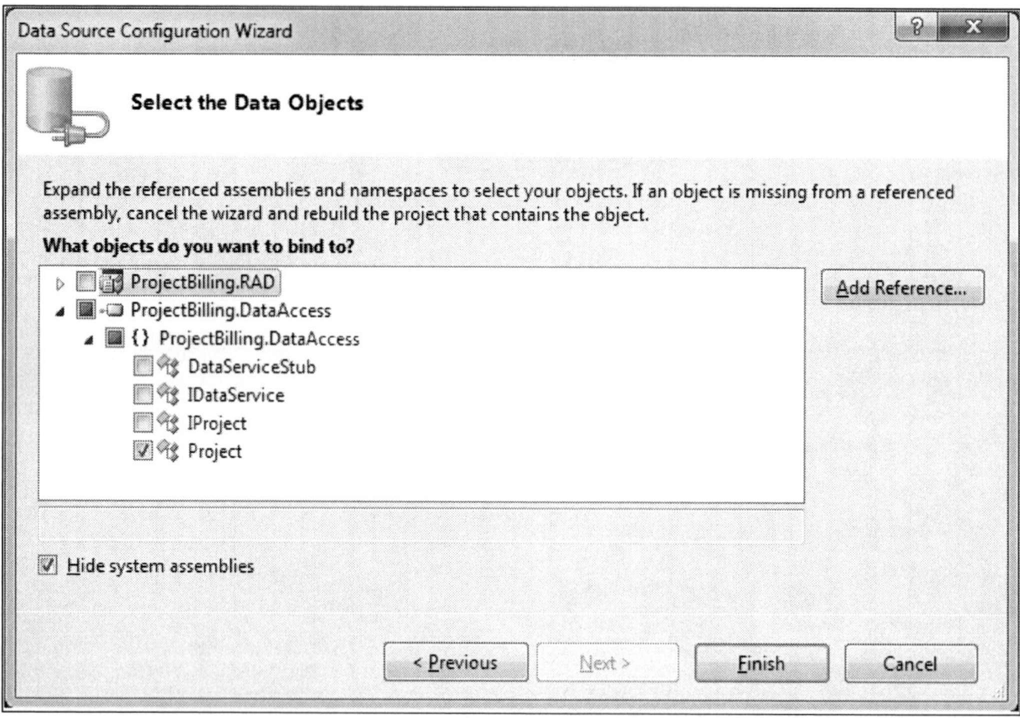

Next, select **ComboBox** from the **Name** drop-down menu, as shown in the following screenshot. This will change the type of generated control to be a combobox for the **Name** property.

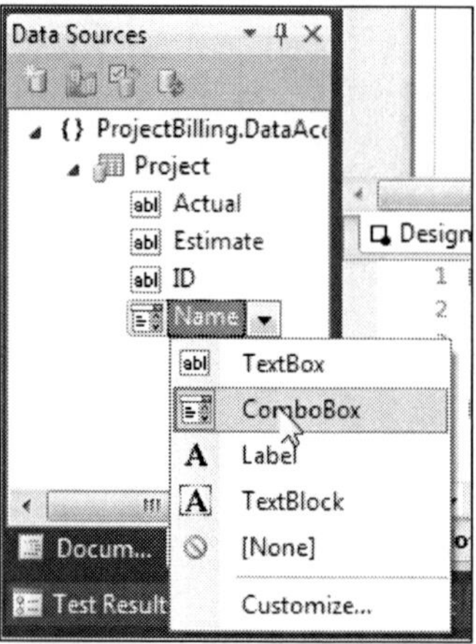

Now drag the **Name** column onto the designer surface so that Visual Studio can generate some code to create a **ComboBox** which will be ready to be bound by an `IList<Product>`.

Change the width of the window to `250` by clicking on the **MainWindow** and setting the width value in the properties. You should now see something similar to what is shown in the following screenshot:

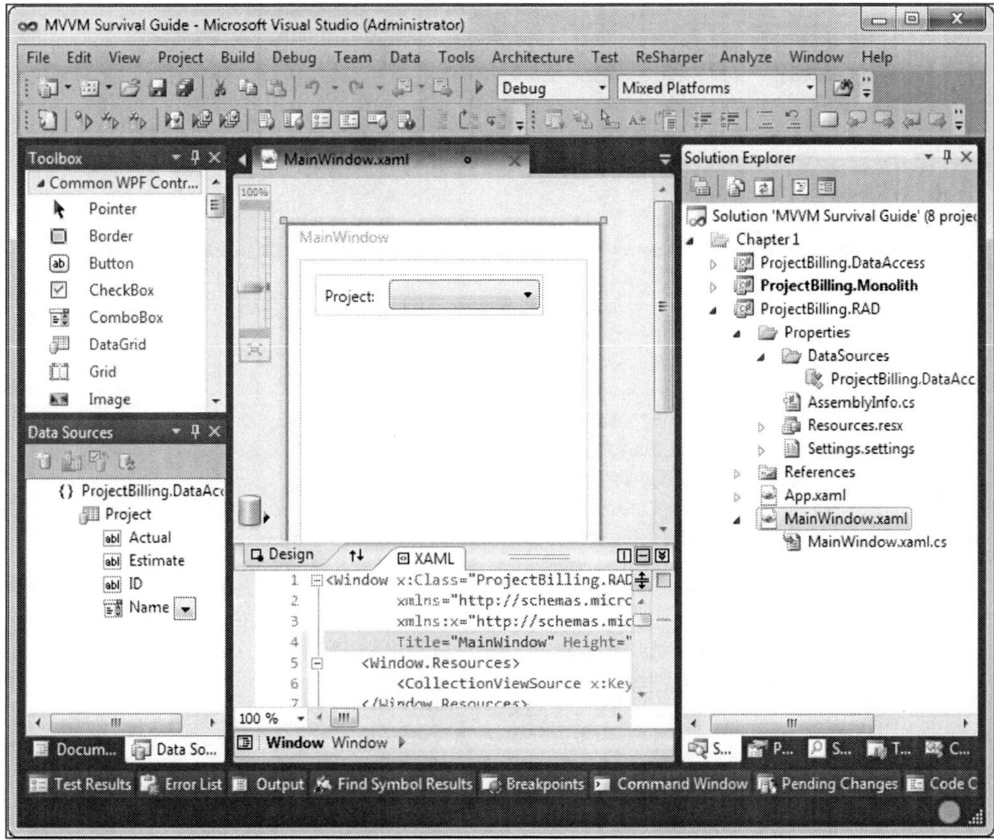

Looking at the XAML in the previous screenshot you will see that some code was generated for you. The important parts are highlighted as follows.

> It is assumed that you are familiar with the basics of WPF's data binding as full details fall outside of the scope of this book. However, see *Appendix B, Binding at a glance*, and/or see *Data Binding (WPF)* on MSDN (`http://msdn.microsoft.com/en-us/library/ms750612.aspx`).

```
<Window x:Class="RadProjectBilling.MainWindow"
        xmlns="http://schemas.microsoft.com/winfx/2006/xaml/
presentation"
        xmlns:x="http://schemas.microsoft.com/winfx/2006/xaml"
        Title="MainWindow" Height="350" Width="250"
        mc:Ignorable="d"
        xmlns:d="http://schemas.microsoft.com/expression/blend/2008"
        xmlns:mc="http://schemas.openxmlformats.org/markup-
compatibility/2006"
        xmlns:my="clr-namespace: ProjectBilling.DataAccess;assembly=Pr
ojectBilling.DataAccess"
        Loaded="Window_Loaded">
    <Window.Resources>
        <CollectionViewSource x:Key="projectViewSource" d:DesignSource
="{d:DesignInstance my:Project, CreateList=True}" />
    </Window.Resources>
    <Grid>
        <Grid DataContext="{StaticResource projectViewSource}"
              HorizontalAlignment="Left"
              Margin="12,12,0,0" Name="grid1"
              VerticalAlignment="Top">
            <Grid.ColumnDefinitions>
                <ColumnDefinition Width="Auto" />
                <ColumnDefinition Width="Auto" />
            </Grid.ColumnDefinitions>
            <Grid.RowDefinitions>
                <RowDefinition Height="Auto" />
            </Grid.RowDefinitions>
            <Label Content="Name:" Grid.Column="0"
                   Grid.Row="0" HorizontalAlignment="Left"
                   Margin="3" VerticalAlignment="Center" />
            <ComboBox DisplayMemberPath="Name" Grid.Column="1"
                      Grid.Row="0" Height="23"
                      HorizontalAlignment="Left"
                      ItemsSource="{Binding}" Margin="3"
                      Name="nameComboBox"
                      VerticalAlignment="Center" Width="120">
                <ComboBox.ItemsPanel>
                    <ItemsPanelTemplate>
                        <VirtualizingStackPanel />
                    </ItemsPanelTemplate>
                </ComboBox.ItemsPanel>
            </ComboBox>
        </Grid>
    </Grid>
</Window>
```

At the top of the file, there is an event handler added for the `Window.Loaded` event which is set to `Window_Loaded`.As you will see soon, `Window_Loaded` was created in the code behind. Next, a new `CollectionViewSource` named `projectViewSource` was added and set to reference to the `DataLayer.Project` class.

A `CollectionViewSource` class wraps a data source and allows you to navigate and display the collection based on sort, filter, and group quires.

The grid, `grid1`, then had its **DataContext** set to `projectViewSource` and a **ComboBox** called `nameComboBox` was added with its **ItemsSource** bound to its **DataContext** with the following code.

```
ItemsSource="{Binding}"
```

Specifying `Binding` with no path in a binding expression will cause the binding target to be bound to the combobox's DataContext property.

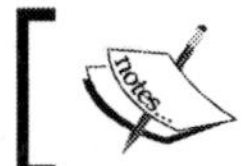

We will be covering bindings and DataContext in more depth later in this book.

`DataContext` is an inherited **DependencyProperty** and inherited `DependencyProperties` will have their values propagated from parents to children in the **Visual Tree** and in this case will result in the DataContext that was set on `grid1` being propagated to all of its children including `nameComboBox`.

For more information on `DependencyProperties` see *Dependency Properties Overview* on MSDN (`http://msdn.microsoft.com/en-us/library/ms752914.aspx`) and for more information on the `Visual Tree` see *Trees in WPF* on MSDN (`http://msdn.microsoft.com/en-us/library/ms753391.aspx`).

If we look in the code behind, `MainWindow.xaml.cs`, we'll see that `projectViewSource` has been initialized in `Window_Loaded()`.

```
private void Window_Loaded(object sender, RoutedEventArgs e)
{

    System.Windows.Data.CollectionViewSource projectViewSource
        = ((System.Windows.Data.CollectionViewSource)
        (this.FindResource("projectViewSource")));
    // Load data by setting the
    // CollectionViewSource.Source property:
    // projectViewSource.Source = [generic data source]
}
```

There is some commented out code created for you.

```
// projectViewSource.Source = [generic data source]
```

By uncommenting the previous line of code, you can easily set the data source to the collection returned by `DataServiceStub.GetProjects`, as shown in the following code.

You will need to add a using statement for `ProjectBilling.DataAccess` to the top of the file.

```
private void Window_Loaded(object sender, RoutedEventArgs e)
{

    System.Windows.Data.CollectionViewSource projectViewSource
        = ((System.Windows.Data.CollectionViewSource)
        (this.FindResource("projectViewSource")));
    // Load data by setting the
    // CollectionViewSource.Source property:
    projectViewSource.Source=new DataServiceStub().GetProjects();

}
```

Now if we run the application, we will see that the **Name** combobox is populated with data shown in the following screenshot:

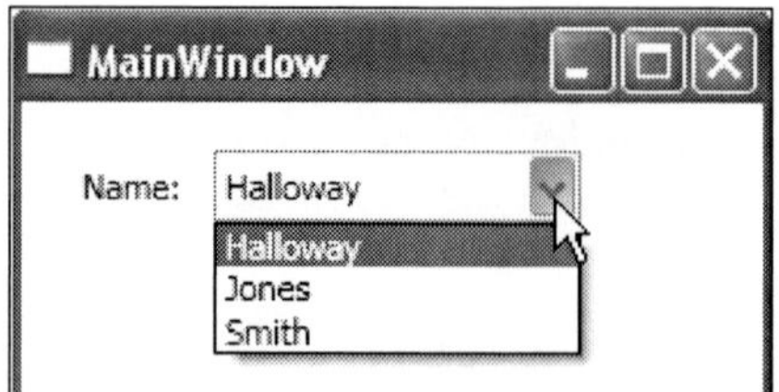

Next we need to add the details controls. The first step is to click on the drop-down menu next to the **Project** data source in the **DataSources** window and change its type to **Details**, as shown in the following screenshot:

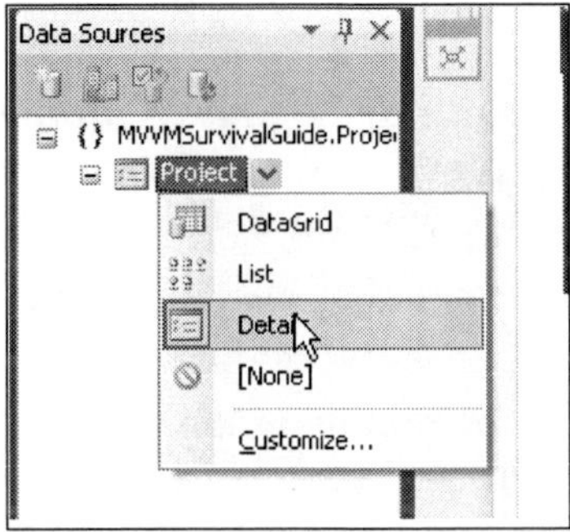

Now we will generate the details controls as shown in the following screenshot:

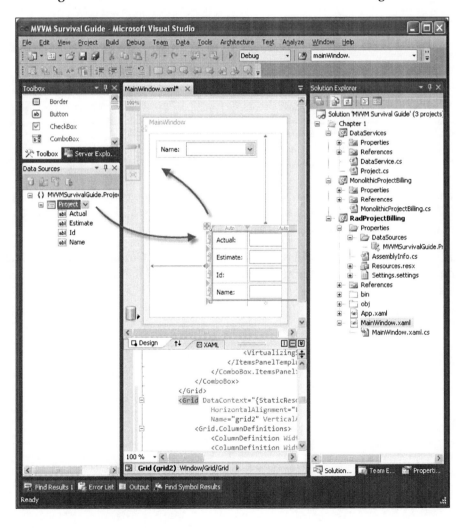

Perform the following steps:

1. Drag the **Project** data source to the **MainWindow** on the `cider` design surface as shown in the previous screenshot. This will create a mini form with the controls for displaying the details.
2. Drag the form that was created by clicking on the drag handles for the grid and move it below the name, as shown in the previous screenshot.
3. Next, clean up the form by removing the labels, textboxes, and rows that are associated with the `Id` and `Name` labels.

Now run `ProjectBilling.RAD` and you should have a working master/details view, as shown in the following screenshot:

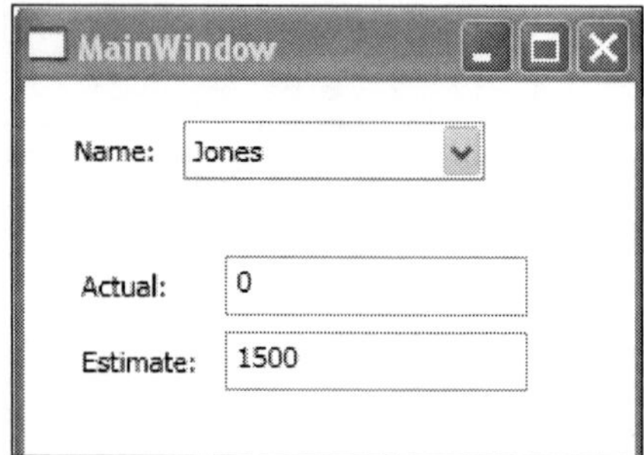

As you can see, it's easy to set up a working master/details form using these tools. It'd need some tweaking to be exactly the same as the monolithic one but I'm sure you get the idea of how this works compared to the monolithic style.

To finish off the application, add a button and change its **Content** to **Update**, **Name** to **UpdateButton**, **IsEnabled** to **false**, and then double-click on the button to create an event handler called `UpdateButton_Click()`.

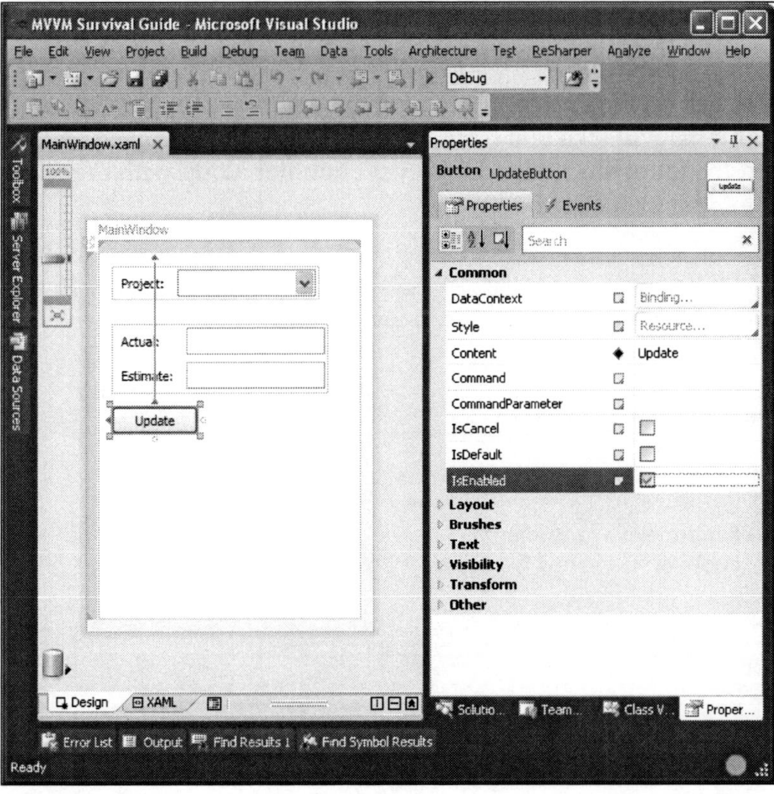

Add the following code to `updateButton_Click()`:

```
private void UpdateButton_Click(object sender,
    RoutedEventArgs e)
{
    Project selectedProject
        = this.nameComboBox.SelectedItem
        as Project;
    if (selectedProject != null)
    {                    selectedProject.Estimate =
            double.Parse(this.estimateTextBox.Text);
        if (!string.IsNullOrEmpty(
            this.actualTextBox.Text))
        {
            selectedProject.Actual
                = double.Parse(
                    this.actualTextBox.Text);
        }
        SetEstimateColor(selectedProject);
    }
}
```

This is almost exactly the same code we saw in the previous monolithic example and works exactly the same way.

Next, double-click on the **Project** combobox to add a `SelectionChanged` event handler. This will take you from the designer to the newly created event handler. Add the following code to this event handler along with the related `SetEstimateColor()` method.

You will need to include the `System.Windows.Controls` and `System.Windows.Media` namespaces.

```
private void nameComboBox_SelectionChanged(object sender,
    SelectionChangedEventArgs e)
{
    ComboBox comboBox = sender as ComboBox;

    // If there is a selected item
    if (comboBox != null && comboBox.SelectedIndex > -1)
    {
        Project selectedProject
            = comboBox.SelectedItem as Project;

        SetEstimateColor(selectedProject);
        this.UpdateButton.IsEnabled = true;
    }
    else
    {
        this.estimateTextBox.IsEnabled = false;
        this.actualTextBox.IsEnabled = false;
        this.UpdateButton.IsEnabled = false;
    }
}

private void SetEstimateColor(Project selectedProject)
{
    if (selectedProject.Actual == 0)
    {
        this.estimateTextBox.Foreground
            = Brushes.Black;
    }
    else if (selectedProject.Actual
        <= selectedProject.Estimate)
    {
        this.estimateTextBox.Foreground
            = Brushes.Green;
    }
    else
```

```
        {
            this.estimateTextBox.Foreground
                = Brushes.Red;
        }
    }
```

The previous code is similar to the monolithic code, except shorter. A lot of the code that was used to update the UI before is now not necessary and has been specified as a part of the XAML.

```
<Window.Resources>
    <CollectionViewSource x:Key="projectViewSource"
            d:DesignSource="{d:DesignInstance my:Project,
                                        CreateList=True}" />
</Window.Resources>
```

The `projectViewSource` is now doing the work we were manually doing before to move data in and out of our details controls, and that is accomplished through the bindings that have been created for us on the details controls.

```
<TextBox Grid.Column="1" Grid.Row="0" Height="23"
        HorizontalAlignment="Left" Margin="3"
        Name="actualTextBox"
        Text="{Binding Path=Actual, Mode=TwoWay,
                ValidatesOnExceptions=true,
                NotifyOnValidationError=true}"
        VerticalAlignment="Center" Width="120" />
```

Each details control will have a binding configured, as shown previously, to allow for two-way communication with the binding source, which in this case is the `Project.Actual` that is exposed from the `projectViewSource` `CollectionViewSource` class.

Takeaways

Looking at the code we just created, we see a situation that is slightly better than with pure monolithic design. The use of a `CollectionViewSource` reduced the amount of code that was created and that would need to be maintained and tested. However, the ease with which these controls allow for creating monolithic designs makes them an overall negative for those who care about design. We still have all the problems of monolithic code here that result from tight coupling and poor separation of concerns. However, we now have the additional problem of Visual Studio encouraging that type of design and we still can't easily support multiple dynamic views of our session state.

MVC

As a result of the problems caused by monolithic design, there has been a movement that started in the 70s towards presentational patterns or "Model View" patterns that provide better SoC and better testability. All this began in 1979 when MVC (Model View Controller) was described by Trygve Reenskaug while he was working on Smalltalk at Xerox PARC. Presentation patterns are notoriously flexible and this flexibility is part of what makes them difficult to master. Because of this there have been numerous versions of the MVC pattern; it's out of the scope of this book to cover all the various types of MVCs. What is important to understand is what these MVC patterns generally looked like and what problems they had which led to MVP. The basic structure of MVC is shown in the following diagram:

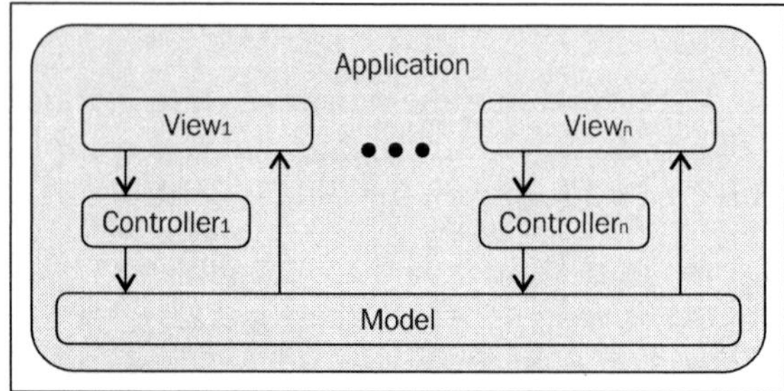

Over the years MVC has taken many forms and it has evolved to where it is now common for the controllers to have a larger scope than just one widget, and under this newer style you'd more likely have one controller per form or user control instead of per widget. The sample used in this book makes use of the more modern style with one controller per window.

We will now cover the responsibilities of each of the components mentioned earlier and as part of that discussion you will see where the components introduced in the *Monolithic* section of this chapter fit into the MVC paradigm.

View

The **view** is responsible for displaying data and collecting user input. The view gets its data from the model including notifications that data has been updated and needs to be refreshed. These notifications are implemented using an observer pattern.

In .NET, events are an implementation of the observer pattern.

When the user interacts with the view through gestures, the view is responsible for collecting those gestures and forwarding them along to the controller for processing.

Controller

The **controller** is responsible for taking user input and communicating it to the model for processing.

The controller doesn't have to pass user input directly to the model and in many cases will instead communicate input gestures to a service layer or business logic layer for processing, which will then update the existing model or return a new model depending on the architecture. These details will be covered more extensively in the section titled *Layered Design* later in this chapter.

The main benefit that the controller provides is the ability to remove as much logic as possible into an external component that can be tested using automated tests.

There are many variations of MVC that we will not be covering where the controller is responsible for collecting input from the user including **Model 2**, which is the pattern that ASP.NET MVC is based on.

Model

In MVC, the model is the in-memory representation of the data that was retrieved from the persistence store (*session state*). The model is also responsible for notifying the view of changes in state which is generally done with an observer pattern. Abstracting the model in this way allows for easily sharing session state among views, as we will discover shortly in the *MVC Project Billing sample* section.

Layered design

The design shown in the previous screenshot is an over-simplification of what is generally done in enterprise applications. Enterprise applications are generally separated into three logical layers as shown in the following diagram:

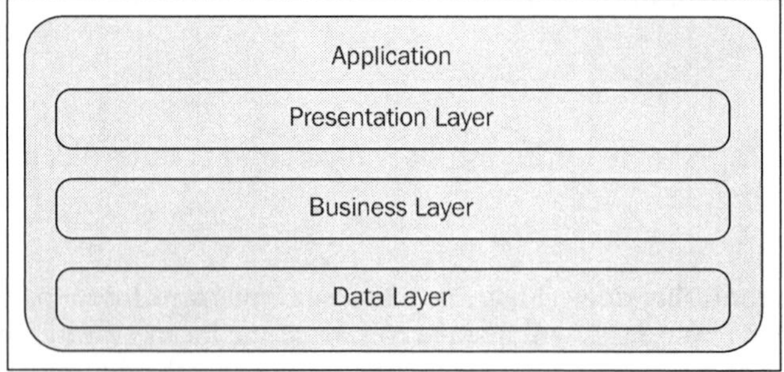

Layering an application in this way provides many benefits including the ability to scale more easily by deploying different layers to different servers and the ability to swap out layers with alternate implementations making the design extensible to change. A full discussion of layered design is outside of the scope of this book. If you'd like to learn more about layered enterprise design then see *Chapter 5, Northwind – Commands and User Inputs*, and *Layered Application Guidelines* from *Microsoft Application Architecture Guide, 2nd Edition* which is freely available online as part of MSDN (`http://msdn.microsoft.com/en-us/library/ff650706.aspx`).

The layers

The common three-layer design shown in the previous screenshot consists of the following layers:

Presentation layer

The **presentation layer** is responsible for

- Displaying data
- Providing feedback to the user
- Collecting user input which is passed along to the business logic layer for processing

Separating the presentation in this way provides the benefits of being able to change the UI or provide a second UI without having to duplicate the code in the lower layers if for example you need to provide a thick client, thin client and a command-line version of your application.

Business layer

The **business layer** or **application layer** is where the core functionality of the system lives. This logic is called the **business logic** or **domain logic** and is applied to the raw data that is fetched from the data access layer for processing. Having the business logic in its own layer allows for scalability as the business logic can be hosted separately from the other layers and allows for extensibility as it provides the flexibility to support multiple types of UIs and multiple types of data stores if needed.

Data layer

The **data layer** is responsible for pulling data from and pushing data to a data store like a database, service or XML file. Having the data access layer provides the benefit of allowing for change in the data store without having to change code in higher layers.

MVC with layered design

Layered design may seem like a similar idea to MVC and it does have some similar ideas but they are not the same. However, they are generally used together in enterprise architecture, as shown in the following diagram:

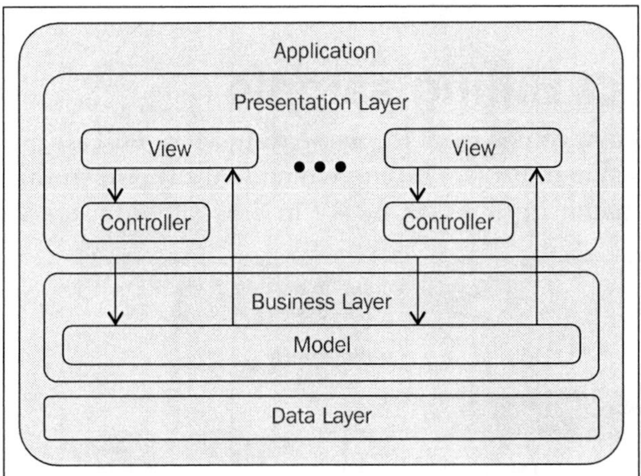

As you can see from the previous screenshot, using MVC with **layered design** results in having the view and controller as part of the presentation layer and the model as part of the business logic layer.

There are various approaches to how the model and business logic can be structured. Martin Fowler describes the most common approaches on his blog and in his book *Patterns of Enterprise Application Architecture*. The patterns Martin describes include the following:

- **Transaction script**: This approach organizes business logic in procedures where each procedure handles a single request from the presentation. Under this design you have one large facade that exposes your business logic through its methods.
- **Domain model**: This approach organizes domain logic into an object model of the domain that incorporates both behavior and data. Under this design you have an object graph that mirrors your domain objects and each of these domain or business objects could provide methods for fetching or manipulating data.
- **Table module**: Under this design you'd have a model that mirrors the database tables instead of the domain objects.

We have barely scratched the surface here because there are so many ways of organizing business logic and the model. Covering all of the options available for the business layer and model is outside of the scope of this book. If you are interested in learning more see *Patterns of Enterprise Application Architecture* by *Martin Fowler*.

MVC Project Billing sample

The increased SoC that comes from implementing MVC will allow us to implement a slightly better version of Project Billing which will support multiple views of the same data with dynamic updates, as shown in the following screenshot:

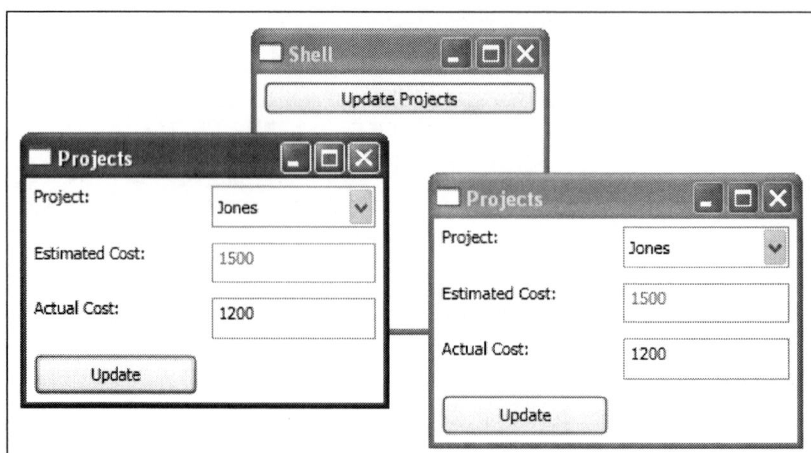

The classes involved in our MVC design are shown in the following screenshot:

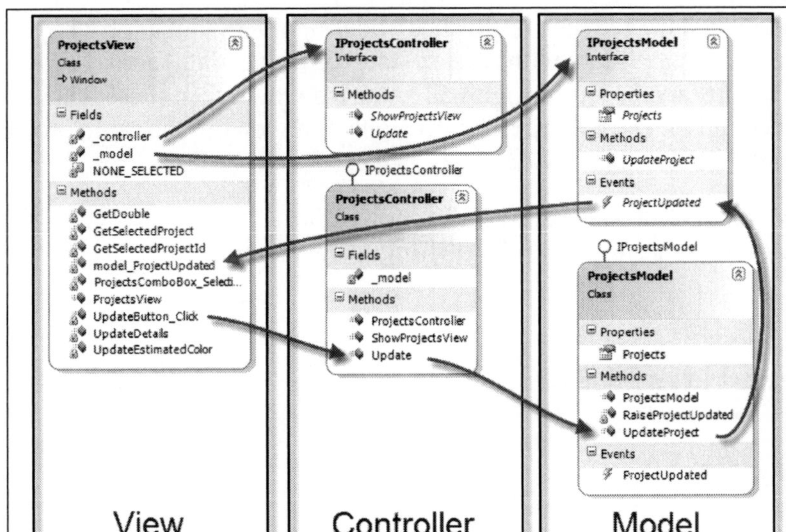

As you can see in the previous screenshot we will have:

- `ProjectsView` that keeps a reference to an `IProjectsController` interface via the `ProjectsView.controller` field and will keep a reference to an `IProjectsModel` interface via the `ProjectsView.model` field
- `ProjectsController` class that implements `IProjectsController`
- `ProjectsModel` that implements `IProjectsModel`

`ProjectsView` will use its reference to `IProjectController` to communicate user gestures to the controller by calling `ProjectsView.controller.Update()`. Internally this will call `ProjectsController.model.UpdateProject()`.

`ProjectsView` could call `ProjectsView.model.UpdateProject()` directly, but then the view logic would not be easily testable.

`ProjectsView` uses its reference to `IProjectModel` so that it can observe the `IProjectsModel.ProjectUpdated` event that will be raised after a call to `ProjectModel.UpdateProject()` finishes updating the model to provide dynamic synchronization of view state with session state (or model data) across all the `ProjectsView` instances. This design will make it so that when a user clicks on the **Update** button, all views that are currently open and viewing the same project will get the update and display the new data.

Let's start by creating a new WPF Application project called `MvcProjectBilling`. Add a project reference to the **ProjectBilling.DataAccess**.

Model

Add a new class to `ProjectBilling.MVC` called `ProjectsModel` and put the following code in it:

```
using System;
using System.Collections.Generic;
using System.Linq;
using ProjectBilling.DataAccess;

namespace ProjectBilling.Business.MVC
{
    public interface IProjectsModel
    {
        IEnumerable<Project> Projects { get; set; }
        event EventHandler<ProjectEventArgs> ProjectUpdated;
        void UpdateProject(Project project);
    }

    public class ProjectsModel : IProjectsModel
    {
        public IEnumerable<Project> Projects { get; set; }

        public event EventHandler<ProjectEventArgs>
            ProjectUpdated = delegate { };

        public ProjectsModel()
        {
            Projects = new DataServiceStub().GetProjects();
        }

        private void RaiseProjectUpdated(Project project)
        {
```

```
            ProjectUpdated(this,
                new ProjectEventArgs(project));
        }

        public void UpdateProject(Project project)
        {
            Project selectedProject
                = Projects.Where(p => p.ID == project.ID)
                      .FirstOrDefault() as Project;
            selectedProject.Name = project.Name;
            selectedProject.Estimate = project.Estimate;
            selectedProject.Actual = project.Actual;
            RaiseProjectUpdated(selectedProject);
        }
    }

    public class ProjectEventArgs : EventArgs
    {
        public Project Project { get; set; }

        public ProjectEventArgs(Project project)
        {
            Project = project;
        }
    }
}
```

This code creates a model for consumption by our view. The view uses the observer pattern to get its updates from the model and the controller passes along user input from the view to the model using an `IProjectsModel` reference.

We have implemented `ProjectsModel` based on the `IProjectModel` so that our design is more extensible and allows using dependency injection. Dependency Injection will allow for increased testability as a fake object (mock or stub) can now be provided during unit tests.

The `IProjectsModel` interface is shown as follows:

```
    public interface IProjectsModel
    {
        IEnumerable<Project> Projects { get; set; }
        event EventHandler<ProjectEventArgs> ProjectUpdated;
        void UpdateProject(Project project);
    }
```

`IProjectsModel` defines the following contract:

- `Projects`: It is a collection of projects that was loaded from persisted state
- `ProjectUpdated`: It is an event for notifying when a project has its data updated
- `UpdateProject()`: It is a method for submitting a project to be updated

The `ProjectModel` class implements the `IProjectModelInterface` and uses `IDataServices.GetProjects()` to fetch the data from our persistence service stub.

The following code is the preferred way of defining events and it allows you to avoid having to check for a null event before raising the event. The code is more concise than the more common null checking pattern and also thread safe.

```
public event EventHandler<ProjectEventArgs>
    ProjectUpdated = delegate { };
```

Controller

Add a class to the `ProjectsBilling.MVC` project called `ProjectsController` and add the code as follows:

```
using System;
using ProjectBilling.Business.MVC;
using ProjectBilling.DataAccess;
using System.Windows;

namespace ProjectBilling.UI.MVC
{
    public interface IProjectsController
    {
        void ShowProjectsView(Window owner);
        void Update(Project project);
    }

    public class ProjectsController : IProjectsController
    {
        private readonly IProjectsModel _model;

        public ProjectsController(IProjectsModel projectModel)
        {
            if (projectModel == null)
                throw new ArgumentNullException(
```

```
                "projectModel");
            _model = projectModel;
        }

        public void ShowProjectsView(Window owner)
        {
            ProjectsView view
                = new ProjectsView(this, _model);
            view.Owner = owner;
            view.Show();
        }

        public void Update(Project project)
        {
            _model.UpdateProject(project);
        }
    }
}
```

We've implemented the controller based on an interface to again take advantage of the benefits of dependency injection. The interface defines the following contract:

- `ShowProjectsView()`: It is a method that allows for displaying a `ProjectsView` to the user
- `Update()`: It is a method that allows for updating a project that delegates the updating of the project to the model

> It was common in older versions of MVC to have the controller responsible for determining the next view and then to display the view. We demonstrated that in the previous code with `ShowProjectsView()`. This is not a responsibility that always is taken on by the controller in MVC.

View

Add a new window to `ProjectBilling.MVC` called `ProjectsView` and add the following code to `ProjectView.xaml`:

```
<Window x:Class="ProjectBilling.UI.MVC.ProjectsView"
        xmlns="http://schemas.microsoft.com/winfx/2006/xaml/
presentation"
        xmlns:x="http://schemas.microsoft.com/winfx/2006/xaml"
        Title="Projects" MinHeight="180" Height="180"
        MinWidth="250" Width="250" Padding="5"
```

```
            FocusManager.FocusedElement
                ="{Binding ElementName=ProjectsComboBox}">
        <UniformGrid Columns="2">
            <Label Content="Project:" />
            <ComboBox Name="ProjectsComboBox" Margin="5"
                    SelectionChanged
                        ="ProjectsComboBox_SelectionChanged" />
            <Label Content="Estimated Cost:" />
            <TextBox Name="EstimatedTextBox" Margin="5"
                     IsEnabled="False" />
            <Label Content="Actual Cost:" />
            <TextBox Name="ActualTextBox" Margin="5"
                     IsEnabled="False" />
            <Button Name="UpdateButton" Content="Update"
                    Margin="5" IsEnabled="False"
                    Click="UpdateButton_Click" />
        </UniformGrid>
    </Window>
```

This XAML creates a simple master/details form, like the one shown in the screenshot at the beginning of the *MVC Project Billing sample* section.

Coverage of the basics of XAML is outside the scope of this book.

Next, add the following code to `ProjectsView.xaml.cs`. Start by adding the fields that will hold a reference to the model and controller.

```
using System.Windows;
using System.Windows.Controls;
using System.Windows.Media;
using ProjectBilling.Business.MVC;
using ProjectBilling.DataAccess;

namespace ProjectBilling.UI.MVC
{
    public partial class ProjectsView : Window
    {
        private readonly IProjectsModel _model;
        private readonly IProjectsController _controller
            = null;
        private const int NONE_SELECTED = -1;
    }
}
```

Initialization

Add the constructor as follows:

```
public ProjectsView(
    IProjectsController projectsController,
    IProjectsModel projectsModel)
{
    InitializeComponent();
    _controller
        = projectsController;
    _model = projectsModel;
    _model.ProjectUpdated
        += model_ProjectUpdated;
    ProjectsComboBox.ItemsSource
        = _model.Projects;
    ProjectsComboBox.DisplayMemberPath
        = "Name";
    ProjectsComboBox.SelectedValuePath
        = "ID";
}
```

This constructor allows for dependency injection by taking an interface for the model and controller as parameters. As previously mentioned, this allows for more isolated unit tests as fake objects (mocks or stubs) can be passed in for testing. The constructor:

1. Wires up the model and controller.
2. Subscribes to the `_model.ProjectUpdated` event.
3. Sets the `projectsComboBox.ItemSource` to `this.Model.Projects` and sets the `DisplayMemberPath` and `SelectedValuePath` so that they resolve to `Project.Name` and `Project.ID` respectively.

Event handlers

Now we will add some event handlers:

- The following `model_ProjectUpdated` code will execute when the `ProjectsModel.ProjectUpdated` event fires:

```
void model_ProjectUpdated(object sender,
    ProjectEventArgs e)
{
    int selectedProjectId = GetSelectedProjectId();

    if (selectedProjectId > NONE_SELECTED)
```

```
    {
        if (selectedProjectId == e.Project.ID)
        {
            UpdateDetails(e.Project);
        }
    }
}
```

- If the project that was updated is currently displayed in the details of this view, then this code will update the details with the project's new data. This allows for multiple synchronized views of the same data.
- The `ProjectsComboBox_SelectionChanged` event handler fires when the user changes the selected project in the `ProjectsComboBox`. This event gets the selected project and then updates the details controls with the newly selected project's data and then calls `UpdateEstimateColor()` to set `estimateTextBox.Foreground` to the appropriate color based on the view logic.

```
private void ProjectsComboBox_SelectionChanged(
    object sender, SelectionChangedEventArgs e)
{
    Project project = GetSelectedProject();
    if (project != null)
    {
        EstimatedTextBox.Text
            = project.Estimate.ToString();
        EstimatedTextBox.IsEnabled = true;
        ActualTextBox.Text
            = project.Actual.ToString();
        ActualTextBox.IsEnabled = true;
        UpdateButton.IsEnabled = true;
        UpdateEstimatedColor();
    }
}
```

- The `UpdateButton_Click` event handler fires when a user clicks on the **UpdateButton**. This event handler simply creates a new `Project` populated with the details data and then passes that project to the controller for processing.

```
private void UpdateButton_Click(object sender,
    RoutedEventArgs e)
{
    Project project = new Project()
    {
```

```
            ID = (int)ProjectsComboBox.SelectedValue,
            Name = ProjectsComboBox.Text,
            Estimate = GetDouble(
                EstimatedTextBox.Text),
            Actual = GetDouble(ActualTextBox.Text)
        };
        _controller.Update(project);
    }
```

Helpers

Add the code that follows as the private helper methods that are called from the event handlers:

- The `UpdateEstimateColor` function will look at the values of the details controls and update the `EstimateTextBox.Foreground` to the appropriate color based on the view logic.

```
private void UpdateEstimatedColor()
{
    double actual
        = GetDouble(ActualTextBox.Text);
    double estimated
        = GetDouble(EstimatedTextBox.Text);
    if (actual == 0)
    {
        EstimatedTextBox.Foreground
            = ActualTextBox.Foreground;
    }
    else if (actual > estimated)
    {
        EstimatedTextBox.Foreground
            = Brushes.Red;
    }
    else
    {
        EstimatedTextBox.Foreground
            = Brushes.Green;
    }
}
```

- The `UpdateDetails` function takes a project and updates the details controls including calling `UpdateEstimateColor()` to update the color of `estimateTextBox.Foreground`.

```
private void UpdateDetails(Project project)
{
```

```
        EstimatedTextBox.Text
            = project.Estimate.ToString();
        ActualTextBox.Text
            = project.Actual.ToString();
        UpdateEstimatedColor();
    }
```

- Next add the following methods which are self explanatory.

```
private double GetDouble(string text)
{
    return string.IsNullOrEmpty(text) ?
        0 : double.Parse(text);
}

private Project GetSelectedProject()
{
    return ProjectsComboBox.SelectedItem
        as Project;
}

private int GetSelectedProjectId()
{
    Project project = GetSelectedProject();
    return (project == null)
        ? NONE_SELECTED : project.ID;
}
```

MainWindow

- Update `MainWindow.xaml` as shown in the following code:

```
<Window x:Class="ProjectBilling.UI.MVC.MainWindow"
        xmlns="http://schemas.microsoft.com/winfx/2006/xaml/
presentation"
        xmlns:x="http://schemas.microsoft.com/winfx/2006/xaml"
        Title="Shell" Height="150" Width="150"
        MinHeight="200" MinWidth="200"
        FocusManager.FocusedElement
            ="{Binding ElementName=ShowProjectsButton}">
    <StackPanel>
        <Button Content="Update Projects"
                Name="ShowProjectsButton" Margin="5"
                Click="ShowProjectsButton_Click" />
    </StackPanel>
</Window>
```

- This will create a window with one button that says **ShowProjects**. Double-click on **ShowProjects** in cider to create an event handler and then add the following code to `MainWindow.xaml.cs`.

```
using System.Windows;
using ProjectBilling.Business.MVC;

namespace ProjectBilling.UI.MVC
{
    /// <summary>
    /// Interaction logic for MainWindow.xaml
    /// </summary>
    public partial class MainWindow : Window
    {
        private IProjectsController _controller;

        public MainWindow()
        {
            InitializeComponent();
            _controller
                = new ProjectsController(new ProjectsModel());
        }

        private void ShowProjectsButton_Click(object sender,
            RoutedEventArgs e)
        {
            _controller.ShowProjectsView(this);
        }
    }
}
```

- This code will serve as the main window of the application and will show a new `ProjectsView` each time the **Show Projects** button is clicked by calling `IProjectsController.ShowProjectsView()`.

How it works

Run the application now. You will see a window like the one shown in the following screenshot:

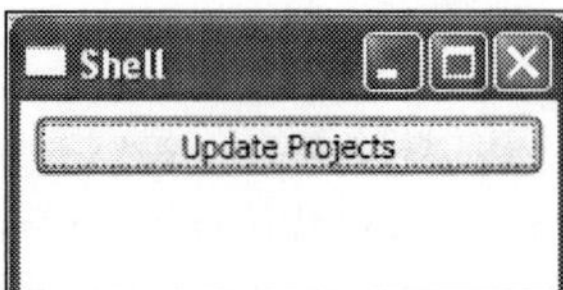

Each time the **Show Projects** button is clicked, a `ProjectsView` will be displayed as shown in the following screenshot:

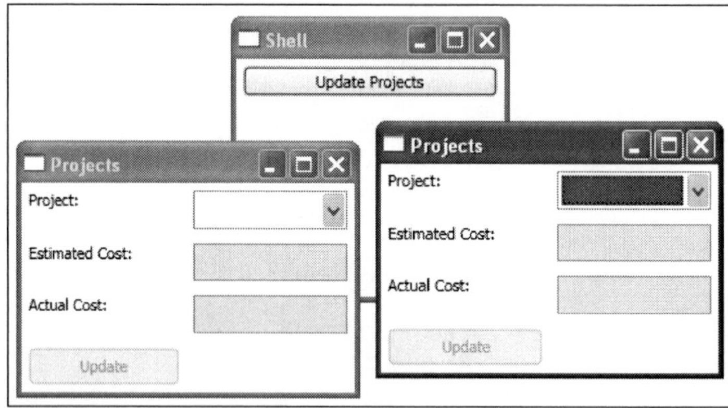

What's interesting about this architecture is that it's now easy to have updates propagate across views as you can see by following these steps:

1. Select the **Jones** account in each view.
2. Change the **Actual Cost** to be 1700 in one of the windows.
3. Click on the **Update** button in the same window that you changed the **Actual Cost** in.

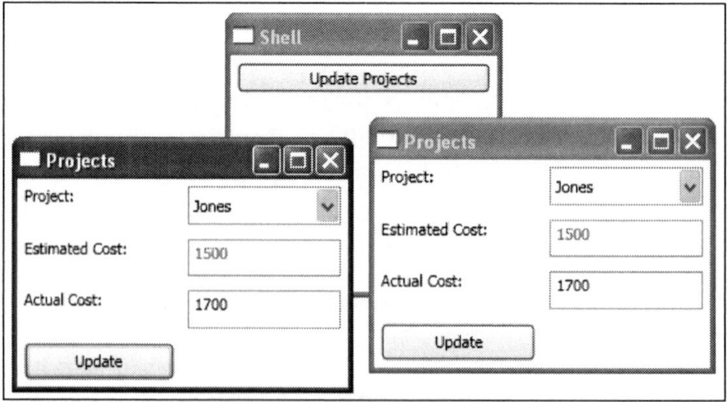

You will now see that both open **ProjectsView** windows update and this is because the model has been abstracted away and the views observes the model. When an update occurs, the windows get their updates in the form of events (the observer pattern). You can also set each window with a different project and then try updating a project in one window. Next, verify that the changes display in the second window when you select the updated project.

Takeaways

MVC makes several improvements over the monolithic approach:

- The increased SoC created by abstracting out a model allowed for easily supporting multiple synchronized views of the same data.
- The **controller** abstraction allows for increased testability of view interactions (gestures).

However, this design also has the following issues:

- The view logic and the view state are both still tightly coupled in the view leaving them difficult to test or share.
- If we wanted to do a thin client for the Web in Silverlight, we'd only be able to reuse the model and not the controller and we'd have to duplicate the view logic and view state.
- The final less obvious issue with this design deals with memory leaks. Details of the memory leaks follow. You can add code to fix the memory leak situation but I've found on the projects that I've worked on that this is often not done and requires higher maintenance than designs that don't rely on events. Having to go through this extra effort required by .NET events makes MVC less desirable than a pattern like MVVM that doesn't require the use of .NET events.

Memory leaks

In the *MVC Project Billing Sample* the view observes the Model using .NET events, which are an implementation of the observer pattern. One thing to watch out for when using .NET events is memory leaks. This is because unfortunately in .NET, events only support using strong references and not weak references. The issue here is that when an observer object (view in our example) subscribes to an event on a subject object (model in our example), the subject keeps a reference in the form of a delegate (or function pointer) to the observer. In .NET, memory management is handled by the **garbage collector** and the garbage collector will not collect any object as long as another object has a strong reference to it. This means that our view subscribing to our model's events will cause those models to hold strong references to the views. These strong references will prevent the garbage collector from collecting the views causing the views to leak.

To see this for yourself, update the previous example as follows. Let's start by adding a button to `MainWindow.xaml`:

```
<Button Content="GC Collect"
        Name="GCCollectButton" Margin="5"
        Click="GCCollectButton_Click" />
```

Next add `gcCollectButton_Click` to `MainWindow.xaml.cs` as follows:

```
private void GCCollectButton_Click(object sender,
    RoutedEventArgs e)
{
    GC.Collect();
    GC.WaitForPendingFinalizers();
    GC.Collect();
}
```

You will need to add the **System** namespace to use GC.

This code will call `GC.Collect()` twice and `GC.WaitForPendingFinalizers()` once. The .NET garbage collector is non-deterministic so there are no guarantees about when it will collect but I find this combination works pretty well at getting it to collect.

Now let's add a **finalizer** to `ProjectsView.xaml.cs` as follows.

Finalizers are called when an object is collected by the garbage collector. Full coverage of .NET memory management is out of the scope of this book. See *C# Via CLR* by *Jeffery Richter* for more details.

```
~ProjectsView()
{
    MessageBox.Show("ProjectsView collected");
}
```

Now when a `ProjectsView` instance is collected by the garbage collector, a message box will pop up and we will know that it was collected.

Go ahead, run the application and follow these steps:

1. Click on the **GC Collect** button as shown in the previous screenshot.
2. Open a few **ProjectsViews** by clicking on the **Show Projects** button and then close them.
3. Click on the **GC Collect** button, in fact click it a few times. Try all you want, you will not be able to get the finalizers to execute from the views that you created because the `ProjectsModel` instance is holding a reference to them.

You will never see the **ProjectsView collected** message box displayed under this design. If you used a memory profiler, you'd see that after each window is closed the memory used by the application doesn't decrease.

To fix this situation add the following code to `ProjectsView.xaml.cs` and then re-run the application repeating the steps listed previously.

```
protected override void OnClosed(EventArgs e)
{
    base.OnClosed(e);
    _model.ProjectUpdated -= model_ProjectUpdated;
}
```

Now you will see that when you click on **GC Collect** the finalizers will execute. This isn't a lot of code to correct this situation but developers do tend to get this wrong from time to time and it can make the code higher maintenance than a design that doesn't require .NET events.

Microsoft recommends using the **weak event pattern** to deal with this situation (`http://msdn.microsoft.com/en-us/library/aa970850.aspx`). However, I prefer the `WeakEvent` class found in *CLR via C#* by *Jeffery Richter* because it's a much lower maintenance approach than the weak event pattern and Richter's `WeakEvent` classes are used almost exactly like regular CLR events, so they require very little training. Please check Richter's blog for the latest version of this code which contains bug fixes to the published version.. These topics will not be covered in this book but feel free to dig deeper on your own.

MVP

MVP or **Model View Presenter** is a pattern that first appeared at IBM and then emerged more prominently at Taligent in the 1990's. MVP was a derivative of MVC that took a slightly different approach. Under MVP, the view is no longer required to observe the model.

Martin Fowler officially retired the MVP pattern on his blog and replaced it with two variations, **Passive View** and **Supervising Controller**. Passive view is what is shown in the following screenshot. Under Supervising Controller, the view still observes the model via an observer but with a much more limited scope than under MVC. For full details see Martin's blog (`http://martinfowler.com/eaaDev/ModelViewPresenter.html`).

The following diagram shows the basic structure of MVP:

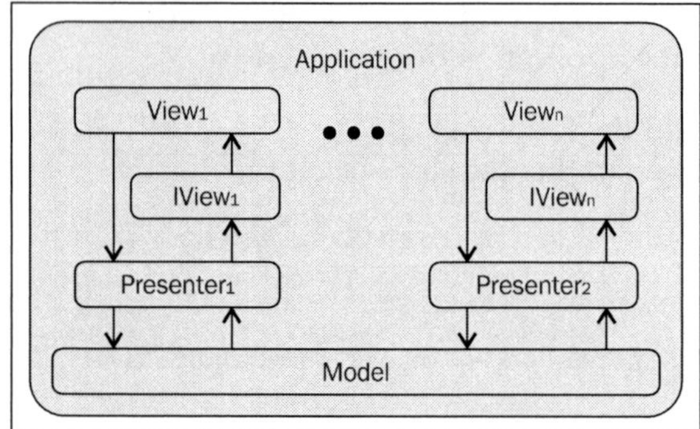

It's more common for presenters to have a larger scope than a single UI widget and to instead have one presenter per form or user control.

As you can see in the previous diagram, the presenter has taken the place of the controller in the triad and is responsible for moving user input from the view to the model as well as being responsible for updating the view about changes that occur in the model. The presenter communicates with the view through an interface which allows for increased testability as the model can be replaced by a fake object (mock or stub) for unit tests. The following diagram shows MVP in a layered architecture:

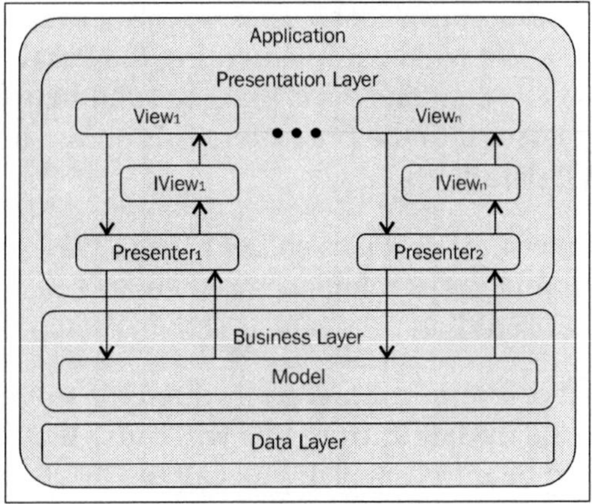

MVP Project Billing sample

We will create an application with the classes shown in the following screenshot:

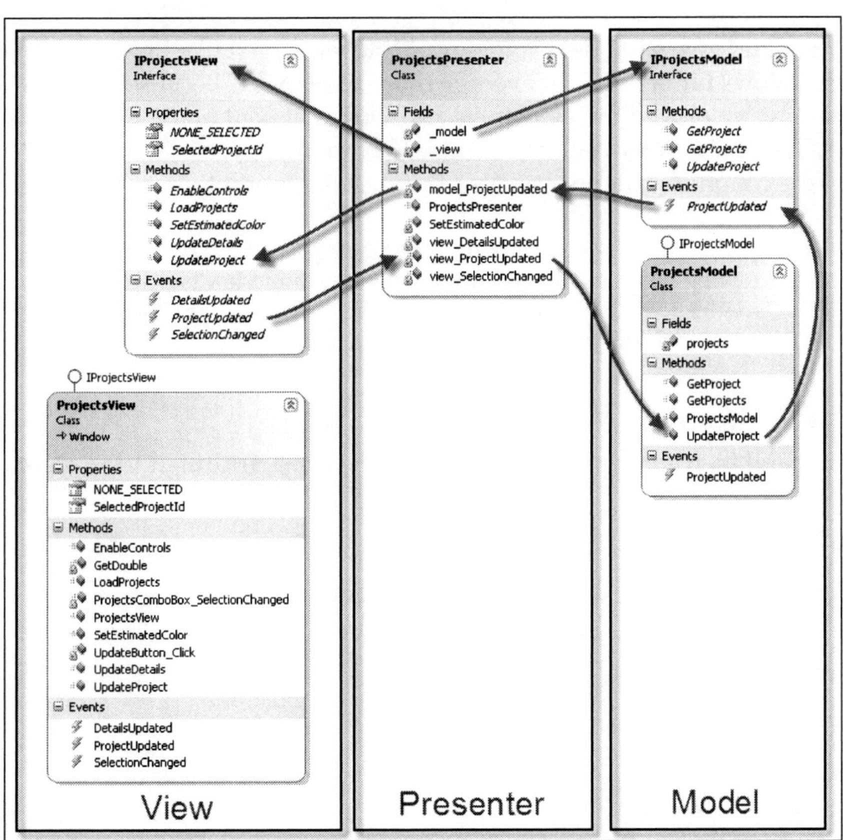

As you can see our view now consists of a class, `ProjectsView` that implements an interface, `IProjectsView`. We will be implementing the **Passive View** version of MVP and so `IProjectsView` contains everything needed to update the view and to communicate user gestures into the presenter. This allows for maximum test coverage under the MVP paradigm.

The presenter, `ProjectsPresenter`, takes an `IProjectsView` and an `IProjectsModel` as constructor arguments and keeps references to them in `ProjectsPresenter.view` and `ProjectsPresenter.model` respectively as shown previously.

This design requires that communications go through the presenter. For example, when the user clicks on the **updateButton**, this will cause the `IProjectView.ProjectUpdated` event to be raised, which will call the `ProjectsPresenter.view_ProjectUpdated()` event handler. `ProjectsPresenter.view_ProjectUpdated` will in turn call `ProjectsPresenter.model.UpdateProject()` which will update the model data and then raise the `IProjectsModel.ProjectUpdated` event to notify presenters that the model has been updated. The Presenters will then call `IView.UpdateProject()`, which will take care of updating the view state and applying view logic to set the color of `estimateTextBox` if necessary. This will allow for dynamic updates to session data across multiple views just like in MVC. However, this design allows for better test coverage than under MVC because the view is passive and we've moved the view logic and view state out of the view and into the presenter. We've also removed direct communication between the view and model and all of the communication is handled through the presenter.

Having no interaction between the model and view is a detail that is specific to the passive view version of MVP. In supervising controller the model and view can still communicate directly.

Let's start by adding a new WPF Application project called `ProjectBilling.MVP` to the solution and then add a project reference to the **ProjectBilling.DataAccess** project.

Model

Add a class called `ProjectsModel` and add the following code:

```
using System;
using System.Collections.Generic;
using System.Linq;
using ProjectBilling.DataAccess;

namespace ProjectBilling.Business
{
```

```
public class ProjectEventArgs : EventArgs
{
    public Project Project { get; set; }
    public ProjectEventArgs(Project project)
    {
        Project = project;
    }
}

public interface IProjectsModel
{
    void UpdateProject(Project project);
    IEnumerable<Project> GetProjects();
    Project GetProject(int Id);
    event EventHandler<ProjectEventArgs> ProjectUpdated;
}

public class ProjectsModel : IProjectsModel
{
    private IEnumerable<Project> projects = null;

    public event EventHandler<ProjectEventArgs>
        ProjectUpdated = delegate { };

    public ProjectsModel()
    {
        projects = new DataServiceStub().GetProjects();
    }

    public void UpdateProject(Project project)
    {
        ProjectUpdated(this,
            new ProjectEventArgs(project));
    }

    public IEnumerable<Project> GetProjects()
    {
        return projects;
    }


    public Project GetProject(int Id)
    {
        return projects.Where(p => p.ID == Id)
```

```
                .First() as Project;
        }
    }
}
```

Our `ProjectsModel` implements the `IProjectsModel` interface for better testability via dependency injection and implements the following contract.

- `UpdateProject()`: This method allows for updating a project across the session state. This design could be extended to support updates across persisted state, but covering that is outside the scope of this book.
- `GetProjects()`: This method will return all projects in the session state.
- `GetProject()`: This method is given a project ID and will return a project from session state.
- `ProjectUpdated`: This event will fire when a project has been updated in the session state.

The `ProjectEventArgs` class is for our events to use to communicate which project has changed.

View

Add a window called **ProjectsView** and add the following code to `ProjectsView.xaml`:

```
<Window x:Class="ProjectBilling.UI.MVP.ProjectsView"
        xmlns="http://schemas.microsoft.com/winfx/2006/xaml/
presentation"
        xmlns:x="http://schemas.microsoft.com/winfx/2006/xaml"
        Title="Projects" MinHeight="180" Height="180"
        MinWidth="250" Width="250" Padding="5"
        FocusManager.FocusedElement
            ="{Binding ElementName=ProjectsComboBox}">
    <UniformGrid Columns="2">
        <Label Content="Project:" />
        <ComboBox Name="ProjectsComboBox" Margin="5"
                SelectionChanged
                    ="ProjectsComboBox_SelectionChanged" />
        <Label Content="Estimated Cost:" />
        <TextBox Name="EstimatedTextBox" Margin="5"
                 IsEnabled="False" />
        <Label Content="Actual Cost:" />
        <TextBox Name="ActualTextBox" Margin="5"
                 IsEnabled="False" />
```

```
        <Button Name="UpdateButton" Content="Update"
                Margin="5" IsEnabled="False"
                Click="UpdateButton_Click" />
    </UniformGrid>
</Window>
```

With the exception of the namespace declaration, this XAML file is exactly the same as that found in the MVC `ProjectsView.xaml`.

Next, add the following code to the `ProjectsView.xaml.cs` file.

```
using System;
using System.Collections.Generic;
using System.Linq;
using System.Windows;
using System.Windows.Controls;
using System.Windows.Media;
using ProjectBilling.Business;
using ProjectBilling.DataAccess;

namespace ProjectBilling.UI.MVP
{
    public interface IProjectsView
    {
        int NONE_SELECTED { get; }
        int SelectedProjectId { get; }
        void UpdateProject(Project project);
        void LoadProjects(IEnumerable<Project> projects);
        void UpdateDetails(Project project);
        void EnableControls(bool isEnabled);
        void SetEstimatedColor(Color? color);
        event EventHandler<ProjectEventArgs> ProjectUpdated;
        event EventHandler<ProjectEventArgs> DetailsUpdated;
        event EventHandler SelectionChanged;
    }

    /// <summary>
    /// Interaction logic for ProjectsView.xaml
    /// </summary>
    public partial class ProjectsView : Window, IProjectsView
    {

        public int NONE_SELECTED { get { return -1; } }
            public event EventHandler<ProjectEventArgs>
```

```
            ProjectUpdated = delegate { };
        public int SelectedProjectId { get; private set; }

        public event EventHandler SelectionChanged
            = delegate { };
        public event EventHandler<ProjectEventArgs>
            DetailsUpdated = delegate { };

        public ProjectsView()
        {
            InitializeComponent();
            SelectedProjectId = NONE_SELECTED;
        }

    }
}
```

This code creates the `IProjectsView` interface, the fields and the events that are needed by **ProjectsView**. **ProjectsView** will implement the `IProjectView` and the contract described as follows:

- `NONE_SELECTED`: This read-only property returns a constant that is used to determine if **SelectedProjectID** currently has a selection
- `SelectedProjectId`: This read-only property returns the currently selected project ID
- `UpdateProject()`: This function allows to update a project in the view state and will take care of updating the details view if needed
- `LoadProjects()`: This function allows for populating the projectsComboBox for the first time
- `UpdateDetails()`: This function allows for updating the details view
- `EnableControls()`: This function allows for setting the details controls and the `IsEnabled` property of **updateButton** to enable and disable these controls
- `SetEstimatedColor()`: This function allows for setting the text color of **estimatedTextBox**
- `ProjectUpdated`: This event will notify the presenter that the user clicked on the **updateButton**
- `DetailsUpdated`: This event will notify the presenter that the details have changed so that the presenter can update the text color of `estimatedColor`
- `SelectionChanged`: This event will notify the presenter that the current selection has changed in the `projectsComboBox`

Event handlers

Now let's add the event handlers that we will need:

- The `UpdateButton_Click` function will fire when a user clicks on **UpdateButton** and will create a new project, populate it with the details control data, and then raise the `IProjectsView.ProjectUpdated` event passing the new project to the constructor of the new ProjectEventArgs that is being passed with the event.

```
private void UpdateButton_Click(object sender,
    RoutedEventArgs e)
{
    Project project = new Project();
    project.Estimate =
        GetDouble(EstimatedTextBox.Text);
    project.Actual =
        GetDouble(ActualTextBox.Text);
    project.ID =
        int.Parse(
            ProjectsComboBox.SelectedValue.
                ToString());
    ProjectUpdated(this,
        new ProjectEventArgs(project));
}
```

- The `ProjectsComboBox_SelectionChanged()` function will fire when the selection changes in the `ProjectsComboBox` and it simply raises the `IProjectsView.SelectionChanged` event to notify the presenter so that it can update the view as needed.

```
private void ProjectsComboBox_SelectionChanged(
    object sender, SelectionChangedEventArgs e)
{
    SelectedProjectId
        = (ProjectsComboBox.SelectedValue == null)
                ? NONE_SELECTED
                : int.Parse(
                    ProjectsComboBox.SelectedValue.
                        ToString());
    SelectionChanged(this,
        new EventArgs());
}
```

Public methods

Add the following public methods:

- The `UpdateProject` function allows for updating a project in the view state by first finding the project in the `ProjectsComboBox.ItemsSource` using a little **Linq**. It then updates the project and if it's the project that is currently selected, it calls `UpdateDetails()` to update the details controls.

```
public void UpdateProject(Project project)
{
    // Null checks excluded
    IEnumerable<Project> projects =
        ProjectsComboBox.ItemsSource as
            IEnumerable<Project>;
    Project projectToUpdate =
        projects.Where(p => p.ID == project.ID)
            .First();
    projectToUpdate.Estimate = project.Estimate;
    projectToUpdate.Actual = project.Actual;
    if (project.ID == SelectedProjectId)
        UpdateDetails(project);
}
```

- The `LoadProjects` function allows for loading a collection of `Projects` as the `ItemsSource` for `projectsComboBox`.

```
public void LoadProjects(IEnumerable<Project> projects)
{
    ProjectsComboBox.ItemsSource = projects;
    ProjectsComboBox.DisplayMemberPath = "Name";
    ProjectsComboBox.SelectedValuePath = "ID";
}
```

- The `EnableControls` function allows for setting the `IsEnabled` state of the details controls and `updateButton`.

```
public void EnableControls(bool isEnabled)
{
    EstimatedTextBox.IsEnabled = isEnabled;
    ActualTextBox.IsEnabled = isEnabled;
    UpdateButton.IsEnabled = isEnabled;
}
```

- The `SetEstimatedColor` function takes a color and will update the `estimateTextBox.Foreground` color to be the passed in color.

```
public void SetEstimatedColor(Color? color)
```

```
{
    EstimatedTextBox.Foreground
        = (color == null)
                ? ActualTextBox.Foreground
                : new SolidColorBrush((Color)color);
}
```

Note that this function doesn't contain view logic and that it's the presenter's responsibility to calculate the correct color.

- The `UpdateDetails` function will update the details controls with the data contained in the project that is passed in.

```
public void UpdateDetails(Project project)
{
    EstimatedTextBox.Text
        = project.Estimate.ToString();
    ActualTextBox.Text
        = project.Actual.ToString();
    DetailsUpdated(this,
        new ProjectEventArgs(project));
}
```

Helpers

The `model_ProjectUpdated` function will get a double from text passed in taking care of null/empty checks.

```
private double GetDouble(string text)
{
    return string.IsNullOrEmpty(text)
        ? 0 : double.Parse(text);
}
```

Presenter

Add a class called `ProjectsPresenter` and add the following code to it:

```
using System;
using System.Windows.Media;
using ProjectBilling.Business;
using ProjectBilling.DataAccess;

namespace ProjectBilling.UI.MVP
```

```
{
    public class ProjectsPresenter
    {
        private readonly IProjectsView _view = null;
        private readonly IProjectsModel _model = null;

        public ProjectsPresenter(IProjectsView projectsView,
            IProjectsModel projectsModel)
        {
            _view = projectsView;
            _view.ProjectUpdated += view_ProjectUpdated;
            _view.SelectionChanged
                += view_SelectionChanged;
            _view.DetailsUpdated += view_DetailsUpdated;
            _model = projectsModel;
            _model.ProjectUpdated += model_ProjectUpdated;
            _view.LoadProjects(
                _model.GetProjects());
        }

    }
}
```

As you can see the presenter takes `IProjectsView` and `IProjectsModel` as constructor arguments and then subscribes to various events and the loads projects into the view from the model with the following code:

```
this.view.LoadProjects(
    this.model.GetProjects());
```

Event handlers

- The `view_DetailsUpdated` function is called in response to the `IProjectsView.DetailsUpdated` event and simply calls `SetEstimateColor()` to update the color of the `estimateTextBox.Foreground`. This allows the view logic to be easily tested.

  ```
  private void view_DetailsUpdated(object sender,
      ProjectEventArgs e)
  {
      SetEstimatedColor(e.Project);
  }
  ```

- `view_SelectionChanged` will be called in response to the `IProjectsView.SelectionChanged` event firing performs the view logic of updating the details controls after a the user changes the selected project. Again, this design allows this view logic to be easily tested.

```
private void view_SelectionChanged(object sender,
    EventArgs e)
{
    int selectedId = _view.SelectedProjectId;
    if (selectedId > _view.NONE_SELECTED)
    {
        Project project =
            _model.GetProject(selectedId);
        _view.EnableControls(true);
        _view.UpdateDetails(project);
        SetEstimatedColor(project);
    }
    else
    {
        _view.EnableControls(false);
    }
}
```

- `model_ProjectUpdated` will be called in response to the `IProjectsModel.ProjectUpdated` event firing and will allow for propagating the changes to session state made in one view to the other views.

```
private void model_ProjectUpdated(object sender,
    ProjectEventArgs e)
{
    _view.UpdateProject(e.Project);
}
```

- The `view_ProjectUpdated` function will fire in response to the `IProjectsView.ProjectsUpdated` event and will notify the model so that it can update the project in the session state and also calls `SetEstimatedColor()` to perform the view logic for updating the color of `estimateTextBox.Foreground` if needed.

```
private void view_ProjectUpdated(object sender,
    ProjectEventArgs e)
{
    _model.UpdateProject(e.Project);
    SetEstimatedColor(e.Project);
}
```

Helpers

Now add the following helper method:

- The `SetEstimateColor` performs the view logic needed to set `estimateColor.Foreground` to the appropriate color and then calls `IProjectsView.SetEstimatedColor()` to apply the needed color again allowing for the view logic to be easily tested.

```
private void SetEstimatedColor(Project project)
{
    if (project.ID == _view.SelectedProjectId)
    {
        if (project.Actual <= 0)
        {
            _view.SetEstimatedColor(null);
        }
        else if (project.Actual
                     > project.Estimate)
        {
            _view.SetEstimatedColor(Colors.Red);
        }
        else
        {
            _view.SetEstimatedColor(Colors.Green);
        }
    }
}
```

Main window

Add the following code to `MainWindow.xaml`:

```
<Window x:Class="ProjectBilling.UI.MVP.MainWindow"
        xmlns="http://schemas.microsoft.com/winfx/2006/xaml/
presentation"
        xmlns:x="http://schemas.microsoft.com/winfx/2006/xaml"
        Title="Shell" Height="150" Width="200"
        MinHeight="150" MinWidth="200"
        FocusManager.FocusedElement
            ="{Binding ElementName=ShowProjectsButton}">
    <StackPanel>
        <Button Content="Show Projects"
                Name="ShowProjectsButton" Margin="5"
                Click="ShowProjectsButton_Click" />
    </StackPanel>
</Window>
```

With the exception of the namespace declaration, this XAML code is exactly the same as the one found in the MVC `MainWindow.xaml`.

Next, add the following code to `MainWindow.xaml.cs`:

```
using System.Windows;
using ProjectBilling.Business;

namespace ProjectBilling.UI.MVP
{
    /// <summary>
    /// Interaction logic for MainWindow.xaml
    /// </summary>
    public partial class MainWindow : Window
    {
        private IProjectsModel _model = null;

        public MainWindow()
        {
            InitializeComponent();
            _model = new ProjectsModel();
        }

        private void ShowProjectsButton_Click(object sender,
            RoutedEventArgs e)
        {
            ProjectsView view = new ProjectsView();
            ProjectsPresenter presenter
                = new ProjectsPresenter(view, _model);
            view.Owner = this;
            view.Show();
        }
    }
}
```

The constructor creates a model that will be shared across all views. The model is used to initialize and update session state.

`ShowProjectsButton_Click()` will be called when the **ShowProjectsButton** is clicked and it will instantiate a new view and pass the new view instance as an argument to the constructor for a new `ProjectsPresenter` instance along with a reference to `MainWindow.model`. `ShowProjectsButton_Click` will then show the view by calling `view.Show()`.

How it works

Running the application you will see that it works the same as our previous MVC application.

Takeaways

MVP represents a big improvement over MVC in a few ways:

- It provides testable view state and view logic by moving them into the presenter allowing the view logic to be easily tested.
- It decouples the view from the model by requiring communication to go through the presenter. Unlike MVC, MVP allows for reuse of the view logic and this is achieved by moving the logic into a presenter and having the presenter communicate with the view through an interface. Now if you wanted to implement a Silverlight version of this application, you would only need to create a view in Silverlight that implements `IProjectsView` and could reuse `IProjectsPresenter` and `IProjectsModel`.

However there are still a few issues as follows:

- We still use a lot of events, and as shown in the *Memory Leaks* section previously, events can cause memory leaks and end up causing code to be higher maintenance than a design that doesn't require events.
- There is still a lot of untested code in the view.

These short comings are all motivators for MVVM or presentation model and we will look at how MVVM addresses each of these issues in the next chapter.

Summary

In this chapter we reviewed the long history of presentation patterns with examples. We started by looking at the state of affairs before applications started having their architectures organized into presentation patterns and were instead written as monoliths. We reviewed the many issues with this approach and looked at how Microsoft is making the situation worse with its RAD toolkit that encourages this kind of monolithic design.

We then looked at how things were improved under MVC and how dynamically sharing the session state across views was made easier by MVC. We also reviewed the shortcomings of MVC including covering issues with .NET events and memory leaks before moving on to discussing how MVP addresses some of the MVC short comings. We finished the chapter by looking at an example of the passive view version of MVP covering all the improvements that it offers over MVC in the area of testing and code reuse while pointing out MVP's shortcomings.

In the next chapter will dive into MVVM and demonstrate how it helps address the shortcomings of all the presentational patterns that came before it by taking advantage of features in Silverlight and WPF.

2

Introduction to MVVM

By Ryan Vice

In this chapter, we will introduce the **Model View View Model** pattern (**MVVM***)* and help you better understand the current state of affairs of *MVVM*. This knowledge will lay a foundation that we will expand on throughout this book, to give you the tools and knowledge you need to take advantage of the many benefits of *MVVM*.

We will start with a brief history of the *MVVM* pattern, and then we will look at the structure of *MVVM*. Next, we will take a look at the features of **WPF** and **Silverlight** that make *MVVM* such an attractive option and follow this by diving into our first MVVM sample. Next, we will look at the benefits of using *MVVM* and discuss how we capitalized on those benefits in the *MVVM* sample that we built. We will follow this by looking at the challenges that can make MVVM difficult; addressing these challenges with various tools and techniques will be covered in the later chapters of this book and will make up a large majority of this book's content. We will finish off this chapter with a brief tour of the **MVVM Light** toolkit that we will be using throughout this book.

History

MVVM is a pattern that emerged to address some of the limitations of *MVC* and *MVP*, and to combine some of their strengths. This pattern first hit the scene as a part of Small Talk's framework, under the name **Application Model**, in the '80s, and was later improved and given the updated name of **Presentation Model**.

Application Model is also used to describe a hierarchical way of implementing MVVM, which will be covered in *Chapter 6, Northwind – Hierarchical View Model and IoC*

In the previous chapter, we reviewed a few shortcomings of MVC and how it dealt with *view state* and *view logic*, including the following:

- The view logic and view state were in the view and therefore difficult to test
- The view state and view logic were tightly coupled to the model and controller and were not reusable

These issues were addressed in the Passive View version of MVP by making the view a humble view and moving the view state and view logic into an external class.

> A humble view is a type of humble object. A humble object is an object that has had its state and functionality extracted to an externalclass, leaving minimal untestable state and logic in the humble object. This is done because, before refactoring to a humble object, the object is hard to test and/or hard to reuse. Restructuring the object in this way allows for automated testing of the extracted state and logic as well as the ability to easily reuse the functionality of the humble object.

Making the view humble was done by having the view implement an interface and only having the view communicate with the presenter through its interface. This worked really well at solving our first issue but created a coupling with our presenter and the view's interface. This requires manually updating the view interface and the presenter for changes, and it'd be nice if there were an easier approach.

Under *MVVM*, a similar approach is taken, where the *view logic* and *view state* are moved into an external class to make the *view humble*. The component that the view logic and state was moved to, got a different name in each variation of the *MVVM* pattern. It was known as **Application Model**, **Presentation Model**, and **View Model**, in the three incarnations of the pattern, and played the role of being the *model of the view*. The *view model* has the responsibility of maintaining the *view state* and executing *view logic*, allowing for the view to be a **humble view**.

Application model and *presentation model* were able to achieve a humble view without the coupling found in *MVP*, between the view and presenter, and originally accomplished this separation by introducing the concept of **property objects** that allowed for storing values of the *view* properties in the properties of external *property objects*.

These *property objects* provided property change updates that allowed them to be observed for changes. These changes allowed for synchronization of the values held in the view's properties with properties found in external classes such as the application model, as shown in the following diagram:

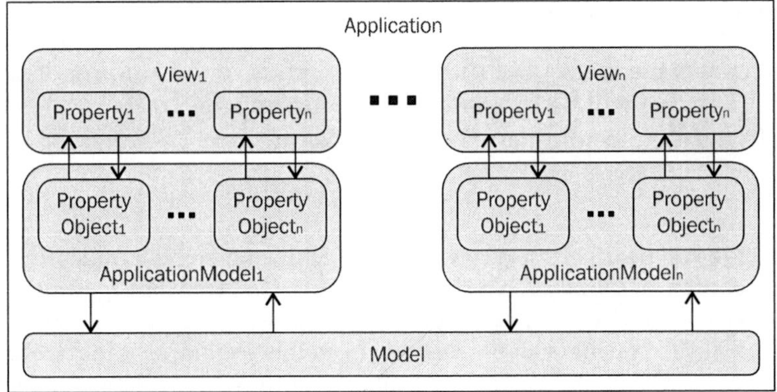

This idea is essentially rich two-way data binding. Property objects allowed for presentation patterns that didn't require the overhead of implementing a view interface for communicating updates, as found in MVP, and additionally didn't require coupling the view and presenter (controller, view model, and so on). But this new approach came at the expense of requiring either writing of a lot of code to create property objects or having a GUI framework that provided rich, two-way data binding.

Robust support for this type of functionality would come in .NET 3.0, with the introduction of Silverlight, for thin client development, and **Windows Presentation Foundation** or **WPF**, for thick client development. These new frameworks were able to eliminate the need to write one's own *property objects* and ushered in the next evolution in the presentational pattern's space, as we will see in the next section.

On a recent project, I was lucky enough to get an opportunity to speak with Sam Bent, who works as the lead for the *WPF Data Services* team at *Microsoft,* and he told me that the *MVVM* style of separated presentation design was what he and his team at Microsoft were trying to accommodate by making such a rich data binding system in *WPF*. John Gossman made this official when he coined the term *MVVM* and published the *presentation model* pattern under the name *MVVM* on his blog, in 2005.

It's debatable as to who deserves credit for inventing *MVVM,* as it was first implemented in Small Talk, first published as *Presentation Model* by Martin Fowler, had its first robust framework support designed by the WPF Data Services team under Sam Bent, and had its name coined by John Gossman. I won't attempt to end that debate here and claim a single inventor for this pattern. Instead, I will simply pay homage to the many important contributors and be thankful for all the hard work that has been put into making this terrific pattern a reality. Once you start using this pattern, you will most likely love it in the same way that I do. It's a really fun and rewarding way to build applications.

Structure

With MVVM comes the concept of purity which refers to the amount of code in the code-behind. Here, we will be focusing on the pure approach—the style where no code is kept in the code-behind, and no references are kept between the view and view model.

We will be covering varying degrees of purity, and the tradeoffs of each, in *Chapter 4, Northwind – Services and Persistence Ignorance*. However, if you are not interested in following the pure approach, you will still benefit from the material from this section, as it introduces the basic MVVM structure and sets up the design that will be used in our first example that will come later in this book.

Pure MVVM

Pure MVVM is structured as shown in the following diagram:

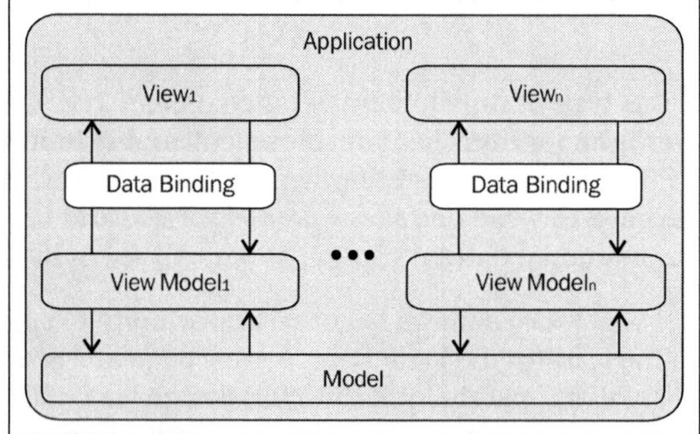

This structure is similar to *MVP*, except that there is no longer the `IView` interface for communicating from presenter to view. All communications between *view* and *view model* are now handled using WPF's and Silverlight's binding systems.

In *MVVM*, the model takes on the same role as found under *MVP*. The model is once again the in-memory representation of the data that was retrieved from the persistence store, which is also called the **session state**. The *model* is also responsible for notifying the *view model* of changes.

It's also common to structure MVVM such that the view gets notified of model updates by using data binding directly. We will cover various approaches to this style in *Chapter 3, Northwind – Foundations*.

View

Under MVVM, the view is still responsible for displaying data, collecting user input, and passing it along, except that now it's passed to the view model. The view now uses the binding system in either WPF or Silverlight for its communications with the view model and no longer contains code in its code behind.

We will cover options that allow more flexibility for the code behind in *Chapter 4, Northwind – Services and Persistence Ignorance*, and cover the trade-offs of the various levels of purity. The sample WPF code in this chapter takes the pure approach. Due to limitations with Silverlight's binding system, we will go with a slightly less pure approach when implementing Project Billing in Silverlight later in this chapter.

The view can also be responsible for mapping *views* to *view models* and for instantiating the *views* under some variations of *MVVM*. We will cover those details later in *Chapter 4, Northwind – Services and Persistence Ignorance*.

View Model

The *view model* or *presentation model* is responsible for *view state* and *view logic* and relies on the binding system for communicating with the view. The *view model* is the middleman in *MVVM* and takes care of:

- Moving data from the model to the view.
- Communicating user gestures to the model from the view.

The view model's role is essentially that of "model of the view" and takes the session state and transforms it into a form that is easily consumable as view state. The view model is also responsible for implementing view logic to transform the view state as needed.

WPF and Silverlight enablers

.NET 3.0 introduced new toolkits for thick and thin client development, which included Silverlight for thin client development and Windows Presentation Foundation (WPF) for thick client development. At the heart of these new frameworks were features that allowed for much greater separation of concerns, including the following:

- A rich data binding system
- A commanding infrastructure
- Support for data templates
- A rich styling system

We will cover these features shortly, but for now it's important to know that these features in WPF and Silverlight made MVVM a practical reality as it provided the framework support needed for separating the view state and view logic from the view without requiring the overhead of writing property objects or using view interfaces.

There are many areas in the framework that could be improved to better support MVVM, and my guess would be that we will be seeing the road map for WPF and Silverlight incorporate more of the techniques and tools found in this book that address limitations in MVVM support. For example, we should be seeing support for linking actions or delegates directly to events, based on data context, which currently has to be accomplished via frameworks or non-trivial patterns. But, at the time of this writing, you definitely can benefit quite a bit by either using open source frameworks or by rolling your own using the techniques we'll review.

Dependency Properties

In WPF, all UI widgets are derived from the type `UIElement`, which is derived from `DependencyObject`, as shown next.

[The object hierarchy is different for Silverlight and WPF.]

Silverlight

```
System.Object
  System.Windows.DependencyObject
    System.Windows.UIElement
```

WPF

```
System.Object
  System.Windows.Threading.DispatcherObject
    System.Windows.DependencyObject
      System.Windows.Media.Visual
```

The `System.Windows.UIElement` classes derive from `DependencyObject` and can take advantage of the property systems that provide many benefits, as described in the following excerpt from *Dependency Properties Overview* on MSDN:

> *Windows Presentation Foundation (WPF) provides a set of services that can be used to extend the functionality of a common language runtime (CLR) property. Collectively, these services are typically referred to as the WPF property system. A property that is backed by the WPF property system is known as a dependency property.*

The same type of property system is used in Silverlight.

Dependency properties make a lot of the new things in WPF and Silverlight possible and provide a lot more features and functionality than we could cover in this book. However, we will be covering the *dependency property* features and functionalities that enable *MVVM*.

For full coverage of dependency properties, see *Dependency Properties Overview* on MSDN (`http://msdn.microsoft.com/en-us/library/ms752914.aspx`).

Dependency property inheritance

Dependency properties are registered with WPF's and Silverlight's property systems, and when they are registered you can configure their behavior. One of the attributes of a dependency property's behavior that can be configured is whether or not the value is inherited by child dependency objects that expose the same dependency property.

Data context

`FrameworkElement` defines a `DataContext` dependency property of type `object`. `FrameworkElement` derives from `UIElement`, as shown next.

Silverlight

```
System.Object
  System.Windows.DependencyObject
    System.Windows.UIElement
      System.Windows.FrameworkElement
```

WPF

```
System.Object
  System.Windows.Threading.DispatcherObject
    System.Windows.DependencyObject
      System.Windows.Media.Visual
        System.Windows.UIElement
          System.Windows.FrameworkElement
```

MSDN describes `FrameworkElement` as:

> **FrameworkElement** *provides a framework of common APIs for objects that participate in Silverlight layout. It also defines APIs related to data binding, object tree, and object lifetime feature areas in Silverlight.*

FrameworkElement works the same in WPF.

This means that every UI widget that derives from `FrameworkElement` can participate in data binding and has a `DataContext` *dependency property* defined on it. This `DataContext` property is configured to be inherited. This is important because if the `DataContext` for a page, window, or user control, is set to a *view model,* all of the controls contained in that page, window, or user control, will inherit that *view model* instance as their `DataContext`. This allows us to easily use data binding to bind control properties to properties of the view model. The framework will then do all the work of synchronizing the properties of the UI widgets with the *view model* properties. This is the same approach that was taken in *application model* which used *property objects* but without requiring any *property object* code to be written. The following diagram shows how this works:

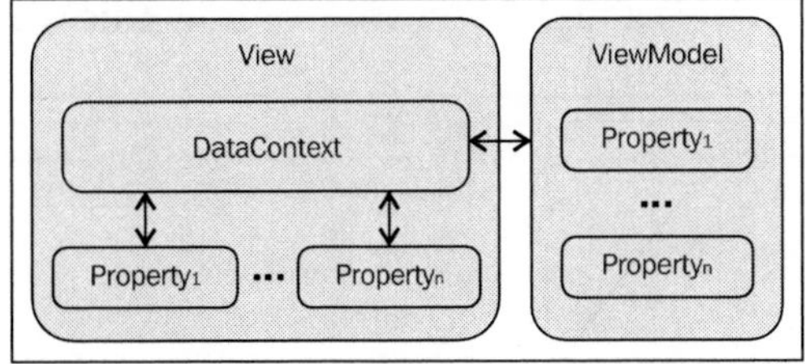

Microsoft has already heavily tested the binding systems so there is no need to be concerned with creating tests for its binding functionality. This greatly reduces the testing burden in the presentation layer. It also greatly reduces the amount of tedious code that needs to be written to do the following:

- Synchronize view properties with view model properties
- Communicate user gestures

We will look at how to use the binding system to communicate user gestures in *Chapter 5, Northwind – Commands and User Inputs*.

And as everyone knows, less code means fewer bugs, less testing, and less maintenance.

Attached behavior pattern

The *property systems in WPF and Silverlight* allow for attaching dependency properties to classes *that the dependency properties aren't defined on*. When *dependency properties* are attached to a *dependency object*, you can subscribe to a property changed event that will get a reference to the class that the dependency property is being attached to. This allows you to do things such as:

- Wiring up event handlers for the events published by `DependencyObject`
- Calling methods on `DependencyObject`
- Executing external code
- Passing the `DependencyObject` instance into external methods for processing

The following diagram shows a high-level view of how this works:

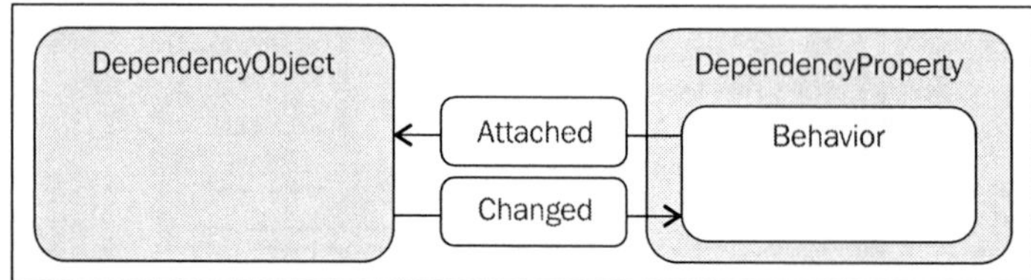

In this diagram, the code that is represented by **Behavior** can execute whenever the property is attached and every time the value of the attached property changes.

This technique is essential to communicating between the *view* and *view model,* if you want to implement a pure MVVM pattern and you don't want to use frameworks (possibly because of workplace policies). We will dive into the details of this pattern in *Chapter 4, Northwind – Services and Persistence Ignorance* and *Chapter 5, Northwind – Commands and User Inputs.*

Rich data binding

WPF and Silverlight brought *data binding* to a whole new level as is described on MSDN:

> *The data binding functionality in WPF has several advantages over traditional models, including a broad range of properties that inherently support data binding, flexible UI representation of data, and clean separation of business logic from UI.*

In data binding, there are two important concepts to understand for MVVM:

- **Binding source**: It is the data that is being bound to the UI
- **Binding target**: It is the `FrameworkElement` class in the UI that will be synchronized in some way with the binding source

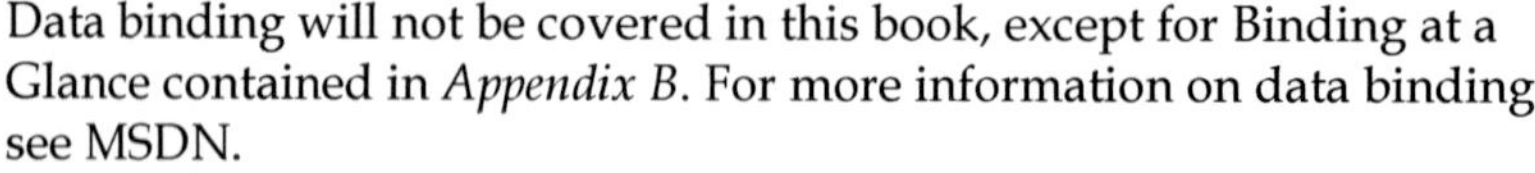

Data binding will not be covered in this book, except for Binding at a Glance contained in *Appendix B*. For more information on data binding, see MSDN.

WPF coverage can be found on MSDN in the article *Data Binding (WPF)* (`http://msdn.microsoft.com/en-us/library/ms750612.aspx`).

Silverlight coverage can be found on MSDN in the article *Data Binding* (`http://msdn.microsoft.com/en-us/library/cc278072(v=vs.95).aspx`).

Data binding is important to MVVM, because it allows for having the framework synchronize the dependency properties of any `FrameworkElement` with properties of other objects. The dependency properties of framework elements can be synchronized with many things, including:

- Properties of other framework elements
- Properties of the framework elements data context

This allows for easily:

- Synchronizing updates from the view model properties to the framework element properties
- Synchronizing properties from one framework element to another in the same view

INotifyCollectionChanged and ObservableCollection<>

`ObservableCollection` implements `INotifyCollectionChanged` and is defined on MSDN as:

> *Represents a dynamic data collection that provides notifications when items get added, removed, or when the whole list is refreshed.*
>
> *You can enumerate over any collection that implements the* `IEnumerable` *interface. However, to set up dynamic bindings so that insertions or deletions in the collection update the UI automatically, the collection must implement the* `INotifyCollectionChanged` *interface. This interface exposes the* `CollectionChanged` *event, an event that should be raised whenever the underlying collection changes.*
>
> *WPF provides the* `ObservableCollection<T>` *class, which is a built-in implementation of a data collection that implements the* `INotifyCollectionChanged` *interface.*

`ObservableCollection` allows for binding to a collection and having the view synchronized with updates to be bound to the collection. This makes `ObservableCollection` very useful for MVVM, as you can bind to `ObservableCollection` in XAML, and the binding target will get updates when the collection changes via the `INotifyCollectionChanged.CollectionChanged` event.

> `INotifyCollectionChanged.CollectionChanged` is handled by WPF's and Silverlight's binding systems in a way that will cause controls to be updated on the same thread that `INotifyCollectionChanged.CollectionChanged` is raised on. This means that updating `ObservableCollection` by adding or removing elements on a background thread will cause the view to be updated by a background thread, which will result in a threading exception being thrown. We will cover options for dealing with this situation when we revisit `ObservableCollection` in *Chapter 3, Northwind – Foundations*.

Another major benefit of this is that as long as each element of your `ObservableCollection` class supports change notifications by implementing `INotifyPropertyChanged`, your binding target will get updated automatically when properties of elements in your collection change.

Automatic dispatching

The binding systems in WPF and Silverlight provide other benefits for MVVM implementations. With the exception of adding and removing elements to and from `ObservableCollection`, there is no need to dispatch changes made to binding sources from background threads. This means that in your view models, you are free-to-run code on a background thread that updates properties that are bound to the view. This greatly reduces the amount of code contained in the middle tier compared to other presentation patterns, which means less testing, less bugs, and easier maintenance.

Triggers

Triggers allow for conditionally setting the values of properties on UI widgets, based on events or property changes. There are three kinds of triggers:

- **Property triggers**: A property trigger is defined using the `Trigger` class and fires when the value of the configured dependency property changes
- **Data triggers**: A data trigger is defined using the `DataTrigger` class and fires when the value of the configured .NET property changes
- **Event Triggers**: An event trigger is defined using the `EventTrigger` class and runs when the configured routed event occurs

You can use any property that you can bind to or any routed event allowing you to map view logic in your markup.

In the *MVVM project billing sample* section that follows in this chapter, we will set the color of the estimated cost based on the actual cost, as seen in all the previous examples in this book. However, we will assign the color purely in XAML markup, by using a style with data triggers.

The view logic in this case is actually in the view model, which exposes a property that indicates the status of the estimate, and the style trigger is used to map a color to the current status.

Triggers also can be used in conjunction with attached properties, to allow for communicating from the view model to the view, which is a technique that will be covered in *Chapter 5, Northwind – Commands and User Inputs*.

Triggers can be used from within:

- Data templates
- Control templates
- Styles
- `FrameworkElement.Triggers` (`EventTriggers` only)

All these topics will not be covered in detail in this book, but that can be freely researched on MSDN.

Styles

Styles in WPF and Silverlight allow for setting properties on elements in a way that can be easily shared throughout your application. This allows for separation of look and feel and allows for centralized changing of appearance in a similar way to what can be done with CSS on the Web. Styles are important for MVVM because they support triggers.

Styles will not be covered in detail in this book, and it is assumed that you know how to use them. If you need more detailed coverage, see *Styling and Templating* (`http://msdn.microsoft.com/en-us/library/ms745683.aspx`), on MSDN.

Control Templates

Control templates in WPF and Silverlight represent the ultimate in separation of look and layout from functionality, as they allow you to specify the look and layout of a control independently of the functionality. This is referred to as **lookless controls**. You can take a standard button and replace its control template to make it simply a round circle, if you like, or something more exotic, say a spinning 3-D cube. Control templates also support triggers, making them useful for MVVM.

One interesting thing about control templates from the MVVM point of view is that they are implemented using the MVVM pattern under the hood. If you think about it, clearly this has to be the case. The ability to completely change the look and layout of a control purely in XAML markup and without touching a line of code follows the MVVM style of using a framework to push data and gestures from the visuals to the code.

Control templates will not be covered in detail in this book, and it is assumed that you know how to use them. If you need more detailed coverage, see *Using Templates to Customize WPF Controls* (http://msdn.microsoft.com/en-us/magazine/cc163497.aspx), in the MSDN magazine.

Data templates

Data templates allow for creating an XAML template and mapping that to a type. Whenever the type is found, it is replaced by the template.

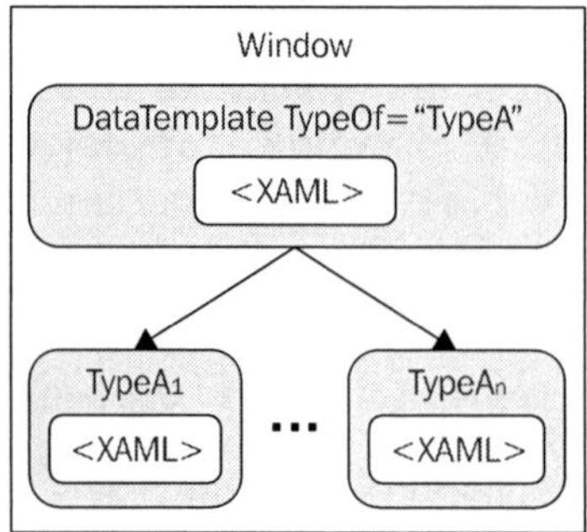

This is very powerful and allows for letting WPF and Silverlight frameworks map views to view models automatically for us, as shown in the following diagram:

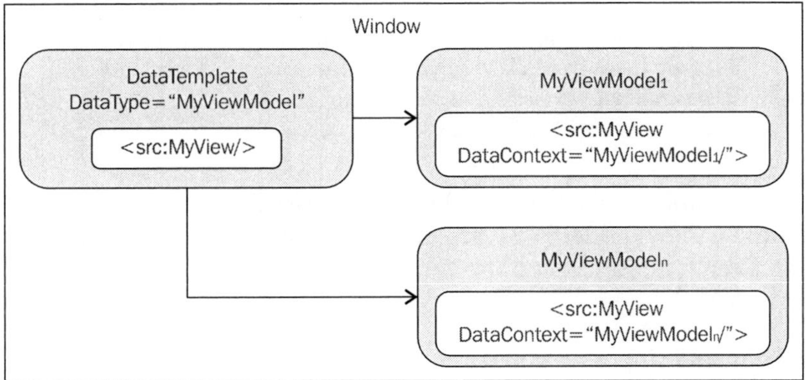

Here, when a `MyViewModel` class is exposed in the window as part of an item source or as the content of a control, the user control `MyView` will replace `MyViewModel` in the XAML and the new `MyView` instance gets its data context set to the `MyViewModel` instance. This allows you to bind to properties of the view model in the user control instances. Additionally this allows for:

- Complete separation of view from view state and view logic
- Designers to work mostly independently of developers on the look and layout of views
- Easily changing the look and layout of views

For more information on data templates, see *Data Templating Overview* web page (`http://msdn.microsoft.com/en-us/library/ms742521.aspx`), on MSDN website.

Commands

The command support found in WPF and Silverlight is an implementation of the command pattern in the *Gang of Four* patterns catalog. Commands are made up of four key elements, as described in the article *Commanding Overview* on MSDN.

- The **command** is the action to be executed
- The **command source** is the object that invokes the command
- The **command target** is the object that the command is being executed on
- The **command binding** is the object that maps the command logic to the command

Commands will not be covered in detail in this book, except for how to apply them in MVVM. If you need to learn the basics, refer to *Commanding Overview* (`http://msdn.microsoft.com/en-us/library/ms752308.aspx#Four_main_Concepts`) on MSDN.

A command from the point of view of MVVM is essentially a way to wrap a delegate from a view model in a command and expose it as a property of the view model. Then, you can assign the command property to a command source (or control) in XAML.

You might be wondering why you'd want to do this, and the answer is simple: it allows you to communicate user gestures directly from view-to-view model without requiring event handlers in your code behind or references from your view model to your view.

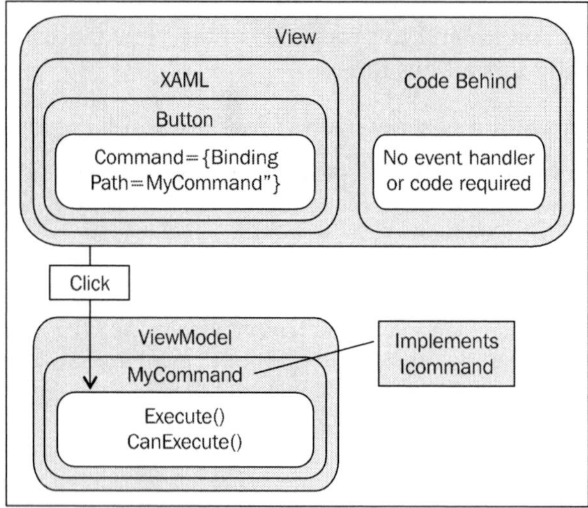

With MVP, you must have each event that you want to react to, wired up through the code-behind approach; this design causes you to have to write more boilerplate code, which is easy to get wrong because it's so mindless and boring to write. It also is more code to test and it also requires references from view-to-view model, which can lead to memory leaks if not properly managed.

Using commands allows for greater separation than what can be achieved in MVP and less code, so then using them should be a no brainer, right? At this point you might be thinking that the future is here and that now we no longer need to worry about code behind. Well, not quite. The commanding implementation from the point of view of MVVM leaves a bit to be desired. The problem is that each command source can have only one command associated with it. So, in our previous diagram, the button's command is bound to the button's `click` event. But what if you wanted to have an action associated with the `Button.KeyDown` event instead? You can't solve this problem by only using commands, however we will explore several options for dealing with this situation in *Chapter 5, Northwind – Commands and User Inputs*.

MVVM project billing sample

Now we will implement project billing using the MVVM pattern. Let's start by discussing the overall design.

MVVM design

The model, view, and view model are shown in the following screenshot, along with their relationships:

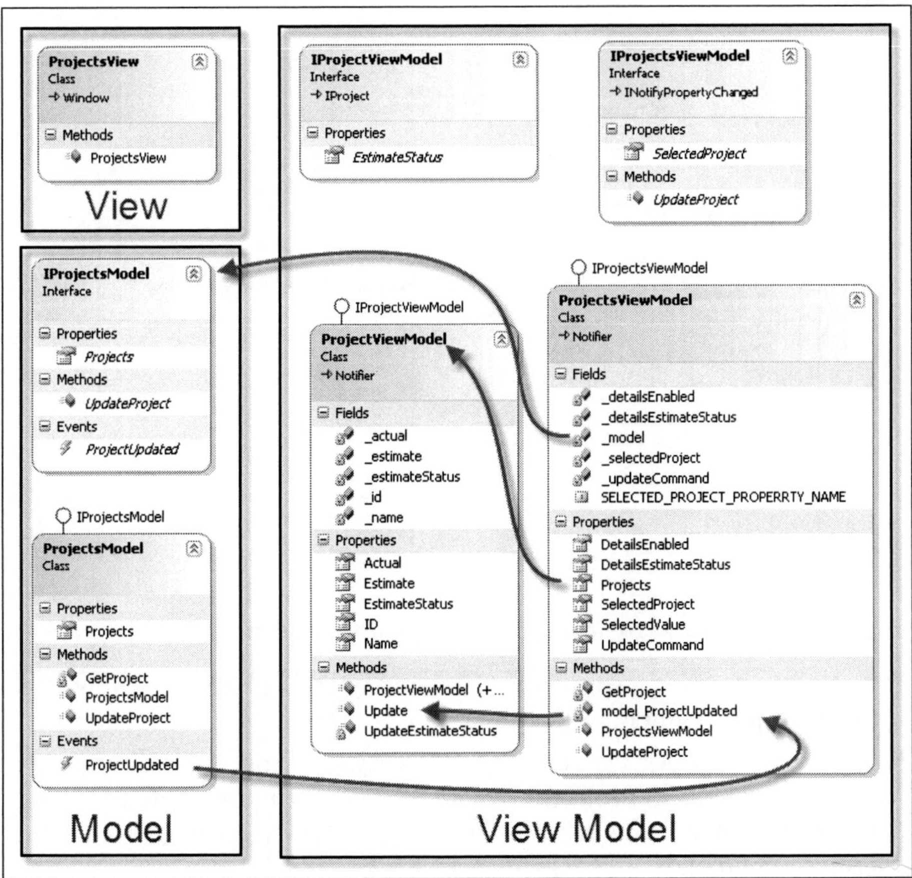

The view is now empty, and all of the explicit relationships that we've created between our classes are between the model and view model.

View Models

We will need two view models for this application. Each view model has its own area of responsibility in the view, as shown in the next screenshot.

Using multiple nested view models in this way is what I call hierarchical view models, and it is a topic that will be explored in more detail in *Chapter 6, Northwind – Hierarchical View Model and IoC.*

ProjectsViewModel

The `ProjectViewModel` view model will contain the view state and view logic for `ProjectsView`. The following screenshot shows the mapping between **Projects** and **ProjectsViewModel**:

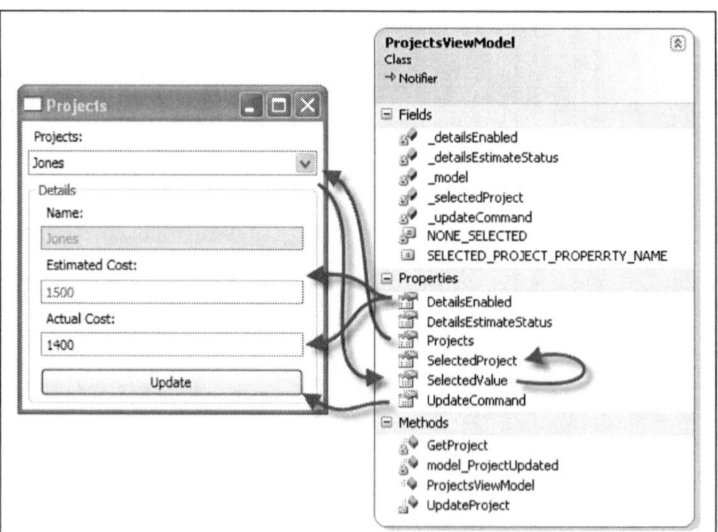

The property bindings and their responsibilities are shown as follows:

- `Projects`: An `ObservableCollection<Project>` object for binding to the **Projects** combobox.
- `SelectedIndex`: An `int` property that is bound with `Binding.Mode` of `OneWayToSource` to **Projects** `ComboBox.SelectedIndex`. This allows us to get notified in **ProjectsViewModel**, when the selection changes in the **Projects** combobox.

- `SelectedProject`: A `PropertyViewModel` object that is bound to the detail's controls in the view. The details of these bindings are shown in the *ProjectViewModel* section that follows. This value gets updated when `ProjectsViewModel.SelectedIndex` changes.
- `DetailsEnabled`: A `bool` value for binding to the `IsEnabled` properties of the **Estimated Cost** textbox and the **Actual Cost** textbox.
- `DetailsEstimateStatus`: A `Status` enum that will be used in combination with style triggers to control the color of the **Estimate** textbox as needed.
- `UpdateCommand`: An `ICommand` interface for binding to the **Update** button that controls the **Update** button's enabled state and reacts to the `Button.Click` event, using WPF's command support. The `UpdateCommand` property returns an instance of `UpdateCommand`, which is a class that implements `ICommand`.

Implementing `ICommand` is one option for taking advantage of commands in MVVM. We will look at some helpers that make this task easier in *Chapter 5, Northwind – Commands and User Inputs.*

ProjectViewModel

This view model will be exposed as the `ProjectsViewModel.SelectedProject` property and will contain the view state and view logic for the detail's controls in our master detail view.

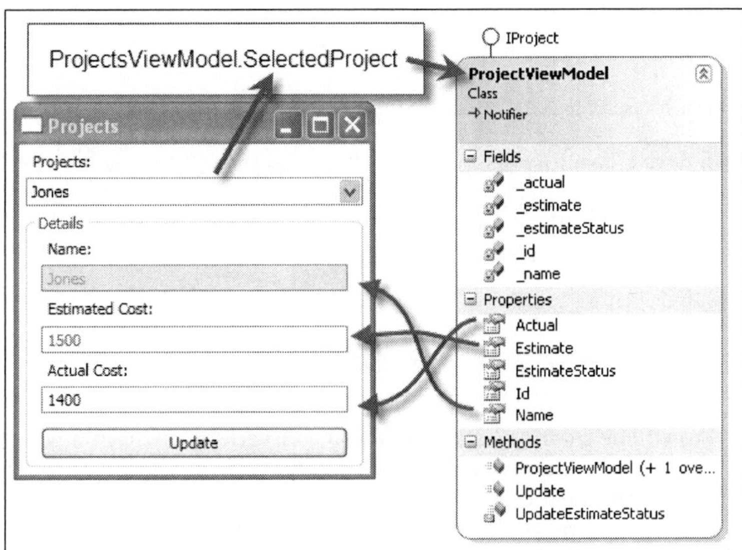

ProjectViewModel will be very similar to our `Project` data object, so we have implemented the `IProject` interface for the common properties. **ProjectViewModel** also contains view state and view logic in the form of the `EstimateStatus` property, which is a `Status` enum that will be used in combination with style triggers to control the color of the **Estimate** textbox.

Model

`ProjectsModel` implements an interface to support dependency injection for easier testing and better extensibility. It's also responsible for communicating changes to the session state to support keeping any number of views synchronized with session state.

The `IProjectsModel` interface exposes:

`Projects`: An `ObservableCollection<ProjectViewModel>` class that is exposed by `ProjectsViewModel` instances via the `ProjectsViewModel.Projects` proxy property. `ProjectsModel.Projects` holds the session state, that is shared across all views. If this application were updated to support adding and removing projects through `ProjectsModel`, then the UI will automatically get these updates without us having to add any code to make it happen.

[ Proxy property is a pattern that will be explored in more detail in *Chapter 3, Northwind – Services and Persistence Ignorance.*]

Code

Let us now take a look at the following steps:

1. Create a new Class Library project called `ProjectBilling.Application.WPF`.
2. Add a project reference to:
    - `ProjectBillingDataAccess`
    - `PresentationCore`
3. Add a class called `Notifier` to `ProjectBilling.Application.WPF`.

[ We will be creating both a WPF and a Silverlight client in this chapter, and later we will be reusing this code in a second project for Silverlight. That is why this project was named `ProjectBilling.Application.WPF`.]

4. We'll start by creating a base class, to be used by our model and view model, that will encapsulate the `INotifyPropertyChanged` functionality. Add the following code to the `Notifier.cs` file:

```
using System.ComponentModel;

namespace ProjectBilling.Application
{
    public class Notifier : INotifyPropertyChanged
    {
        public event PropertyChangedEventHandler
            PropertyChanged = delegate { };

        protected void NotifyPropertyChanged(
            string propertyName)
        {
            PropertyChanged(this,
                                new PropertyChangedEventArgs(
                                    propertyName));
        }
    }
}
```

   This class provides an implementation of `INotifyPropertyChanged` and adds the `NotifyPropertyChanged()` method, to raise `INotifyPropertyChanged.PropertyChanged`.

ProjectsModel

We will now create the model, so let's start by adding a class called `ProjectsModel` to our project. Add the following code to the `ProjectsModel.cs` file:

```
using System;
using System.Collections.ObjectModel;
using System.Linq;
using ProjectBilling.DataAccess;

namespace ProjectBilling.Application
{
    public interface IProjectsModel
    {
        ObservableCollection<Project> Projects
            { get; set; }

        event EventHandler<ProjectEventArgs> ProjectUpdated;
```

```
        void UpdateProject(IProject updatedProject);
    }

    public class ProjectEventArgs : EventArgs
    {
        public IProject Project { get; set; }
        public ProjectEventArgs(IProject project)
        {
            Project = project;
        }
    }

    public class ProjectsModel : IProjectsModel
    {
    }
}
```

> You may prefer to keep each item in its own file, which wasn't done here, to keep things short.

This code adds the following items to the file:

- `IProjectsModel`: The interfaces that the `ProjectsModel` class will implement are as follows:
    - `Projects`: An `ObservableCollection<Project>` class, which will hold our session state that will be shared across all views
    - `ProjectUpdated`: It indicates that our project was updated in the session state and allows for our view models to update their details controls, if the project that was updated is currently being displayed
    - `UpdateProject()`: It allows for notifying the model that a project was updated
- `ProjectsEventArgs`: `EventArgs` derived class that is used by `IProjectsModel.ProjectUpdated`
- `Project`: It holds a reference to the project that was updated

Next, update the `ProjectsModel` class, as shown in the following code:

```
public class ProjectsModel : IProjectsModel
{
    public ObservableCollection<Project> Projects
        { get; set; }
    public event EventHandler<ProjectEventArgs>
        ProjectUpdated = delegate { };

    public ProjectsModel(IDataService dataService)
    {
        Projects = new ObservableCollection<Project>();
        foreach (Project project
            in dataService.GetProjects())
        {
            Projects.Add(project);
        }
    }

    public void UpdateProject(IProject updatedProject)
    {
        GetProject(updatedProject.ID)
            .Update(updatedProject);
        ProjectUpdated(this,
            new ProjectEventArgs(updatedProject));
    }

    private Project GetProject(int projectId)
    {
        return Projects.FirstOrDefault(
            project => project.ID == projectId);
    }
}
```

This class simply implements the `IProjectsModel` interface. Here are a few points of interest.

- Constructor: The constructor populates `IProjectsModel.Projects` by iterating over the collection returned from `DataService.GetProjects()`
- `UpdateProjects()`: The implementation of `IProjectsModel.UpdateProjects` will first update the `IProjectsModel.Projects` collection and then raise the `IProjectsModel.ProjectUpdated` event to notify other view models of the change. This is done so that the view models can update `ProjectsViewModel.SelectedProject`, if it currently contains the project that was updated.

ProjectViewModel

Now, add a class called `ProjectViewModel` and add the following code:

```
using ProjectBilling.DataAccess;

namespace ProjectBilling.Application
{
    public interface IProjectViewModel : IProject
    {
        Status EstimateStatus { get; set; }
    }

    public class ProjectViewModel : Notifier,
        IProjectViewModel
    {
        private int _id;
        private string _name;
        private double _estimate;
        private double _actual;
        private Status _estimateStatus
            = Status.None;

        public int Id
        {
            get { return _id; }
            set
            {
                _id = value;
                NotifyPropertyChanged("Id");
            }
        }

        public string Name
        {
            get { return _name; }
            set
            {
                _name = value;
                NotifyPropertyChanged("Name");
            }
        }

        public double Estimate
        {
```

```
            get { return _estimate; }
            set
            {
                _estimate = value;
                NotifyPropertyChanged("Estimate");
            }
        }

        public double Actual
        {
            get { return _actual; }
            set
            {
                _actual = value;
                UpdateEstimateStatus();
                NotifyPropertyChanged("Actual");
            }
        }

        public Status EstimateStatus
        {
            get { return _estimateStatus; }
            set
            {
                _estimateStatus = value;
                NotifyPropertyChanged("EstimateStatus");
            }
        }
    }
}
```

We first add the `IProjectViewModel` interface, which inherits the `IProject` interface and adds the `EstimateStatus` property that will be used to control the color of the estimate in the UI by returning the appropriate `Status` enum. This class contains the properties that will be bound to the details controls in the view. Next, update the `ProjectViewModel` class by adding the following code:

```
public ProjectViewModel()
{}

public ProjectViewModel(IProject project)
{
    if (project == null)
        return;
    Id = project.Id;
```

```
        Update(project);
    }

    public void Update(IProject project)
    {
        Id = project.Id;
        Name = project.Name;
        Estimate = project.Estimate;
        Actual = project.Actual;
    }

    private void UpdateEstimateStatus()
    {
        if (Actual == 0)
            EstimateStatus = Status.None;
        else if (Actual <= Estimate)
            EstimateStatus = Status.Good;
        else
            EstimateStatus = Status.Bad;
    }
```

Here, we've added a constructor that takes an `IProject` interface and updates itself by using the `Update()` method. The `Update()` method is public to allow for easily updating `ProjectViewModel` and the details controls that it is bound to. The details' controls will automatically be updated as the properties of the `ProjectViewModel` class implement `INotifyPropertyChanged` via `ProjectViewModel`, subclassing the `Notifier` class.

We've also added an `UpdateEstimateStatus()` method that performs the view logic of determining the estimate status by comparing the actual and estimate properties.

ProjectsViewModel

At this point, we have run out of code that can be shared with a Silverlight client. This is because we will need to now add a class called `ProjectsViewModel` to the project. We'll start by adding the following enum to `ProjectsViewModel.cs`:

```
public enum Status
{
    None,
    Good,
    Bad
}
```

The `Status` enum is used to indicate the status of an estimate and has three values.

- `None`: Indicates that there is no actual data at this time and that we can't determine if the estimate is good or bad
- `Good`: Indicates that the actual cost was equal to or less than the estimated cost
- `Bad`: Indicates that the actual cost was greater than the estimated cost

Now we will add an interface to the file.

```
public interface IProjectsViewModel
  : INotifyPropertyChanged
{
        IProjectsViewModel SelectedProject { get; set; }
    void UpdateProject();
}
```

This will be used shortly by `UpdateCommand,` which we will implement and expose only those methods which are needed by the `UpdateCommand` property to keep the sample short. The interface inherits `INotifyPropertyChanged` to allow `UpdateCommand` access to the `INotifyPropertyChanged.PropertyChanged` event. The interface also exposes the `SelectedProject` property, which will be bound to the details controls and `UpdateProject()` method for updating the details controls.

Next, add the fields and properties:

```
using System;
using System.Collections.ObjectModel;
using System.ComponentModel;
using System.Linq;
using System.Windows.Input;
using ProjectBilling.DataAccess;

namespace ProjectBilling.Application
{
    public class ProjectsViewModel : Notifier,
        IProjectsViewModel
    {
        public const string SELECTED_PROJECT_PROPERRTY_NAME
            = "SelectedProject";
        private readonly IProjectsModel _model;
        private IProjectViewModel _selectedProject;
        private Status _detailsEstimateStatus
            = Status.None;
        private bool _detailsEnabled;
```

```
private readonly ICommand _updateCommand;


public ObservableCollection<Project>
    Projects { get { return _model.Projects; } }

public int? SelectedValue
{
    set
    {
        if (value == null)
            return;
        Project project = GetProject((int)value);
        if (SelectedProject == null)
        {
            SelectedProject
                = new ProjectViewModel(project);
        }
        else
        {
            SelectedProject.Update(project);
        }
        DetailsEstimateStatus =
            SelectedProject.EstimateStatus;
    }
}

public IProjectViewModel SelectedProject
{
    get { return _selectedProject; }
    set
    {
        if (value == null)
        {
            _selectedProject = value;
            DetailsEnabled = false;
        }
        else
        {
            if (_selectedProject == null)
            {
                _selectedProject =
                    new ProjectViewModel(value);
            }
```

```
                    _selectedProject.Update(value);
                    DetailsEstimateStatus =
                        _selectedProject.EstimateStatus;
                    DetailsEnabled = true;
                    NotifyPropertyChanged(
                        SELECTED_PROJECT_PROPERRTY_NAME);
                }
            }
        }

        public Status DetailsEstimateStatus
        {
            get { return _detailsEstimateStatus; }
            set
            {
                _detailsEstimateStatus = value;
                NotifyPropertyChanged("DetailsEstimateStatus");
            }
        }

        public bool DetailsEnabled
        {
            get { return _detailsEnabled; }
            set
            {
                _detailsEnabled = value;
                NotifyPropertyChanged("DetailsEnabled");
            }
        }

        public ICommand UpdateCommand
        {
            get { return _updateCommand; }
        }
    }
}
```

This code adds the properties and fields that we need. Items of interest include:

- `Notifier`: This class derives from `Notifier` to provide `INotifyPropertyChanged` support.
- `_model`: This holds a reference to a `ProjectsModel` instance. Only one `ProjectsModel` will be created and it will be shared by all `ProjectsViewModel` instances.

- `Projects`: `ObservableCollection<Project>` is a proxy to `IProjectsModel.Projects` and simply returns a reference to it. This allows for shared session state, as updates to `IProjectsModel.Projects` will be shared by all views.
- `SelectedValue`: This property will be bound to the `Projects` `ComboBox.SelectedIndex` property in the view with `Binding.Mode = OneWayToSource` causing this property setter to be called whenever the selection of the `Projects` combobox changes.
  When that happens this code does two things:
    - It updates `SelectedProject` with the newly selected project
    - It updates the `DetailsEstimateStatus` property
- `SelectedProject`: This property is a `ProjectsViewModel` instance that gets updated by `SelectedValue`, to hold the currently selected project as a `ProjectViewModel` instance. The `SelectedProject` object instance will be bound to the details controls in the view and provide the view state for those controls.
- `DetailsEstimateStatus`: This property returns the current estimate status. See the description of the `Status` enum previously, for details.
- `DetailsEnabled`: It is a Boolean value that specifies whether the details controls should be enabled or disabled.
- `UpdateCommand`: It is an `ICommand` interface that will be bound to the **Update** button on the view. It handles:
    - Communicating the click event to the view model
    - Enabling and disabling the **Update** button

Now we will add the constructor.

```
public ProjectsViewModel(IProjectsModel projectModel)
{
    _model = projectModel;
    _model.ProjectUpdated +=
        model_ProjectUpdated;
    _updateCommand = new UpdateCommand(this);
}
```

The constructor does the following:

- It takes an `IProjectModel` argument to support dependency injection for easier testing and better extensibility.
- It sets `projectsModel` to `_model`.

- It subscribes to the `IProjectsModel.ProjectUpdated` event.
- It instantiates an `UpdateCommand` property and assigns it to `_updateCommand`. `_updateCommand` is the field that backs the `UpdateCommand` property. `UpdateCommand` takes this reference as a constructor argument so that it has access to the view model that it is responsible for communicating the `Update Button.Click` event to. Details of `UpdateCommand` will be explained shortly.

We will finish `ProjectsViewModel` by adding the event handler and helper methods, as follows:

```
public void UpdateProject()
{
    DetailsEstimateStatus =
        SelectedProject.EstimateStatus;
    _model.UpdateProject(SelectedProject);
}

private void model_ProjectUpdated(object sender,
                                  ProjectEventArgs e)
{
    GetProject(e.Project.Id).Update(e.Project);
    if (SelectedProject != null
        && e.Project.Id == SelectedProject.Id)
    {
        SelectedProject.Update(e.Project);
        DetailsEstimateStatus =
            SelectedProject.EstimateStatus;
    }
}

private Project GetProject(int projectId)
{
    return (from p in Projects
            where p.Id == projectId
            select p).FirstOrDefault();
}
```

These methods are described as follows:

- `UpdateProjects()`: This method allows for the `UpdateCommand` property to pass the `Update.Button.Click` event to the `ProjectsViewModel` class instance that it is responsible for. This is one of many areas in which C# will benefit from a `friend` modifier found in C++, but I digress.

- `model_ProjectUpdated()`: This is an event handler that will be called when the `IProjectsModel.ProjectUpdated` event is raised. It first updates the updated project in the `Projects` collection, and then it will update the `SelectedProject` view model if its ID is the same as the updated project. This code demonstrates one reason the `IProject` interface is useful—it allows for passing `Project` or `ProjectModel` instances to `Project.Update()` and `ProjectViewModel.Update()`, respectively, as they both use `IProject` to perform their updates.
- `GetProject()`: This is a helper method that finds a project in `Projects`, by ID, and returns it.

Now, we will add the `UpdateCommand` property to the `ProjectsViewModel.cs` file, as follows:

```
internal class UpdateCommand : ICommand
{
    private const int ARE_EQUAL = 0;
    private const int NONE_SELECTED = -1;
    private IProjectsViewModel _vm;

    public UpdateCommand(IProjectsViewModel viewModel)
    {
        _vm = viewModel;
        _vm.PropertyChanged += vm_PropertyChanged;
    }

    private void vm_PropertyChanged(object sender,
        PropertyChangedEventArgs e)
    {
        if (string.Compare(e.PropertyName,
                           ProjectsViewModel.
                           SELECTED_PROJECT_PROPERRTY_NAME)
            == ARE_EQUAL)
        {
            CanExecuteChanged(this, new EventArgs());
        }
    }

    public bool CanExecute(object parameter)
    {
        if (_vm.SelectedProject == null)
            return false;
        return ((ProjectViewModel) _vm.SelectedProject).Id
                > NONE_SELECTED;
```

```
        }

        public event EventHandler CanExecuteChanged
            = delegate { };

        public void Execute(object parameter)
        {
            _vm.UpdateProject();
        }
    }
```

The `UpdateCommand` property is an `ICommand` implementation that allows for binding to a command source. Most controls in WPF and Silverlight are command sources and will call the `ICommand.Execute()` method when the event that they associate with `ICommandSource.Command` fires. There can be only one event that is associated with `ICommandSource.Command`, for any control instance, and the event that is associated varies from control to control. In some controls, such as buttons, the event mapping is configurable. For example, `Button.ClickMode` allows for changing the input that fires `Button.Click`, which also changes what input fires `Command.Execute`. Things to note about `UpdateCommand` include:

- The constructor takes an `IProjectsViewModel` enum, which it saves a reference to in the `_vm` property. It then subscribes to `INotifyPropertyChanged.PropertyChanged`, so that it can raise `ICommand.CanExecuteChanged` whenever `ProjectsViewModel.SelectedProject` changes. `IComand.CanExecuteChanged` will indicate to the command source that it should call `ICommand.CanExecute()` as it may have changed.
- `CanExecute()`: This is an implementation of `ICommand.CanExecute()`. `ICommand.CanExecute()` is called by command sources to determine if they can currently execute the associated command. Controls will generally disable themselves when `ICommand.CanExecute()` returns `false`, and in our case this is used to control when the **Update** button is enabled or disabled by returning false when there is no `ProjectsViewModel.SelectedProject`.
- `CanExecuteChanged`: This event is an implementation of `ICommand.CanExecuteChanged`.
- `Execute()`: This is an implementation of `ICommand.Execute()` and will be called by the command source when the command source's associated event fires. In this implementation, we simply notify `ProjectsViewModel` by calling `ProjectsViewModel.UpdateProject`.

WPF UI

Now we will create a WPF UI to consume our model and view model. Start by:

1. Adding a new project WPF Application project called `ProjectBilling.UI.WPF`
2. Opening `App.Xaml.cs` and changing the class definition from:

   ```
   public partial class App : Application
   ```

   To:

   ```
   public partial class App
   ```

3. Removing the explicit sub-classing of application in this way will prevent the compiler from complaining about the name clash between the `ProjectBilling.Application` namespace and the `System.Windows.Application` class.

ProjectsView

Now add a new window called **ProjectsView**. The following is the code that we need in the code-behind approach:

```
using System.Windows;

namespace ProjectBilling.UI.WPF
{
    public partial class ProjectsView : Window
    {
        public ProjectsView()
        {
            InitializeComponent();
        }
    }
}
```

For those of you who are new to MVVM, this may be a surprise as there is no code, other than that generated by Visual Studio, needed in the code-behind approach, but when implementing pure MVVM, you will find that the you can have an empty code behind most of the time. In fact you can delete the code behinds which is a practice that I follow on my projects.

> Empty code-behind approaches are the result of implementation of pure MVVM. Just like anything else in development, there are tradeoffs to the various approaches to code in the code behind. I prefer implementing pure MVVM whenever possible, and I'm yet to find a scenario where pure MVVM isn't possible. I like the benefits of pure MVVM, and the challenge of keeping MVVM pure keeps things fun and interesting for me. However, we will cover all the tradeoffs of the various levels of purity as well as approaches for implementing each level throughout this book and leave it to you to decide what level of purity makes the most sense for you and your project.

Now add the following code shown to `ProjectsView.xaml`.

```
<Window x:Class="ProjectBilling.UI.WPF.ProjectsView"
        xmlns="http://schemas.microsoft.com/winfx/2006/xaml/
presentation"
        xmlns:x="http://schemas.microsoft.com/winfx/2006/xaml"
        Title="Projects" MinHeight="180" Height="180"
        MinWidth="250" Width="250" Padding="5"
        FocusManager.FocusedElement
            ="{Binding ElementName=ProjectsComboBox}">
    <UniformGrid Columns="2">
        <Label Content="Project:" />
        <ComboBox Margin="5" Name="ProjectsComboBox"
                SelectedValue="{Binding Path=SelectedValue,
                    Mode=OneWayToSource}"
                ItemsSource="{Binding Path=Projects}"
                DisplayMemberPath="Name"
                SelectedValuePath="ID" />
        <Label Content="Estimated Cost:" />
        <TextBox Margin="5" Grid.Row="1" Grid.Column="1"
                IsEnabled="{Binding Path=DetailsEnabled}"
                Text="{Binding Path=SelectedProject.Estimate}"
                Style="{StaticResource EstimateStyle}" />
        <Label Content="Actual Cost:" />
        <TextBox Margin="5"
                IsEnabled="{Binding Path=DetailsEnabled}"
                Text="{Binding
                    Path=SelectedProject.Actual}" />
        <Button Content="Update" Margin="5"
                Command="{Binding Path=UpdateCommand}" />
    </UniformGrid>
</Window>
```

The preceding code wires up our view model to the controls of our view. One thing you might notice is that we no longer need to name our elements, as the binding will take care of updates and no code is required.

> We still added a name to `ProjectsComboBox` to allow us to set the focus. The point to take away from this is that it's not necessary to name controls in order to communicate with depended-upon components such as the view model.

The interesting parts are how we are binding from view dependency properties to model `INotifyPropertyChanged` properties. We will now review the bindings and what they are for:

- `Projects ComboBox`
    - `ItemsSource`: This binding connects to the `ProjectsViewModel.Projects` collection and will populate the combobox with items contained in that collection. We've set `ComboBox.DisplayMemberPath="Name"` and `ComboBox.SelectedValuePath="ID"` so that the combobox will display `Project.Name` when expanded and assign `Project.Id` as the value of each item.
    - `SelectedValue`: This binding connects `ComboBox.SelectedValue` to `ProjectsViewModel.SelectedValue`, using `Binding.Mode="OneWayToSource"`. This will make it so that whenever the user changes the selection, the binding system will update `ProjectsViewModel.SelectedValue`, giving us a chance to update the window accordingly. We've done a `OneWayToSource` binding, because we only need to push data from the combobox to the view model and not the other way.
- Details Controls
    - `TextBox`: The details textbox controls are bound to the property `ProjectsViewModel.SelectedProject` allowing for the data to flow back and forth between the view model and view. This should all be straightforward except for the **Estimate** textbox's `Style` property. We will cover that style shortly.
- Update Button
    - `Command`: The **Update** button has it's command set to `ProjectsViewModel.UpdateCommand`, and this binding will use that command to manage its enabled state (view logic) and will call `UpdateCommand.Execute()` when clicked.

Now, add the following style to the `Windows.Resources` collection:

```
<Window.Resources>
    <!-- Update estimate color -->
    <Style x:Key="EstimateStyle"
            TargetType="{x:Type TextBox}">
        <Style.Triggers>
            <DataTrigger Binding="{Binding
                        DetailsEstimateStatus}"
                    Value="None">
                <Setter Property="Foreground"
                        Value="Black" />
            </DataTrigger>
            <DataTrigger Binding="{Binding
                        DetailsEstimateStatus}"
                    Value="Good">
                <Setter Property="Foreground"
                        Value="Green" />
            </DataTrigger>
            <DataTrigger Binding="{Binding
                        DetailsEstimateStatus}"
                    Value="Bad">
                <Setter Property="Foreground"
                    Value="Red" />
            </DataTrigger>
        </Style.Triggers>
    </Style>
</Window.Resources>
```

The preceding style is the style that is used by our **Estimate** textbox. This style uses data triggers to update the color of text in the **Estimate** textbox. The data triggers are all bound to `DetailsEstimateStatus` and will set the `Foreground` property to a color. When the value of `DetailsEstimateStatus` is `Status.None`, we set the text to `Brushes.Black`; when it is `Status.Good`, we set it to `Brushes.Green`; and when it is `Status.Bad`, we set it to `Brushes.Red`.

In previous examples, we set the color to the **Estimated Cost** textbox's `Foreground` color, which we could have done here by using an `ElementName` binding in the trigger. I decided not to do that here, because functionally the application will work the same, and earlier I wanted to make the point about how naming the controls is not necessary a lot of the time with MVVM.

This allows us to translate our `DetailsEstimateStatus` value to the correct color and to easily manage our view logic in a decoupled design.

MainWindow

Update `MainWindow.Xaml`, as follows:

```
<Window x:Class="ProjectBilling.UI.WPF.MainWindow"
        xmlns="http://schemas.microsoft.com/winfx/2006/xaml/
presentation"
        xmlns:x="http://schemas.microsoft.com/winfx/2006/xaml"
        Title="Shell" Height="150" Width="200"
        MinHeight="150" MinWidth="200"
        FocusManager.FocusedElement
            ="{Binding ElementName=ShowProjectsButton}">
    <StackPanel>
        <Button Content="Update Projects"
                Name="ShowProjectsButton" Margin="5"
                Click="ShowProjectsButton_Click" />
    </StackPanel>
</Window>
```

And update the code behind, as follows:

```
using System.Windows;
using ProjectBilling.Application;
using ProjectBilling.DataAccess;

namespace ProjectBilling.UI.WPF
{
    public partial class MainWindow : Window
    {
        private IProjectsModel _projectModel;

        public MainWindow()
        {
            InitializeComponent();
            _projectModel = new ProjectsModel(
                new DataServiceStub());
        }
```

```
        private void ShowProjectsButton_Click(object sender,
            RoutedEventArgs e)
        {
            ProjectsView view = new ProjectsView();
            view.DataContext
                = new ProjectsViewModel(_projectModel);
            view.Owner = this;
            view.Show();
        }
    }
}
```

MainWindow does not implement MVVM. To implement MVVM, MainWindow will have to use a command instead of using a button click handler for the ShowProjectsButton.Click event. We would also have had to move the showing of ProjectsView to the view model of MainWindow. Having UI elements in view models breaks the MVVM pattern. There are MVVM-friendly ways of dealing with this situation, however we won't be covering those techniques until *Chapter 3, Northwind – Foundations*. So, to avoid introducing that material at this point in the book, we have not implemented MVVM for MainWindow.

Now, run the project by setting it as startup project and click on *F5*; you should see the same application that we built several times in the last chapter.

Silverlight UI

Now, we will create a Silverlight client and attempt to reuse our non-view code from our WPF implementation.

If you will be using Silverlight in this book then you will need to install Microsoft Silverlight 4 Tools for Visual Studio 2010, available for free download at www.Microsoft.com (http://www.microsoft.com/downloads/en/details.aspx?FamilyID=b3deb194-ca86-4fb6-a716-b67c2604a139).

Porting assemblies to Silverlight

We must start by creating versions of our assemblies that can be consumed by a Silverlight client. Silverlight is often described as a subset of WPF, which is not correct, as shown in the following diagram:

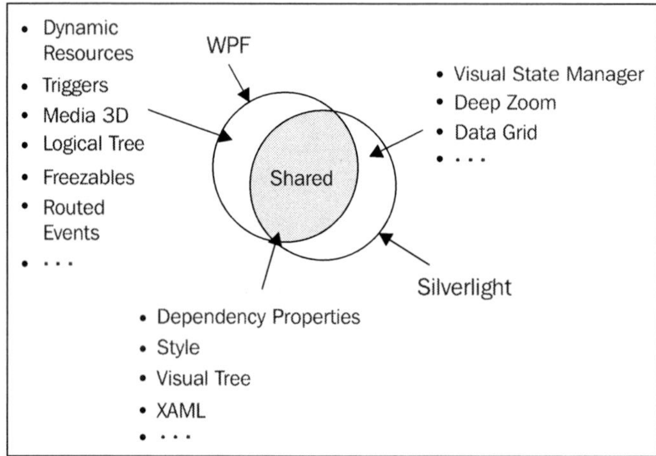

As you can see, there is an intersection of these functionalities, but there is functionality from each technology that isn't available in the other. Even with things that are shared, such as binding markup extensions, you will find that only a subset of functionality is available across both platforms. For example, Silverlight does not support binding by element name or relative bindings.

Microsoft has attempted to make porting between WPF and Silverlight easier by making the following assemblies portable in WPF 4.0 and Silverlight 4.0.

- `Mscorlib`
- `System`
- `System.Core`
- `System.ComponentModel.Composition`
- `Microsoft.VisualBasic`

> There are various techniques suggested by Microsoft for sharing assemblies between Silverlight and WPF; see MSDN for more details. For now, we will take an approach that I found to be appropriate for our example.

Perform the following steps to create Silverlight versions of the assemblies needed:

1. Add two new **Silverlight Class Library** projects, called `ProjectBilling.DataAccess.SL` and `ProjectBilling.Application.SL`, to your solution.
2. Right-click on `ProjectBilling.DataAccess.SL` in **Solution Explorer** and select **Add | Existing Item**.
3. You will be presented with a dialog that allows for adding items. Browse to the `ProjectBilling.DataAccess` project directory that we created in *Chapter 1, Presentation Patterns* and select `DataService.cs` and `Project.cs`, but don't click on the **Add** button. Instead, click the arrow on the **Add** button and select **Add As Link**, as shown in the following screenshot. This will cause the `ProjectBilling.DataAccess.SL` project to use the files in the `ProjectBilling.DataAccess` project. This is very helpful, because the assemblies that contain things like `ObservableCollection` are different for Silverlight and WPF but the namespaces are the same. Now when you build, each project will build against its framework assemblies, and this will result in a working version of our code for each technology based on one set of source files.
4. Add a reference from `ProjectBilling.Application.SL` to `ProjectBilling.DataAccess.SL`.
5. Add all of the files in `ProjectBilling.Application` to `ProjectBilling.Application.SL` as links, in the same way that we did in step 3, from `ProjectBilling.DataAccess.SL`.
6. Build and make sure that there are no errors. If you get errors then double check the previous steps to make sure that you've followed them exactly, got the project types correct, and only added files as links.

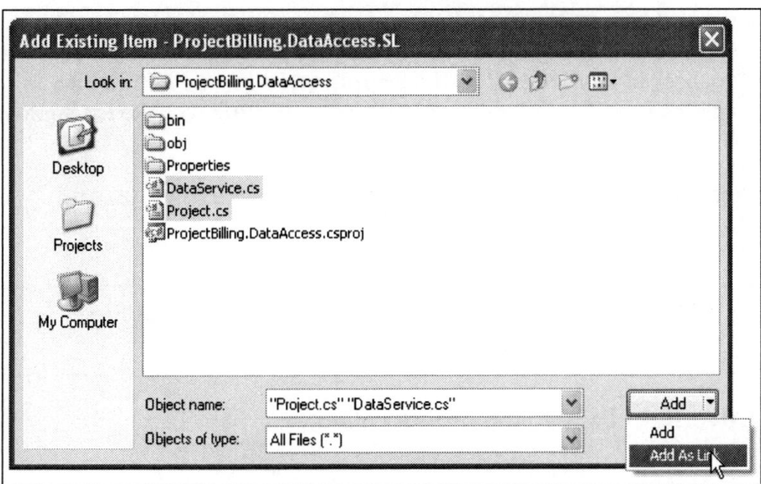

ProjectsView

Add a **Silverlight Application** project, called `ProjectBilling.UI.SL`, to your solution. You will be presented with the dialog that follows. In that dialog, perform the following steps as shown in the following screenshot:

1. Uncheck the **Host the Silverlight application in a new Web site** checkbox.
2. Select **Silverlight 4** from the drop-down menu.
3. Click on the **OK** button.

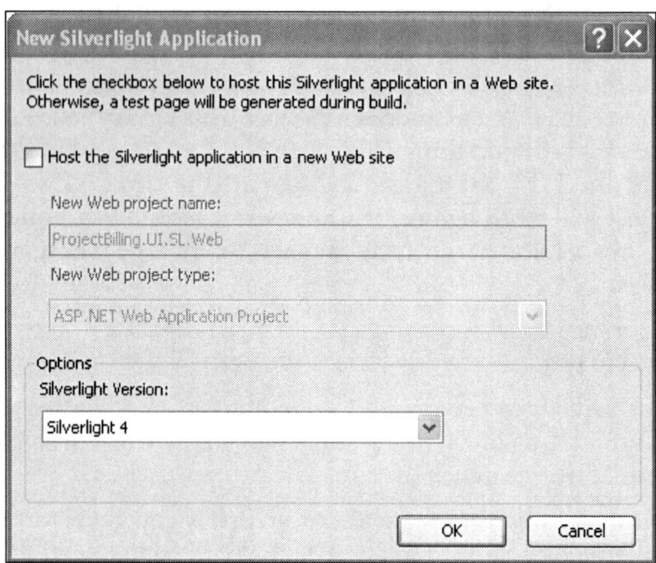

We will be running our Silverlight application through Visual Studio, and because of that, we don't need to create a hosting website; this is why we unchecked **Host the Silverlight application in a new Web site**. In real applications, you would want to create a hosting website for deployment.

Next, add project references to `ProjectBilling.DataAccess.SL` and `ProjectBilling.Application.SL`.

Be sure to reference the Silverlight versions of these assemblies.

Add a new **Silverlight Page** to the project called `ProjectView`.

Add the following code shown to `ProjectView.xaml`.

```
<UserControl
    x:Class="ProjectBilling.UI.SL.ProjectsView"
    xmlns="http://schemas.microsoft.com/winfx/2006/xaml/presentation"
    xmlns:x="http://schemas.microsoft.com/winfx/2006/xaml"
    xmlns:local="clr-namespace:ProjectBilling.UI.SL"
    MinHeight="180" Height="180" MinWidth="250" Width="250">

    <UserControl.Resources>
        <local:StatusToBrushConverter x:Key="StatusToBrush" />
    </UserControl.Resources>
    <Border BorderBrush="Blue" BorderThickness="5"
            Margin="10" Padding="5" CornerRadius="5">
        <Grid Margin="5">
            <Grid.RowDefinitions>
                <RowDefinition />
                <RowDefinition />
                <RowDefinition />
                <RowDefinition />
            </Grid.RowDefinitions>
            <Grid.ColumnDefinitions>
                <ColumnDefinition />
                <ColumnDefinition />
            </Grid.ColumnDefinitions>

            <TextBlock Text="Project:" />
            <ComboBox Margin="5" Grid.Column="1"
                    SelectionChanged
                      ="ComboBox_SelectionChanged"
                    ItemsSource="{Binding Path=Projects}"
                    DisplayMemberPath="Name"
                    SelectedValuePath="ID" />
            <TextBlock Text="Estimated Cost:" Grid.Row="1"/>
            <TextBox Margin="5" Grid.Row="1" Grid.Column="1"
                    IsEnabled="{Binding
                        Path=DetailsEnabled}"
                    Text="{Binding
                        Path=SelectedProject.Estimate,
                        Mode=TwoWay}"
                    Foreground="{Binding
                        Path=DetailsEstimateStatus,
                        Converter={StaticResource
                            StatusToBrush}}"/>
```

```
            <TextBlock Text="Actual Cost:" Grid.Row="2" />
            <TextBox Margin="5" Grid.Row="2" Grid.Column="2"
                     IsEnabled="{Binding
                        Path=DetailsEnabled}"
                     Text="{Binding
                        Path=SelectedProject.Actual,
                        Mode=TwoWay}" />
            <Button Content="Update" Margin="5" Grid.Row="3"
                    Command="{Binding Path=UpdateCommand}" />
        </Grid>
    </Border>
</UserControl>
```

You should notice a lot of similarities between this code and the `ProjectsView.xaml` file from our WPF example. The main difference in the approach here boils down to three features that are not available in Silverlight.

- Style triggers
- Binding using OneWayToSource mode
- `UniformGrid`

The absence of these features has caused us to take a slightly different approach when wiring up our `ProjectsViewModel`.

The first difference is that, instead of using a style in our resources, we are now using a custom converter that is instantiated in the resources, as follows:

```
<UserControl.Resources>
    <local:StatusToBrushConverter x:Key="StatusToBrush" />
</UserControl.Resources>
```

And then, we use this converter in the binding for the **Estimated Cost** textbox, as shown in the following code:

```
<TextBox Margin="5" Grid.Row="1" Grid.Column="1"
        IsEnabled="{Binding
            Path=DetailsEnabled}"
        Text="{Binding
            Path=SelectedProject.Estimate,
            Mode=TwoWay}"
        Foreground="{Binding
            Path=DetailsEstimateStatus,
            Converter={StaticResource
                StatusToBrush}}"/>
```

As you can see, we have associated the `StatusToBrush` converter with the `Foreground` binding, and this takes the place of using a style to control the color of the **Estimated Cost** textbox.

We will cover the converter code shortly.

We've also changed the binding mode of our **Estimated Cost** and **Actual Cost** `TextBox` controls to be explicitly `TwoWay`, as shown in the code previously. This is because in Silverlight all controls are `OneWay`, by default. In WPF, the binding mode varies by control and `TextBox` has a default value of `TwoWay`.

The next difference is one that causes us to break with pure MVVM and add code to our code behind:

```
<ComboBox Margin="5" Grid.Column="1"
        SelectionChanged
            ="ComboBox_SelectionChanged"
        ItemsSource="{Binding Path=Projects}"
        DisplayMemberPath="Name"
        SelectedValuePath="ID" />
```

As you can see, we've added an event handler for `SelectionChanged`. This was done because Silverlight doesn't support `OneWayToSource` bindings. We previously used a `OneWayToSource` binding to allow us to take advantage of a bound property setter to avoid using an event handler. However, the only binding that can be used in this way is `OneWayToSource`. Attempting to use a `TwoWay` binding mode in this scenario leads to a stack overflow exception. We will look at the code behind shortly, to see what this event handler does.

There are several options for both Silverlight and WPF that allow avoiding using event handlers, which we will look at in *Chapter 5, Northwind – Commands and User Inputs*.

Add the following code to `ProjectsView.xaml.cs`.

```
using System.Windows.Controls;
using ProjectBilling.Application;

namespace ProjectBilling.UI.SL
{
    public partial class ProjectsView : UserControl
    {
        public ProjectsView()
```

```
        {
            InitializeComponent();
        }

        private void ComboBox_SelectionChanged(object sender,
            SelectionChangedEventArgs e)
        {
            ((ProjectsViewModel) DataContext).SelectedValue
                = (int?)((ComboBox) sender).SelectedValue;
        }
    }
}
```

As you can see, we've now got an event handler and are no longer implementing a pure no-code-behind approach. In this event handler, we avoid storing an explicit reference to our view model by taking advantage of `DataContext` and casting it to `ProjectsViewModel`. We then explicitly set `SelectedValue`. We've effectively done the same thing that we did previously in our WPF example, allowing us to use our existing view model as is.

MainPage

To keep things simple, **MainPage** displays each ProjectsView in the same page by adding user controls to a StackPanel.

> Displaying multiple windows in Silverlight and synchronizing the content will not be covered here, and it's not the only option one might use to achieve a dialog feel in Silverlight. There are many in-browser dialog options out there, and I will leave exploring those techniques and tools up to you. However, what I did want to illustrate here is implementing MVVM for the ProjectsView.

```
<UserControl x:Class="ProjectBilling.UI.SL.MainPage"
    xmlns="http://schemas.microsoft.com/winfx/2006/xaml/presentation"
    xmlns:x="http://schemas.microsoft.com/winfx/2006/xaml"
    xmlns:d="http://schemas.microsoft.com/expression/blend/2008"
    xmlns:mc="http://schemas.openxmlformats.org/markup-
compatibility/2006"
    mc:Ignorable="d">
    <Grid>
        <Grid.ColumnDefinitions>
            <ColumnDefinition Width="150" />
            <ColumnDefinition Width="*" />
        </Grid.ColumnDefinitions>
```

```
        <Button Content="Update Projects"
            VerticalAlignment="Top" Height="Auto"
            Margin="10" Click="Button_Click" />
        <StackPanel x:Name="MainStackPanel" Grid.Column="1"
            HorizontalAlignment="Left"/>
    </Grid>
</UserControl>
```

This code simply creates a grid that has two columns and puts a button for showing `ProjectsView` in the left column and a `StackPanel` that the `ProjectsView` will be placed in the right column.

> We have chosen to not implement MVVM in `MainPage` in the same way we didn't implement it in WPF's `MainWindow`. This was done to avoid diving into some advanced topics that will be covered later in this book.

Next, we will look at the code behind.

```
using System.Windows;
using System.Windows.Controls;
using ProjectBilling.Application;
using ProjectBilling.DataAccess;

namespace ProjectBilling.UI.SL
{
    public partial class MainPage : UserControl
    {
        private IProjectsModel _model;
        public MainPage()
        {
            InitializeComponent();
            _model = new ProjectsModel(new DataServiceStub());
        }

        private void Button_Click(object sender,
            RoutedEventArgs e)
        {
            ProjectsView view = new ProjectsView();
            view.DataContext = new ProjectsViewModel(_model);
            MainStackPanel.Children.Add(view);
        }
    }
}
```

Here we keep a reference to our model in the `_model` property, which is set to a new instance in the constructor. We also have an event handler, `Button_Click()`, that will be called in response to our **Update Projects** button being clicked. This event handler creates new `ProjectsView`, sets its `DataContext` property to a new instance of `ProjectsViewModel`, and then adds this new view to the `MainStackPanel.Childern` collection by calling `Add()`.

Now, set `ProjectBilling.UI.Silverlight` as the **StartUp Project** and press *F5* to launch the site; you will see a version of **Project Billing**, as shown in the following screenshot:

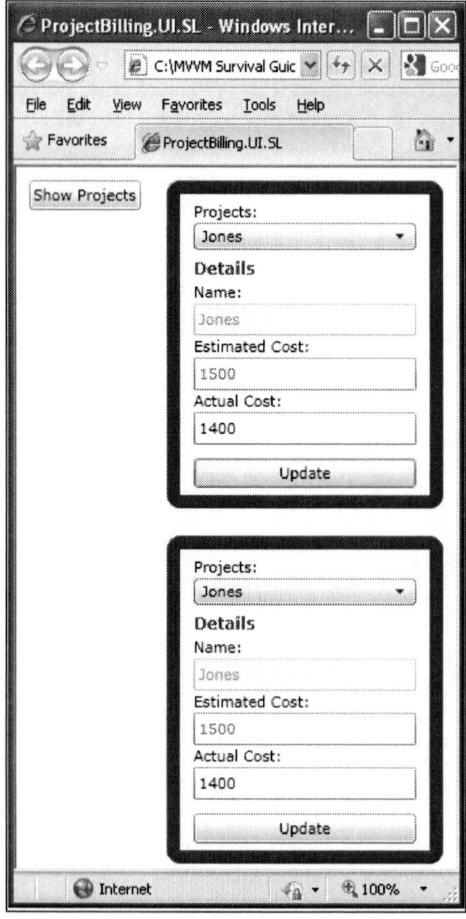

Clicking on **Show Projects** will display an additional `ProjectsView`. Functionally, this version of Project Billing is the same as the other project billing applications we've built, with some minor exceptions.

Benefits of MVVM

MVP had been the dominant presentational pattern for most UI development, with MVC still having a strong presence in web UIs before .NET 3.0 introduced some new technologies that made MVVM or Presentation Model an attractive option for WPF and Silverlight.

The benefits of MVVM include the following:

- **Increased testability**: Testability is improved as all view logic is now easily testable from unit tests.
- **Less code**: I've found that the amount of code required to manage the view has decreased quite a bit, as you no longer have to deal with boilerplate code behind code. This code involves a lot of casting and error checking in production quality code. Less code means fewer bugs, less code to maintain, and fewer unit tests to write.
- **Increased decoupling**: When using the pure approach, you no longer need to have the view and mediator (view model, presenter, or controller) be explicitly aware of each other. The view does have a reference to the view model via its `DataContext` property. However, under pure MVVM, it's not necessary for the view to be aware of the type of the view model.
- **Allows for streamlined development processes**: Now developers and designers can work independently on the same application views. This is because of the decoupling in this pattern and also because Blend doesn't execute constructors of the view's code behind but executes the constructor of your view model. You can create a view model that exposes the needed data points and have the view model properties return design-time data. This allows designers to work on the look of the application while the view model and model are being built. This is much harder in other patterns, as we will see later, in *Chapter 7, Dialogs and MVVM*.

I generally start my projects by creating a view model stub that returns fake design-time data. I then use that design-time view model to create a rough mock UI in Blend. Once I can tell that functionally the view model supports what is needed in the view, it's very easy to hand off the UI to a designer. Then, you can also delegate the building of the model and updating of the view model to support real data to other developers, if desired. For the current project I'm working on, we use outsourced labor; this approach allows me as the architect to quickly create the overall design and then delegate the remaining pieces to others, to be fleshed out. When I hand off the work, the wiring between the view and view model has already been created, and once the model and view model are updated to use real data, the UI will work as expected. The designer and backend programmers don't need to interact, because they are both working off the view model and they are not dependent on each other. This approach allows the view model to essentially define a contract for both sides to work off of.

- **Allows for some interesting design approaches**: Convention over configuration can be leveraged and lead to some interesting designs, as demonstrated by *Rob Eisenberg* in his *Mix10 presentation, Build Your Own MVVM Framework* (`http://live.visitmix.com/MIX10/Sessions/EX15`). His approach is similar to what is found in ASP.NET MVC—to establish naming conventions for elements of the MVVM design triad and then create a framework that allows for automatically connecting all the pieces at runtime. In his demonstration, Rob was able to create an impressive demo application that had no binding code in the XAML and had no code outside of his framework code to connect views to view models. Rob is the man behind the Caliburn and Caliburn Micro MVVM frameworks. He has added built-in support for this style of convention over configuration in those frameworks. More on this can be found in *Appendix A*, .
- Another interesting approach that we will explore in *Chapter 6, Northwind—Hierarchical View Model and IoC*, is the idea of hierarchical view model design, where you create a large main view model (or application model) that aggregates all of the other view models used in the application. Doing this effectively creates an object graph representation of your view state. One benefit of this approach is that you can serialize your application model to effectively persist the view state of your application. Then, on application start up, you can deserialize the view state and restore the UI to its previous state without having to write a settings framework.
- MVVM provides for well-organized, easy-to-understand designs. Your bindings are clear and easy to understand, as each view has a view model that it is bound to.

- **Improved developer experience**: If you're new to MVVM, then there's a good chance that you and your team will find this new approach refreshing and energizing. After you get comfortable with the pattern, working in the view model feels much more natural than the code-behind approach. This has been my experience and that of many others. However, results may vary.

MVVM and humble views

Under this design, it's debatable whether the view is always completely humble as it's common to bind from one control to another or to use the framework binding system to visually interpret view state and view logic.

Previously, under MVP, the presenter told the view what color to apply to the **Estimated Cost** text, but in the example in this chapter, we only defined a status for **Estimated Cost** and used WPF's style triggers to map a color to the **Estimated Cost** status.

Under both designs, the view logic is contained in the middle component (presenter or view model) and is therefore testable. However, looking at the MVVM approach, you might conclude that the view isn't truly humble, as it's still performing some small degree of view logic by mapping a color to a state. But upon further examination, you will likely reach the same conclusion that I arrived at, that the mapping of color to status is essentially styling the look of the application and based on the view logic and view state. The view logic that determined the view state is still in the view model and is therefore testable.

There will most certainly be grey areas when it comes to the issue of how much view logic and view state remains in the view under MVVM and whether the view is in fact truly humble. As you have seen, you can also use triggers and binding to do things like disabling controls based on the state of the view model, the state of other controls, or even the state of other view resources. Many of these techniques will beg the question *Is the view really a humble view*?

However, this will mostly be an academic exercise. You will most likely find, as I did, that these behaviors that are defined in XAML don't need to be verified via unit tests, because as long as they are properly defined and configured, they will work as expected, every time. In the same way that we don't write unit tests to verify that a CSS style in a web page is correct, there is no need to write unit tests to verify that the estimated cost mapping is correct. We have now removed the responsibility for visually presenting the view state and view logic from the programmers and moved it to the designers, with whom it belongs.

An additional benefit of having the code organized in this way is the freedom it gives designers to communicate view logic and view state to the users. Designers can use tools such as Expression Blend to tweak the visual representation of the estimate status in any way they like, without the need to involve programmers. Designers can take the view's logical state and communicate that in whatever visual way they want.

To add to this, the WPF and Silverlight framework code has been heavily tested by Microsoft. Therefore, there is no need for us to write unit tests that confirm the binding system's behavior. It is sufficient to test our view models to verify that the view logic and view state are correct and to leave the representation of that state in the hands of the designers and analysts.

The end result of all of this is that we will be able to achieve the same confidence and stability in our code with our unit tests under MVVM that we could under passive view, with the added benefit of less coupling and a lower maintenance design.

Issues and pain points of MVVM

There are some issues and pain points to implementing MVVM which include the following:

- **Lack of direction from Microsoft**: Microsoft hasn't given clear directions on this pattern yet, and the various non-Microsoft resources available on the topic can send mixed messages, leaving developers and architects confused.
- **Need for boilerplate code, complicated techniques and/or frameworks**: There are many areas in WPF and Silverlight where MVVM support can be improved. Things like property changed notifications and commands require lots of boilerplate code and potentially brittle designs that require using "magic strings". There are many frameworks and techniques out there that help address these issues. However, you may not want to or may not be allowed to use open source frameworks. Also, implementing the techniques that allow you to avoid using the frameworks can be complicated and require a good bit of boilerplate code to implement, as you will see later in this book.
- **Paradigm shift requiring retraining**: MVVM requires a new way of thinking about UI programming and a new approach to design that will likely be unfamiliar to developers coming from a WinForms or ASP.NET background that are used to the code-behind style of programming. This can impose training and enforcement burdens when moving to MVVM.

- **Only supported in WPF and Silverlight**: This pattern doesn't transfer well to technologies such as ASP.NET or WinForms easily, which makes it a very specialized skill.
- **Long learning curve**: To learn everything you will need to be able to effectively implement the pattern in a real-world enterprise application, takes a good bit of ramp-up time.

This book will give you the tools you need to overcome a lot of these issues and pain points, but it is worth noting that there can be some bumps in the road. Hopefully the situation will improve in the future as Microsoft embraces the pattern and introduces more support. I was told by Sam Bent from Microsoft that they are considering adding support for things like linking events directly to actions, eliminating the need for commands and the techniques and tools that allow for linking commands to events. I'd expect that with future releases we will see more and more tools coming with WPF and Silverlight that help alleviate the issues and pain points that exist at the time of writing this book.

MVVM Light

There are many great MVVM frameworks out there, and we review many of them in *Appendix A*, but throughout this book we will be using the MVVM Light toolkit by Laurent Bugnion and GalaSoft. The toolkit is available for free on Code Plex (`http://mvvmlight.codeplex.com/`) and offers many features, including:

- A lean framework that offers only what is needed for MVVM
- Project templates for both WPF and Silverlight, in both Visual Studio and Blend
- Blendability support is written into the templates
- Service locator pattern is written into the templates
- Item templates for Visual Studio and Blend
    - Create a new view model
    - Create a new view
    - Create a new view model locator, a class that holds and manages references to view models
- Code snippets to help increase productivity when implementing MVVM
    - `mvvminpc` adds a new bindable property to a view model
    - `mvvmlocatorproperty` adds a new view model to a view mode locator

  - `mvvmpropa` adds a new attached property to a dependency object (WPF only)
  - `mvvmpropdp` adds a new dependency property to a dependency object (WPF only)
  - `mvvmslpropa` adds a new attached property to a dependency object (Silverlight only)
  - `mvvmslpropdp` adds a new dependency property to a dependency object (Silverlight only)

- `EventToCommand`: The `EventTrigger` property allows for connecting events to commands, purely in XAML
- `DipatcherHelper`: A lightweight class that helps you to create multithreaded applications

You can find a getting started guide on MVVM Light's Code Plex page (`http://www.galasoft.ch/mvvm/getstarted/`). You are not required to use this framework, and we will cover options that don't require frameworks for each topic covered in this book. But if you are interested in using MVVM Light, please take the time to visit the **Get Started** page on Code Plex and to set up MVVM Light in your environment.

Summary

In this chapter, we got our feet wet with MVVM. We started things off with a quick review of the history of the pattern and its basic structure. We then covered the technologies in WPF and Silverlight that enable MVVM. Next, we built a version of the Project Billing sample application using MVVM and followed this by looking at the benefits of the pattern. We talked briefly about some of the issues and pain points with implementing MVVM and then finished off the chapter by looking at the MVVM Light toolkit that we will use later in this book.

3

Northwind – Foundations

By Ryan Vice

Now that we've laid a solid foundation by covering the history of presentation patterns and by building the Project Billing sample in MVVM, we are ready for a deeper dive that will take us beyond "Hello World" applications and into the real world of enterprise MVVM development. One of the key goals of this book is to provide comprehensive coverage of MVVM that will guide you through the many architectural decisions that need to be made when designing and building MVVM applications. If you are a one-man team building an internal intranet application that serves a small number of users, then you should have a much simpler design than if you were building the next `http://www.amazon.com/`.

Our goal is to educate you on not just the "hows" but also the "whys" of each technique that we introduce. This will allow you to find the right balance in your design, and help you to avoid over-engineering or under-engineering your solution. To help us accomplish this goal, we are going to build an N-Tier, LOB enterprise application on top of the Northwind sample database over the course of the next four chapters. These chapters will show a natural architectural progression, and as the application gets more complex, the need for techniques to manage that complexity will become apparent. In the agile parlance, this is known as evolutionary design.

In this chapter we will:

- Review Northwind's requirements
- Use Entity Framework to interact with Northwind's database
- Add our first unit tests
- Use MVVM style design to easily create a tabbed interface
- Explore Entity Framework's built-in change notifications

Northwind requirements

Northwind is a sample database released by Microsoft that contains the sales data for a fictitious company called **Northwind Traders**, which imports and exports specialty foods from around the world. We will be building an application based on the Northwind database that will support:

- Selecting a customer from a list of current customers, and viewing the selected customer's details and order history with support for editing the customer's details
- Selecting an order by ID and viewing the order details including the company's information, sales contact and an invoice summary (products purchased, quantities, prices, and so on)
- Ability to create a new order

This is far from a complete application, but is complex enough to allow us to demonstrate all the tools and techniques that would be needed to create a full LOB application using MVVM.

The UI of this application is shown in the following screenshot:

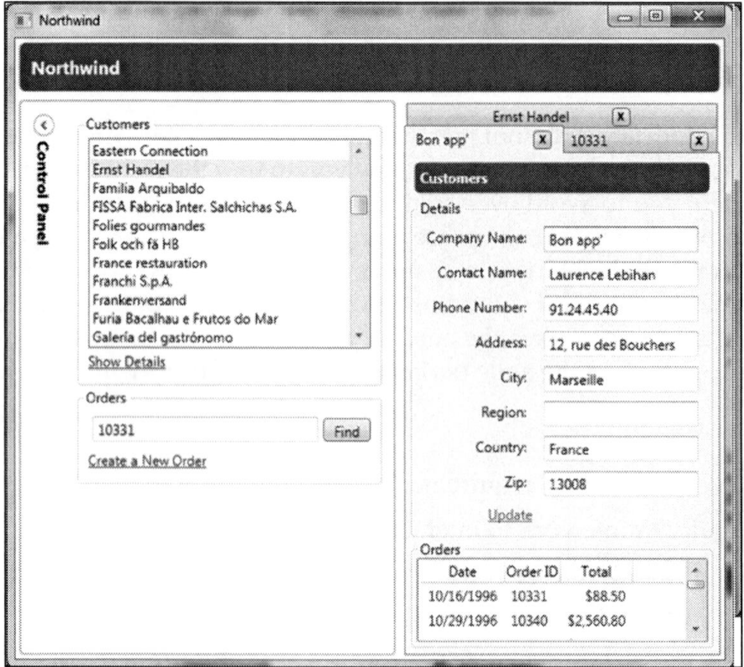

Presentation tier foundation

Let's start things off by creating the visual layout of our application by following these steps:

1. Start a new Visual Studio instance.
2. Create a new WPF application project called `Northwind.UI.WPF`, and name the solution `Northwind`.
3. Add a folder to `Northwind.UI.WPF` called `Skins`, and add a new `Resource Dictionary (WPF)` file to that folder called `MainSkin.xaml`.
4. Open `MainWindow.xaml` for editing and update it as follows:

```
<Window x:Class="Northwind.UI.WPF.MainWindow"
        xmlns="http://schemas.microsoft.com/winfx/
        2006/xaml/presentation"
        xmlns:x="http://schemas.microsoft.com/winfx/2006/xaml"
        Title="MainWindow"
        MinHeight="350"
        MinWidth="525"
        xmlns:ViewModel="clr-namespace:Northwind.ViewModel;
        assembly=Northwind.ViewModel"
        DataContext="{Binding
            Source={x:Static
            ViewModel:ViewModelLocator
                .MainWindowViewModelStatic}}">
    <Window.Resources>
        <ResourceDictionary>
            <ResourceDictionary.MergedDictionaries>
                <ResourceDictionary
                    Source="Skins/MainSkin.xaml" />
            </ResourceDictionary.MergedDictionaries>
        </ResourceDictionary>
    </Window.Resources>
    <DockPanel>
        <Border DockPanel.Dock="Top"
                Padding="10"
                Margin="4"
                CornerRadius="5"
                Background="{StaticResource mainBlueBrush}">
            <TextBlock Text="Northwind"
                       Foreground="White"
                       FontWeight="Bold"
                       FontSize="16" />
        </Border>
```

```
        <Grid>
            <Grid.ColumnDefinitions>
                <ColumnDefinition Width="auto" />
                <ColumnDefinition Width="*" />
            </Grid.ColumnDefinitions>
            <Grid.RowDefinitions>
                <RowDefinition Height="*" />
            </Grid.RowDefinitions>
            <Expander Padding="10"
                      Margin="4"
                      BorderBrush="DarkGray"
                      ExpandDirection="Right"
                      Grid.Row="0"
                      Grid.Column="0"
                      IsExpanded="True">
                <Expander.Header>
                    <TextBlock Text="Control Panel"
                               FontSize="14"
                               FontWeight="Bold">
                    <TextBlock.LayoutTransform>
                        <RotateTransform Angle="90" />
                    </TextBlock.LayoutTransform>
                    </TextBlock>
                </Expander.Header>

            </Expander>
            <TabControl Margin="4"
                        Grid.Row="0"
                        Grid.Column="1"
                        IsSynchronizedWithCurrentItem="True">
            </TabControl>
        </Grid>
    </DockPanel>
</Window>
```

5. Open `MainSkin.xaml` for editing and update it as follows:

```
<ResourceDictionary xmlns="http://schemas.microsoft.com/winfx/
                    2006/xaml/presentation"
                    xmlns:x="http://schemas.microsoft.com/
                    winfx/2006/xaml">
    <Color x:Key="mainBlue">#FF145E9D</Color>
    <SolidColorBrush x:Key="mainBlueBrush"
                     Color="{StaticResource mainBlue}" />
</ResourceDictionary>
```

6. Add a new class library project called `Northwind.ViewModel`, and rename the file `Class1.cs` to `MainWindowViewModel.cs`.
7. Add a new class called `ViewModelLocator.cs`.
8. Open `MainWindowViewModel.cs` for editing and update it as follows:

```
namespace Northwind.ViewModel
{
    public class MainWindowViewModel
    {
    }
}
```

9. Open `ViewModelLocator.cs` for editing and update it as follows:

```
namespace Northwind.ViewModel
{
    public class ViewModelLocator
    {
        private static MainWindowViewModel
            _mainWindowViewModel;
        public static MainWindowViewModel
            MainWindowViewModelStatic
        {
            get
            {
                if (_mainWindowViewModel == null)
                {
                    _mainWindowViewModel
                        = new MainWindowViewModel();
                }

                return _mainWindowViewModel;
            }
        }
    }
}
```

10. Add a project reference from `Northwind.UI.WPF` to `Northwind.ViewModel`.

11. Build and run the application, and you should see an application similar to the following:

What we've done here is create a main window that uses:

- `MainWindowViewModel` as its view model, which currently doesn't do anything.
- `MainSkin.xaml` as its resource dictionary, which is currently providing the dark blue color, but will be expanded to provide a lot more as we progress. For more details on creating this kind of application layout see Sams Teach Yourself WPF in 24 Hours by Rob Eisenberg.
- `ViewModelLocator` to resolve its view model, which exposes the static `MainWindowViewModelStatic` property that is then bound to `MainWindow.DataContext` using the following code:

```
DataContext="{Binding
            Source={x:Static
            ViewModel:ViewModelLocator
            .MainWindowViewModelStatic}}">
```

Locator pattern

`ViewModelLocator` is a specialization of the **Service Locator pattern** (Martin), which has been adopted by the MVVM community, and is commonly called the **View Model Locator** or simply **Locator**. This pattern consists of a class that exposes properties for accessing your view models, and is responsible for abstracting away the logic for instantiating the view models. `ViewModelLocator` can be used to perform clean up as well. Later in this book, we will see that this pattern also allows us to easily integrate an IoC framework.

MVVM Light framework will create a view model locator as part of its project templates for you.

Data access tier

Now we need to get our data access sorted out. We will show a few different options for data access throughout this book. For our first pass, we will keep things simple and use the entity framework to get up and running quickly. Let's start by following these steps:

If you are not running Visual Studio as an administrator, then you need to close it and restart it as the administrator. On Windows 7, this is done by right-clicking on the program icon in the **Start** menu, and then selecting **Run as administrator**.

1. Download Northwind database.

At the time of writing this book, the database could be downloaded from `http://archive.msdn.microsoft.com/northwind/Release/ProjectReleases.aspx?ReleaseId=1401`. If that URL is no longer working, then use your favorite search engine to find the Northwind sample database and download it.

2. Unzip the downloaded file and take note of the location of the `Northwind.mdf` file that was a part of the download.

If you are not running Visual Studio as an administrator, then close Visual Studio, reopen Visual Studio as an administrator, then reopen the solution.

3. Add a new Class Library project called `Northwind.Data`.
4. Delete the `Class1.cs` file that was created by the Project template.
5. Use the context menu to add an existing item to the `Northwind.Data` project, and browse to the `Northwind.MDF` file that you located in *step* 2. If you can't see the file in the location from *step* 2, then make sure that the file filter is set to **All Files (*)** in the visual studio **Add Existing Item** dialog box.

6. You will then be shown the following dialog box. Select **Entity Data Model** and click on **Next**.

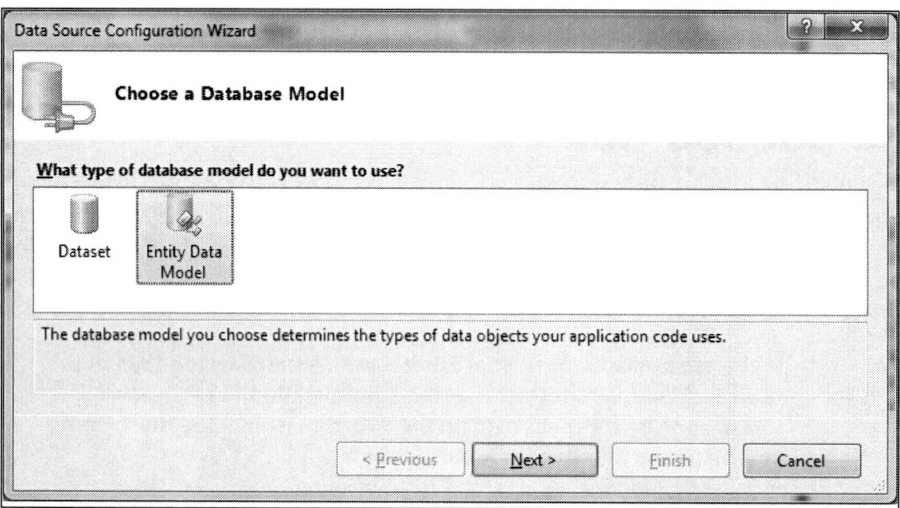

7. Select **Generate from database** and click on **Next**.

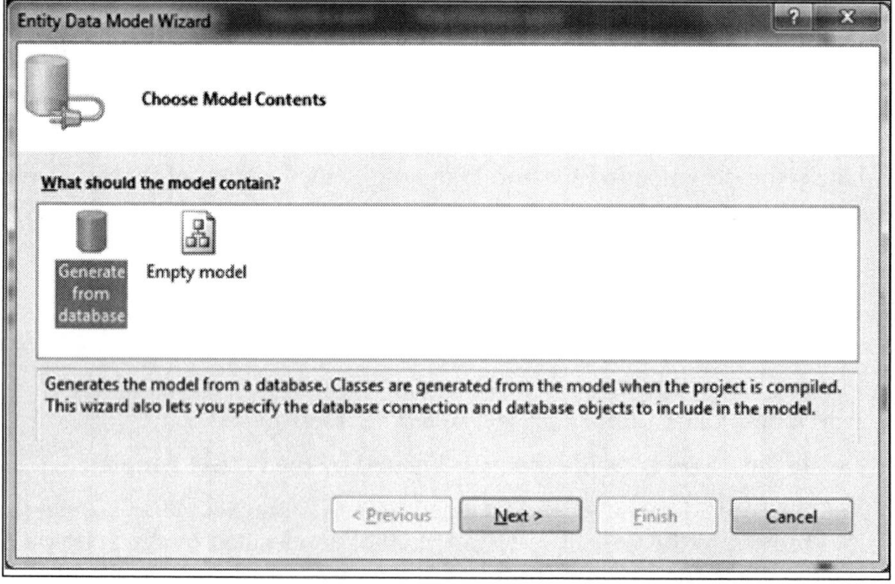

8. Configure the **Choose Your Data Connection** dialog box as shown in the following screenshot:

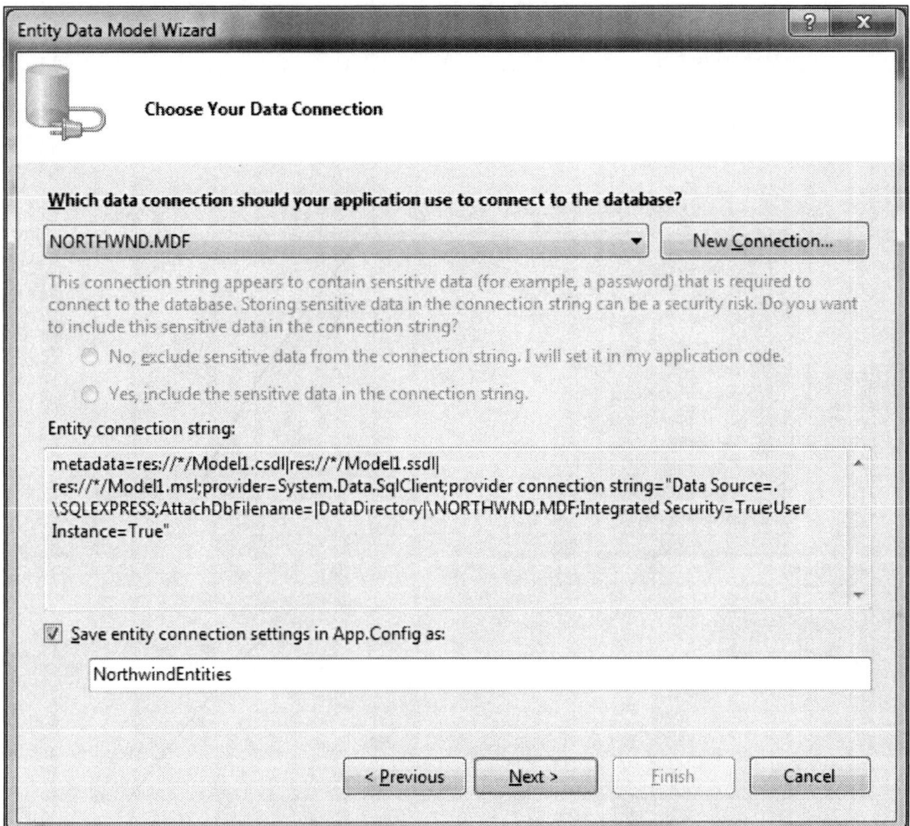

By default, this dialog box should work. I changed the name of the connection string, but other than that I just accepted the defaults. However, if you've added Northwind to SQL Express before, then you may have more than one `NORTHWND.MDF` connection listed in the drop-down list. If that is the case, then you will have to make sure that there is a connection in the list that has the correct connection string, and if not, then you will need to create a new one by clicking on the **New Connection...** button. Another, possibly easier way, is to cancel the wizard, delete the `.mdf` file from the project, open **Server Explorer**, delete all the `NORTHWND*.MDF` type connections, and then repeat all of the steps listed here starting from *step 5*.

9. In the **Choose Your Database Objects** dialog box,select the `Customers`, `Employees`, `Order Details`, `Orders`, and `Products` tables as shown in the following screenshot:

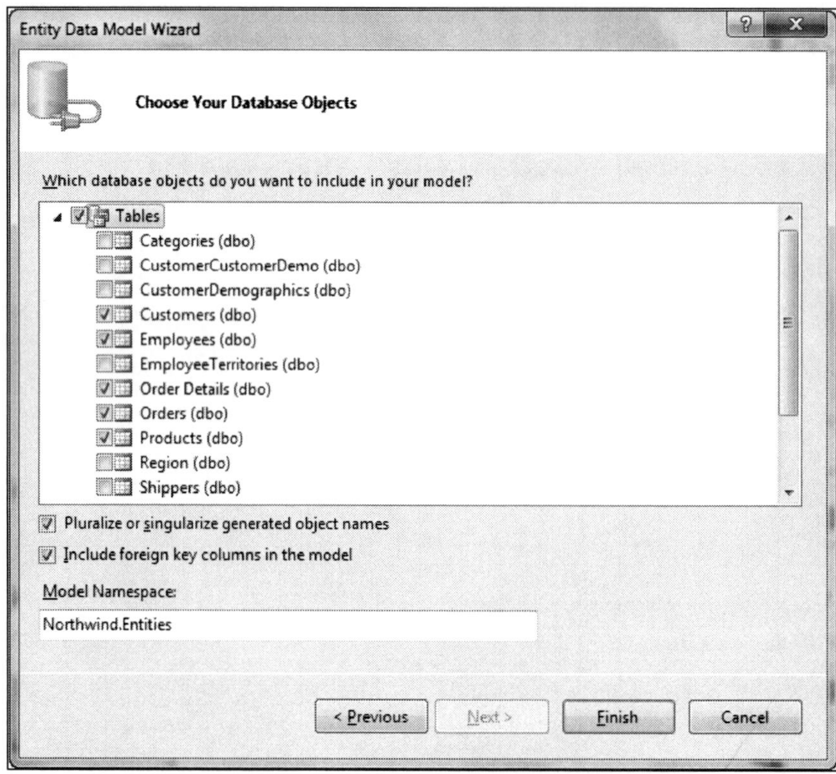

You should now see a data model similar to the following:

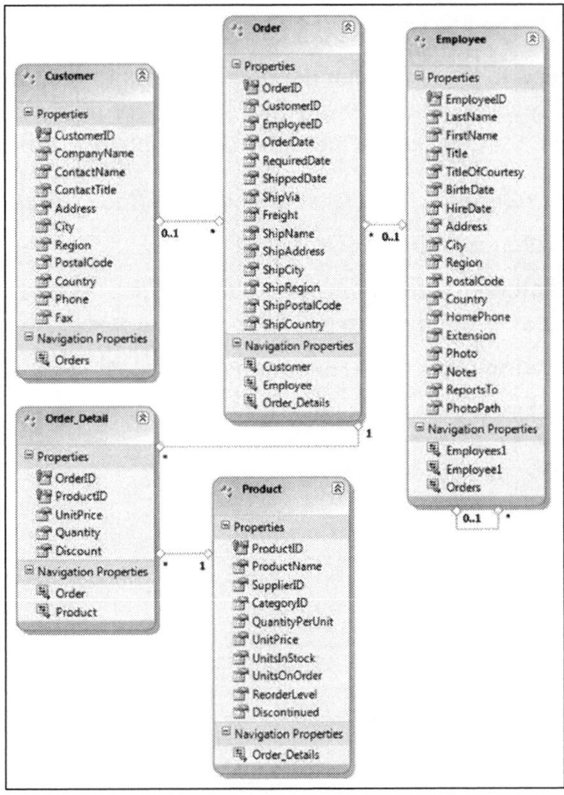

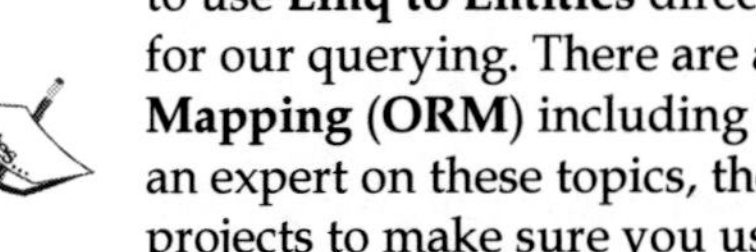
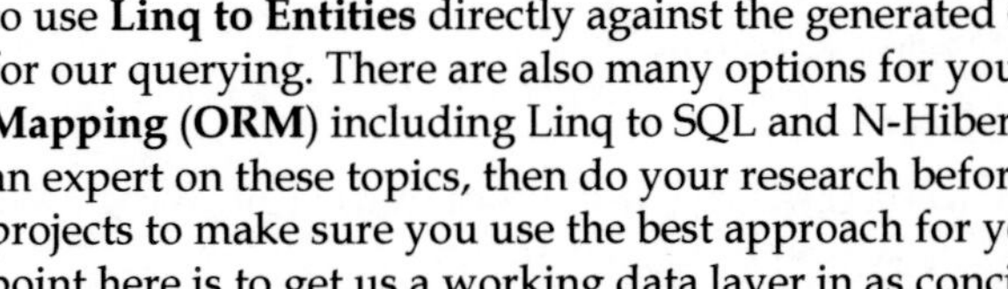

There are a lot of options and details surrounding both entity framework and design choices for creating a data access tier. For example, the `Northwind` database ships with many built-in stored procedures and views that we could take advantage of, but for simplicity, we are going to use **Linq to Entities** directly against the generated `ObjectContext` for our querying. There are also many options for your **Object Relational Mapping (ORM)** including Linq to SQL and N-Hibernate. If you are not an expert on these topics, then do your research before you start your projects to make sure you use the best approach for your situation. The point here is to get us a working data layer in as concise a way as possible. MVVM is a presentation architecture and isn't concerned with where the data comes from or what technologies are used to fetch the data. You could be working on top of an SOA architecture and not even be concerned with database access (which we will cover later in this book).

Listing the customers

The next thing we need to do is to get a list of customers to display in the UI. Our approach will be to create a data provider that will query the entity framework to get our entities, which we will use as our models. To accomplish this, follow these steps:

1. Add a project reference from `Northwind.ViewModel` to `Northwind.Data`.
2. Add a .NET reference to `System.Data.Entity`.
3. Add `using` statements for `System.Collections.Generic`, `Northwind.Data`, and `System.Data.Objects` to `MainWindowViewModel`.
4. Add the following code to `MainWindowViewModel`:

```
private IList<Customer> _customers;

public IList<Customer> Customers
{
    get
    {
        if (_customers == null)
        {
            GetCustomers();
        }
        return _customers;
    }
}

private void GetCustomers()
{
    _customers
        = new NorthwindEntities()
            .Customers.ToList();
}
```

5. Update `Expander` in `MainWindow` as shown in the following code:

```
<Expander Padding="10"
          Margin="4"
          BorderBrush="DarkGray"
          ExpandDirection="Right"
          Grid.Row="0"
          Grid.Column="0"
          IsExpanded="True">
    <Expander.Header>
        <!-- Omitted Code -->
    </Expander.Header>
```

```
    <ListBox ItemsSource="{Binding Customers}"
             DisplayMemberPath="CompanyName"
             VerticalAlignment="Top"
             Height="180"
             Width="250" />
</Expander>
```

6. Add an `App.Config` file to `Northwind.UI.WPF`.
7. Find the connection string that was created in *step 7* in the *Data Access Tier* section. It will be in the `App.Config` config file of `Northwind.Data`, and should be called `NorthwindEntities`. Copy it to `App.Config` of `Northwind.UI.WPF`, which was created in *step 2*. You will need to modify the `AttachDBFilename` property of the connection string to replace the `|DataDirectory|` token with an absolute path to your `Northwnd.MDF` file, which was copied to your `Northwind.Data` project's directory. On my machine, that meant changing `|DataDirectory|` to `C:\Code\Northwind\Northwind.Data\`.

You could also leave the connection string as it is in *step 3* after copying it over to `App.Config` of `Northwind.UI.WPF`, and updating the `DataDirectory` value in the code instead. To do this, you could add the following code to `App.xaml.cs`:

```
public partial class App : Application
{
    // Code to update DataDirectory
    protected override void OnStartup(StartupEventArgs
e)
    {
        string dataDirectory
            = @"C:\Code\Northwind\Northwind.Data";
        AppDomain.CurrentDomain.
SetData("DataDirectory",
            dataDirectory);
        base.OnStartup(e);
    }
}
```

8. Build and run the application, and verify that you see a list of customers as shown in the following screenshot:

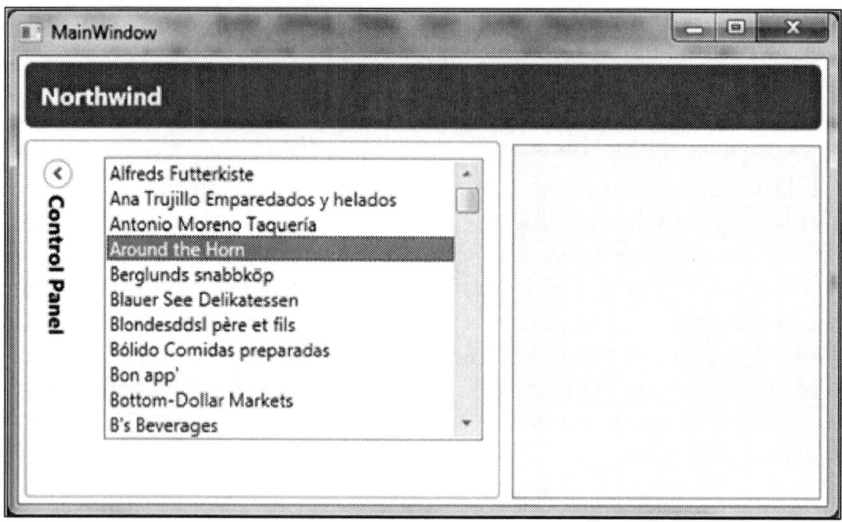

Your solution should look similar to the following screenshot:

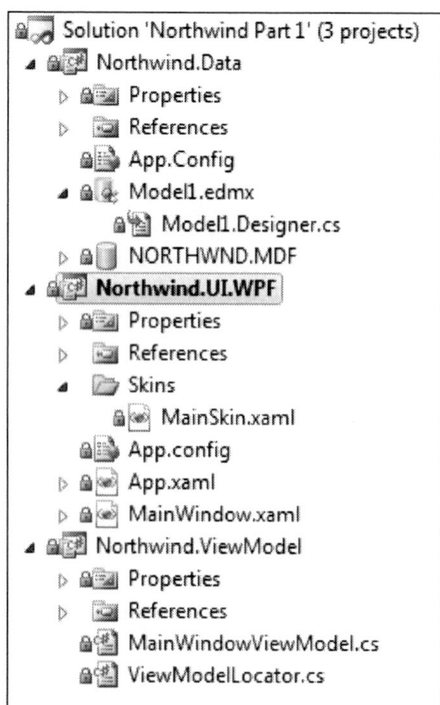

What we've done here is:

- Added a **Data Access Layer (DAL)** using Visual Studio's built-in support
- Updated `MainWindowViewModel` to use the `NorthwindEntities` object context to retrieve a list of all customers and expose them to `MainWindow` as the `Customers` collection

In a real application, you wouldn't want to pull back the entire `Customer` object just to get a list of `Customer.CompanyName` to display in the UI, and would instead want to return an object that only has the `CompanyName` and `CustomerID` properties. There are numerous ways of doing this (using Service Packs, anonymous types with Linq, and so on), Later, when we look at the idea of persistence ignorance, we will take a closer look at some approaches.

- Added a list box to `MainWindow` and bound it to the `Customers` collection, setting `DisplayMemberPath` to `CompanyName`, and enabling the customers to be displayed as a list of company names.

Unit testing getting customers

Our code works fine as is, but let's go ahead and get some unit tests in place for what we have so far, and see how adding unit tests as a client will require us to refactor our design.

Feel free to test first in your own applications or use whatever style that is appropriate for your projects. In this book, we will talk about unit tests after the code is written, to allow us to point out architectural concerns with MVVM and unit testing.

Looking at our `MainWindowViewModel`, the only scenario to test is verifying the `Customers` population logic.

We will assume that you are familiar with the basics of using MSTest and with unit testing principles. If you want or need to learn more, see *The Art of Unit Testing* by *Roy Osherove* (*Osherove*).We will be following *The Art of Unit Testing* approach, including the naming convention for tests that are used. Our tests will be named in this style:

```
<Method>_<Scenario>_<ExpectedResult>
```

To create the first two tests, follow these steps:

We don't want to test the database, because we want our test to be easily repeatable from any computer and isolated from dependencies. We will need to rethink our code to be able to accomplish this. What we are going to do is add a layer of abstraction between our data source and our view model, which will allow us to use various techniques to fake out the fetching of customers. We will call this new class `UIDataProvider`, and it will also be responsible for defining the interface needed by the UI to get its data. This will allow us to:

1. Test our view model in isolation without testing the dependencies. We will be able to use a variety of techniques and tools to inject fake objects (stubs and mocks), allowing for isolated testing.
2. More easily change our data source. If we wanted to scale, it would now be easier to add a WCF service layer by updating UIDataProvider to use the new service layer instead of Entity Framework. To really maximize this benefit we would need to make our design **persistence ignorant** which we will look at in *Chapter 6, Northwind – Services and Persistence Ignorance*.
3. Aggregate multiple sources of data if needed. For example, if we later need to integrate with an external product catalog service to retrieve additional product details, we could consume this catalog service under `UIDataProvider`, and easily hide those details from the rest of the presentation layer. Additionally, if we assume that this catalog service is still under development, we can use a stub in `UIDataProvider` and allow presentation development to continue while the dependent catalog service is being built. I find this technique invaluable on large SOA projects were different teams are responsible for different services.

We will explore these many benefits as we progress, but for now follow these steps to get started:

1. Add a new class library project to your solution called `Northwind.Application`.
2. Add a project reference from `Northwind.Application` to `Northwind.Data` and a .Net reference to `System.Data.Entity`.
3. Rename the file `Class1.cs` in `Northwind.Application` to `IUIDataProvider.cs`, allow Visual Studio to update references, and update the `IUIDataProvider.cs` file as follows:

```
using System.Collections.Generic;
using Northwind.Data;

namespace Northwind.Application
```

```
{
    public interface IUIDataProvider
    {
        IList<Customer> GetCustomers();
    }
}
```

4. Add a new class to `Northwind.Application` called `UIDataProvider.cs`, and update the code in that file as follows:

```
using System.Collections.Generic;
using System.Linq;
using Northwind.Data;

namespace Northwind.Application
{
    public class UIDataProvider : IUIDataProvider
    {
        public IList<Customer> GetCustomers()
        {
            return new NorthwindEntities()
                    .Customers.ToList();
        }
    }
}
```

5. Add a reference from `Northwind.ViewModel` to `Northwind.Application`.
6. Update `MainWindowViewModel.cs` as follows:

```
using System.Collections.Generic;
using Northwind.Data;
using Northwind.Application;

namespace Northwind.ViewModel
{
    public class MainWindowViewModel
    {
        private readonly IUIDataProvider _dataProvider;

        public string Name
            { get { return "Northwind"; } }
        public string ControlPanelName
            { get { return "Control Panel"; } }

        private IList<Customer> _customers;
```

```
            public IList<Customer> Customers
            {
                get
                {
                    if (_customers == null)
                    {
                        GetCustomers();
                    }
                    return _customers;
                }
            }

            public MainWindowViewModel(
                IUIDataProvider dataProvider)
            {
                _dataProvider = dataProvider;
            }


            private void GetCustomers()

            {

                _customers = _dataProvider.GetCustomers();
            }
        }
    }
```

7. Open `ViewModelLocator.cs`, add a `using` statement for `Northwind.Application`, and update the code that instantiates the `MainWindoViewModel` as follows:

```
_mainWindowViewModel
    = new MainWindowViewModel(new UIDataProvider());
```

8. Add a new test project to the solution called `Northwind.ViewModel.Tests`.
9. Add a project reference from `Northwind.ViewModel.Tests` to `Northwind.ViewModel`, `Northwind.Data`, and `Northwind.Application`.
10. Add a .Net reference from `Northwind.ViewModel.Tests` to `System.Data.Entity`.
11. Rename the file `UnitTest1.cs` to `MainWindowViewModelTests.cs`, allow Visual Studio to rename all references in the code, and update the file as follows:

```
using System.Collections.Generic;
using Microsoft.VisualStudio.TestTools.UnitTesting;
```

```
using Northwind.Data;
using Northwind.Application;

namespace Northwind.ViewModel.Tests
{
    [TestClass]
    public class MainWindowViewModelTests
    {

        [TestMethod]
        public void Customers_Always_CallsGetCustomers()
        {
            // Create stub
            IList<Customer> expected = GetCustomers();
            UIDataProviderStub uiDataProviderStub
                = new UIDataProviderStub
                {
                    Customers = expected
                };

            // Inject stub
            MainWindowViewModel target
                = new MainWindowViewModel(uiDataProviderStub);

            CollectionAssert.AreEquivalent(
                (List<Customer>)expected,
                (List<Customer>)target.Customers);
        }

        private IList<Customer> GetCustomers()
        {
            const int numberOfCustomers = 10;
            IList<Customer> customers
                = new List<Customer>();
            for (int i = 0; i < numberOfCustomers; i++)
            {
                customers.Add(new Customer
                    {
                        CustomerID = "CustomerID " + i,
                        CompanyName = "CompanyName " + i
                    });
            }

            return customers;
```

```
            }

            private class UIDataProviderStub : IUIDataProvider
            {
                public IList<Customer> Customers
                { private get; set; }

                public IList<Customer> GetCustomers()
                {
                    return Customers;
                }
            }
        }
    }
```

12. Run the test and verify that it passes.

To run all the tests, put your cursor on the `TestClass` attribute, and do one of the following:

1. Right-click on the `TestClass` attribute and select **Run Tests**.
2. Use *Ctrl+R, T*.
3. Use the **Test** menu or toolbar.

To avoid false positives, you should always run a negative test that fails. It's best if you do this before putting the correct expected data in your unit test and passing it.

Now, we are confirming that `MainWindowViewModel.Customers` is populated by calling `IUIDataProvider.GetCustomers()` while not coupling `MainWindowViewModel` to any concrete implementation of IUIDataProvider. Using this approach we are able to verify that our MainWindowViewModel gets it's data in the expected way. However, we are not testing the actual fetching of the data in the way you would in an integration test. We are instead injecting a fake object into our MainWindowViewModel instance using constructor injection allowing us to test this behavior in isolation. This design allows us to support both the WPF UI client and the MSTest client code, and was accomplished using the following techniques:

- Adding a layer of abstraction to our data access (`UIDataProvider`).
- Implementing that abstraction on an interface (`IUIDataProvider`).
- Adding a stubbed implementation of `IUIDataProvider` for testing, which was added as a private nested class to `MainWindowViewModelTests`.

- Updating `MainWindowViewModel` to use dependency injection, allowing us to inject `UIDataProvider` from the `ViewModelLocator`, and to inject `UIDataProviderStub` from our unit tests. We did this by adding a constructor that takes a `IUIDataProvider` as an argument, which is called **Constructor Dependency Injection**.

The image that follows shows the relationship between `UIDataProvider` and `MainWindowViewModel`:

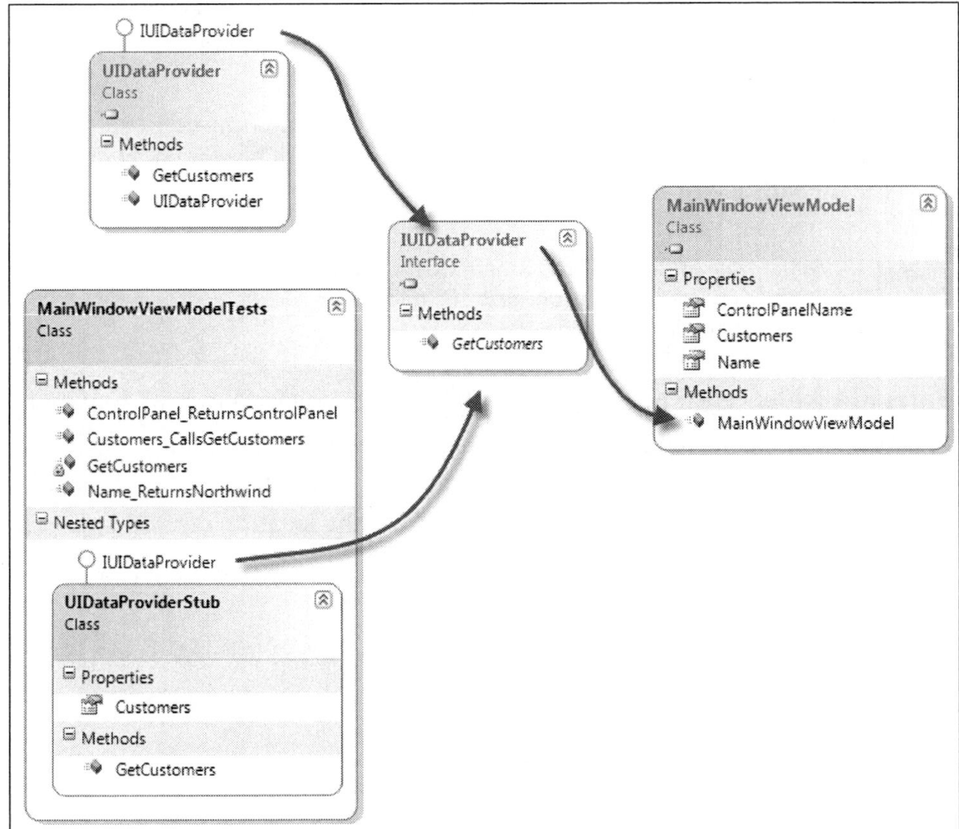

As you can see, `MainWindowViewModel` can now take any implementation of `IUIDataProvider`.

Using an isolation framework

Currently we are using a manual stub, `UIDataProviderStub`, which gets the job done, but we can save ourselves some code by using an isolation framework.

Isolation frameworks allow for creating fake objects (stubs and mocks) for use in testing, and there are many out there to choose from. See *The Art of Unit Testing* by *Roy Osherove* for complete details.

We are going to update our implementation to use Rhino Mocks to dynamically create an `IUIDataProvider` stub in our tests by following these steps:

1. Remove the code for `UIDataProviderStub` class and for the `MainWindowViewModelTests.GetCustomer` method as we will no longer be needing it.
2. Download the latest version of Rhino Mocks to your computer or if you prefer using Nuget then install the Rhino Mocks Nuget package in Northwind.ViewModel.Tests and skip to step 7..

At the time of this writing, Rhino Mocks could be downloaded from `http://hibernatingrhinos.com/open-source/rhino-mocks`. We are using Version 3.5.

3. Add a folder called `Lib` to your solution's directory in Windows Explorer.
4. Add `RhinoMocks.dll` and `RhinoMocks.xml` to the `Lib` folder.
5. Add a solution folder to Northwind called `Lib`, and then add `RhinoMocks.dll` and `RhinoMocks.xml` to that folder from the location created in *step 3*.
6. Add a browse reference from `RhinoMocks.dll` to `Northwind.ViewModel.Tests`.
7. Add `using Rhino.Mocks` to the top of `MainWindowViewModelTests.cs`.
8. Update `MainWindowViewModel` as follows:

```
[TestClass]
public class MainWindowViewModelTests
{
    [TestMethod]
    public void Customers_Always_CallsGetCustomers()
    {
        IUIDataProvider uiDataProviderMock
            = MockRepository
                .GenerateMock<IUIDataProvider>();
        uiDataProviderMock.Expect(c => c.GetCustomers());

        // Inject stub
        MainWindowViewModel target
```

```
                = new MainWindowViewModel(uiDataProviderMock);
            IList<Customer> customers = target.Customers;

            uiDataProviderMock.VerifyAllExpectations();
        }
    }
```

9. Run all the tests and verify that they pass.

As you can see, we were able to reduce the amount of code needed by quite a bit here. In all fairness, we are performing a behavior verification test now, whereas before, we were performing a state verification test. However, the point being that it doesn't take long to learn to appreciate the benefits of an isolation frameworks when writing unit tests. Note that:

- **State verification** is a style of unit testing where you perform some action on the component under test, and then verify that the state of the application is as expected. In our first attempt we were verifying the state of our MainWindowViewModel.Customers property.
- **Behavior verification** is a style of unit testing where you perform some action on the component under test, and use a mock object to verify that the component under test behaved as expected. In our example, we verified that `MainWindowViewModel` called `IUIDataProvider.GetCustomers`. There is a canonical example given as to why you would test in this way. Imagine that you were tasked with creating tests for a software that controls a sprinkler system. Each time you ran a test, you wouldn't want to have to run the sprinkler system, then try and collect all the water that was dispersed and verify that the correct amount of water was dispersed for the correct amount of time [Osherove]. Instead, you would want to create tests that verify that the sprinkler controller called into the hardware with the correct values (or its behavior), and would leave it to the hardware manufacture to test the hardware.

Interaction verification is what we did in our second attempt at testing MainWindowViewModel using Rhino Mocks to create our mock object.
The line

```
uiDataProviderMock.Expect(c =>
c.GetCustomers());
```

sets an expectation that GetCustomers will be called on our mocked IUiDataProvider instance that was then injected into our MainWindowViewModel instance's constructor. When we call

```
uiDataProviderMock.VerifyAllExpectations()
```

on our mock object at the end of our test, Rhino Mocks then will verify that the uiDataProviderMock.GetCustomers method was called during the test run. However, Rhino Mocks will throw an exception if the uiDataProviderMock. GetCustomers method was not called and this exception will cause our test to fail. And that is how we were able to use interaction verification to test our MainWindowViewModel.GetCustomers functionality.

Adding tabs

As shown in the requirements section earlier, in this chapter, our Northwind application needs to support a tabbed display. MVVM greatly simplifies the creating and managing of tabs as you can have the binding system map views to view models. This makes adding a tabbed interface to our UI a simple matter of using the **Hierarchical View Model** approach along with some basic OOD techniques.

Hierarchical View Model will be discussed in detail in *Chapter 6, Hierarchical View Model and IoC.*

To accomplish this, follow the steps listed here:

1. Add a new class called `ToolViewModel.cs` to the `Northwind.ViewModel` project, and update the code as follows:

```
namespace Northwind.ViewModel
{
    public class ToolViewModel
    {
        public string DisplayName { get; set; }
    }

    public class AToolViewModel  : ToolViewModel
    {
        public AToolViewModel()
        {
            DisplayName = "A";
        }
    }

    public class BToolViewModel  : ToolViewModel
    {
        public BToolViewModel()
        {
            DisplayName = "B";
```

```
            }
        }
    }
```

2. Open `MainWindowViewModel.cs`, add a using for `System.Collections.ObjectModel`, and update `MainWindowViewModel` as follows:

```
        public ObservableCollection<ToolViewModel>
            Tools { get; set; }

        public MainWindowViewModel(
            IUIDataProvider dataProvider)
        {
            _dataProvider = dataProvider;
            Tools = new ObservableCollection<ToolViewModel>();
            Tools.Add(new AToolViewModel());
            Tools.Add(new BToolViewModel());
        }
```

3. Update `TabControl` in `MainWindow.xaml` as follows:

```
<TabControl ItemsSource="{Binding Tools}"
            Margin="4"
            Grid.Row="0"
            Grid.Column="1">
    <TabControl.ItemTemplate>
        <DataTemplate>
            <ContentPresenter Content="{Binding DisplayName}" />
        </DataTemplate>
    </TabControl.ItemTemplate>
</TabControl>
```

4. Add a new `UserControl` to `Northwind.UI.WPF` called `ATool.xaml`, and add the following code to it:

```
<UserControl x:Class="Northwind.UI.WPF.ATool"
             xmlns="http://schemas.microsoft.com/winfx/2006/xaml/
presentation"
             xmlns:x="http://schemas.microsoft.com/winfx/2006/
xaml"
             xmlns:mc="http://schemas.openxmlformats.org/markup-
compatibility/2006"
             xmlns:d="http://schemas.microsoft.com/expression/
blend/2008"
             mc:Ignorable="d"
             d:DesignHeight="300" d:DesignWidth="300">
    <Grid>
```

```
        <TextBlock Text="{Binding DisplayName}" />
    </Grid>
</UserControl>
```

5. Add a new `UserControl` to `Northwind.UI.WPF` called `BTool.xaml`, and add the following code to it:

```
<UserControl x:Class="Northwind.UI.WPF.BTool"
             xmlns="http://schemas.microsoft.com/winfx/2006/xaml/
presentation"
             xmlns:x="http://schemas.microsoft.com/winfx/2006/
xaml"
             xmlns:mc="http://schemas.openxmlformats.org/markup-
compatibility/2006"
             xmlns:d="http://schemas.microsoft.com/expression/
blend/2008"
             mc:Ignorable="d"
             d:DesignHeight="300" d:DesignWidth="300">
    <StackPanel>
        <TextBox Text="{Binding DisplayName}" />
    </StackPanel>
</UserControl>
```

6. Add the following namespaces to `MainSkin.xaml`:

```
xmlns:ViewModel="clr-namespace:Northwind.
ViewModel;assembly=Northwind.ViewModel"
xmlns:WPF="clr-namespace:Northwind.UI.WPF"
```

7. Update `MainSkin.xaml` as follows:

```
<DataTemplate
    DataType="{x:Type ViewModel:AToolViewModel}">
    <WPF:ATool/>
</DataTemplate>
<DataTemplate
    DataType="{x:Type ViewModel:BToolViewModel}">
    <WPF:BTool />
</DataTemplate>
```

8. Update the included namespaces in `MainSkin.xaml` to include the following:

```
xmlns:WPF="clr-namespace:Northwind.UI.WPF"
xmlns:ViewModel="clr-namespace:Northwind.ViewModel;
assembly=Northwind.ViewModel"
```

9. Build and run the application.

   You should see an application similar to the following screenshot:

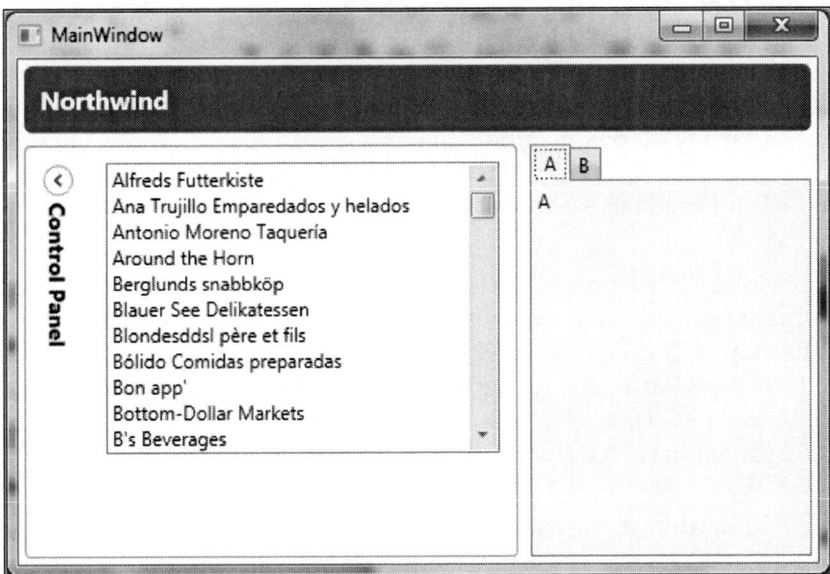

   Notice how changing the tabs presents a different view in the screenshot that follows:

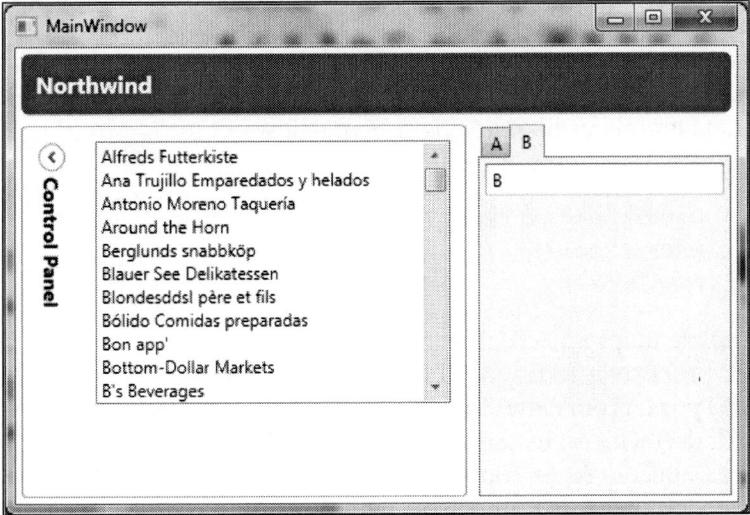

As you can see, we've now created a tabbed layout that supports showing different types of views in each tab. We accomplished this in the following manner:

1. In *step 1* and *step 2*, we created a common base view model type - `ToolViewModel`, and added an `ObservableCollection<ToolViewModel> Tools` to our `MainWindowViewModel`. We also created two derived types of ToolViewModel, `AToolViewModel` and `BToolViewModel`. We then added one of each type of view model to our `MainViewModel.Tools` collection in the constructor of `MainWindowViewModel` allowing us to provide the view models for each tab we want to display in an easily consumable format for our view.
2. Next, in *step 3*, we bound the `MainWindowViewModel.Tools` collection to `TabControl.ItemSource` of MainWindow. This will expose our collection of Tools to our view and allow each ToolViewModel instance to be mapped to a view using WPFs data template support. We also added a `TabControl.ItemTemplate`, which allowed us to format how `DisplayName` is displayed in each tab.

In a tab control, you control the look and layout of the tab by styling `TabItem`, and you control the look and layout of the tab content by styling `TabControl`. The `TabControl.ItemTemplate` property allows you to specify a control template for `TabItem`, which is what we did above. The same result could be accomplished by applying a style to `TabItem`.

3. In *step 4*, *step 5*, and *step 6* we created `ATool` and `BTool` views as WPF `UserControls`. Next we mapped the ATool view to the AToolViewModel and the BTool view to the BToolViewModel by updating MainSkin.xaml to add data templates like the one shown below.

```
<DataTemplate
        DataType="{x:Type ViewModel:AToolViewModel}">
        <WPF:ATool/>
</DataTemplate>
```

This data template maps an ATool instance view to an AToolViewModel instance. The DataType property is letting WPF know that if it finds an instance of the specified DataType (AToolViewModel), that it is to replace that DataType instance (AToolViewModel) with an instance of the DataTemplate.Content (ATool) and set that instance's DataContext (ATool.DataContext) to the instance of the DataType (AToolViewModel) that was found. This would result in code equivalent to the XAML shown below being generated for us.

```
<WPF:ATool DataContext={Binding aToolViewModelInstance} />
```

This is an extremely powerful technique as you can easily use it to create views that display collections of different views (tabs, MDIs, and so on) simply by:

1. Having all your view models derive from the same type.
2. Creating derived view model types for each type of view you want to support.
3. Creating a user control for each view type you are supporting.
4. Mapping the views to the view models using a data template.

Using data templates to instantiate views is a very powerful and useful technique. When you do this, the view is created for you by the binding system, and its data context is set to be the newly created instance of the datatype that it is mapped. See *Chapter 2, Introduction to MVVM* for more details.

We will now use this technique to display customer details. Before moving on, first perform the following actions:

1. Delete `ATool.xaml` and `BTool.xaml`.
2. Remove the data templates from `MainSkin.xaml` that were added in *step 6*.
3. Remove the classes `AToolViewModel` and `BToolViewModel` from `ToolViewModel.cs`.
4. Remove the following highlighted code from `MainWindowViewModel`:

```
public MainWindowViewModel(
    IUIDataProvider dataProvider)
{
    _dataProvider = dataProvider;
    Tools = new ObservableCollection<ToolViewModel>();
    Tools.Add(new AToolViewModel());
    Tools.Add(new BToolViewModel());
}
```

Viewing customer details

Next, we will be updating Northwind to allow us to view customer details.

Viewing details for one customer

We will view the details for one customer by opening a tab for each customer detail in the UI using the technique that we just covered. We will start things off by creating the `ToolViewModel` derived view model and its associated view (UserControl). We will then connect the pieces using a data template to map our view to our view model. To do this, perform the following steps:

1. Update the `IUIDataProvider` interface to add the following method:

   ```
   Customer GetCustomer(string customerID);
   ```

2. Update `UIDataProvider` as follows:

   ```
   public class UIDataProvider : IUIDataProvider
   {
       private NorthwindEntities _northwindEntities
           = new NorthwindEntities();

       public IList<Customer> GetCustomers()
       {
           return _northwindEntities.Customers.ToList();
       }

       public Customer GetCustomer(string customerID)
       {
           return
               _northwindEntities.Customers.Single(
                   c => c.CustomerID == customerID);
       }
   }
   ```

3. Add a new class called `CustomerDetailsViewModel` to `Northwind.ViewModel`, and update it as follows:

   ```
   using Northwind.Application;
   using Northwind.Data;

   namespace Northwind.ViewModel
   {
       public class CustomerDetailsViewModel : ToolViewModel
       {
           private readonly IUIDataProvider _dataProvider;
           public Customer Customer { get; set; }

           public CustomerDetailsViewModel(
               IUIDataProvider dataProvider,
   ```

```
                string customerID)
            {
                _dataProvider = dataProvider;
                Customer = _dataProvider.GetCustomer(customerID);
                DisplayName = Customer.CompanyName;
            }
        }
    }
```

4. Add a new `UserControl` to `Northwind.UI.WPF` called `CustomerDetails`, and update it as follows:

```
<UserControl x:Class="Northwind.UI.WPF.CustomerDetails"
             xmlns="http://schemas.microsoft.com/winfx/2006/xaml/
presentation"
             xmlns:x="http://schemas.microsoft.com/winfx/2006/
xaml"
             xmlns:mc="http://schemas.openxmlformats.org/markup-
compatibility/2006"
             xmlns:d="http://schemas.microsoft.com/expression/
blend/2008"
             mc:Ignorable="d"
             d:DesignHeight="300" d:DesignWidth="300">
    <UserControl.Resources>
        <ResourceDictionary>
            <ResourceDictionary.MergedDictionaries>
                <ResourceDictionary Source="Skins/MainSkin.xaml"
/>
            </ResourceDictionary.MergedDictionaries>
        </ResourceDictionary>
    </UserControl.Resources>
    <Grid>
        <Grid.RowDefinitions>
            <RowDefinition Height="Auto" />
            <RowDefinition Height="Auto" />
            <RowDefinition Height="*" />
        </Grid.RowDefinitions>
        <Border Padding="5"
                Margin="4"
                CornerRadius="5"
                Background="{StaticResource
                    mainBlueBrush}">
            <TextBlock Text="Customer Details"
                       Foreground="White"
                       FontWeight="Bold"
                       FontSize="12" />
```

```
</Border>
<GroupBox Header="Details"
          MinHeight="240"
          Grid.Row="1"
          DockPanel.Dock="Bottom">
    <Grid Margin="4">
        <Grid.ColumnDefinitions>
            <ColumnDefinition Width="Auto" />
            <ColumnDefinition Width="6" />
            <ColumnDefinition Width="*" />
        </Grid.ColumnDefinitions>

        <Grid.RowDefinitions>
            <RowDefinition Height="Auto" />
            <RowDefinition Height="30" />
            <RowDefinition Height="Auto" />
            <RowDefinition Height="30" />
            <RowDefinition Height="Auto" />
            <RowDefinition Height="30" />
            <RowDefinition Height="Auto" />
            <RowDefinition Height="30" />
        </Grid.RowDefinitions>
        <Label Content="Company Name:"
               HorizontalAlignment="Right" />
        <TextBox Text="{Binding Customer.CompanyName,
                 UpdateSourceTrigger=PropertyChanged}"
                 Grid.Column="2" />
        <Label Content="Contact Name:"
               Grid.Row="1"
               HorizontalAlignment="Right" />
        <TextBox Text="{Binding Customer.ContactName,
                 UpdateSourceTrigger=PropertyChanged}"
                 Grid.Row="1"
                 Grid.Column="2" />
        <Label Content="Phone Number:"
               Grid.Row="2"
               HorizontalAlignment="Right" />
        <TextBox Text="{Binding Customer.Phone,
                 UpdateSourceTrigger=PropertyChanged}"
                 Grid.Row="2"
                 Grid.Column="2" />
        <Label Content="Address:"
               Grid.Row="3"
               HorizontalAlignment="Right" />
```

```
                <TextBox Text="{Binding Customer.Address,
                         UpdateSourceTrigger=PropertyChanged}"
                         Grid.Row="3"
                         Grid.Column="2" />
                <Label Content="City:"
                       Grid.Row="4"
                       HorizontalAlignment="Right" />
                <TextBox Text="{Binding Customer.City,
                         UpdateSourceTrigger=PropertyChanged}"
                         Grid.Row="4"
                         Grid.Column="2" />
                <Label Content="Region:"
                       Grid.Row="5"
                       HorizontalAlignment="Right" />
                <TextBox Text="{Binding Customer.Region,
                         UpdateSourceTrigger=PropertyChanged}"
                         Grid.Row="5"
                         Grid.Column="2" />
                <Label Content="Country:"
                       Grid.Row="6"
                       HorizontalAlignment="Right" />
                <TextBox Text="{Binding Customer.Country,
                         UpdateSourceTrigger=PropertyChanged}"
                         Grid.Row="6"
                         Grid.Column="2" />
                <Label Content="Zip:"
                       Grid.Row="7"
                       HorizontalAlignment="Right" />
                <TextBox Text="{Binding Customer.PostalCode,
                         UpdateSourceTrigger=PropertyChanged}"
                         Grid.Row="7"
                         Grid.Column="2" />
            </Grid>
        </GroupBox>
    </Grid>
</UserControl>
```

5. Update `MainSkin.xaml` as follows:

```
<DataTemplate
    DataType="{x:Type
        ViewModel:CustomerDetailsViewModel}">
    <WPF:CustomerDetails/>
</DataTemplate>
```

6. Update `MainWindowViewModel` as follows:

```
public MainWindowViewModel(
    IUIDataProvider dataProvider)
{
    _dataProvider = dataProvider;
    Tools = new ObservableCollection<ToolViewModel>();
    Tools.Add(new CustomerDetailsViewModel(
                  _dataProvider, "ALFKI"));
}
```

7. Build and run the solution, and you should see something similar to the following screenshot:

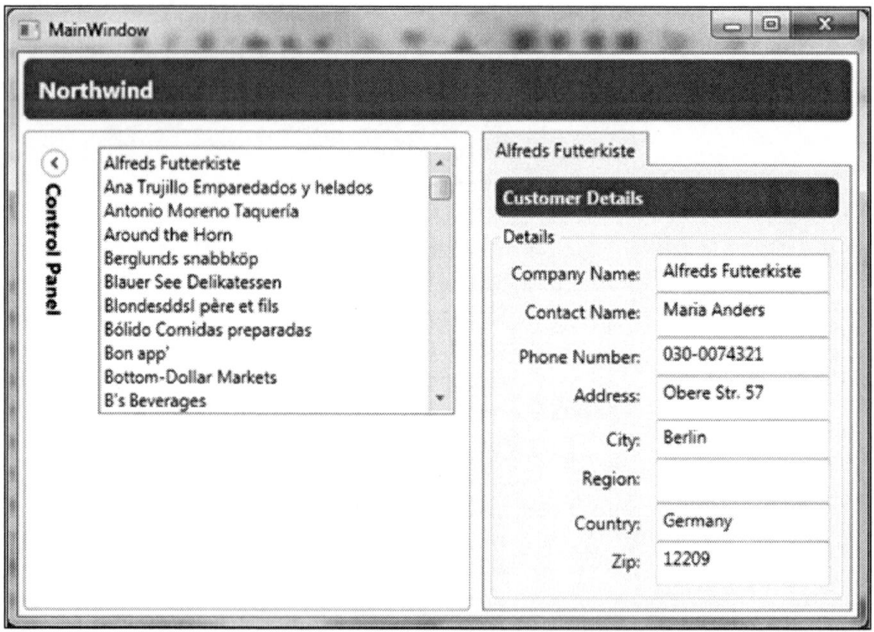

We still have some work to do, but what we've accomplished so far is adding one `CustomerDetails` view to our UI. To accomplish this we perform the following steps:

1. Update our `UIDataProvider` to allow us to get a customer by customer ID in *steps 1* and 2 above.
2. Create a `CustomerDetails` view and a `ToolViewModel` derived view model, `CustomerDetailsViewModel`.
3. Map `CustomerDetails` to `CustomerDetailsViewModel` in `MainSkin.xaml`.

4. Update `MainWindowViewModel` to instantiate a new `CustomerDetailsViewModel` that was passed a hardcoded customer ID, and then add it to the Tools collection.

We passed a hard-coded customer ID to get up and running quickly. Soon we will refactor this code to allow the ID to be passed from the customer listbox selection to the main window view model.

Testing CustomerDetailsViewModel

Now, let's add some unit tests by doing the following steps:

1. Add a new **Basic Unit Test** to `Northwind.ViewModel.Tests` by right-clicking on the project and selecting **Add** and then **New Test** called `CustomerDetailsViewModelTests`.
2. Add `using` **statements for** `Northwind.Application`, `Rhino.Mocks`, and `Northwind.Data`.
3. And update `CustomerDetailsViewModelTests` as follows:

```
[TestMethod]
public void Ctor_Always_CallsGetCustomer()
{
    // Arrange
    IUIDataProvider uiDataProviderMock
        = MockRepository
            .GenerateMock<IUIDataProvider>();
    const string expectedID = "EXPECTEDID";
    uiDataProviderMock.Expect(
        c => c.GetCustomer(expectedID)).Return(
            new Customer());

    // Act
    CustomerDetailsViewModel target
        = new CustomerDetailsViewModel(
            uiDataProviderMock, expectedID);

    // Assert
    uiDataProviderMock.VerifyAllExpectations();
}

[TestMethod]
public void
    Customer_Always_ReturnsCustomerFromGetCustomer
    ()
```

```
{
    // Arrange
    IUIDataProvider uiDataProviderStub
        = MockRepository
            .GenerateStub<IUIDataProvider>();
    const string expectedID = "EXPECTEDID";
    Customer expectedCustomer
        = new Customer
            {
                CustomerID =
                    expectedID
            };
    uiDataProviderStub.Stub(
        c => c.GetCustomer(expectedID)).Return(
            expectedCustomer);

    // Act
    CustomerDetailsViewModel target
        = new CustomerDetailsViewModel(
            uiDataProviderStub, expectedID);

    // Assert
    Assert.AreSame(expectedCustomer, target.Customer);
}

[TestMethod]
public void DisplayName_Always_ReturnsCompanyName()
{
    // Arrange
    IUIDataProvider uiDataProviderStub
        = MockRepository
            .GenerateStub<IUIDataProvider>();
    const string expectedID = "EXPECTEDID";
    const string expectedCompanyName = "EXPECTEDNAME";
    Customer expectedCustomer
        = new Customer
            {
                CustomerID =
                    expectedID,
                CompanyName =
                    expectedCompanyName
            };
    uiDataProviderStub.Stub(
        c => c.GetCustomer(expectedID)).Return(
```

```
                expectedCustomer);

        // Act
        CustomerDetailsViewModel target
            = new CustomerDetailsViewModel(
                uiDataProviderStub, expectedID);

        // Assert
        Assert.AreEqual(expectedCompanyName,
                        target.DisplayName);
    }
```

4. Run all the tests and verify that they pass.

What we did here was tested the following three scenarios:

- The constructor will always call `IUIDataProvider.GetCustomers()`
- Verify that `CustomerDetailsViewModel.Customer` returns the value that was fetched from `IUIDataProvider.GetCustomers()`
- Verify that `CustomerDetailsViewModel.DisplayName` returns `Customer.CompanyName` for the customer that was returned from `IUIDataProvider.GetCustomers()`

These tests should be self-explanatory. You might find yourself writing more tests or using a different testing style, however, the point here is to demonstrate that we can unit test, not to teach unit testing.

Wiring up the customer list box

Now, we need to make the tabs dynamic and wire them up to the customer list box. To do this follow these steps:

1. Update `MainWindow.xaml` as follows:

```
</Expander.Header>
<StackPanel>
    <ListBox ItemsSource="{Binding Customers}"
                DisplayMemberPath="CompanyName"
                SelectedValuePath="CustomerID"
                VerticalAlignment="Top"
                SelectedValue="{Binding
                    SelectedCustomerID}"
                Height="180"
                Width="250" />
```

```
        <ContentControl Margin="0, 3">
            <Hyperlink Click="Hyperlink_Click">
                <TextBlock Text="Show Details" />
            </Hyperlink>
        </ContentControl>
    </StackPanel>
</Expander>
```

2. Add a `using` statement for `Northwind.ViewModel` in `MainWindow.xaml.cs`.
3. Add the following function to `MainWindow` in `MainWindow.xaml.cs`.

```
private MainWindowViewModel ViewModel
{
    get { return (MainWindowViewModel) DataContext; }
}

private void Hyperlink_Click(object sender,
                             RoutedEventArgs e)
{
    ViewModel.ShowCustomerDetails();
}
```

> We are using the code behind style here, and not implementing a pure "no code behind" style of MVVM. If you are going to use this approach, then it's good to define what is and what isn't allowed in the code behind. A rule of thumb that you could use is "No conditional logic in the code behind" [Smith]. Using this rule you can be pretty sure that there is no view logic contained in the code behind. However, later in this book, we will show how to update this code to use pure MVVM with no code behind.

4. Open `MainWindowViewModel.cs`, and add a `using` statement for `System.Linq`.
5. Update `MainWindowViewModel` as follows:

```
public string SelectedCustomerID { get; set; }

public MainWindowViewModel(
    IUIDataProvider dataProvider)
{
    _dataProvider = dataProvider;
    Tools = new ObservableCollection<ToolViewModel>();
}
```

```
public void ShowCustomerDetails()
{
    if (string.IsNullOrEmpty(SelectedCustomerID))
        throw new InvalidOperationException(
            "SelectedCustomerID can't be null");

    CustomerDetailsViewModel customerDetailsViewModel
        = GetCustomerDetailsTool(SelectedCustomerID);
    if (customerDetailsViewModel == null)
    {
        customerDetailsViewModel
            = new CustomerDetailsViewModel(
                _dataProvider, SelectedCustomerID);
        Tools.Add(customerDetailsViewModel);
    }
    SetCurrentTool(customerDetailsViewModel);
}

private CustomerDetailsViewModel GetCustomerDetailsTool(
    string customerID)
{
    return Tools
        .OfType<CustomerDetailsViewModel>()
        .FirstOrDefault(c =>
                        c.Customer.CustomerID ==
                        customerID);
}

private void SetCurrentTool(ToolViewModel currentTool)
{
    ICollectionView collectionView =
        CollectionViewSource.GetDefaultView(Tools);
    if (collectionView != null)
    {
        if (collectionView.MoveCurrentTo(currentTool) !=
            true)
        {
            throw new InvalidOperationException(
                "Could not find the current tool.");
        }
    }
}
```

6. Add a .Net reference from `Northwind.ViewModel` to `PresentationFramework` and `WindowsBase`.
7. Build and run the application.
8. Select a few different customers, and click on **Show Details** for each one selected.
9. Verify that you see something similar to the following screenshot:

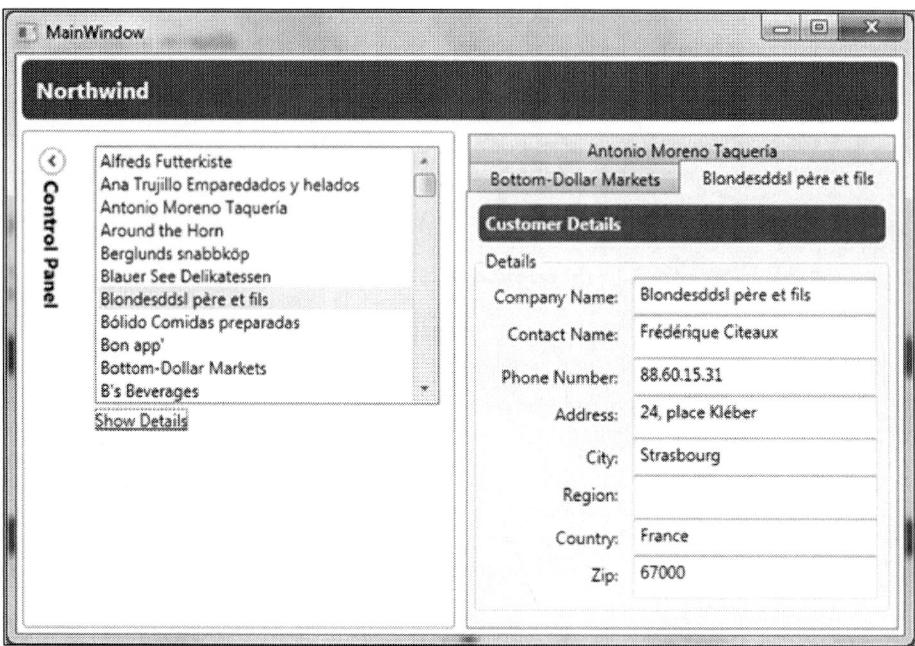

What we did here was:

- Used the code behind approach to wire up an event handler to the `Hyperlink.Click` event
- Accessed the view model of `MainWindow` by adding a property that cast `MainWindow.DataContext` to a `MainWindowViewModel`
- Added `MainWindowViewModel.SelectedCustomerID`
- Added `MainWindowViewModel.ShowCustomerDetails()` that handles either creating a new `CustomerDetailsViewModel` or selecting the existing one if it's already been opened

One interesting thing to point out at this time is the entity framework's built-in support for Change Notifications. Open up the `Customer` class in Visual Studio's class view, expand the **Base Types**, and you will see something similar to the following screenshot:

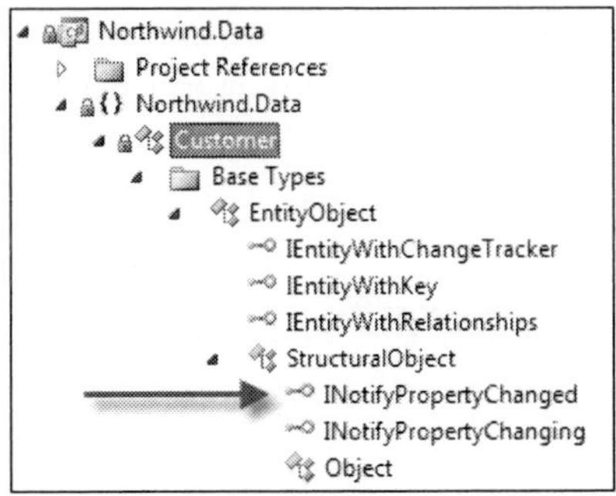

As you can see, `Customer` is dervied from `StructuralObject`, which implements `INotifyPropertyChanged` and provides support for binding updates. We can easily verify this by performing the following steps:

1. Launch Northwind.
2. Open a **Customer Details** tab.
3. Change the **Company Name** by adding the word `changed` to the end; and as you type, notice how the **Company Name** is also updated in the customer list box, as shown in the following screenshot:

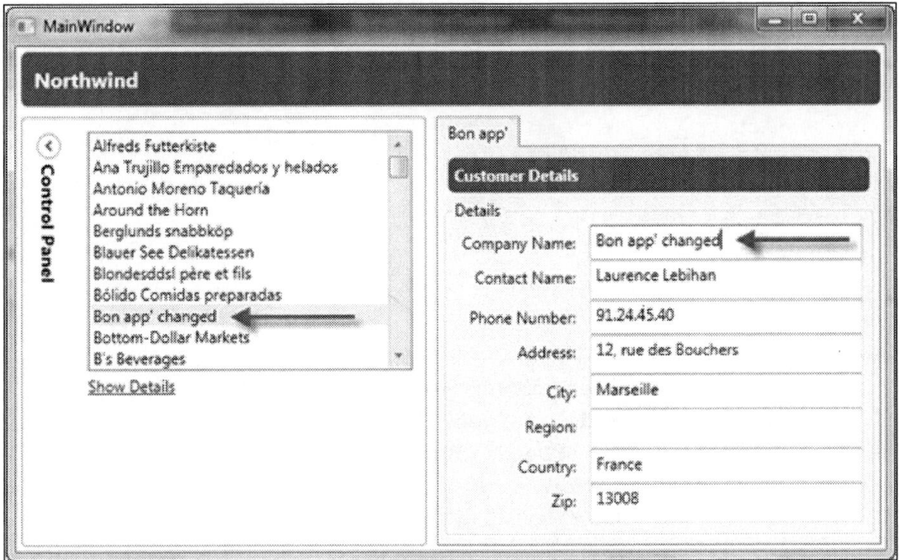

We didn't have to add any code to get this change notification support in our model. This is definitely a huge benefit of using entity framework with Silverlight and WPF. Later, we will see how WCF also supports built-in change notifications. There is, of course, a downside to getting change notifications for free in this way. We have now tightly coupled our UI to Entity Framework and our generated schema. Later, we will be looking into the idea of persistence ignorance, the extra work that it involves, and the additional benefits that it provides over solutions that don't provide persistence ignorance. For now, it is just important to note that the entity framework allows for getting your change notifications working very easily.

Testing ShowCustomerDetails()

Let's update our code to test `MainWindowViewModel.ShowCustomerDetails()` by performing the following steps:

1. Add .Net references to `WindowsBase` and `PresentationFramework`.
2. Add a `using` statement for `System` and `System.Windows.Data`.
3. Adding the following code to `MainWindowViewModelTests`:

```
[ExpectedException(typeof (InvalidOperationException))]
[TestMethod]
public void
ShowCustomerDetails_SelectedCustomerIDIsNull_
ThrowsInvalidOperationException
    ()
{
    // Arrange
    MainWindowViewModel target
        = new MainWindowViewModel(null);

    // Act
    target.ShowCustomerDetails();
}

[TestMethod]
public void ShowCustomerDetails_ToolNotFound_AddNewTool()
{
    // Arrange
    const string expectedCustomerID = "EXPECTEDID";
    MainWindowViewModel target =
        GetShowCustomerDetailsTarget(
            new Customer
                { CustomerID = expectedCustomerID});
```

```
    // Act
    target.ShowCustomerDetails();

    // Assert
    CustomerDetailsViewModel actual =
        target.Tools.Cast<CustomerDetailsViewModel>().
            FirstOrDefault(
                viewModel =>
                viewModel.Customer.CustomerID ==
                expectedCustomerID);
    Assert.IsNotNull(actual);
}

[TestMethod]
public void ShowCustomerDetails_Always_ToolIsSetToCurrent
    ()
{
    // Arrange
    Customer expected = new Customer
                        {
                            CustomerID =
                                "EXPECTEDID"
                        };
    MainWindowViewModel target =
        GetShowCustomerDetailsTarget(expected);

    // Act
    target.ShowCustomerDetails();

    // Assert
    CustomerDetailsViewModel actual =
        CollectionViewSource.GetDefaultView(target.Tools)
            .CurrentItem as CustomerDetailsViewModel;

    Assert.AreSame(expected, actual.Customer);
}

private static MainWindowViewModel
    GetShowCustomerDetailsTarget(
    Customer customer)
{
    IUIDataProvider uiDataProviderStub
        = MockRepository
            .GenerateStub<IUIDataProvider>();
```

```
        MainWindowViewModel target
            = new MainWindowViewModel(uiDataProviderStub);
        target.SelectedCustomerID = customer.CustomerID;
        uiDataProviderStub.Stub(
            d => d.GetCustomer(customer.CustomerID)).Return(
                customer);
        return target;
    }
```

4. Now, run all the tests and verify that they pass.

We now added tests for the following scenarios for `ShowCustomerDetails`:

1. Not setting a `MainWindowViewModel.SelectedCustomerID` will result in `InvalidOperationException` being thrown.
2. If there is no tool for `MainWindowViewModel.SelectedCustomerID`, then create one and add it.
3. Verify that `MainWindowViewModel.SelectedCustomerID` is always set to the current tool.

We could easily have tested more scenarios here, but again, the point here is to demonstrate that we have a testable architecture, and not to tryand teach unit testing.

Summary

In this chapter, we've laid the foundation for our application. We started things off by introducing the requirements of the Northwind application. Next, we demonstrated a quick way to get up and running with a database-driven MVVM application by using Microsoft's entity framework. We followed this up by refactoring our design to improve testability, and added our first unit tests. We then looked at how to easily create dynamic workspaces using MVVM by adding a tabbed interface to Northwind. We finished the chapter by looking at the entity framework's support for change notifications.

4

Northwind—Services and Persistence Ignorance

By Ryan Vice

We are off to a good start, but what about performance and scalability? Our current design isn't very scalable and places a large processing load on the client that would make more sense if it was placed on a server. Enterprise applications will generally need to be crafted differently for scalability, performance, and component-based development. They need to be service-oriented, enabling different applications to reuse the same functionalities across the enterprise. The easiest way to improve our design so that it's more enterprise-ready is by adding a **Service Layer** by *Fowler* between our presentation tier and our application tier. This will allow us to move our business logic processing to a server which we can easily scale in server farms or on the cloud.

Another consideration for moving to a more enterprise-scale design is around Persistence ignorance. Persistence ignorance is achieved in a design when the persistence store can be changed without requiring changes to the consumers of the data coming out of the persistence store. Having multiple consumers in an enterprise SOA environment creates a compelling scenario for considering adding persistence ignorance to your design, as you wouldn't want changes in persistence to affect downstream dependencies.

In this chapter, we will refactor the `Northwind` database to add a Service Layer. As we do our refactoring, we will take note of some difficulties that our current design has around refactoring our data access code and will take a look at how this situation can be improved by making our design Persistence ignorant. We will then look at the testability of our design and will finish off the chapter by refactoring our design to a more testable approach that will allow us to add some unit tests.

Adding a Service Layer

In this section, we will add a Service Layer to our design.

Decision Point: Service Layer

You should only introduce a service layer in your project if it's needed. Each new architectural feature we will cover in this text will provide benefits for a cost. It's extremely important that you are familiar with the trade-offs and only add what you need. If you are writing an internal tool, adding a Service Layer might be overkill and provide no ROI to your project.

To add a Service Layer to Northwind, perform the following steps:

1. Add a new **WCF Service Library** project to your solution called `Northwind.Service` and delete the files `IService1.cs` and `Service1.cs` ,from the project.
2. Add a project reference from `Northwind.Service` to `Northwind.Data` and a .NET reference from `System.Data.Entity` to `Northwind.Data`.
3. Add a file called `Customer.cs` to `Northwind.Service` and update it, as shown in the following code:

```
using System.Runtime.Serialization;

namespace Northwind.Service
{
    [DataContract]
    public class Customer
    {
        [DataMember]
        public string CustomerID { get; set; }
        [DataMember]
        public string CompanyName { get; set; }
        [DataMember]
        public string ContactName { get; set; }
        [DataMember]
        public string Address { get; set; }
        [DataMember]
        public string City { get; set; }
        [DataMember]
        public string Region { get; set; }
        [DataMember]
        public string PostalCode { get; set; }
```

```
            [DataMember]
            public string Country { get; set; }
            [DataMember]
            public string Phone { get; set; }
        }
    }
```

This class is a Data Transfer Object by *Fowler* in WCF. We will soon see that WCF will generate entities on the client from this class and that these generated entities will come with built-in support for change notification.

4. Add a file called `ICustomer.cs` to your project and update it, as shown in the following code:

```
using System.Collections.Generic;
using System.ServiceModel;

namespace Northwind.Service
{
    [ServiceContract]
    public interface ICustomerService
    {
        [OperationContract]
        IList<Customer> GetCustomers();
        [OperationContract]
        Customer GetCustomer(string customerID);
    }
}
```

This interface is our WCF **Service Contract** which will be used to generate a client-side proxy. In our design, this contract is essentially a Transaction Script by *Fowler* that will be **customer-centric** and will be expanded to allow for getting related customer data such as orders.

Decision Point: Data Access

In Domain-Driven Design or DDD, a domain model is created by constructing an object graph from domain objects. The object graph is a *Fowler* Domain Model and it mimics the real world domain language and relationships in code. One of the key goals in DDD is creating a ubiquitous language between the stake holders and developers to reduce communication friction and increase code quality. The domain model can be organized into aggregates where an aggregate is a group ofassociated objects which are considered as one unit with regard to data changes. So for example, if you deleted a customer, you'd likely want to delete their orders too, and when you fetch a customer it would also make sense to retrieve the associated orders. For this reason, it makes sense for orders to share a repository with customers where the customer entity is the central focus or "aggregate". However, this kind of relationship wouldn't exist between employee and customer in our domain model, so it might not make sense to have them aggregated together in the same repository if we were taking a domain driven approach. But this leads us to another point of debate. You will need to decide, in your project how you want to organize your data access and services. For a simple project, you might want to design around a single repository, an approach that Martin Fowler calls **Transaction Script**. But if your domain model and logic get complex, you will find that you get more benefits from segmenting your design around multiple repositories and taking more of a domain model-driven approach, such as Domain-Driven Design, using multiple well-organized repositories with aggregates.

Service Oriented Architecture (**SOA**) introduces a whole host of design considerations. We will not be covering SOA concepts in depth in this book, as we are mainly concerned with the implication that having a Service Layer can place on an MVVM design. For more information on SOA patterns, see `http://www.soapatterns.org`.

5. Add a file called `CustomerService.cs` to `Northwind.Service` and update it, as shown in the following code:

```
using System.Collections.Generic;
using System.Linq;
using Northwind.Data;

namespace Northwind.Service
{
    public class CustomerService : ICustomerService
    {
        private readonly NorthwindEntities _northwindEntities
```

```
                = new NorthwindEntities();

            public IList<Northwind.Service.Customer>
                GetCustomers()
            {
                return _northwindEntities.Customers
                    .Select(
                        c => new Northwind.Service.Customer
                                {
                                    CustomerID = c.CustomerID,
                                    CompanyName = c.CompanyName
                                }).ToList();
            }

            public Northwind.Service.Customer GetCustomer(
                string customerID)
            {
                Northwind.Data.Customer customer
                    = _northwindEntities
                    .Customers.Single(
                        c => c.CustomerID == customerID);
                return new Northwind.Service.Customer
                            {
                                CustomerID = customer.CustomerID,
                                CompanyName = customer.CompanyName,
                                ContactName = customer.ContactName,
                                Address = customer.Address,
                                City = customer.City,
                                Country = customer.Country,
                                Region = customer.Region,
                                PostalCode = customer.PostalCode,
                                Phone = customer.Phone
                            };
            }
        }
    }
```

This class implements the same logic that was previously implemented in `UIDataProvider` but makes that logic available as a WCF service.

6. Add a folder called `App_Data` to `Northwind.Service`, and then copy the `NORTHWND.MDF` file in **Solution Explorer** from `Northwind.Data` and paste it into `App_Data`.

7. Open `App.config` in `Northwind.Service` and update it, as shown in the following code:

By adding our database to a folder named `App_Data`, we are able to use the `DataDirectory` attribute in our connection string to resolve our MDF file.

```
<?xml version="1.0" encoding="utf-8"?>
<configuration>
  <connectionStrings>
    <add name="NorthwindEntities"
         connectionString="metadata=res://*/Model1.csdl|
         res://*/Model1.ssdl|res://*/Model1.msl;
         provider=System.Data.SqlClient;
         provider connection string=&quot;
         data source=.\SQLEXPRESS;
         attachdbfilename=|DataDirectory|\NORTHWND.MDF;
         integrated security=True;user instance=True;
         multipleactiveresultsets=True;App=EntityFramework&quot;"
         providerName="System.Data.EntityClient" />
  </connectionStrings>
  <system.web>
    <compilation debug="true" />
  </system.web>
  <system.serviceModel>
    <services>
      <service name="Northwind.Service.CustomerService">
        <host>
          <baseAddresses>
            <add
              baseAddress="http://localhost:8080/CustomerService"
/>
          </baseAddresses>
        </host>
        <endpoint address="" binding="basicHttpBinding"
                  contract="Northwind.Service.ICustomerService" />
        <endpoint address="mex" binding="mexHttpBinding"
                  contract="IMetadataExchange" />
      </service>
    </services>
    <behaviors>
      <serviceBehaviors>
        <behavior>
```

```
            <serviceMetadata httpGetEnabled="True" />
            <serviceDebug includeExceptionDetailInFaults="True" />
          </behavior>
        </serviceBehaviors>
      </behaviors>
    </system.serviceModel>
  </configuration>
```

8. Set `Northwind.Service` as the `StartUp` project, build the solution, and then run it in debug mode.

You should now get the **WCF Test Client** window and be able to verify that the services are working correctly by invoking the service operations, as shown in the following screenshot:

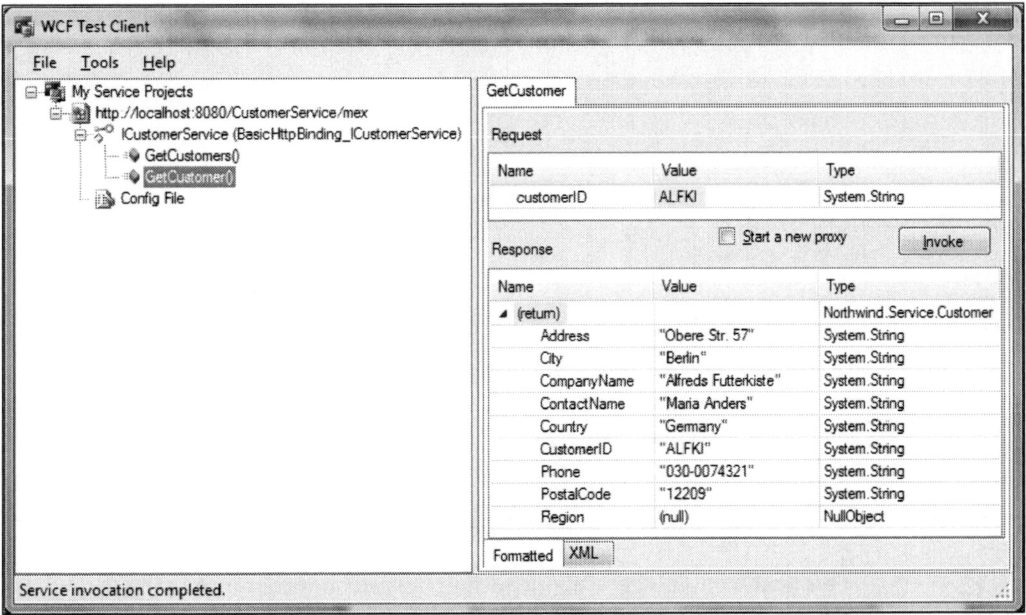

Integrating the Service Layer

Now that we've got our Service Layer working, let's refactor our presentation code to use it by following these steps:

1. Remove the reference from `Northwind.Application` to `Northwind.Data`.
2. Right-click on **Northwind.Application** in **Solution Explorer** and select **Add a Service Reference**.

3. In the dialog that pops up, click on the **Discover** button and set **Namespace** to **CustomerService**, as shown in the following screenshot and then click on the **OK** button.

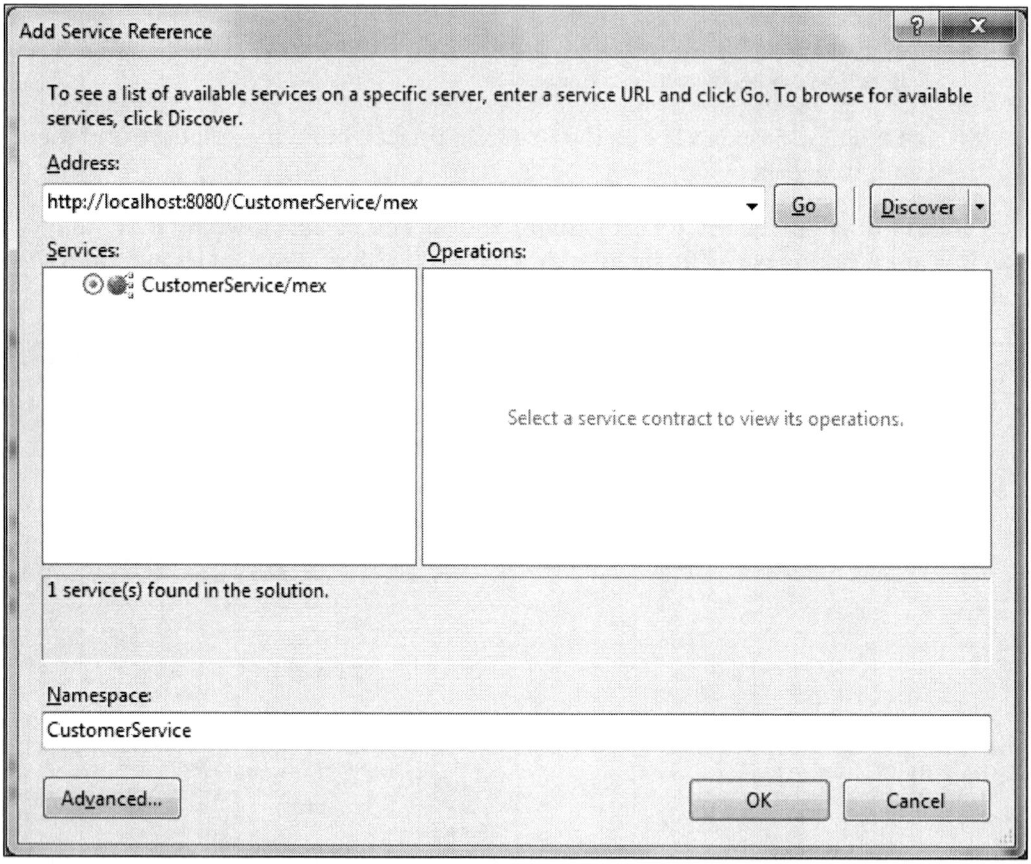

Add Service Reference
To see a list of available services on a specific server, enter a service URL and click Go. To browse for available services, click Discover.
Address:
http://localhost:8080/CustomerService/mex
Go
Discover
Services:
CustomerService/mex
Operations:
Select a service contract to view its operations.
1 service(s) found in the solution.
Namespace:
CustomerService
Advanced...
OK
Cancel

> Our next section will be about adding Persistence Ignorance to the design. Persistence ignorance is the decoupling of the presentation tier from the lower data tiers. It will minimize the refactoring needed for the presentation when changing your data providers (services, database, ORM, and so on). To appreciate the value of persistence ignorance, take note of how much refactoring we have to do in the next few steps, in the presentation tier, to change our application to use services. If our application were persistence ignorant, most of these steps would not be required.

4. Open `IUIDataProvider.cs` and replace the using statement for `Northwind.Data` with one for `Northwind.Application.CustomerService`. This will update the interface to use the `CustomerService` generated entities instead of using the `Northwind.Data` generated entities, which would not be necessary if our design were persistence ignorant and based on **POCOs (Plain Old CLR Objects)**.
5. Open `UIDataProvider.cs` and update it, as shown in the following code, taking care to update the namespaces correctly:

```
using System.Collections.Generic;
using System.Linq;
using Northwind.Application.CustomerService;

namespace Northwind.Application
{
    public class UIDataProvider : IUIDataProvider
    {

        private IList<Customer> _customers;
        private readonly CustomerServiceClient
            _customerServiceClient
                = new CustomerServiceClient();

        public IList<Customer> GetCustomers()
        {
            return _customers ??
                   (_customers =
                    _customerServiceClient.GetCustomers());
        }

        public Customer GetCustomer(string customerID)
        {
            Customer customer
                = _customers.First(
                    c => c.CustomerID == customerID);
            return customer.Update(
                _customerServiceClient.GetCustomer(
                    customer.CustomerID));
        }
    }

    internal static class CustomerExtensions
    {
        public static Customer Update(this Customer customer,
```

```
                Customer existingCustomer)
            {
                customer.ContactName =
                    existingCustomer.ContactName;
                customer.Address = existingCustomer.Address;
                customer.City = existingCustomer.City;
                customer.Region = existingCustomer.Region;
                customer.Country = existingCustomer.Country;
                customer.Phone = existingCustomer.Phone;
                return customer;
            }
        }
    }
```

> If you build the solution at this point, you will see that `Northwind.ViewModel`, `Northwind.ViewModel.Tests`, and `Northwind.UI.WPF` will have build errors and need additional refactoring. These steps would not be required, if we had already implemented persistence ignorance and had a design that used POCOs.

6. Remove the reference from `Northwind.ViewModel` to `Northwind.Data`.
7. Add a reference to `Northwind.Service` and `System.Runtime.Serialization`.
8. Replace all occurrences of `using Northwind.Data;` with `using Northwind.Application.CustomerService;` in `Northwind.ViewModel` and in `Northwind.UI.WPF`.
9. Add a reference to `System.Runtime.Serialization` in `Northwind.ViewModel.Tests`.
10. Open the `App.config` file in `Northwind.UI.WPF` and update it, as shown in the following code (which can be copied from the `App.config` file in `Northwind.Application`):

```
<?xml version="1.0" encoding="utf-8"?>

<configuration>
  <system.serviceModel>
    <bindings>
      <basicHttpBinding>
        <binding
          name="BasicHttpBinding_ICustomerService"
          closeTimeout="00:01:00"
          openTimeout="00:01:00"
          receiveTimeout="00:10:00"
```

```
            sendTimeout="00:01:00"
            allowCookies="false"
            bypassProxyOnLocal="false"
            hostNameComparisonMode="StrongWildcard"
            maxBufferSize="65536"
            maxBufferPoolSize="524288"
            maxReceivedMessageSize="65536"
            messageEncoding="Text"
            textEncoding="utf-8"
            transferMode="Buffered"
            useDefaultWebProxy="true">
            <readerQuotas maxDepth="32"
                          maxStringContentLength="8192"
                          maxArrayLength="16384"
                          maxBytesPerRead="4096"
                          maxNameTableCharCount="16384" />
            <security mode="None">
              <transport clientCredentialType="None"
                         proxyCredentialType="None"
                         realm="" />
              <message clientCredentialType="UserName"
                       algorithmSuite="Default" />
            </security>
          </binding>
        </basicHttpBinding>
      </bindings>
      <client>
        <endpoint
          address="http://localhost:8080/CustomerService"
          binding="basicHttpBinding"
          bindingConfiguration
                  ="BasicHttpBinding_ICustomerService"
          contract="CustomerService.ICustomerService"
          name="BasicHttpBinding_ICustomerService" />
      </client>
    </system.serviceModel>
  </configuration>
```

11. Build and run the application.

If you run the application, you will see that it works as it did before. In step 5, we had to do some slightly unusual things to accommodate the differences between a WCF proxy and Entity Framework object context. The object context maintains a collection for us that we used as our session state. After updating to WCF we needed to maintain a collection of customers locally to create the same type of session state. Neither of the two implementations is ideal for the approach being taken and both could be improved if they were choosen as the path you wanted to go down. However, for the purposes of this book, they show the options available and allow for us to demonstrate how you get to change notifications for free when integrating directly with Entity Framework or WCF. If you decide to take these types of approaches, make sure that you are comfortable with the technologies you are using and the various best practices for their use.

Persistence ignorance and custom models

So far, we have used generated classes as our models. We will now look at creating a custom model and will add persistence ignorance to our design.

Trade-offs of generated models

The Microsoft technology stack provides plenty of solutions that allow for getting up and running with models that support change notifications via `INotifyPropertyChanged`. As with everything in software development, there are trade-offs to be considered when determining what type of architecture you need; the advantages and disadvantages of using generated models are shown as follows:

Advantages	Disadvantages
Quick to develop	Couples Presentation with data access
Models are generated for you	Changing data access requires difficult refactoring of presentation code.
Generated code for change notification	Encourages database centric model

You should be familiar with the advantages listed previously at this point, so let's talk a bit about the disadvantages. When we needed to change our design to support services we had to refactor not only the application layer but also the UI layer, because we were using generated models. While this saved us time up-front, we ended up having to modify the presentation code when we decided to upgrade our data access to include a Service Layer. Another minor negative is, with technology such as the Entity Framework, there is the temptation to simply drag over your tables from the database into the designer and use the database schema as your model. This type of data access approach where your model mimics the database structure is called **Table Module** by *Fowler*. There are many projects where this approach will work perfectly fine, however you will find that as your domain model and logic get complex, an approach like Domain-Driven Design might make more sense. You can most certainly accomplish this in Entity Framework, but at this point, the amount of effort saved begins to deteriorate a bit over writing your own model, as you end up having to create your model in the designer and then configure the mapping. So even though Entity Framework supports Domain-Driven Design, you will get the most productivity gains from taking the table module approach.

There is no "best approach" for all situations. If you have a project that is an internal application that will not be around for 10 years, or that won't be updated too often, you probably don't want to put the extra effort into decoupling your model from your data access. However, if you are building a new enterprise application for a company that stays up on the technology curve and this application will likely be around for 10 years and will need to scale up easily, it would likely be worth the extra effort to decouple your presentation and make it persistence ignorant and therefore easier to update in the future. Also, if you have complex domain logic or if you are in an environment where you must aggregate data from various sources (services, DBs, and so on), you might want to make your application persistence ignorant with a domain model approach like Domain-Driven Design.

There is a POCO T4 template for Entity Framework that will allow you to create POCO models. This is a tool that we won't be covering in this book but that is worth knowing and that I'd encourage you to investigate if you find yourself exploring options for data access and are favoring generated models. Additionally, there is a T4 template that supports mocking of the `ObjectContext` which is also worth looking at.

Adding persistence ignorance

In order to add persistence ignorance to our UI, we are going to:

1. Add a custom model to our project which will be made up of POCOs and be ignorant to the persistence technology that we are using.
2. Update `IUIDataProvider` to use our new persistence ignorant model.
3. Update the UI to consume our new model and to no longer be dependent on generated models.

To accomplish this, perform the following steps:

1. Add a new `Class Library` project to the solution called `Northwind.Model` and delete the `Class1.cs` file that is added by default.
2. Add a class called `ModelBase.cs` and update it, as shown in the following code. This class provides change notification support and includes debug code that will verify that property names exist in debug builds.

```
using System;
using System.Diagnostics;
using System.ComponentModel;

namespace Northwind.Model
{
    public class ModelBase : INotifyPropertyChanged
    {
        public event PropertyChangedEventHandler
            PropertyChanged = delegate { };

        public void RaisePropertyChanged(string propertyName)
        {
            VerifyPropertyName(propertyName);
            PropertyChanged(this,
                new PropertyChangedEventArgs(propertyName));
        }

        [DebuggerStepThrough]
        [Conditional("DEBUG")]
        private void VerifyPropertyName(string propertyName)
        {
            if (TypeDescriptor
                .GetProperties(this)[propertyName] == null)
                throw new InvalidOperationException(
                    "Property " + propertyName +
                    " wasn't found in "
                    + GetType().Name + ".");
        }
    }
}
```

3. Add a class called `Customer.cs` and update it, as shown in the following code:

```
namespace Northwind.Model
{
```

```
        public class Customer : ModelBase
        {
            private string _customerID;
            public string CustomerID
            {
                get { return _customerID; }
                set
                {
                    if (string.Compare(_customerID, value) == 0)
                        return;
                    _customerID = value;
                    RaisePropertyChanged("CustomerID");
                }
            }
            private string _companyName;
            public string CompanyName
            {
                get { return _companyName; }
                set
                {
                    if (string.Compare(_companyName, value) == 0)
                        return;
                    _companyName = value;
                    RaisePropertyChanged("CompanyName");
                }
            }
           // Add all properties needed here
        }
    }
```

We didn't list all the properties needed to save space, but add properties for `ContactName`, `Address`, `Region`, `Country`, `PostalCode`, and `Phone`, in your code. Make sure to follow the same pattern that is used for `CustomerID`. This class inherits from our `ModelBase` and is a simple POCO model with change notifications added.

4. Add a project reference from `Northwind.Application` to `Northwind.Model`.
5. In `IUIDataProvider.cs`, remove the `using` statement for `Northwind.Application.CustomerService` and add a `using` statement for `Northwind.Model`.

6. Add a class called `DataMapper.cs` to `Northwind.Application` and update it as shown in the following code:

```
using Service = Northwind.Application.CustomerService;

namespace Northwind.Application
{
    public static class DataMapper
    {
        public static Model.Customer Update(
            this Model.Customer model, Service.Customer dto)
        {
            model.CustomerID = dto.CustomerID;
            model.CompanyName = dto.CompanyName;
            model.ContactName = dto.CompanyName;
            model.Address = dto.Address;
            model.Region = dto.Region;
            model.Country = dto.Region;
            model.PostalCode = dto.PostalCode;
            return model;
        }
    }
}
```

This is a static class that provides an extension method that allows for updating a `Northwind.Model.Customer` instance from a `Northwind.Application.CustomerService.Customer` instance.

7. Update `UIDataProvider.cs`, as shown in the following code:

```
using System.Collections.Generic;
using System.Linq;
using Northwind.Application.CustomerService;

namespace Northwind.Application
{
    public class UIDataProvider : IUIDataProvider
    {
        private readonly CustomerServiceClient
            _customerServiceClient
                = new CustomerServiceClient();

      public IList<Model.Customer> GetCustomers()
```

```
        {
            return _customerServiceClient.GetCustomers()
                .Select(c => new Model.Customer().Update(c))
                .ToList();
        }

        public Model.Customer GetCustomer(string customerID)
        {

            return new Model.Customer()
                .Update(_customerServiceClient
                    .GetCustomer(customerID));
        }
       }
   }
```

This update changes to using our persistence ignorant model and uses our DataMapper extensions to allow for concise code, allowing us to call `Update()` off our `Northwind.Model.Customer` instance.

8. Add a reference to `Northwind.Model` in both `Northwind.ViewModel` and `Northwind.ViewModel.Tests`.
9. Do a Find and Replace for `using Northwind.Application.CustomerService;` with `using Northwind.Model;` in both `Northwind.ViewModel` and `Northwind.ViewModel.Tests`.
10. Build and run the project.

It should work the same as before and you can easily verify that the change notifications are still working as expected. It should be apparent that this design allows for easier updates to your data access, as now when you change your data access, you won't need to change anything above the `Northwind.Application` layer.

Note that we haven't implemented persistence ignorance in our DAL, only in our presentation tier. If you are interested in achieving a persistence-ignorant DAL, search the web for the **Repository Pattern** and **Unit of Work (UoW)** patterns for your data access technology. It's fairly easy to find detailed examples for Linq to SQL, Entity Framework, NHibernate, and so on of achieving persistence ignorance using Repository and UoW.

Decision Point: Exposing the Model through the View Model

In our current design, we are aggregating our model in our view model and then binding to the model in the UI. I call this approach **Aggregate Model**. Another option you can consider is to create proxy properties in your view model for each model property. This technique is known as **Proxy Property**. The proxy properties simply pass along the model property and implement `INotifyPropertyChanged` (and potentially `IDataErrorInfo`, which will be covered in the validations chapter). The advantages of Proxy Property include simplifying the view model, as you don't need to go through an intermediate object when binding, and simplifying your models as they no longer need to worry about change notification. The main disadvantage is that it requires more code. Another option for the relationship between your model and view model is the use of dynamic properties. This approach combines the Proxy Property and Aggregated Model approaches by exposing the model properties through the view model using the new Dynamic feature in .NET 4.0 and reflection. The big benefit of this approach is that it doesn't require the additional work that goes into writing proxy properties but still provides some of the benefits of Proxy Property. We won't cover this technique here, but it's well documented in the MSDN Magazine article *Problems and Solutions with Model-View-ViewModel* by *Robert McCarter*, freely available on the web (`http://msdn.microsoft.com/en-us/magazine/ff798279.aspx`, at the time of writing this book).

Adding unit tests

Let's go ahead and add some tests to our `Northwind.Application` layer, now that we've settled on a data access approach. We will have to update our `UIDataProvider` to support dependency injection for its data provider. Taking a look at our current implementation of `UIDataProvider`, we find that it's not easily testable for a few reasons.

One issue is with our service dependency.

```
private readonly CustomerServiceClient
    _customerServiceClient
        = new CustomerServiceClient();
```

We are not using **Dependency Injection(DI)** on this dependency and need to refactor our code so that it properly uses DI for this dependency.

Another issue is the `Update` extension method shown in the following code:

```
public IList<Model.Customer> GetCustomers()
{
    return _customers ??
        (_customers =
        _customerServiceClient.GetCustomers()
            .Select(
                c => new Model.Customer().Update(c))
            .ToList());
}

public Model.Customer GetCustomer(string customerID)
{

    return _customers
        .First(c => c.CustomerID == customerID)
        .Update(_customerServiceClient
            .GetCustomer(customerID));
}
```

To properly isolate our tests we should test the `Update` functionality separately from `UIDataProvider` and use interaction verification style testing to verify that the `Update` method was called in the `UIDataProvider` context. However, this is not an easy way to do this under the current design, so we will need to refactor our code to improve the testability of this logic.

To add a unit test, follow these steps.

1. Delete `DataMapper.cs`.
2. Add a new interface called `IEntityTranslator.cs` to `Northwind.Application`, and update it as shown in the following code:

```
using Northwind.Model;

namespace Northwind.Application
{
    public interface IEntityTranslator<M, D>
        where M : ModelBase
    {
        M CreateModel(D dto);
        M UpdateModel(M model, D dto);
        D CreateDto(M model);
        D UpdateDto(D dto, M model);
    }
}
```

Here we are using the EntityTranslator pattern which is a simple data mapping pattern for mapping entities to models (business objects). We've started by creating a generic interface that our translators will implement and that allows for two-way translations between entities and models. Note that you can also consider using AutoMapper by Jimmy Bogard which is a great open source tool for doing entity translations (`http://automapper.org/`).

3. Add a class called `CustomerTranslator.cs` to `Northwind.Application`. Take care to add code for updating all the properties as some of that code was omitted for brevity.

```
using Service = Northwind.Application.CustomerService;

namespace Northwind.Application
{
    public class CustomerTranslator
        : IEntityTranslator<Model.Customer, Service.Customer>
    {
        internal static IEntityTranslator<Model.Customer,
            Service.Customer> _instance;

        public static IEntityTranslator<Model.Customer,
            Service.Customer> Instance
        {
            get
            {
                return _instance ??
                       (_instance = new CustomerTranslator());
            }
        }

        public Model.Customer CreateModel(
            CustomerService.Customer dto)
        {
            return UpdateModel(new Model.Customer(), dto);
        }

        public Model.Customer UpdateModel(Model.Customer model,
                                          CustomerService.
                                              Customer dto)
        {
            if (model.CustomerID != dto.CustomerID)
                model.CustomerID = dto.CustomerID;
```

```
            if (model.CompanyName != dto.CompanyName)
                model.CompanyName = dto.CompanyName;
           // Update all properties
            return model;
        }

        public CustomerService.Customer CreateDto(
            Model.Customer model)
        {
            return UpdateDto(new Service.Customer(), model);
        }

        public CustomerService.Customer UpdateDto(
            CustomerService.Customer dto, Model.Customer model)
        {
            if (dto.CustomerID != model.CustomerID)
                dto.CustomerID = model.CustomerID;
            if (dto.CompanyName != model.CompanyName)
                dto.CompanyName = model.CompanyName;
            // Update all properties
            return dto;
        }
    }
}
```

This class simply moves the data from our entities to our models, and vice versa.

4. Update `UIDataProvider`, as shown in the following code:

```
public class UIDataProvider : IUIDataProvider
{
    private IList<Model.Customer> _customers;

    private readonly ICustomerService
        _customerServiceClient;

    public UIDataProvider(ICustomerService customerService)
    {
        _customerServiceClient = customerService;
    }

    public IList<Model.Customer> GetCustomers()
```

```
        {
            return _customers ??
                    (_customers =
                     _customerServiceClient.GetCustomers()
                         .Select(
                             c =>
                             CustomerTranslator.Instance.
                                 CreateModel(c))
                         .ToList());
        }

        public Model.Customer GetCustomer(string customerID)
        {
            return
                CustomerTranslator.Instance.UpdateModel(
                    _customers
                        .First(c => c.CustomerID ==
                            customerID),
                    _customerServiceClient
                        .GetCustomer(customerID));
        }
    }
```

Here, we have introduced constructor dependency injection for the customer service and have updated to using our new `CustomerTranslator`.

5. Add a .NET reference from `Northwind.ViewModel` to `System.ServiceModel` and update `ViewModelLocator` as shown in the following code:

```
using Northwind.Application;
using Northwind.Application.CustomerService;

namespace Northwind.ViewModel
{
    public class ViewModelLocator
    {
        private static MainWindowViewModel
            _mainWindowViewModel;

        public static MainWindowViewModel
            MainWindowViewModelStatic
        {
```

```
                get
                {
                 return _mainWindowViewModel ??
                        (_mainWindowViewModel =
                         new MainWindowViewModel(
                             new UIDataProvider(
                                 new
                                 CustomerServiceClient())));
                }
            }
        }
    }
```

> What we've done here is to update our view model locator to manually inject `CustomerServiceClient`. We will see how to improve this approach using inversion of control frameworks, in the next chapter.

6. Add a new `Test Project` called `Northwind.Application.Tests`, delete the `UnitTest1.cs` class (which is created by default), add a project reference to `Northwind.Application`, add a browse reference to `Rhino.Mocks.dll`, and then create a new class called `UIDataProviderTests.cs` and update it, as shown in the following code:

```
using Microsoft.VisualStudio.TestTools.UnitTesting;
using Northwind.Application.CustomerService;
using Rhino.Mocks;
using Service = Northwind.Application.CustomerService;

namespace Northwind.Application.Tests
{
    [TestClass()]
    public class UIDataProviderTest
    {
        /// <summary>
        ///A test for GetCustomer
        ///</summary>
        [TestMethod()]
        public void GetCustomers_Always_CallsGetCustomers()
        {
            // Arrange
            ICustomerService customerServiceMock =
                MockRepository.GenerateMock<ICustomerService>();
            UIDataProvider target =
```

```
            new UIDataProvider(customerServiceMock);
        var customerDtos = new Service.Customer[]
                                {new Service.Customer()};
        customerServiceMock.Stub(c => c.GetCustomers()).
            Return(customerDtos);

        // Act
        target.GetCustomers();

        // Assert
        customerServiceMock.AssertWasCalled(
            c => c.GetCustomers());
    }

    /// <summary>
    ///A test for GetCustomer
    ///</summary>
    [TestMethod()]
    public void
        GetCustomers_ServiceReturnsDto_DtoPassedToTranslator()
    {
        // Arrange
        ICustomerService customerServiceStub =
            MockRepository.GenerateStub<ICustomerService>();
        CustomerTranslator._instance
            = MockRepository.GenerateStub<
                IEntityTranslator
                    <Model.Customer,
                        Service.Customer>>();
        UIDataProvider target =
            new UIDataProvider(customerServiceStub);
        var expected = new Service.Customer();
        var customerDtos = new Service.Customer[] {expected};
        customerServiceStub.Stub(c => c.GetCustomers()).
            Return(customerDtos);

        // Act
        target.GetCustomers();

        // Assert
        CustomerTranslator.Instance.AssertWasCalled(
            c => c.CreateModel(expected));
    }
```

```
        /// <summary>
        ///A test for GetCustomer
        ///</summary>
        [TestMethod()]
        public void
            GetCustomers_ServiceReturnsDto_
ModelReturnedFromTranslator
            ()
        {
            // Arrange
            ICustomerService customerServiceStub =
                MockRepository.GenerateStub<ICustomerService>();
            CustomerTranslator._instance
                = MockRepository.GenerateStub<
                    IEntityTranslator
                        <Model.Customer,
                            Service.Customer>>();
            UIDataProvider target =
                new UIDataProvider(customerServiceStub);
            var dto = new Service.Customer();
            var expected = new Model.Customer();
            var customerDtos = new Service.Customer[] {dto};
            customerServiceStub.Stub(c => c.GetCustomers()).
                Return(customerDtos);
            CustomerTranslator.Instance.Stub(
                c => c.CreateModel(dto)).Return(expected);

            // Act
            var actual = target.GetCustomers();

            // Assert
            Assert.AreSame(expected, actual[0]);
        }

        /// <summary>
        ///A test for GetCustomers
        ///</summary>
        [TestMethod()]
        public void GetCustomer_Always_CallsGetCustomer()
        {
            // Arrange
            const string expectedID = "expectedID";
            ICustomerService customerServiceMock =
                MockRepository.GenerateMock<ICustomerService>();
```

```
                CustomerTranslator._instance
                    = MockRepository.GenerateStub<
                        IEntityTranslator
                            <Model.Customer,
                                Service.Customer>>();
                UIDataProvider target =
                    new UIDataProvider(customerServiceMock);
                var dto = new Service.Customer
                              {CustomerID = expectedID};
                var model = new Model.Customer
                                {CustomerID = expectedID};
                var customerDtos = new Service.Customer[] {dto};
                customerServiceMock.Stub(c => c.GetCustomers()).
                    Return(customerDtos);
                CustomerTranslator.Instance.Stub(
                    c => c.CreateModel(dto)).Return(model);
                target.GetCustomers(); // Load session data

                // Act
                target.GetCustomer(expectedID);

                // Assert
                customerServiceMock.AssertWasCalled(
                    c => c.GetCustomer(expectedID));
            }
        }
    }
```

Here we are testing four scenarios using interaction verification style tests. We could add more tests and provide full coverage, but we have shown that all of our dependencies are injectable with fake objects and that our design has good testability.

7. Run all the tests and verify that they pass.

We are not going to walk through testing the entity translator here, as there isn't anything complicated about testing it and it should be easy to see that this class has a testable design.

If you use Entity Translator or other mapping patterns, I would encourage you to provide testing coverage for your translators. Getting the translations right is critical and can easily get messed up during bug fixing or refactorings. Because of this, these tests will provide high ROI.

Summary

In this chapter, we refactored our architecture to make it more scalable by introducing a service layer. We saw how not having a persistence ignorant design causes us to have to refactor presentation code in order to change our data access approach, and we discussed the trade-offs of using generated models. We learned how to make our presentation code persistent ignorant and what benefits that would provide us. We then looked at the testability of our approach and finished off the chapter by refactoring our code to be more testable, which allowed us to add some unit tests.

5

Northwind—Commands and User Inputs

By Ryan Vice

Getting user input from the **view** to the **view model** is one of the many challenges of implementing MVVM especially when you want to keep it pure and go with a no code-behind approach. In this chapter, we will look at how the command infrastructure helps make this task easier and where the command infrastructure falls short. We will look at several ways of dealing with the shortcomings of the commanding infrastructure, examining both code-behind and no code-behind approaches as well as looking at how the MVVM Light framework can make our life easier.

Pure MVVM

Currently, we are wiring up our event handlers in the code behind instead of taking advantage of the command infrastructure to pass user input from the view to the view model. There's a lot of talk in the development community as to how much code is alright in the code behind and I won't attempt to end that debate here, instead what I will do is, provide the tools and techniques that allow for taking the pure approach. This will allow you to decide what the best approach for your project is and use whatever level of purity makes the most sense.

That said, in my projects I prefer to keep it as pure as possible and I am yet to find a situation where I had to put code in the code behind. The following are a few reasons that I favor the pure approach apart from just being a bit of a purist at heart:

- **Enforcement**: On a large project, you will have developers with differing levels of skill and ambition and what happens without fail is that if you allow for the code-behind approach, it ends up getting abused and before long you will end up with developers abusing the references from your view to your view model and/or you will end up with view gunk in your view models making them difficult to test. Because of this I like to have a best practice on my projects that states that code-behinds need to be deleted.
- **Less code, fewer bugs**: In my projects, I've found up to 80 percent reduction in code needed in some cases. This is because when using the code-behind approach you have to add a lot of unnecessary code to pass input from the view to the view model. You will do a good bit of casting and null checks before you can pass along the event to the view model for processing, while in a pure approach all of this code becomes unnecessary. Less code means lower maintenance and fewer bugs. Not to mention that this code is boilerplate code that tends to be boring to write.

On the flip side, if you are going to allow for code in your code behinds, then I'd strongly encourage you to be explicit about what kind of code is allowed and my recommendation would be that you use the following rules:

- **No conditional logic**: This will prevent from having any untestable business or view logic in the code behind
- **No view controls in the view model**: This requires that only value types and POCOs can be passed from the view to the view model, which will allow your view models to remain testable

So now let's refactor our code to allow for a pure MVVM implementation by following these steps:

1. Add a reference to `PresentationCore` in `Northwind.Application`.
2. Add a new class called `Command` to `Northwind.Application` and update it as shown in the following code. This code creates a generic `command` that can be instantiated with lambdas for specifying `ICommand.Execute` and `ICommand.CanExecute` logic. It also provides `RaiseCanExecute` for raising the `ICommand.CanExecute` event to notify the view that it should call `CanExecute`:

```
using System;
using System.Windows.Input;
```

```
namespace Northwind.Application
{
    public class Command : ICommand
    {
        private readonly Action<object> _execute;
        private readonly Func<object, bool> _canExecute;

        public Command(Action<object> execute)
            : this(execute, null)
        {}

        public Command(Action<object> execute,
            Func<object, bool> canExecute)
        {
            _execute = execute;
            _canExecute = canExecute;
        }

        public void Execute(object parameter)
        {
            _execute(parameter);
        }

        public bool CanExecute(object parameter)
        {
            return (_canExecute == null)
                || _canExecute(parameter);
        }

        public event EventHandler CanExecuteChanged
            = delegate {};

        public void RaiseCanExecuteChanged()
        {
            CanExecuteChanged(this, new EventArgs());
        }
    }
}
```

3. Open the `MainWindowViewModel.cs` file and update it as shown in the following code. What we've done here is that we've added a command property that uses our new `Command` class, which is instantiated with two lambdas. The first will be called when the `ICommand.Execute` event is executed and the second will be called when the `ICommand.CanExecute` event is executed. We've also updated the `SelectedCustomerID` class so that it will call `Command.RaiseCanExecutedChanged`, which will in turn raise `ICommand.CanExecuteChanged` to notify the view that it needs to call `ICommand.CanExecute` again. This will make it so that our link will be enabled and disabled for us after we wire it up to use commands in the next step.

```
private Command _showDetailsCommand;
public Command ShowDetailsCommand
{
    get
    {
        return _showDetailsCommand ??
               (_showDetailsCommand =
                new Command(
                    ShowCustomerDetails,
                    IsCustomerSelected));
    }
}

private string _selectedCustomerID;
public string SelectedCustomerID
{
    get { return _selectedCustomerID; }
    set
    {
        _selectedCustomerID = value;
        ShowDetailsCommand.RaiseCanExecuteChanged();
    }
}

public void ShowCustomerDetails()
{
    if (!IsCustomerSelected())
```

```
            throw new InvalidOperationException(
                "Unable to show customer because no "
                + "customer is selected.");

        CustomerDetailsViewModel customerDetailsViewModel
            = GetCustomerDetailsTool(SelectedCustomerID);
        if (customerDetailsViewModel == null)
        {
            customerDetailsViewModel
                = new CustomerDetailsViewModel(
                    _dataProvider, SelectedCustomerID);
            Tools.Add(customerDetailsViewModel);
        }
        SetCurrentTool(customerDetailsViewModel);
    }
    public bool IsCustomerSelected()
    {
        return !string.IsNullOrEmpty(SelectedCustomerID);
    }
```

4. Open the `MainWindow.xaml` file and update `Hyperlink` as shown in the following code. Here we will now use a command instead of the code-behind approach and we get the added benefit of having our link to be disabled when no selection is made and then be enabled when a selection is made.

   ```
   <Hyperlink Command="{Binding ShowDetailsCommand}">
   ```

5. Open the `MainWindow.xaml.cs` file and remove the `Hyperlink_Click` method and the `ViewModel` property as neither is required now that we are moving to pure MVVM and using commands. It should look like it did right after it was created as shown in the following code:

   ```
   public partial class MainWindow : Window
   {
       public MainWindow()
       {
           InitializeComponent();
       }
   }
   ```

6. Build and run the application.

When running the application, everything should work as before with one difference. Now when the application starts for the first time and no customer is selected, the **Show Details** link will be disabled as shown in the following screenshot:

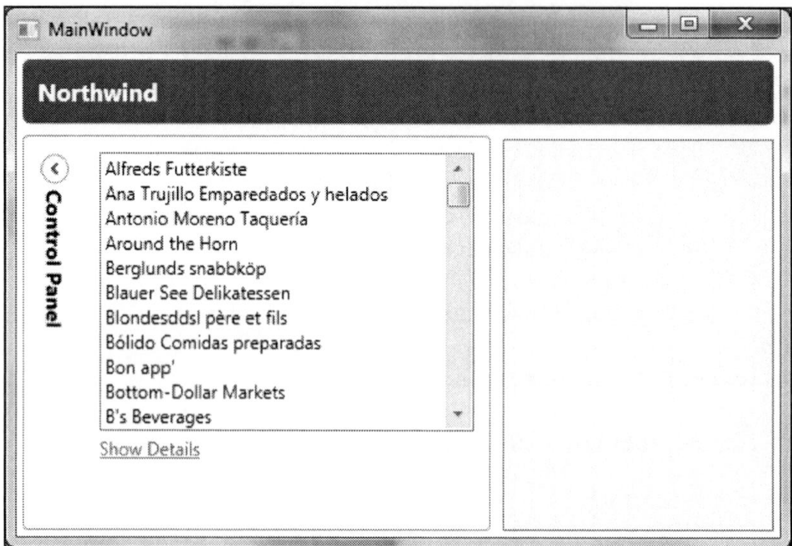

Making it easier with frameworks

We can save ourselves a little effort by taking advantage of one of the many MVVM frameworks freely available on the Web.

See *Appendix A, MVVM Frameworks* for a list of frameworks.

We are now going to update our code to use the MVVM Light framework by following the steps mentioned next:

If you haven't downloaded the MVVM Light framework then download the framework. See *Chapter 2, Introduction to MVVM* for details. Also note that there is now an MVVM Light Nuget package (`http://nuget.org/packages/mvvmLight`) available, which would be the preferred way to install the framework..

1. Copy `GalaSoft.MvvmLight.WPF4.dll` to the `Lib` directory in the solution, as shown in the following screenshot. This assembly contains the `RelayCommand` class that we will be using.

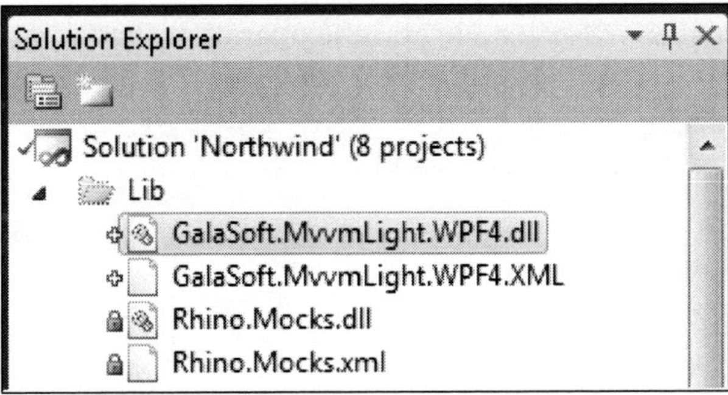

2. Add browse reference from `Northwind.ViewModel` to `GalaSoft.MvvmLight.WPF4.dll`.
3. Delete the `Command.cs` file from `Northwind.Application`.
4. Open `MainWindowViewModel.cs`, add a using statement for `GalaSoft.MvvmLight.Command` and then update the class as shown in the following code:

```
private RelayCommand _showDetailsCommand;
public RelayCommand ShowDetailsCommand
{
    get
    {
        return _showDetailsCommand ??
               (_showDetailsCommand =
                new RelayCommand(
                    ShowCustomerDetails,
                    IsCustomerSelected));
    }
}
```

5. Build and run the application and verify that it still works the same as before.

The relay command has made life a little easier as now we don't have to bother with creating a command wrapper class.

Updating customer details

Let's go ahead and add some code to allow for updating customer details by following these steps:

1. Update `ICustomerService` to add the operation shown in the following code:

   ```
   [OperationContract]
   void Update(Customer customer);
   ```

2. Update `CustomerService` to implement the new operation as shown in the following code:

   ```
   public void Update(Customer customer)
   {
       Data.Customer customerEntity
           = _northwindEntities
               .Customers.Single(
                   c => c.CustomerID == customer.CustomerID);
       customerEntity.CompanyName = customer.CompanyName;
       customerEntity.ContactName = customer.ContactName;
       customerEntity.Address = customer.Address;
       customerEntity.City = customer.City;
       customerEntity.Country = customer.Country;
       customerEntity.Region = customer.Region;
       customerEntity.PostalCode = customer.PostalCode;
       customerEntity.Phone = customer.Phone;
       _northwindEntities.SaveChanges();
   }
   ```

3. Build and then right-click on the **CustomerService** file in the **Service References** folder in **Northwind.Application** and select **Update Service Reference**, as shown in the following screenshot. This will update the `WCF` proxy classes to reflect our new update operation.

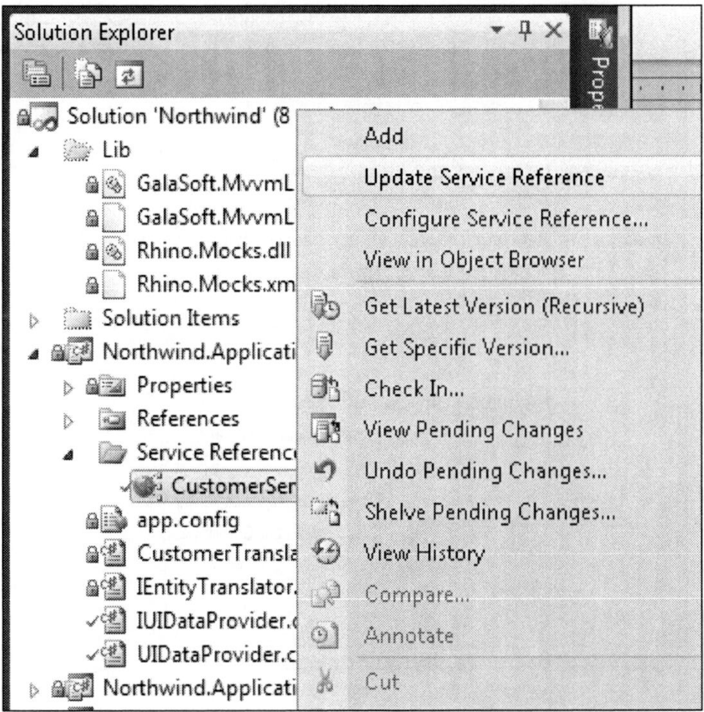

4. Update `IUIDataProvider` to add the operation shown in the following code:

```
[OperationContract]
void Update(Customer customer);
```

5. Update `UIDataProvider` to implement this new operation as shown in the following code:

```
public void Update(Customer customer)
{
    _customerServiceClient.Update(
        CustomerTranslator.Instance.CreateDto(customer));
}
```

6. Update `CustomerDetailsViewModel` as shown in the following code. This will expose an update command and implement the logic needed to perform updates when the command fires.

```
using System.ComponentModel;
using GalaSoft.MvvmLight.Command;
using Northwind.Application;
using Northwind.Model;

namespace Northwind.ViewModel
```

```
{
    public class CustomerDetailsViewModel : ToolViewModel
    {
        private readonly IUIDataProvider _dataProvider;
        public Customer Customer { get; set; }
        private bool _isDirty;

        private RelayCommand _updateCommand;
        public RelayCommand UpdateCommand
        {
            get
            {
                return _updateCommand ??
                       (_updateCommand =
                        new RelayCommand(
                            UpdateCustomer,
                            CanUpdateCustomer));
            }
        }

        private bool CanUpdateCustomer()
        {
            return _isDirty;
        }

        private void UpdateCustomer()
        {
            _dataProvider.Update(Customer);
        }

        public CustomerDetailsViewModel(
            IUIDataProvider dataProvider,
            string customerID)
        {
            _dataProvider = dataProvider;
            Customer = _dataProvider.GetCustomer(customerID);
            Customer.PropertyChanged
                += Customer_PropertyChanged;
```

```
            DisplayName = Customer.CompanyName;
        }

        void Customer_PropertyChanged(object sender,
            PropertyChangedEventArgs e)
        {
            _isDirty = true;
            UpdateCommand.RaiseCanExecuteChanged();
        }
    }
}
```

7. Update `CustomerDetails.xaml` as shown in the following code to add a new row to the layout:

```
<Grid.RowDefinitions>
    <RowDefinition Height="Auto" />
    <RowDefinition Height="30" />
    <RowDefinition Height="Auto" />
    <RowDefinition Height="30" />
    <RowDefinition Height="Auto" />
    <RowDefinition Height="30" />
    <RowDefinition Height="Auto" />
    <RowDefinition Height="30" />
    <RowDefinition Height="Auto" />
</Grid.RowDefinitions>
```

8. Update `CustomerDetails.xaml` as shown in the following code to add an update button.

```
    <TextBox Text="{Binding Customer.PostalCode,
             UpdateSourceTrigger=PropertyChanged}"
             Grid.Row="7"
             Grid.Column="2" />
    <Button Command="{Binding UpdateCommand}"
            Grid.Row="8"
            Content="Update" />
</Grid>
```

9. Build and run the application; now open a customer and verify whether you can update the customer details, as shown in the following screenshot:

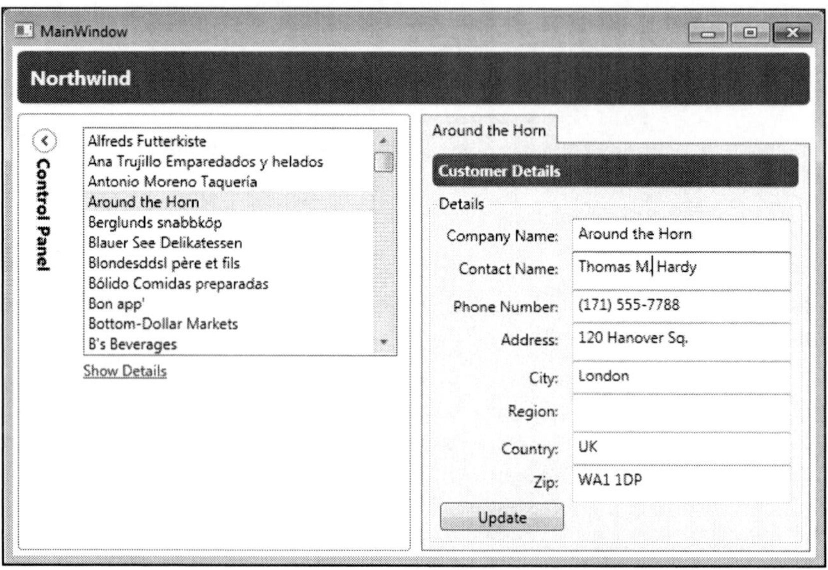

You'll find that the **Update** button enables as expected and if you update a customer's details and then restart the application you will find that your changes were persisted.

Testing and updating customer details

Using commands not only allows us to get rid of the code behind and easily enable/disable controls, we can also very easily test this logic. Add the following tests to `CustomerDetailsViewModelTest`:

```
[TestMethod]
public void UpdateCustomer_Always_CallsUpdateWithCustomer()
{
    // Arrange
    IUIDataProvider uiDataProviderMock
        = MockRepository
            .GenerateMock<IUIDataProvider>();
    Customer expectedCustomer = new Customer();
    uiDataProviderMock.Stub(
        u => u.GetCustomer(Arg<string>.Is.Anything))
        .Return(expectedCustomer);
    CustomerDetailsViewModel viewModel
```

```
        = new CustomerDetailsViewModel(
            uiDataProviderMock, string.Empty);
    RelayCommand target = viewModel.UpdateCommand;

    // Act
    target.Execute(null);

    // Assert
    uiDataProviderMock.AssertWasCalled(
        u => u.Update(expectedCustomer));
}
```

1. This first test shows how easy it is to test user interaction using commands. Here we are getting `UpdateCommand` and then calling its `Execute` method which is the same as what will happen when the application is run. We can easily verify that `update` is called on the `UIDataProvider` by using interaction verification against our `uiDataProviderMock`, which was injected into a `CustomerDetailsViewModel` instance using constructor injection.

```
[TestMethod]
public void CanUpdateCustomer_NotDirty_ReturnsFalse()
{
    // Arrange
    IUIDataProvider uiDataProviderMock
        = MockRepository
            .GenerateMock<IUIDataProvider>();
    Customer expectedCustomer = new Customer();
    uiDataProviderMock.Stub(
        u => u.GetCustomer(Arg<string>.Is.Anything))
        .Return(expectedCustomer);
    CustomerDetailsViewModel viewModel
        = new CustomerDetailsViewModel(
            uiDataProviderMock, string.Empty);
    RelayCommand target = viewModel.UpdateCommand;

    // Act
    bool actual = target.CanExecute(null);

    // Assert
    Assert.IsFalse(actual);
}
```

2. Our second test allows us to verify that can execute is `false` when our view model is not dirty, meaning that `CustomerDetailsViewModel.Customer` hasn't been changed.

   Our implementation of "dirty" could easily be improved. Currently we are simply flipping the `CustomerDetailsViewModel._isDirty` in response to `CustomerDetailsViewModel.Customer.PropertyChanged`. You might want to use something like the **Memento Pattern** to improve the approach.

```
[TestMethod]
public void CanUpdateCustomer_IsDirty_ReturnsTrue()
{
    // Arrange
    IUIDataProvider uiDataProviderMock
        = MockRepository
            .GenerateMock<IUIDataProvider>();
    Customer expectedCustomer = new Customer();
    uiDataProviderMock.Stub(
        u => u.GetCustomer(Arg<string>.Is.Anything))
        .Return(expectedCustomer);
    CustomerDetailsViewModel viewModel
        = new CustomerDetailsViewModel(
            uiDataProviderMock, string.Empty);
    RelayCommand target = viewModel.UpdateCommand;
    expectedCustomer.RaisePropertyChanged("CompanyName");

    // Act
    bool actual = target.CanExecute(null);

    // Assert
    Assert.IsTrue(actual);
}
```

3. Our final test is just like the previous one except that we raised `PropertyChanged` method to cause our dirty flag to be set before calling `CanExecute`.

Gestures, events, and commands

Classes that expose a command property in WPF and Silverlight are implementing the `ICommandSource` interface that is shown in the following code:

```
//     Defines an object that knows how to invoke a command.
public interface ICommandSource
{
```

```
    //      The command that will be executed when the command
            source is invoked.
    ICommand Command { get; }
    //      Represents a user defined data value that can be
            passed to the command when it is executed.
    object CommandParameter { get; }
    //      The object that the command is being executed on.
    IInputElement CommandTarget { get; }
}
```

One major limitation of the commanding infrastructure is that `ICommandSource` only allows for one action on a command source to be associated with a command. So, for example, if you want to have commands executed for both left-click and right-click on a button, you wouldn't be able to accomplish that using the `Button.Command` property. This limitation is one of the areas that you will find MVVM implementers breaking with pure MVVM by putting code to forward events to the View Model, as we showed earlier in this book. In this section, we will cover many techniques that can be used to keep your implementation pure when dealing with MVVM and events.

InputBindings

One option available for using commands to route user input from the View to the View Model is using `InputBindings`. `UIElement.InputBindings` is an `InputBindingCollection`, which can be populated with `InputBinding` elements.

MSDN defines:

> "*InputBinding as representing a binding between an InputGesture and a command*".

What this allows us to do is to associate an `InputGesture` like a `MouseGesture` or a `KeyGesture` with a command. We accomplish this by:

1. Creating an instance of an `InputBinding` derived class
2. Setting `InputBinding.Gesture`
3. Adding the `InputBinding` instance to a `UIElements.InputBindings` collection

There are two `InputBinding` derived classes included in WPF and Silverlight that we can use.

KeyBinding

KeyBinding allows for associating a `KeyGesture` with a command. A `KeyGesture` is a combination of a `Key` and `Modifiers`. For example, updating `MainWindow.xaml` as shown in the following code will associate `ShowDetailsCommand` with the *Ctrl* + *D* keyboard combination.

```
<Window.InputBindings>
    <KeyBinding Modifiers="Ctrl" Key="d"
                Command="{Binding ShowDetailsCommand}" />
</Window.InputBindings>
```

The `Gesture` property uses a convertor allowing for easier syntax in XAML. `Gesture` requires a string that is made up of a key and one or more modifiers. Each modifier and key must be delimited with a + sign. The following code shows how to wire up *Ctrl* + *D* to `ShowDetailsCommand` using the `Gesture` property:

```
<Window.InputBindings>
    <KeyBinding Gesture="Ctrl+d"
                Command="{Binding ShowDetailsCommand}" />
</Window.InputBindings>
```

Note that there are exceptions to the rule that you must provide one or more modifiers when defining a `KeyGesture`.

MSDN states that:

> *"In most cases, a KeyGesture must be associated with one or more ModifierKeys. The exceptions to this rule are the function keys and the numeric keypad keys, which can be a valid KeyGesture by themselves. For example, you can create a KeyGesture by using only the F12 key, but to use the X key in a KeyGesture it must be paired with a modifier key".*

Modifiers are defined in the `ModifierKeys` enumeration and are mapped in XAML via a converter to the modifier strings, as shown in the following table:

Modifier	Description
Alt	The Alt key.
Ctrl	The Control key.
Shift	The Shift key.
Windows	The Windows logo key.

MouseBinding

Another type of `InputBinding` is a `MouseBinding` which allows for mapping a `MouseAction` to a command. For example, adding the following code to `MainWindow.xaml` will associate the `ShowCustomerCommand` with the right-click button.

```
<Hyperlink Command="{Binding ShowDetailsCommand}">
    <Hyperlink.InputBindings>
        <MouseBinding MouseAction="RightClick"
                      Command="{Binding
                          ShowDetailsCommand}" />
    </Hyperlink.InputBindings>
    <TextBlock Text="Show Details" />
</Hyperlink>
```

Similar to the `KeyBinding.Gesture`, `MouseBinding.Gesture` is a `MouseGesture` that combines a `MouseAction` and a modifier. So if we wanted to allow *Shift* + right-click on our **Show Details** hyperlink to execute the `ShowDetailsCommand` then we'd use the XAML file that follows:

```
<Hyperlink Command="{Binding ShowDetailsCommand}">
    <Hyperlink.InputBindings>
        <MouseBinding Gesture="Shift+RightClick"
                      Command="{Binding
                          ShowDetailsCommand}" />
    </Hyperlink.InputBindings>
    <TextBlock Text="Show Details" />
</Hyperlink>
```

The `MouseAction` values are shown in the table that follows:

Action	Description
LeftClick	A left mouse button click.
RightClick	A right mouse button click.
MiddleClick	A middle mouse button click.
WheelClick	A mouse wheel rotation.
LeftDoubleClick	A left mouse button double-click.
RightDoubleClick	A right mouse button double-click.
MiddleDoubleClick	A middle mouse button double-click.

However, having two ways of showing a customer's details when clicking the **Show Details** link isn't very useful. Let's now update our application to use this technique in a way that makes more sense. It'd be nice to allow showing a customer's details when a user double-clicks the customer's name in the listbox on the main window. The following code looks like it would do the job nicely, but if you add it to your application and run it you will find that it doesn't work:

```
<ListBox>
    <ListBox.InputBindings>
        <MouseBinding Gesture="LeftDoubleClick"
                      Command="{Binding
                          ShowDetailsCommand}" />
    </ListBox.InputBindings>
</ListBox>
```

The chatter I've seen on the Internet about this seems to indicate that this is a known bug in WPF. So how can we move forward? One approach is to break with pure MVVM and use the code-behind approach with a style.

Using code behind

We will now update `Northwind` to use code behind for `ListBox.MouseDoubleClick`. To do this perform the following steps:

1. Update `MainWindowViewModel.xaml` as shown in the following code. This is a work around that allows us to attach an event handler to double-click by applying a style to the `ListBoxItem` type.

```
<ListBox ItemsSource="{Binding Customers}"
         DisplayMemberPath="CompanyName"
         SelectedValuePath="CustomerID"
         VerticalAlignment="Top"
         SelectedValue="{Binding
                SelectedCustomerID}"
         Height="180"
         Width="250">
    <ListBox.ItemContainerStyle>
        <Style TargetType="{x:Type ListBoxItem}"
               BasedOn="{StaticResource {x:Type
                   ListBoxItem}}">
            <EventSetter Event="MouseDoubleClick"
               Handler="ListBoxItem_MouseDoubleClick" />
        </Style>
    </ListBox.ItemContainerStyle>
</ListBox>
```

2. Add a reference from `Northwind.WPF.UI` to `GalaSoft.MvvmLight.WPF4.dll`.
3. Update `MainWindow.xaml.cs` as shown in the following code:

```
using System.Windows;
using System.Windows.Input;
using Northwind.ViewModel;

namespace Northwind.UI.WPF
{
    public partial class MainWindow : Window
    {
        public MainWindow()
        {
            InitializeComponent();
        }

        private void ListBoxItem_MouseDoubleClick(
            object sender,
            MouseButtonEventArgs e)
        {
            ((MainWindowViewModel)DataContext)
                .ShowDetailsCommand.Execute(null);
        }
    }
}
```

4. Run the application and verify that we can now show a customer's details by double-clicking on their name in the listbox.

This approach works and is a perfectly fine approach to take when mapping events to commands if you are comfortable with using the code-behind approach. However, we will now look at some options that will allow us to keep our MVVM pure and eliminate the need for the code behind.

Event to command

It doesn't take long in WPF or Silverlight to find yourself in need of a way to connect an event to a command especially when wanting to keep your MVVM pure. We are now going to look at two options for accomplishing this. The first option is a technique using the **Attached Behavior** pattern where no frameworks are required. The second approach will show how to use the MVVM Light framework to easily accomplish the same pattern concisely in XAML.

Attached Behavior

The Attached Behavior pattern takes advantage of the dependency property infrastructure in WPF and Silverlight. It makes use of the attached property feature of this infrastructure to allow for attaching behaviors to `UIElements`. The way the pattern works is by taking advantage of the property by changing the callback functionality of attached properties (see *Chapter 2, Introduction to MVVM* for more details). When you register an attached property, you can register a callback to be called whenever the attached property's value is changed and in the property changed event handler you get access to `DependencyObject` that the attached property was attached to, which in our case will be the `ListBox` instance. You can then subscribe to events on `DependencyObject`. We will be subscribing to the `MouseDoubleClick` routed event and then whenever the `MouseDoubleClick` event is received our event handler will be called. In our event handler, we will forward the call along by calling `ICommand.Execute` on the command that was attached to our `ListBox` instance.

Now, let's do this by following these steps:

1. Remove the code that was added in the previous section for handling double-click events.
2. Add a new class to `Northwind.UI.WPF` called `ListBoxBehaviors` and update it as shown in the following code. The `PropertyChanged` callback subscription is highlighted as it's the key to making this pattern work.

```
using System.Windows;
using System.Windows.Controls;
using System.Windows.Input;

namespace Northwind.UI.WPF
{
    static class ListBoxBehaviors
    {
        public static readonly DependencyProperty
            DoubleClickCommandProperty
            = DependencyProperty.RegisterAttached(
              "DoubleClickCommand",
              typeof(ICommand),
              typeof(ListBoxBehaviors),
              new PropertyMetadata(null,
                  new PropertyChangedCallback(
                      DoubleClickCommand_PropertyChanged)));

        public static void SetDoubleClickCommand(
            UIElement element, ICommand value)
```

```
        {
            element.SetValue(DoubleClickCommandProperty,
                value);
        }

        public static ICommand GetDoubleClickCommand(
            UIElement element)
        {
            return (ICommand)element.GetValue(
                DoubleClickCommandProperty);
        }

        private static void DoubleClickCommand_PropertyChanged(
            DependencyObject d,
            DependencyPropertyChangedEventArgs e)
        {
            UIElement target = d as UIElement;
            if (e.OldValue != null)
            {
                target.RemoveHandler(
                    ListBox.MouseDoubleClickEvent,
                  new RoutedEventHandler(ListBox_DoubleClick));
            }
            if (e.NewValue != null)
            {
                target.AddHandler(
                    ListBox.MouseDoubleClickEvent,
                  new RoutedEventHandler(ListBox_DoubleClick));
            }
        }

        private static void ListBox_DoubleClick(object sender,
            RoutedEventArgs routedEventArgs)
        {
            ListBox listBox = sender as ListBox;
            ICommand doubleClickCommand =
                GetDoubleClickCommand(listBox);
            if (doubleClickCommand.CanExecute(routedEventArgs))
            {
                doubleClickCommand.Execute(routedEventArgs);
            }
        }
    }
}
```

3. Add the namespace shown in the following code to `MainWindow.xaml`.

```
xmlns:WPF="clr-namespace:Northwind.UI.WPF"
```

4. Update `MainWindow.xaml` as shown in the following code:

```
<ListBox ItemsSource="{Binding Customers}"
         DisplayMemberPath="CompanyName"
         SelectedValuePath="CustomerID"
         VerticalAlignment="Top"
         SelectedValue="{Binding
               SelectedCustomerID}"
         Height="180"
         Width="250"
         WPF:ListBoxBehaviors.DoubleClickCommand
             ="{Binding ShowDetailsCommand}">
</ListBox>
```

5. Build and run the code and verify that double-click works for selecting customer details.
6. The key to making this work is highlighted again in the following code:

```
public static readonly DependencyProperty
    DoubleClickCommandProperty
    = DependencyProperty.RegisterAttached(
      "DoubleClickCommand",
      typeof(ICommand),
      typeof(ListBoxBehaviors),
      new PropertyMetadata(null,
          new PropertyChangedCallback(

           DoubleClickCommand_PropertyChanged)));
```

You might be wondering why we didn't put our code in `SetDoubleClickCommand` which is our dependency properties setter function. The reason for this is that when a dependency property is set in XAML, the binding system directly calls `DependencyObject.SetValue` and won't use `SetDoubleClickCommand`. `SetDoubleClickCommand` will only be used when the dependency property is set from code. This is why we must use the property changed event instead.

7. In the previous code, we are registering the callback method, `DoubleClickCommand_PropertyChanged` and it is shown in the following code. `DoubleClickCommand_PropertyChanged` will be called whenever our attached property's value changes.

```
private static void DoubleClickCommand_PropertyChanged(
    DependencyObject d,
    DependencyPropertyChangedEventArgs e)
{
    UIElement target = d as UIElement;
    if (e.OldValue != null)
    {
        target.RemoveHandler(
            ListBox.MouseDoubleClickEvent,
            new RoutedEventHandler(
                ListBox_DoubleClick));
    }
    if (e.NewValue != null)
    {
        target.AddHandler(
            ListBox.MouseDoubleClickEvent,
            new RoutedEventHandler(
                ListBox_DoubleClick));
    }
}
```

8. In our callback method, we are updating the routed event subscriptions for our target `DependencyObject` which will be our `ListBox` instance. Now our target `ListBox` instances will call `ListBox_DoubleClick` (shown in the following code) when `ListBox.MouseDoubleClick` is raised.

```
private static void ListBox_DoubleClick(object sender,
    RoutedEventArgs routedEventArgs)
{
    ListBox listBox = sender as ListBox;
    ICommand doubleClickCommand =
        GetDoubleClickCommand(listBox);
    if (doubleClickCommand.CanExecute(routedEventArgs))
    {
        doubleClickCommand.Execute(routedEventArgs);
    }
}
```

9. `ListBox_DoubleClick` takes advantage of the fact that our attached property is an `ICommand` and fetches the attached command using our `GetDoubleClickCommand` accessor and then calls `ICommand.Execute` on the returned command allowing us to route the event to the command.

The point of the code in this section was to introduce the basics of using attached behaviors to implement an Event to Command pattern and not to create the best possible implementation of the Event to Command pattern. This approach can be improved in a lot of ways and if you are thinking about using this approach in production code, I'd recommend taking a look at Samuel Jack's blog post titled *Hooking up Commands to Events in WPF* (`http://blog.functionalfun.net/2008/09/hooking-up-commands-to-events-in-wpf.html`), which shows a great generic version of this pattern that he calls `EventBehaviourFactory`. The `EventBehaviourFactory` class is also available for download from the MSDN code gallery (`http://archive.msdn.microsoft.com/eventbehaviourfactor`).

Using MVVM Light

Fortunately, the MVVM Light framework includes an implementation of the Event to Command pattern that can be easily configured in XAML. The MVVM Light version of Event to Command takes advantage of the **Microsoft Expression Blend SDK** and you will need to download the SDK before you are able to use the Event to Command support in MVVM Light.

Microsoft recommends redistributing any Microsoft Expression Blend SDK DLLs that you need in your application as part of your Application's install package. Following this recommendation will give you more control over your Application's environment and will make sure that updates to the SDK don't break your application.

Let's take a look at the following steps to see how we can simplify our approach by using the MVVM Light framework:

1. Remove any code you have from the previous section.
2. If you don't have the Microsoft Expression Blend SDK, then download and install it so that you can have a local copy of `System.Windows.Interactivity.resources.dll`.
3. Add a reference from `Northwind.UI.WPF` to `GalaSoft.MvvmLight.Extras.WPF4.dll` and to `System.Windows.Interactivity.resources.dll` (part of Blend SDK).

You will want to add these to your solution's `Lib` folder first to make your code portable in a source-controlled environment.

4. Add the namespaces shown in the following code to `MainWindow.xaml`:

```
xmlns:ViewModel="clr-namespace:Northwind.ViewModel;
assembly=Northwind.ViewModel"
xmlns:Command="clr-namespace:GalaSoft.MvvmLight.Command;
assembly=GalaSoft.MvvmLight.Extras.WPF4"
```

5. Update `MainWindow.xaml` as shown in the following code. The highlighted code is wiring up the `MouseDoubleClick` event to `ShowDetailsCommand` in the current `DataContext` and will implement the Event to Command pattern and forward `MouseDoubleClick` events to the `Execute` method of whatever command is bound at runtime.

```
<ListBox ItemsSource="{Binding Customers}"
         DisplayMemberPath="CompanyName"
         SelectedValuePath="CustomerID"
         VerticalAlignment="Top"
         SelectedValue="{Binding
                SelectedCustomerID}"
         Height="180"
         Width="250">
    <i:Interaction.Triggers>
        <i:EventTrigger EventName="MouseDoubleClick">
            <Command:EventToCommand Command="{Binding
                ShowDetailsCommand}" />
        </i:EventTrigger>
    </i:Interaction.Triggers>
</ListBox>
```

6. Build and run the solution and verify that double-clicking a customer will show the customer's details.

I really like this approach for Event to Command and would recommend it for your projects if you don't have any restrictions on using open source frameworks. However, we also looked at how to handle routing events to command targets using the code-behind approach and the attached behavior pattern so it's up to you to figure out what approach makes the most sense in your projects.

Summary

We are now well-equipped to handle user interactions. We have reviewed a variety of approaches for dealing with the shortcomings of the commanding infrastructure. On your own projects you will need to figure out what is the best approach for your team and requirements.

6

Northwind—Hierarchical View Model and IoC

By Ryan Vice

In this chapter, we will explore the power of using the Hierarchical View Model approach for building XAML applications. We will use this approach to add the ability to show order details in our application. As we begin to add this functionality, we will take some time to reconsider our design, and look at using an **IoC** (**Inversion of Control**) framework to improve our productivity.

Adding orders to customer details

Let's update **Northwind** to show the orders for each customer in the `CustomerDetails.xaml` view as shown in the following screenshot:

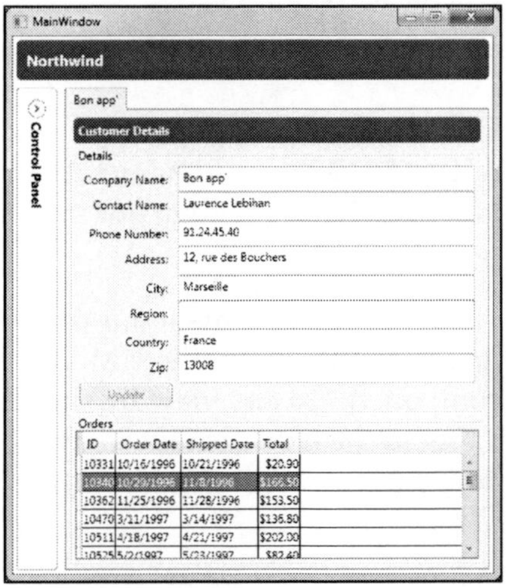

The approach we are going to use here is one that I call the Hierarchical View Model or HVM. We've already seen this approach briefly in *Chapter 2, Introduction to MVVM*, but in this chapter we are going to take a deeper look at this very useful technique.

The way this technique works is by taking advantage of data templates to map Views to View Models. By using this approach, we will be able to add the order details by following these simple steps:

1. Create `OrdersViewModel`.
2. Create an `Orders` View.
3. Add `DataTemplate` to map `OrdersViewModel` to `OrdersView`.
4. Add a `OrdersViewModel` property called `Orders` to `CustomeDetailsViewModel`.
5. Add `ContentControl` to `CustomerDetailsView` and bind it to `CustomerDetailsViewModel.Orders`.

You might be wondering why we didn't simply add a collection of `OrderViewModel` classes directly to `CustomerDetailsViewModel` class and keep our design simpler. Instead we added an abstraction for our `Orders` collection through `OrdersViewModel` and added an `Orders` View that contains our grid markup in XAML. We could have achieved the same result with a simpler design, however, the point of this chapter is to demonstrate organizing our presentation layer using HVM. By using the HVM approach here, we have created a self-contained control and are allowing reuse of the `Orders` grid in other areas of our application; all we have to do to reuse the `Orders` grid is to expose an `OrderViewModel` property in a content control. Additionally, we've encapsulated the grid functionality, and if we started expanding our grid functionality we'd have a nice clean separation in `OrdersViewModel` that would allow us to encapsulate that logic and state.

By following these steps all we have to do is populate `CustomerDetailsViewModel.Orders`, which will raise an `INotifyPropertyChanged.PropertyChanged` event. The binding system will then map `OrdersView` to our `OrdersViewModel` and we will be done.

Following this approach will allow us to segment our presentation logic into small components that are each made up of a View, View Model, and DataTemplate. We can then easily add these components to any view by simply adding a property to the View Model corresponding to the type of view we want to add. We can then bind the View Model property to the `Content` property of a `ContentControl`. Using this approach we can build a class hierarchy that models our UI needs. Then if we want to change the structure of the application all we need to do is move the associated ContentControl(s) to where they are needed in our XAML.

> There are a lot of controls other than `ContentControl` that allow for this approach. WPF supports the idea of **Content Model** which allows for placing arbitrary types into views, which can then be mapped to Views using `DataTemplates`. For more details see *WPF Content Model* or *Control Content Model* (for Silverlight) on MSDN (`http://msdn.microsoft.com/en-us/library/bb613548.aspx` and `http://msdn.microsoft.com/en-us/library/cc838221(v=vs.95).aspx`). Note that Silverlight 4 and below don't support implicit data templates but that at the time of writing this book support has been added to Silverlight 5.0 developer preview. In later chapters, we will look at techniques that allow for improving the lack of implicit data template support in Silverlight.

We can also use OOD techniques to easily create different views using collections of base class View Models. For example, in this chapter we will update our tabbed UI to support having an **Order Detail** tab by simply subclassing `ToolViewModel` to create our `OrderDetailViewModel` and then adding instances of `OrderDetailViewModel` to `MainWindow.Tools`. This approach also allows us to easily change the view as we could switch from a tabbed UI to some other style (MDI, and so on) by mostly updating our data templates and XAML. We will take a look at using this technique in *Chapter 7, Dialogs and MVVM*.

Service layer

To get started let's get our service update so that they return the orders when we call `ICustomerService.GetCustomer()`.

1. The first thing we need is some new DTOs (Data Transfer Objects) [Fowler] for the order details. Let's create those in `Northwind.Service`. Add a new class called `Order.cs` and update it as shown in the following code:

```
using System;
using System.Collections.Generic;
using System.Runtime.Serialization;

namespace Northwind.Service
{
    [DataContract]
    public class Order
    {
```

```
        [DataMember]
        public int OrderID { get; set; }
        [DataMember]
        public DateTime? OrderDate { get; set; }
        [DataMember]
        public DateTime? ShippedDate { get; set; }
        [DataMember]
        public decimal? Freight { get; set; }
        [DataMember]
        public IEnumerable<OrderDetail> OrderDetails { get; set; }
    }
}
```

2. Add a class called `OrderDetails.cs` and update it as shown in the following code:

```
using System.Runtime.Serialization;

namespace Northwind.Service
{
    [DataContract]
    public class OrderDetail
    {
        [DataMember]
        public Product Product { get; set; }
        [DataMember]
        public int Quantity { get; set; }
        [DataMember]
        public decimal UnitPrice { get; set; }
    }
}
```

3. Add a class called `Product.cs` and update it as shown here:

```
using System.Runtime.Serialization;

namespace Northwind.Service
{
    [DataContract]
    public class Product
    {
        [DataMember]
        public int ProductID { get; set; }
        [DataMember]
        public string ProductName { get; set; }
    }
}
```

4. Open `Customer.cs` and add the following property to it:

   ```
   [DataMember]
   public IEnumerable<Order> Orders { get; set; }
   ```

   Now that we have the DTOs that we need let's update our service to return those as part of `ICustomerService.GetCustomer()` as shown below.

5. Open `CustomerService.cs` and update it as shown in the following code. We've added two helper methods that allow for populating the orders when fetching customers.

   ```
   public Service.Customer GetCustomer(string customerID)
   {
       Data.Customer customer
           = _northwindEntities
               .Customers.Single(
                   c => c.CustomerID == customerID);
       return new Service.Customer
                  {
                      CustomerID = customer.CustomerID,
                      CompanyName = customer.CompanyName,
                      ContactName = customer.ContactName,
                      Address = customer.Address,
                      City = customer.City,
                      Country = customer.Country,
                      Region = customer.Region,
                      PostalCode = customer.PostalCode,
                      Phone = customer.Phone,
                      Orders
                       = GetOrders(customer.Orders)
                  };
   }

   private static IEnumerable<Service.Order> GetOrders(
       IEnumerable<Data.Order> order)
   {
       return order.Select(o => new Service.Order
           {
               OrderID = o.OrderID,
               OrderDate = o.OrderDate,
               OrderDetails = GetOrderDetails(o),
               Freight = o.Freight,
               ShippedDate = o.ShippedDate
           }).ToList();
   }
   ```

```
private static IEnumerable<Service.OrderDetail> GetOrderDetails(
    Data.Order order)
{
    return order.Order_Details.Select(
        o => new Service.OrderDetail
        {
            Product
                = new Service.Product
                {
                    ProductID
                        = o.Product.ProductID,
                    ProductName
                        = o.Product.ProductName
                },
            Quantity = o.Quantity,
            UnitPrice = o.UnitPrice
        }).ToList();
}
```

We are calling `ToList()` on our queries to cause them to execute immediately causing them to populate our collections before we send them across the wire.

6. Open `App.config` in the `Northwind.Service` project and update it as shown in the following highlighted code. Note that most of this file has been left out and we are only looking at the necessary changes. These changes will allow for us to return a larger amount of data giving us enough room to return all of the customer orders.

```
<system.web>
  <httpRuntime maxRequestLength="1000000" />
  <compilation debug="true" />
</system.web>


  <behaviors>
    <endpointBehaviors>
      <behavior>
        <dataContractSerializer maxItemsInObjectGraph="10000000"
/>
      </behavior>
    </endpointBehaviors>
    <serviceBehaviors>
```

```
        <behavior>
          <dataContractSerializer maxItemsInObjectGraph="10000000"
/>
          <serviceMetadata httpGetEnabled="true" />
          <serviceDebug includeExceptionDetailInFaults="true" />
        </behavior>
      </serviceBehaviors>
    </behaviors>
</system.serviceModel>
```

More details on WCF configurations can be found on MSDN.

7. Now set `Northwind.Services` as the startup project and run it in the debugger. You should now be able to execute `ICustomerService.GetCustomers()` from WCF Test Client and get orders as shown in the following screenshot:

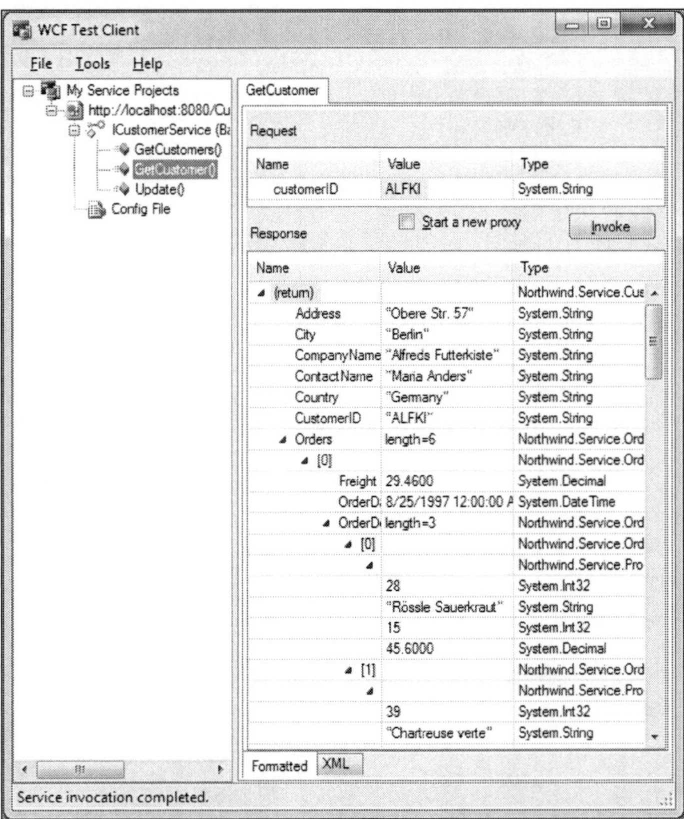

You can execute `GetCustomers()` to get a list of customers with IDs and then you can use any of the customer IDs to call `GetCustomer()`.

Application layer

Now let's get our application layer updated by opening `Northwind.Application` and following these steps:

1. Regenerate the service proxies using the following steps:
   - Expanding the `Service References` folder
   - Right-clicking on **CustomerService**
   - Selecting **Update Service Reference**

2. Add a class called `Product` to `Northwind.Model` and update it as shown in the following code:

```
public class Product : ModelBase
{
    public const string ProductIDPropertyName = "ProductID";
    private int _productID;
    public int ProductID
    {
        get { return _productID; }
        set
        {
            if (_productID == value)
                return;
            _productID = value;
            RaisePropertyChanged(ProductIDPropertyName);
        }
    }

    public const string ProductNamePropertyName
        = "ProductName";
    private string _productName;
    public string ProductName
    {
        get { return _productName; }
        set
        {
            if (_productName == value)
                return;
```

```
                _productName = value;
                RaisePropertyChanged(ProductNamePropertyName);
            }
        }
    }
```

3. Add a class called `OrderDetails` to `Northwind.Model` and update it as shown in the following code:

```
public class OrderDetail : ModelBase
{
    public const string ProductPropertyName = "Product";
    private Product _product;
    public Product Product
    {
        get { return _product; }
        set
        {
            if (_product == value)
                return;
            _product = value;
            RaisePropertyChanged(ProductPropertyName);
        }
    }

    public const string QuanityPropertyName = "Quanity";
    private int _quanity;
    public int Quanity
    {
        get { return _quanity; }
        set
        {
            if (_quanity == value)
                return;
            _quanity = value;
            RaisePropertyChanged(QuanityPropertyName);
        }
    }

    public const string UnitPricePropertyName = "UnitPrice";
    private decimal _unitPrice;
    public decimal UnitPrice
    {
        get { return _unitPrice; }
        set
```

```
            {
                if (_unitPrice == value)
                    return;
                _unitPrice = value;
                RaisePropertyChanged(UnitPricePropertyName);
            }
        }
    }
```

4. Add a class called `Order` to `Northwind.Model` and update it as follows:

```
public class Order : ModelBase
{
    public const string OrderIDPropertyName = "OrderID";
    private int _orderID;
    public int OrderID
    {
        get { return _orderID; }
        set
        {
            if (_orderID == value)
                return;
            _orderID = value;
            RaisePropertyChanged(OrderIDPropertyName);
        }
    }

    public const string OrderDatePropertyName = "OrderDate";
    private DateTime? _orderDate;
    public DateTime? OrderDate
    {
        get { return _orderDate; }
        set
        {
            if (_orderDate == value)
                return;
            _orderDate = value;
            RaisePropertyChanged(OrderDatePropertyName);
        }
    }

    public const string ShippedDatePropertyName = "ShippedDate
    private DateTime? _shippedDate;
    public DateTime? ShippedDate
    {
```

```
        get { return _shippedDate; }
        set
        {
            if (_shippedDate == value)
                return;
            _shippedDate = value;
            RaisePropertyChanged(ShippedDatePropertyName);
        }
    }

    public const string FreightPropertyName = "Freight";
    private decimal? _freight;
    public decimal? Freight
    {
        get { return _freight; }
        set
        {
            if (_freight == value)
                return;
            _freight = value;
            RaisePropertyChanged(FreightPropertyName);
        }
    }

    public IEnumerable<OrderDetail> OrderDetails { get; set; }
}
```

5. Open `Model.Customer` and update it by adding the property shown in the following code:

```
    private ObservableCollection<Order> _orders;
    public ObservableCollection<Order> Orders
    {
        get { return _orders; }
        set
        {
            if (_orders == value)
                return;
            _orders = value;
            RaisePropertyChanged("Orders");
        }
    }
```

6. Update `CustomerTranslator.cs` as shown in the following code. Here we are simply copying the data across from our DTOs to our Model.

> There are tools out there to make implementing the entity translation pattern easier. On my current project, we are using `AutoMapper` which will automatically maps properties with the same names (`https://github.com/AutoMapper/AutoMapper`).

```
public Model.Customer UpdateModel(Model.Customer model,
                                  CustomerService.
                                      Customer dto)
{
    if (model.CustomerID != dto.CustomerID)
        model.CustomerID = dto.CustomerID;
    if (model.CompanyName != dto.CompanyName)
        model.CompanyName = dto.CompanyName;
    if (model.ContactName != dto.ContactName)
        model.ContactName = dto.ContactName;
    if (model.Address != dto.Address)
        model.Address = dto.Address;
    if (model.City != dto.City)
        model.City = dto.City;
    if (model.Region != dto.Region)
        model.Region = dto.Region;
    if (model.Country != dto.Country)
        model.Country = dto.Country;
    if (model.PostalCode != dto.PostalCode)
        model.PostalCode = dto.PostalCode;
    if (model.Phone != dto.Phone)
        model.Phone = dto.Phone;
    if (dto.Orders != null)
    {
        model.Orders = GetOrdersFromDto(dto);
    }

    return model;
}

private static ObservableCollection<Order>
    GetOrdersFromDto(Customer dto)
{
    IEnumerable<Order> orders
        = dto.Orders.Select(o => new Model.Order
```

```
            {
                OrderID = o.OrderID,
                OrderDate = o.OrderDate,
                OrderDetails = GetOrderDetailsFromDto(o),
                Freight = o.Freight,
                ShippedDate = o.ShippedDate
            });
        return new ObservableCollection<Order>(orders);
    }

    private static IEnumerable<Model.OrderDetail>
        GetOrderDetailsFromDto(
        CustomerService.Order order)
    {
        return order.OrderDetails.Select(
            od => new Model.OrderDetail
            {
                Product
                    = GetProductFromDto(od),
                Quantity = od.Quantity,
                UnitPrice = od.UnitPrice
            });
    }

    private static Product GetProductFromDto(
        OrderDetail od)
    {
        return new Product
                   {
                       ProductID = od.Product.ProductID,
                       ProductName = od.Product.ProductName
                   };
    }
```

Now we are ready to consume our new data in the UI.

Presentation layer

We've got two updates that we need to make now. First we need to get our View Models updated to support the new functionality using the HVM approach and next we need to wire up those View Models into our views.

View Models

Open `Northwind.ViewModel` and follow these steps:

1. Add a class called `OrderViewModel` and update it as shown in the following code:

```
using System.ComponentModel;
using System.Linq;
using GalaSoft.MvvmLight;
using Northwind.Model;

namespace Northwind.ViewModel
{
    public class OrderViewModel : ViewModelBase
    {
        public const string ModelPropertyName = "Model";
        private Order _model;
        public Order Model
        {
            get { return _model; }
            set
            {
                if (_model == value)
                    return;
                _model = value;
                RaisePropertyChanged(ModelPropertyName);
                RaisePropertyChanged(TotalPropertyName);
            }
        }

        public const string TotalPropertyName = "Total";
        public decimal Total
        {
            get
            {
                return _model.OrderDetails.Sum(
                    o => o.Quantity + o.UnitPrice);
            }
        }

        public OrderViewModel(Order model)
        {
            _model = model;
            SubscribeToOrderDetailsChanged(_model);
```

```
        }

        private void SubscribeToOrderDetailsChanged(
            Order order)
        {
            order.PropertyChanged += Order_PropertyChanged;
            foreach(var orderDetail in order.OrderDetails)
            {
                orderDetail.PropertyChanged
                    += Order_PropertyChanged;
            }
        }

        private void UnSubscribeToOrderDetailsChanged(
            Order order)
        {
            order.PropertyChanged -= Order_PropertyChanged;
            foreach (var orderDetail in order.OrderDetails)
            {
                orderDetail.PropertyChanged
                    -= Order_PropertyChanged;
            }
        }

        void Order_PropertyChanged(
            object sender, PropertyChangedEventArgs e)
        {
            switch (e.PropertyName)
            {
                case Order.FreightPropertyName:
                case OrderDetail.QuantityPropertyName:
                case OrderDetail.UnitPricePropertyName:
                    RaisePropertyChanged(TotalPropertyName);
                    break;
            }
        }

        public override void Cleanup()
        {
            UnSubscribeToOrderDetailsChanged(Model);
            base.Cleanup();
        }
    }
}
```

What we've done here is use model aggregation to expose our model via the `OrderViewModel.Model` property. However, our model doesn't contain a property for `Total`, which we need for display in the UI so we've added this calculated property as `OrderViewModel.Total`. We then take `Model.Order` as a constructor argument and we wire up property changed notifications. This is so that we can raise a property change notification for `OrderViewModel.Total` when properties on `Model.Order` change allowing us to have our UI properly updated. We also subclassed `MVVMLight.ViewModelBase` and this allows us to easily unsubscribe from the notification updates in `MVVMLight.ViewModelBase.Cleanup` overridden method preventing us from leaking. Note that it's debatable whether `Total` belongs to the entity or the View Model and we will revisit this approach later in this chapter. For now, it's providing us a great way of demonstrating using View Models for managing view state and view logic but later we will look at what happens if it becomes session state and session logic.

2. Add a class called `OrdersViewModel.cs` and update it as shown in the following code. This View Model takes a collection of `Model.Order` objects as a constructor argument and then exposes them as a collection of `OrderViewModel` instances for consumption by the view.

```
using System.Collections.Generic;
using System.Collections.ObjectModel;
using System.Linq;
using Northwind.Model;

namespace Northwind.ViewModel
{
    public class OrdersViewModel : ViewModelBase
    {
        public ObservableCollection<OrderViewModel>
            Orders { get; set; }

        public OrdersViewModel(
            IEnumerable<Model.Order> orders)
        {
            Orders = new ObservableCollection<OrderViewModel>(
                orders.Select(o => new OrderViewModel(o)));
        }
    }
}
```

3. Open `CustomerDetailsViewModel.cs` and add the following property to it. This property is lazy instantiated and when its getter is called it will create a new `OrderViewModel`, if one hasn't been created, and pass it to `Customers.Orders`.

```
private OrdersViewModel _orders;
public OrdersViewModel Orders
{
    get
    {
        if (Customer == null)
            return null;
        return _orders ?? (_orders
            = new OrdersViewModel(Customer.Orders));
    }
}
```

You should now be able to see how the HVM approach works as our `CustomerDetailsViewModel` contains `OrdersViewModel` which in turn contains a collection of `OrderViewModels`. Because of the Content Model in WPF and Silverlight, we can now easily map views to any of these new View Models to get the results we desire.

Views

Now we will update our Views to consume the new View Models by following these steps in the `Northwind.WPF.UI` project:

1. Add a new WPF user control called `Orders.xaml` and update it as shown here. Here we have created a simple view that binds a `DataGrid` to a collection of orders. Most of the markup is for controlling the look and layout of the data.

```
<UserControl.Resources>
    <Style TargetType="{x:Type TextBlock}" x:Key="rightAlign" >
        <Setter Property="TextAlignment" Value="Right" />
    </Style>
    <Style TargetType="{x:Type TextBlock}" x:Key="leftAlign" >
        <Setter Property="TextAlignment" Value="Left" />
    </Style>
</UserControl.Resources>
<Grid>
    <DataGrid ItemsSource="{Binding Orders}"
              AutoGenerateColumns="False">
        <DataGrid.Columns>
            <DataGridTextColumn Header="ID"
```

```
                                      Binding="{Binding Model.OrderID}"
                                      ElementStyle
                                          ="{StaticResource leftAlign}"
/>
                    <DataGridTextColumn Header="Order Date"
                                      Binding="{Binding Model.OrderDate,
                                          StringFormat=d}"
                                      ElementStyle
                                          ="{StaticResource leftAlign}"
/>
                    <DataGridTextColumn Header="Shipped Date"
                                      Binding="{Binding Model.
ShippedDate,
                                          StringFormat=d}"
                                      ElementStyle
                                          ="{StaticResource leftAlign}"
/>
                    <DataGridTextColumn Header="Total"
                                      Binding="{Binding Total,
                                          StringFormat=c}"
                                      ElementStyle
                                          ="{StaticResource rightAlign}"
/>
            </DataGrid.Columns>
        </DataGrid>
</Grid>
```

2. Open `MainSkin.xaml` and add `DataTemplate` as shown in the following code. This `DataTemplate` will map an `OrdersViewModel` instance to an `Orders` view and will set `Orders.DataContext` to the `OrdersViewModel` instance.

```
<DataTemplate DataType="{x:Type ViewModel:OrdersViewModel}">
    <WPF:Orders/>
</DataTemplate>
```

3. Open `CustomerDetails.xaml` and update it by adding the following code to the bottom of the outermost `Grid`. Here we have placed `ContentControl` on the page and bound it's content to `Orders`, which will bind to `CustomerDetailsViewModel.Orders` resulting in our `DataTemplate` being used to map the `Orders` view to our nested `OrdersViewModel`.

```
    <GroupBox Header="Orders"
              Grid.Row="2">
        <ContentControl Content="{Binding Orders}" />
    </GroupBox>
```

4. Build and run `Northwind` and verify that you get `Orders` back when opening any customer's details.

Take aways

Now we've seen how we can add functionality to our WPF and Silverlight applications using a Hierarchical View Model approach. This is a very powerful and useful technique to learn. Next, we will look at how we can take advantage of this technique to easily support tabbed layouts that support loading different views.

Viewing order details

The next thing we are going to do is add the ability to open an order's details in a new tabbed window and add the ability to close tabs as shown in the following screenshot:

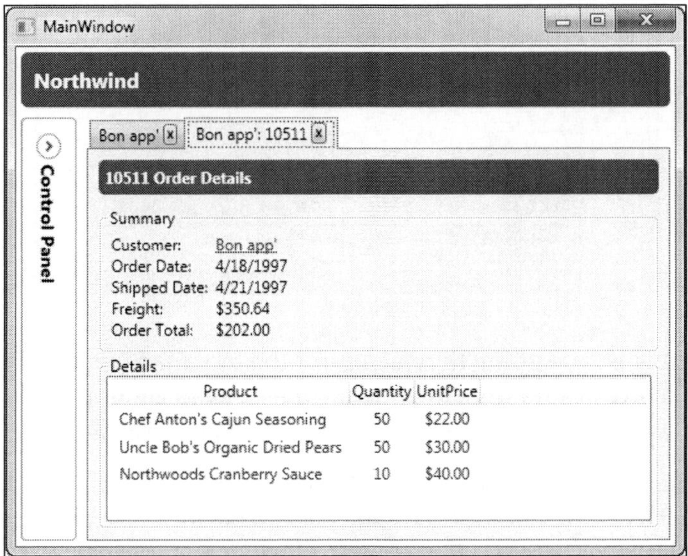

The **Order Details** view will display all the order line items along with details about the order such as the **Shipped Date**, **Freight**, and so on. It allows the user to click on a customer link that will open the that customer's **Customer Details** view.

We are going to take advantage of HVM to make this easy to accomplish. I have seen people go to great lengths to accomplish tabs in WPF and Silverlight. However, using an MVVM design with HVM makes tabbed interfaces very easy to implement.

ToolManager

Currently, our `MainWindowViewModel` owns the responsibility for opening tools but under our new design we want to be able to open an order's details from the order details row as shown in the following screenshot:

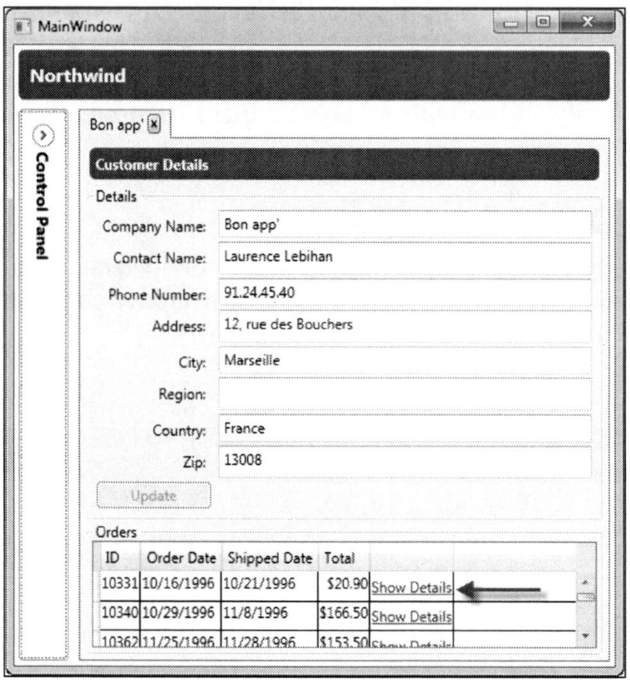

To accomplish this we are going to refactor out the tool management behind a new `IToolManager` interface and use dependency injection to get implementations of `IToolManager` to the places it's needed by following these steps:

1. Add a new `Interface` to `Northwind.ViewModel` called `IToolManager` and update it as shown in the following code. This interface exposes `Tools`: an `ObservableCollection` that contains the current tools, `OpenTool`: a method that takes two functions, `predicate` that will be used as a predicate to find the desired tool if it exists and `toolFactory` that will be called if the tool isn't found and needs to be created, and `CloseTool`: a method for closing a tool if it is opened.

```
public interface IToolManager
{
    ObservableCollection<ToolViewModel>
        Tools { get; set; }
    void OpenTool<T>(Func<T, bool> predicate,
```

```
                      Func<T> toolFactory)
            where T : ToolViewModel;
        void CloseTool(ToolViewModel tool);
    }
```

To keep things really solid, we'd want to extract an interface from `ToolViewModel` to use in the `IToolManager` interface but we skipped that step here.

2. Add a class to `Northwind.ViewModel` called `ToolManager` and update it as shown in the following code. Here we are implementing `IToolManager` by simply manipulating `ObservableCollection` of `ToolViewModel` (`Tools`) and adding `ICollectionView` which is initialized to `Tool/Tools`, default collection view in the constructor. The most complex part is the `OpenTool` method which will first attempt to find the requested tool in the `Tools` collection using `Predicate`. If this fails it will then use `toolFactory` to create an instance of the desired tool and then it will call `SetCurrentTool` with the tool to make it an active tool.

```
public class ToolManager : IToolManager
{
        private readonly ICollectionView _toolCollectionView;
        public ObservableCollection<ToolViewModel>
            Tools { get; set; }

        public ToolManager()
        {
            Tools = new ObservableCollection<ToolViewModel>();
            _toolCollectionView =
                CollectionViewSource.GetDefaultView(Tools);
        }

        public void OpenTool<T>(Func<T, bool> predicate,
            Func<T> toolFactory)
                where T : ToolViewModel
        {
            var tool = Tools
                .Where(t => t.GetType() == typeof (T))
                .FirstOrDefault(t => predicate.Invoke((T)t));
            if (tool == null)
            {
                tool = toolFactory.Invoke();
                Tools.Add(tool);
            }
```

```
            SetCurrentTool(tool);
        }

        public void CloseTool(ToolViewModel tool)
        {
            Tools.Remove(tool);
        }

        private void SetCurrentTool(ToolViewModel currentTool)
        {
            if (_toolCollectionView.MoveCurrentTo(currentTool)
                != true)
            {
                throw new InvalidOperationException(
                    "Could not find the current tool.");
            }
        }
}
```

3. Open `MainWindowViewModel`, delete the `SetCurrentTool` and `GetCustomerDetailsTool` methods, and then update it as shown in the following code. Note that only modified and new code is shown here. This code simply updates `MainWindowViewModel` so that it takes `IToolManager` via constructor injection and then delegates tool management to that interface.

```
private readonly IToolManager _toolManager;

public ObservableCollection<ToolViewModel> Tools
    { get { return _toolManager.Tools; } }

public MainWindowViewModel(
    IUIDataProvider dataProvider,
    IToolManager toolManager)
{
    _dataProvider = dataProvider;
    _toolManager = toolManager  ;
}

public void ShowCustomerDetails()
{
    if (!IsCustomerSelected())
        throw new InvalidOperationException(
            "Unable to show customer because no "
            + "customer is selected.");
```

```
    _toolManager.OpenTool(
        c => c.Customer.CustomerID
            == SelectedCustomerID,
        () => new CustomerDetailsViewModel(
                    _dataProvider, SelectedCustomerID,
                    _toolManger));
}

public bool IsCustomerSelected()
{
    return !string.IsNullOrEmpty(SelectedCustomerID);
}
```

4. Next open `ViewModelLocator` and update it as shown in the following code. This will create an instance of `ToolManager` and inject it into our `MainWindowViewModel` via constructor injection.

```
public static MainWindowViewModel
    MainWindowViewModelStatic
{
    get
    {
        return _mainWindowViewModel ??
               (_mainWindowViewModel =
                new MainWindowViewModel(
                    new UIDataProvider(
                        new CustomerServiceClient()),
                    new ToolManager()));
    }
}
```

5. Open `ToolViewModel` and update it as follows. This will add the ability to close a tool. This code exposes `CloseCommand`, which is a relay command that will close a tool when it's executed by calling the `Close` method which delegates to the `_toolManager`.

```
public class ToolViewModel : ViewModelBase
{
    private readonly IToolManager _toolManager;
    public string DisplayName { get; set; }

    private ICommand _closeCommand = null;

    public ICommand CloseCommand
    {
        get
```

```
            {
                return _closeCommand ??
                       (_closeCommand =
                        new RelayCommand(Close));
            }
        }

        public ToolViewModel(IToolManager toolManager)
        {
            _toolManager = toolManager;
        }

        protected void Close()
        {
            _toolManager.CloseTool(this);
        }
    }
```

6. Update `CustomerDetailsViewModel` as follows. This refactoring allows `CustomerDetailsViewModel` to take `IToolManager` via constructor injection and passes it to new `OrderDetailsViewModel` instances again via constructor injection. Note that only new and changed code is shown.

```
    private readonly IToolManager _toolManager;

    private OrdersViewModel _orders;
    public OrdersViewModel Orders
    {
        get
        {
            if (Customer == null)
                return null;
            return _orders ?? (_orders
                = new OrdersViewModel(
                    Customer, _toolManager));
        }
    }

    public CustomerDetailsViewModel(
        IUIDataProvider dataProvider,
        string customerID,
        IToolManager toolManager = null)
        : base(toolManager)
    {
        _dataProvider = dataProvider;
```

```
        Customer = _dataProvider.GetCustomer(customerID);
        Customer.PropertyChanged
            += Customer_PropertyChanged;
        DisplayName = Customer.CompanyName;
    }
```

7. Next open `OrdersViewModel` and update it as shown in the following code. Here again the update is a simple matter of passing `IToolManager` to new instances of `OrderViewModel`.

```
public ObservableCollection<OrderViewModel>
    Orders { get; set; }

public OrdersViewModel(
    Model.Customer model,
    IToolManager toolManager)
{
    Orders = new ObservableCollection<OrderViewModel>(
        model.Orders.Select(o =>
            new OrderViewModel(o, model, _toolManager)));
}
```

8. Now open `OrderViewModel` and update it as shown in the following code. All we are doing here is holding a reference to `IToolManager` and `Customer` so that we can use it when we add the ability to open an order's details from an order line item in the grid on a **Customer Details** tab, which we will implement shortly.

```
private readonly Customer _customer;
private readonly IToolManager _toolManager;

public OrderViewModel(Order order,
    Customer customer, IToolManager toolManager)
{
    _customer = customer;
    _order = order;
    _toolManager = toolManager;
    SubscribeToOrderDetailsChanged(_order);
}
```

9. Open `MainWindow` and update it as shown in the following code. Here we have updated the tab's `DataTemplate` to add a button that can be used to close the window and bound that button's command to `ToolViewModel.CloseCommand` that was created previously.

```
<TabControl ItemsSource="{Binding Tools}"
            Margin="4"
```

```
                Grid.Row="0"
                Grid.Column="1"
                IsSynchronizedWithCurrentItem="True">
        <TabControl.ItemTemplate>
            <DataTemplate>
            <DockPanel>
                <Button
                    Command="{Binding Path=CloseCommand}"
                    Content="X"
                    DockPanel.Dock="Right"
                    FontSize="8"
                    Focusable="False"
                    FontWeight="Bold"
                    Margin="3, 0, 0, 0"/>
                   <ContentPresenter
                       Content="{Binding DisplayName}" />
                </DockPanel>
            </DataTemplate>
        </TabControl.ItemTemplate>
    </TabControl>
```

10. At this point, you should be comfortable with unit testing as it relates to this style of architecture so we will no longer be updating unit tests. If you are following along, several tests will need updating at this point. Feel free to update the tests as an exercise or delete them based on your preference.
11. Build and launch the application and verify that it works as it did before with the additional feature of being able to close tabs by clicking on the **x** button located on the tab as shown at the beginning of this section.

We are now ready to add the ability to open order details using the new `IToolManager` infrastructure. However, you may have noticed that a lot of code we added was simply to allow us to pass the `IToolManager` instance from one place to the next. Many classes that don't need to use `IToolManager` still have to deal with the interface causing the **greedy constructor** code smell.

> Greedy constructor is the term for when a constructor takes more dependencies than are needed by the class. It can also be taking dependencies as constructor arguments that aren't cross-cutting concerns for that class but following the Single Responsibility principle would limit this type of the smell.

We've made our code more extensible and testable by using this approach but it also feels more complex than it needs to be in some places. Simplifying this situation is what we will look at next.

Inversion of Control frameworks

To help avoid the greedy constructor smell and to make using dependency injection easier, many Inversion of Control frameworks (IoC) have emerged. An IoC framework generally provides an infrastructure tool commonly referred to as a container that can take the place of the `new` operator in your code. Unlike the `new` operator, an IoC container is configured to know how to create objects using non-default constructors and the IoC container will take care of instantiating the dependencies that the constructor needs (and the dependencies of the dependencies and so on).

> There are an awful lot of details and things to learn when using IoC containers and if you are not well versed in this area, I'd encourage you to take a look at the book *Dependency Injection in .Net* by *Mark Seemann*.

IoC designs

There are a few principles and best practices to keep in mind when using IoC containers and they address design choices that must be made when using IoC containers that include:

1. Where and how do you create the IoC container?
2. How do you make the IoC functionality available to the components that need it?
3. What components should have direct access to the IoC container?

The way IoC containers usually work is by following this heuristic.

1. Configure IoC container to know about the classes that it will need to create instances of and to know about the dependencies of those classes.
2. Once configured, the code calls a generic factory method such as `Get<MyType>()` on the container to create an instance with its dependencies populated.

Without any guidance or best practices these frameworks can lead to designs that don't capture all of the benefits of Dependency Injection and Dependency Inversion.

Service Locator anti-pattern

Since the IoC containers work in the way described previously, it's common to take an approach similar to the following approach:

1. Create your IoC as close to application start up as possible.
2. Create a wrapper interface (or use an existing interface that is a part of the IoC implementation) for the IoC container and register it with the IoC container so that any class that needs to create types can have the container interface injected as a dependency. The container interface being used in this way is known as **Service Locator**.
3. Create types using the `IoC.Get<MyType>()` method and for any class that needs to create types you simply specify your IoC's interface as a constructor argument allowing for the container to be injected.

   This approach is known as using the Service Locator pattern. Mark Seemann has called this approach a dependency injection anti-pattern [Seemann], and I agree. In our application this pattern would change this code:

```
public CustomerDetailsViewModel(
    IUIDataProvider dataProvider,
    string customerID,
    IToolManager toolManager,
    IOrdersViewModelFactory ordersViewModelFactory)
    : base(IToolManager)
{
    _dataProvider = dataProvider;
    _ordersViewModelFactory = ordersViewModelFactory;
    Customer = _dataProvider.GetCustomer(customerID);
    Customer.PropertyChanged
        += Customer_PropertyChanged;
    DisplayName = Customer.CompanyName;
}
```

   To be like this code:

```
public CustomerDetailsViewModel(
    string customerID,
    IContainer container)
    : base(IContainer)
{
    _dataProvider = container.Get<IUIDataProvider>();
    _ordersViewModelFactory
        = container.Get<IOrdersViewModelFactory>();
    Customer = _dataProvider.GetCustomer(customerID);
```

```
            Customer.PropertyChanged
                += Customer_PropertyChanged;
            DisplayName = Customer.CompanyName;
        }
```

What we have done here is taken an interface to our container as a constructor argument and been able to eliminate all of our other dependencies. Now as long as we instantiate this class with a properly configured container, our object instance will get passed a container reference. This allows for easily creating the needed types.

At this point, you might be wondering why this is an anti-pattern? The code is still testable and dependencies are replaceable at runtime so it still makes for extensible code. The reason that this approach is an anti-pattern is because dependency injection is a tool that enables a more solid design. The D in solid stands for **Dependency Inversion**, which states that the responsibility for creating dependencies should belong to the component that creates the object, not to the object itself. The reason is that it not only allows your design to be extensible but also makes it clear what dependencies are needed where. It's considered a good practice to have a constructor clearly define the dependencies that are needed by that class. If your class only takes an `IContainer` interface as a constructor argument, then consuming classes have no idea what dependencies are needed in the IoC container when consuming that component and problems can pop up in mysterious ways at runtime. This problem is magnified when working on larger teams and consuming component created by others. If you are given a task that involves consuming a component built by other engineers who may have already left the project, you will be more productive if those components have constructors letting you know what they need at compile time, instead of taking `IContainer` and then blowing up at runtime when they aren't able to resolve what is needed.

Earlier in this book, we saw Service Locator also being used to describe View Model Locator that we used to create our Main Window View Model. The View Model Locator, as we implemented, doesn't exhibit the same issues as the Service Locator anti-pattern as it only creates one type and so the dependency that is being used is clearly defined. In that sense, it's actually more of an abstract factory than a Service Locator. However, if I had implemented the View Model Locator in the same way that it is done automatically by MVVM Light, which is why I kept the name Locator, so that it could create more than one View Model then we would be introducing the same anti-pattern. We will see shortly the best practice approach I recommend for avoiding the Service Locator anti-pattern when implementing MVVM.

IoC best practices

Now let's look at the best practices that we should follow which address the needs introduced previously in the *IoC designs* introduction. We will start by introducing a concept called **Composite Root** [Seemann]. Mark Seemann defines Composite Root as:

> *A Composition Root is a (preferably) unique location in an application where modules are composed together.*

And Mark recommends the following:

- Only the Composite Root and abstract factories can access to the IoC container
- The Composite Root is located as close as possible to the application's entry point
- A class should only take dependencies that represent cross-cutting concerns for that class as constructor arguments and not take any dependencies that are going to be passed through to its dependencies
- Objects that require runtime values in order to be created should be created using abstract factories that can be injected where they are needed

Abstract factory is a creational pattern from the Gang of Four patterns that allows for creating a specific type.

Next we will look at an example of following these best practices in a WPF application.

Adding an IoC container to Northwind

Let's take a look at updating our code to use StructureMap as our IoC container while following the previously mentioned best practices. Let's keep in mind that our motivation here is to get `IToolManager` to the classes that need it without introducing the greedy constructor smell and to remove the need for using `new` for creating dependencies.

The first thing we need to do is to introduce a Composite Root to our architecture.

Remember that the Composite Root is a location as close as possible to our application's startup where we can use our IoC container to instantiate our application's object graph.

We are going to introduce a new component called a `BootStrapper` as our composite root and have that component own the responsibility of composing our application graph using StructureMap. To do this follow these steps:

1. The first thing we need to do is introduce StructureMap to our application. To accomplish this either use nuget or download the StructureMap DLLs and put them in the application's `Lib` directory.
2. Delete `ViewModelLocator.cs` from `Northwind.ViewModel`.
3. Add a reference to `StructureMap.dll` in `Northwind.WPF.UI`.
4. Add `BootStrapper.cs` to `Northwind.WPF.UI` and update it as shown in the following code. You will also need to bring in the `StructureMap` namespace. We will look more closely at the following code:

```
public class BootStrapper
{
    public MainWindowViewModel MainWindowViewModel
    {
        get
        {
            return ObjectFactory
                .GetInstance<MainWindowViewModel>();
        }
    }

    public BootStrapper()
    {
        ObjectFactory.Initialize(
            o => o.Scan(
                a =>
                {
                    a.WithDefaultConventions();
                    a.AssembliesFromApplicationBaseDirectory(
                        d => d.FullName
                            .StartsWith("Northwind"));
                    a.LookForRegistries();
                }));
    }
}
```

5. Update `App.xaml` as follows:

```
<Application.Resources>
    <ObjectDataProvider x:Key="BootStrapper"
                        ObjectType="src:BootStrapper" />
</Application.Resources>
```

6. Update `MainWindow.xaml` as shown in the following code:

```
<Window x:Class="Northwind.UI.WPF.MainWindow"
        xmlns="http://schemas.microsoft.com/winfx/2006/xaml/
presentation"
        xmlns:x="http://schemas.microsoft.com/winfx/2006/xaml"
        Title="MainWindow" MinHeight="350" MinWidth="525"
        xmlns:Command="clr-
            namespace:GalaSoft.MvvmLight.Command;
            assembly=GalaSoft.MvvmLight.Extras.WPF4"
        xmlns:i="clr-namespace:System.Windows.Interactivity;
            assembly=System.Windows.Interactivity"
        DataContext="{Binding Path=MainWindowViewModel,
            Source={StaticResource BootStrapper}}">
```

What we have done here is essentially to replace our `ViewModelLocator` with our `BootStrapper`. There are two parts to this code. In our constructor, we are configuring our IoC container using StructureMap's `scan` functionality to scan all assemblies that start with **Northwind** and to use default conventions when mapping types to interfaces. This will cause StructureMap to map classes to interfaces that share the same name. So `ICustomType` would map to `CustomType`. And then we've also configured it to look for registries.

> For more information on StructureMap see its online documentation.

Registries, as we will see shortly, are classes that provide explicit configurations for our container. In our case, we are doing this so that we can configure some of our types as **Singletons**.

> Singleton is a Gang of Four design pattern that allows for creating types that can only have a single instance created [GOF]. By properly configuring StructureMap, we are able to delegate that responsibility to our IoC container.

This might seem like pointless academic exercise but upon looking closer we can see that there is a significant difference in what our `BootStrapper` is responsible for. The first obvious difference is that our `BootStrapper` is using an IoC container but we could have updated our `ViewModelLocator` to do the same and saved some effort. However, in a real application you will most likely need to create infrastructure components that aren't View Models and aren't used by View Models. While `ViewModelLocator` was responsible for creating View Models only, a `BootsStrapper` is responsible for initializing all the resources that our application needs. BootStrapper is responsible for application composition while ViewModelLocator is only responsible for creating View Models. Additionally, if we want to avoid the Service Locator anti-pattern then our ViewModelLocator is also extremely limited in what it can do. For these reasons, this refactoring will improve our architecture and make it better communicate its intended use.

We still haven't addressed getting our IToolManager interface to the components that need it deep in the object graph or eliminated the use of new. Let's take a look at how we can accomplish this now by looking at MainWindowViewModel.ShowCustomerDetails.

```
public void ShowCustomerDetails()
{
    if (!IsCustomerSelected())
        throw new InvalidOperationException(
            "Unable to show customer because no "
            + "customer is selected.");

    _toolManager.OpenTool(
        c => c.Customer.CustomerID
            == SelectedCustomerID,
        () => new CustomerDetailsViewModel(
                        _dataProvider, SelectedCustomerID,
                        _toolManger));
}
```

As you can see, this method is using a lambda expression to provide a factory that will use new to create a CustomerDetailsViewModel instance. This lambda will pass its IToolManager instance via a closure.

Next, we will take a look at the following CustomerDetailsViewModel.Order code and we will find that the IToolManager instance is only used to construct OrdersViewModel in the Orders property and never directly used by CustomerDetialsViewModel:

```
public OrdersViewModel Orders
{
    get
    {
        if (Customer == null)
            return null;
        return _orders ?? (_orders
            = new OrdersViewModel(
                Customer,
                _toolManager));
    }
}
```

This clearly violates our Dependency Injection best practices as it's a greedy constructor smell, so let's review our available options to see how we can fix this situation. The best practice listed here is our answer.

> Objects that require runtime values in order to be created should be created using abstract factory that can be injected where they are needed.

So now let's update our code so that we use an abstract factory to construct `CustomerDetailsViewModel` instead of using new by following these steps:

1. Add an interface called `ICustomerDetailsViewModelFactory.cs` to `Northwind.ViewModel` and update it as shown in the following code:

   ```
   public interface ICustomerDetailsViewModelFactory
   {
       CustomerDetailsViewModel CreateInstance(
           string customerID);
   }
   ```

2. Add a reference to `StructureMap.dll` in `Northwind.ViewModel`.
3. Add a class called `CustomerDetailsViewModelFactory.cs` to `Northwind.ViewModel` and update it as shown in the following code. Here we are taking `IContainer` as a constructor argument allowing `StructureMap` to inject a reference to its container. We then use this container reference to create an instance of `CustomerDetailsViewModel` passing it the runtime values needed using the `With` and `EqualTo` methods (see StructureMap online documentation for full details).

> As you may recall, earlier in this chapter we explained that this approach allows us to avoid the problems of the Service Locator anti-pattern as we are using abstract factory to ensure that our types have their dependencies properly inverted. When a class takes a dependency on `ICustomerDetailsViewModelFactory` we are clearly defining the dependencies needed to be available at runtime. If we instead took an `IContainer` and created the instances we needed internal to our class we would no longer be advertising our dependencies to consumers.

```
public class CustomerDetailsViewModelFactory
    : ICustomerDetailsViewModelFactory
{
    private readonly IContainer _container;

    public CustomerDetailsViewModelFactory(
```

```
        IContainer container)
    {
        _container = container;
    }

    public CustomerDetailsViewModel CreateInstance(
        string customerID)
    {
        return _container
            .With("customerID")
            .EqualTo(customerID)
            .GetInstance<CustomerDetailsViewModel>();
    }
}
```

4. Open `IToolManager` and update it as shown in the following code. Here we've removed the generic `OpenTool` method and replaced it with `OpenCustomerDetails`. The reasons we've done this is because knowing how to create `CustomerDetailsViewModel` shouldn't be the responsibility of `MainWindowViewModel`. It makes more sense to have those details hidden behind `IToolManager` (as `ToolManager` becomes more complex it might make sense to have a separate `ToolFactory` but that's something that we won't explore in this book).

```
public interface IToolManager
{
    ObservableCollection<ToolViewModel>
        Tools { get; set; }
    void OpenCustomerDetails(string customerId);
    void CloseTool(ToolViewModel tool);
}
```

5. Open `ToolManager` and update it as follows:

```
    private readonly ICustomerDetailsViewModelFactory
        _customerDetailsFactory;
    private readonly ICollectionView _toolCollectionView;
    public ObservableCollection<ToolViewModel>
        Tools { get; set; }

    public ToolManager(
        ICustomerDetailsViewModelFactory
            customerDetailsFactory)
    {
        _customerDetailsFactory = customerDetailsFactory;
        Tools = new ObservableCollection<ToolViewModel>();
```

```
            _toolCollectionView =
                CollectionViewSource.GetDefaultView(Tools);
        }

        public void OpenCustomerDetails(string customerId)
        {
            OpenTool(
                c => c.Customer.CustomerID
                    == customerId,
                () => _customerDetailsFactory
                    .CreateInstance(customerId));
        }

    ...

        private void OpenTool<T>(Func<T, bool> predicate,
            Func<T> toolFactory)
                where T : ToolViewModel
        {
            var tool = Tools
                .Where(t => t.GetType() == typeof (T))
                .FirstOrDefault(t => predicate.Invoke((T)t));
            if (tool == null)
            {
                tool = toolFactory.Invoke();
                Tools.Add(tool);
            }
            SetCurrentTool(tool);
        }
    ...
    }
```

6. Update `MainWindowViewModel.ShowCustomerDetails` as shown in the following code:

```
public void ShowCustomerDetails()
{
    if (!IsCustomerSelected())
        throw new InvalidOperationException(
            "Unable to show customer because no "
            + "customer is selected.");

    _toolManager.OpenCustomerDetails(SelectedCustomerID);
}
```

Now instead of having a call to `new` that passes all the dependencies needed to create `CustomerDetailsViewModel`, we simply call `IToolManager.OpenCustomerDetails` and pass the runtime parameter. `SelectedCustomerID`. `ToolManager` takes `ICustomerDetailsViewModelFactory` as a constructor argument and our IoC container will resolve this dependency for us. This allows `ToolManager` to create `CustomerDetailsViewModel` using `ICustomerDetailsViewModelFactory`.

In this context, a runtime parameter is a value that is only available at runtime. Our abstract factory is only necessary because of this runtime parameter as without it we could have let the container build our type for us but because there are values that can't be known until the user makes a selection at runtime our best option becomes using an abstract factory.

Before we move on, let's look a little closer at why we decided to make `IToolManager` responsible for creating the View Models that it is responsible for opening in the preceding step 3.

Consider the View Model Hierarchy that we are trying to build as shown in the following diagram and keep in mind that we are going to add a **Customer** link on the **Order Details** view that will allow for opening that customer's details when viewing an order's detail.

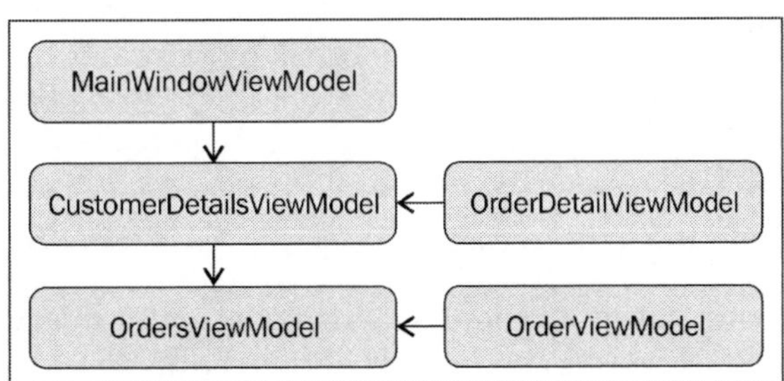

This diagram shows the dependencies we have. Each arrow represents the need for a factory that will create the next View Model in the hierarchy. If our View Models owned the responsibility for providing the factories needed by `IToolManager` to create View Models then `OrderDetailViewModel` would need to have access to `ICustomerDetailsViewModelFactory`. This would result in us having created a circular dependency. If we proceeded down this path we would have reached a point where StructureMap would throw an exception because it can't resolve object graphs that contain circular dependencies.

If you are familiar with IoC containers then you might be aware that there is one other option we could have considered. We could have `OrderDetailViewModel` use property injection for `ICustomerDetailsViewModelFactory` instead of constructor injection.

> property injection is another form of dependency injection where dependencies are injected into public properties on classes. Any IoC container worth its salt will support this form of dependency injection. However, we should try to use it sparingly as it doesn't allow for easily making dependencies needed by a class a requirement in the same way that you can with constructor injection. It could be argued that for concerns that aren't cross cutting for the class, you shouldn't use constructor injection to avoid the greedy constructor smell and should consider property injection in those cases. However, in those cases **method injection** should be considered first as you can better communicate and enforce dependencies with this approach. Method injection is yet another form of dependency injection where you take your dependencies as method parameters, which is what we were doing with `IToolManager.Open` tool previously. Method injection allows for easily guarding against missing dependencies and for clearly defining what dependencies are needed to callers but in our case would have led to a circular dependency.

Using property injection would successfully break our circular dependency and would prevent StructureMap from throwing exceptions. However, this approach just doesn't feel right. Would we really want to alternate between constructor injection and property injection to avoid circular dependencies in our code? That would be confusing and difficult to maintain.

Instead, we changed our design to theone using constructor injection in `IToolManager` for the factories it needs. This allowed our View Models to be no longer concerned with how to create the tools that they wanted to open and broke the circular dependency displayed previously. This approach provides the benefit of breaking our circular dependency concerns and also improving our design from an SRP point of view as now our ViewModels no longer need to be concerned with how to create tools. However, now we are taking dependencies in `IToolManager` that aren't cross-cutting concerns as constructor arguments are making our constructor arguably greedier than they need to be. There are lots of approaches we have considered here and the most important thing for us to get from this is an understanding of our options and what the tradeoffs are so that we can make the choice that best fits our needs.

Now that we are creating `CustomerDetailsViewModel` in an IoC best practices way, we next need clean up the rest of our application. We need to:

1. Refactor `CustomerDetailsViewModel` to not have a greedy constructor smell by removing the `IToolManager` constructor injection.
2. Refactor `CustomerDetailsViewModel` to not `use` the `new` operator to create `OrdersViewModel`.
3. Perform the same refactorings listed previously on `OrdersViewModel`.

Let's refactor our code now to address these needs by updating our `Norhwind.ViewModel` project as follows:

1. Add an interface called `IOrdersViewModelFactory` and update it as shown in the following code:

   ```
   public interface IOrdersViewModelFactory
   {
       OrdersViewModel CreateInstance(Customer customer);
   }
   ```

2. Add a class called `OrdersViewModelFactory` and update it as shown in the following code:

   ```
   public class OrdersViewModelFactory
       : IOrdersViewModelFactory
   {
       private readonly IContainer _container;

       public OrdersViewModelFactory(
           IContainer container)
       {
           _container = container;
       }

       public OrdersViewModel CreateInstance(
           Customer customer)
       {
           return _container
               .With("model")
               .EqualTo(customer)
               .GetInstance<OrdersViewModel>();
       }
   }
   ```

3. Open `CustomerDetailsViewModel` and update it as follows. Note that only the modified parts have been shown for brevity.

```
public class CustomerDetailsViewModel : ToolViewModel
{
    private readonly IUIDataProvider _dataProvider;
    private readonly IOrdersViewModelFactory
        _ordersViewModelFactory;
    private bool _isDirty;

...

    private OrdersViewModel _orders;
    public OrdersViewModel Orders
    {
        get
        {
            if (Customer == null)
                return null;
            return _orders
                ?? (_orders
                    = _ordersViewModelFactory
                    .CreateInstance(Customer));
        }
    }

...

    public CustomerDetailsViewModel(
        IUIDataProvider dataProvider,
        string customerID,
        IToolManager toolManager,
        IOrdersViewModelFactory ordersViewModelFactory)
        : base(toolManager)
    {
        _dataProvider = dataProvider;
        _ordersViewModelFactory = ordersViewModelFactory;
        Customer = _dataProvider.GetCustomer(customerID);
        Customer.PropertyChanged
            += Customer_PropertyChanged;
        DisplayName = Customer.CompanyName;
    }

...

}
```

4. Add an interface called `IOrderViewModelFactory` and update it as shown in the following code:

```
public interface IOrderViewModelFactory
{
    OrderViewModel CreateInstance(Order order,
        Customer customer);
}
```

5. Add a class called `OrderViewModelFactory` and update it as follows:

```
public class OrderViewModelFactory
    : IOrderViewModelFactory
{
    private readonly IContainer _container;

    public OrderViewModelFactory(
        IContainer container)
    {
        _container = container;
    }

    public OrderViewModel CreateInstance(
        Order order, Customer customer)
    {
        return _container
            .With("model")
            .EqualTo(order)
            .With("customer")
            .EqualTo(customer)
            .GetInstance<OrderViewModel>();
    }
}
```

6. Open `OrdersViewModel` and update it as follows:

```
public OrdersViewModel(
    Model.Customer model,
    IOrderViewModelFactory orderViewModelFactory)
{
    Orders = new ObservableCollection<OrderViewModel>(
        model.Orders.Select(o =>
            orderViewModelFactory
                .CreateInstance(o, model)));
}
```

7. Add a class called `RepositoryRegistry` and update it as shown in the following code. This registry will be picked up by the StructureMap scan and will configure `IToolManager` and our abstract factories to all be singletons.

```
using StructureMap.Configuration.DSL;

namespace Northwind.ViewModel
{
    public class RepositoryRegistry : Registry
    {
        public RepositoryRegistry()
        {
            For<IToolManager>()
                .Singleton();
            For<ICustomerDetailsViewModelFactory>()
                .Singleton();
            For<IOrderViewModelFactory>()
                .Singleton();
            For<IOrdersViewModelFactory>()
                .Singleton();
        }
    }
}
```

Now we've created the additional abstract factories we needed to allow us to compose our application in a best-practices way. We no longer need to have `OrdersViewModel` deal with the `IToolManager` interface as `OrderViewModelFactory` is capable of resolving the dependencies needed by `OrderViewModel`. By doing this, we've taken the responsibility for creating the `OrderViewModel` instances away from `OrdersViewModel`, improving our application's adherence to Single Responsibility Principal and avoiding the greedy constructor smell.

One additional thing we did was add a `RepositoryRegistry`, which is a class that contains our IoC container configurations for StructureMap. As we saw earlier, we had configured StructureMap in `BootStrapper` to scan the `Northwind` assemblies and look for registries. This provides us an opportunity to provide non-default configurations and in this case, we use this feature to configure `IToolManager` and our abstract factories to be singletons.

We could build our application at this point but we still have some refactorings to do in order to get our entire application integrated with our IoC container. We are injecting `IUIDataProvider` using our IoC container and this should be a singleton. We also need to configure `ICustomerService` to be a singleton and we need to explicitly configure the mapping between `ICustomerService` and

`CustomerServiceClient` as it doesn't follow StructureMap's naming convention and won't be mapped for us. Let's do these final refactorings by adding a class to `Northwind.Application` called `RepositoryRegistry.cs` and then update it as follows:

```
public class RepositoryRegistry : Registry
{
    public RepositoryRegistry()
    {
        For<IUIDataProvider>()
            .Singleton();
        For<ICustomerService>()
            .Singleton()
            .Use(() => new CustomerServiceClient());
    }
}
```

This code should be fairly self-explanatory. `IUIDataProvider` and `ICustomerService` are both configured as singletons and then `ICustomerService` is explicitly mapped using the `.Use()` overload which takes a lambda for the construction logic.

There is also a generic overload of `.Use<CustomerServiceClient>()` that would allow us to configure our type mapping more concisely. However, this method will use the most greedy constructor by default and for a WCF proxy this would mean that we'd need to explicitly configure the proxy by passing in the channel configurations. However, by using the lambda version of `.Use()` we were able to configure StructureMap to use the default constructor which will pull our WCF configurations out of our `App.config` file automatically for us.

Now if we build our application and run it, we should see the same behavior as before except with all the architectural benefits of using an IoC container and following dependency injection best practices.

Order details

We are now ready to add support for showing order details by following these steps:

1. Open `IToolManager` and update it as shown in the following code:

```
public interface IToolManager
{
    ObservableCollection<ToolViewModel>
        Tools { get; set; }
    void OpenCustomerDetails(string customerId);
```

```
    void OpenOrderDetails(OrderViewModel order);
    void CloseTool(ToolViewModel tool);
}
```

2. Open `ToolManager` and update it as follows. This will add a method that allows for opening **Order Details**.

```
public class ToolManager : IToolManager
{
    private readonly ICustomerDetailsViewModelFactory
        _customerDetailsFactory;
    private readonly IOrderDetailsViewModelFactory
        _orderDetailsFactory;
    private readonly ICollectionView _toolCollectionView;
    public ObservableCollection<ToolViewModel>
        Tools { get; set; }

    public ToolManager(
        ICustomerDetailsViewModelFactory
            customerDetailsFactory,
        IOrderDetailsViewModelFactory
            orderDetailsFactory)
    {
        _customerDetailsFactory = customerDetailsFactory;
        _orderDetailsFactory = orderDetailsFactory;
        Tools = new ObservableCollection<ToolViewModel>();
        _toolCollectionView =
            CollectionViewSource.GetDefaultView(Tools);
    }

...

    public void OpenOrderDetails(OrderViewModel order)
    {
        OpenTool(
            p => p.Order.Model.OrderID
                 == order.Model.OrderID,
            () => _orderDetailsFactory
                     .CreateInstance(order));
    }
...
}
```

3. Add a new interface to `Northwind.ViewModel` called `IOrderDetailsViewModelFactory` and update it as follows:

```
public interface IOrderDetailsViewModelFactory
{
    OrderDetailsViewModel CreateInstance(
        OrderViewModel order);
}
```

4. Add a new class to `Northwind.ViewModel` called `OrderDetailsViewModelFactory` and update it as shown in the following code. This factory is being injected into the preceding `ToolManager` and will allow for creating `OrderDetailsViewModel`.

```
public class OrderDetailsViewModelFactory
    : IOrderDetailsViewModelFactory
{
    private readonly IContainer _container;

    public OrderDetailsViewModelFactory(
        IContainer container)
    {
        _container = container;
    }

    public OrderDetailsViewModel CreateInstance(
        OrderViewModel order)
    {
        return _container
            .With("order")
            .EqualTo(order)
            .GetInstance<OrderDetailsViewModel>();
    }
}
```

5. Add a new class to `Northwind.ViewModel` called `OrderDetailsViewModel` and update it as follows:

```
public class OrderDetailsViewModel : ToolViewModel
{
    private readonly IToolManager _toolManager;
    public ICustomerDetailsViewModelFactory
        CustomerDetailsFactory { get; set; }
    public OrderViewModel Order { get; set; }

    public ICommand ShowCustomerDetailsCommand
    {
```

```
            get
            {
                return new RelayCommand(() =>
                    _toolManager.OpenCustomerDetails(
                    Order.Customer.CustomerID));
            }
        }

        public OrderDetailsViewModel(OrderViewModel order,
            IToolManager toolManager)
            : base(toolManager)
        {
            _toolManager = toolManager;
            Order = order;
            DisplayName = Order.Customer.CompanyName
                + ": " + Order.Model.OrderID.ToString();
        }
    }
```

6. Add `UserControl` to `Northwind.UI.WPF` called `OrderDetails` and update it as shown in the following code. It was a bit difficult to fit this code in the width of the book but we should be able to get the idea of what's being presented here. This will add our `OrderDetails` view that can be displayed.

```
<UserControl x:Class="Northwind.UI.WPF.OrderDetails"
             xmlns="http://schemas.microsoft.com/winfx/2006/xaml/
presentation"
             xmlns:x="http://schemas.microsoft.com/winfx/2006/
xaml"
             xmlns:mc="http://schemas.openxmlformats.org/markup-
compatibility/2006"
             xmlns:d="http://schemas.microsoft.com/expression/
blend/2008"
             mc:Ignorable="d">
    <UserControl.Resources>
        <ResourceDictionary>
            <ResourceDictionary.MergedDictionaries>
                <ResourceDictionary
                    Source="Skins/MainSkin.xaml" />
            </ResourceDictionary.MergedDictionaries>
        </ResourceDictionary>
    </UserControl.Resources>
    <Grid>
        <Grid.RowDefinitions>
            <RowDefinition Height="Auto" />
            <RowDefinition />
```

```
        </Grid.RowDefinitions>
        <Border Padding="5"
                Margin="4" CornerRadius="5"
                Background="{StaticResource mainBlueBrush}">
            <TextBlock Text="{Binding Order.Model.OrderID,
                StringFormat={}{0} Order Details}"
                       Foreground="White"
                       FontWeight="Bold"
                       FontSize="12" />
        </Border>
        <Grid Margin="4" Grid.Row="1">
            <Grid.RowDefinitions>
                <RowDefinition Height="Auto" />
                <RowDefinition Height="*" />
            </Grid.RowDefinitions>
            <GroupBox Header="Summary">
                <Grid Margin="4" Grid.Row="1">
                    <Grid.ColumnDefinitions>
                        <ColumnDefinition Width="Auto" />
                        <ColumnDefinition Width="6" />
                        <ColumnDefinition Width="*" />
                    </Grid.ColumnDefinitions>
                    <Grid.RowDefinitions>
                        <RowDefinition Height="Auto" />
                        <RowDefinition Height="Auto" />
                        <RowDefinition Height="Auto" />
                        <RowDefinition Height="Auto" />
                        <RowDefinition Height="Auto" />
                    </Grid.RowDefinitions>
                    <TextBlock Text="Customer:" />
                    <TextBlock Grid.Column="2">
                        <Hyperlink
                            Command="{Binding
                                ShowCustomerDetailsCommand}">
                            <TextBlock
                                Text="{Binding
                                    Order.Customer
                                        .CompanyName}"/>
                        </Hyperlink>
                    </TextBlock>
                    <TextBlock Text="Order Date:"
                        Grid.Row="1" />
                    <TextBlock
                        Text="{Binding Order.Model.OrderDate,
```

```
                    StringFormat=d}"
                Grid.Row="1"
                Grid.Column="2" />
            <TextBlock Text="Shipped Date:"
                Grid.Row="2"/>
            <TextBlock Text="{Binding
                Order.Model.ShippedDate,
                    StringFormat=d}" Grid.Row="2"
                    Grid.Column="2" />
            <TextBlock Text="Freight:" Grid.Row="3"/>
            <TextBlock
                Text="{Binding Order.Model.Freight,
                    StringFormat=c}" Grid.Row="3"
                    Grid.Column="2" />
            <TextBlock Text="Order Total:"
                Grid.Row="4"/>
            <TextBlock Text="{Binding Order.Total,
                    StringFormat=c}" Grid.Row="4"
                    Grid.Column="2" />
        </Grid>
    </GroupBox>
    <GroupBox Header="Details" Grid.Row="1">
        <ListView ItemsSource="{Binding
            Order.Model.OrderDetails}">
            <ListView.Resources>
                <Style TargetType="ListViewItem">
                    <Setter
                 Property="HorizontalContentAlignment"
                        Value="Stretch" />
                </Style>
            </ListView.Resources>
            <ListView.View>
                <GridView>
                    <GridView.Columns>
                        <GridViewColumn
                            Header="Product">
                            <GridViewColumn
                                    .CellTemplate>
                                <DataTemplate>
                                    <TextBlock
                                  TextAlignment="Left"
                                  Text="{Binding
                                    Product
                                   .ProductName}"/>
```

```
                                    </DataTemplate>
                                </GridViewColumn
                                        .CellTemplate>
                            </GridViewColumn>
                            <GridViewColumn
                                        Header="Quantity">
                                <GridViewColumn
                                        .CellTemplate>
                                    <DataTemplate>
                                        <TextBlock
                                    TextAlignment="Center"
                                    Text="{Binding
                                        Quantity}"/>
                                    </DataTemplate>
                                </GridViewColumn
                                        .CellTemplate>
                            </GridViewColumn>
                            <GridViewColumn
                                       Header="UnitPrice">
                                <GridViewColumn
                                        .CellTemplate>
                                    <DataTemplate>
                                        <TextBlock
                                    TextAlignment="Center"
                                    Text="{Binding
                                        UnitPrice,
                               StringFormat='{}{0:C}'}" />
                                    </DataTemplate>
                                </GridViewColumn
                                        .CellTemplate>
                            </GridViewColumn>
                        </GridView.Columns>
                    </GridView>
                </ListView.View>
            </ListView>
        </GroupBox>
    </Grid>
</Grid>
</UserControl>
```

7. Open `MainSkin.xaml` and add the following template to it. This will map our View to our View Model.

```
<DataTemplate DataType="{x:Type ViewModel:OrderDetailsViewModel}">
    <WPF:OrderDetails/>
</DataTemplate>
```

8. Open `OrderViewModel` and update it as follows:

```
public class OrderViewModel : ViewModelBase
{
    public const string ModelPropertyName = "Model";
    private Order _model;
    public Customer Customer { get; set; }
    private readonly IToolManager _toolManager;

    public ICommand ShowOrderDetailsCommand
    {
        get
        {
            return new RelayCommand(
                () => _toolManager.OpenOrderDetails(this));
        }
    }

...

    public OrderViewModel(Order model,
        Customer customer, IToolManager toolManager)
    {
        _model = model;
        Customer = customer;
        _toolManager = toolManager;
        SubscribeToOrderDetailsChanged(_model);
    }
...
}
```

9. Open `Orders.xaml` and update the `DataGrid` as shown in the following code. This will add a **Show Details** link to our grid that will open the related order details when clicked.

```
<DataGrid ItemsSource="{Binding Orders}"
          AutoGenerateColumns="False">
    <DataGrid.Columns>
        <DataGridTextColumn Header="ID"
            Binding="{Binding Model.OrderID}"
            ElementStyle
                ="{StaticResource leftAlign}" />
        <DataGridTextColumn Header="Order Date"
            Binding="{Binding Model.OrderDate,
                StringFormat=d}"
            ElementStyle
                ="{StaticResource leftAlign}" />
        <DataGridTextColumn Header="Shipped Date"
            Binding="{Binding Model.ShippedDate,
                StringFormat=d}"
            ElementStyle
                ="{StaticResource leftAlign}" />
        <DataGridTextColumn Header="Total"
            Binding="{Binding Total,
                StringFormat=c}"
            ElementStyle
                ="{StaticResource rightAlign}" />
        <DataGridTemplateColumn Header="Details">
            <DataGridTemplateColumn.CellTemplate>
                <DataTemplate>
                    <TextBlock>
                        <Hyperlink
                            Command="{Binding
                                ShowOrderDetailsCommand}">
                             <TextBlock
                                Text="Show Details" />
                        </Hyperlink>
                    </TextBlock>
                </DataTemplate>
            </DataGridTemplateColumn.CellTemplate>
        </DataGridTemplateColumn>
    </DataGrid.Columns>
</DataGrid>
```

Now if you build and run the application, you will get the application that was shown at the beginning of this chapter.

Summary

This brings us to the end of our implementation of Northwind. In this chapter, we saw how, as the complexity of our application grew, we could make things easier by using the HVM approach and using an IoC container to help with application composition. We looked at IoC's best practices and looked at a lot of the issues that can pop up when using IoC containers along with approaches for avoiding these issues.

7
Dialogs and MVVM

By Muhammad Shujaat Siddiqi

In WPF, dialogs are similar to those in Winform. The only way to show dialogs is by using either `Window.Show()` (modeless) or `Window.ShowDialog()` (modal) methods.

This includes built-in dialogs, such as `MessageBox`, `OpenFileDialog`, `SaveFileDialog`, and `PrintDialog`.

Since we need our view model logic to be able to initiate the display of these dialogs, we might be tempted to call these methods directly from our view models. The problem with calling `Show()` or `ShowDialog()` directly is that it requires the `System.Windows.Window` references to be held by view model coupling `ViewModel` to `System.Windows`. This breaks down the desired separation of concerns in MVVM and makes things like testing our code more difficult than it needs to be.

There is another issue around dialog ownership as you must set a dialog's owner to be the window that will be its parent. Even if we show our dialogs directly from our view models, we still will not be able to set the ownership directly from our view models unless we have a reference from our view to our view model.

Another consideration is multitargeting. Even though there are gaps in achieving multitargeting without compromising on some features, you might want to take on those gaps and use the same view model for your Silverlight/WPF and WP7 applications. You will likely be handling dialogs differently in each platform and so having dialog management abstracted in some way will be very useful. If we show views directly from view models then we severely limit our code reuse across platforms.

It should now be obvious that there are a lot of things that we need to consider before adding dialogs to our applications in an MVVM-friendly way. We will now take a look at how we can deal with these challenges.

Should we make a compromise?

The preceding discussion might lead you to think that we have no solution to display dialogs in an MVVM fashion or you might think that it's not worth the effort. As we will see there are definitely options and we've already looked at the benefits that will be provided by putting in that extra effort. The MVVM community has devised many different ways to deal with this problem and just like everything in development there are tradeoffs to each approach. In this chapter, we are going to discuss some of these approaches. We will be discussing how we can show both, modal and modeless dialogs with these technique. We will also discuss how these dialogs can return data, which can be used by the view model using these techniques. The options we are going to explore in this chapter are as follows:

- Dialog service
- Mediators
- Attached behavior

Dialog service

Dialog service is an approach where a layer of abstraction is used to show dialog boxes. View models delegate the responsibility of showing the dialogs to a dialog service and simply provide the service the data needed for display. The dialog service owns the responsibility of showing dialogs and we are able to keep our view models decoupled from `System.Windows` and avoid the need for references from our views to our view models. In unit tests, we can inject a fake dialog service instance instead of showing the actual dialog and use our fake object for stubbing and mocking.

Let's consider a simple example WPF `MVVMLight` project to show a dialog box using dialog service. The following view has a `TextBlock` and a `Button`. Clicking on the button should display a dialog box.

The XAML definition of the view can be as follows:

```
<Window x:Class="MVVMBasedDialogs.MainWindowDialogService"
        xmlns="http://schemas.microsoft.com/winfx/2006/xaml/
presentation"
        xmlns:x="http://schemas.microsoft.com/winfx/2006/xaml"
        xmlns:d="http://schemas.microsoft.com/expression/blend/2008"
        xmlns:mc="http://schemas.openxmlformats.org/markup-
compatibility/2006"
        xmlns:vm="clr-namespace:MVVMBasedDialogs.ViewModel"
        mc:Ignorable="d"
        Height="300"
        Width="355"
        Title="MVVM Survival Guide">
    <Window.DataContext>
        <vm:MainViewModelWithDialogService />
    </Window.DataContext>
    <Grid x:Name="LayoutRoot">
        <Grid.RowDefinitions>
            <RowDefinition Height="*" />
            <RowDefinition Height="0.25*" />
        </Grid.RowDefinitions>
        <TextBlock FontSize="36" Grid.Row="0"
                   FontWeight="Bold"
                   Text="{Binding Welcome}"
                   VerticalAlignment="Center"
                   HorizontalAlignment="Center"
                   TextWrapping="Wrap" />
        <Button Grid.Row="1" Content="Show Dialog"
                Command="{Binding ShowDialogCommand}" />
    </Grid>
</Window>
```

In the following view model definition, we are using `DialogService` to show our message box. Here we are instantiating `DialogService` as an instance member. Although this approach is still unit testable, it is generally preferred to use an IoC-based mechanism for injecting/locating the `DialogService` instance. We are not discussing that in order to minimize the noise.

[See *Chapter 6, Northwind – Hierarchical View Model and IoC*, for details on how to set up IoC in your application.]

```
namespace MVVMBasedDialogs.ViewModel{
   using GalaSoft.MvvmLight;
   using System.Windows.Input;
   using GalaSoft.MvvmLight.Command;
   using System.Windows;

   internal class MainViewModelWithDialogService : ViewModelBase
   {
       IDialogService _applicationDialogService;
       public IDialogService ApplicationDialogService
       {
           get
           {
               if (_applicationDialogService == null)
               {
                   _applicationDialogService = new DialogService();
               }
               return _applicationDialogService;
           }
           internal set
           {
               _applicationDialogService = value;
           }
       }
       string _welcome = "Dialogs & MVVM";
       public string Welcome
       {
           get
           {
               return _welcome;
           }
           set
           {
               _welcome = value;
               RaisePropertyChanged("Welcome");
           }
       }
       ICommand _showDialogCommand;
       public ICommand ShowDialogCommand
       {
           get
           {
               if (_showDialogCommand == null)
               {
```

```
                _showDialogCommand = new RelayCommand(ShowMessage);
            }
            return _showDialogCommand;
        }
    }
    internal void ShowMessage()
    {
        MessageBoxResult result =
            ApplicationDialogService.ShowMessageBox("Message",
                            "Message Header", MessageBoxButton.OK);
        Welcome = EvaluateText(result);
    }
    protected virtual string EvaluateText(MessageBoxResult result)
    {
        string msg =
     System.Enum.GetName(typeof(MessageBoxResult), result);
        return msg;
    }
  }
}
```

Here `IDialogService` just provides functionality to display `MessageBox`. It can also be used to display any specialized window. The definition of the `IDialogService` interface and the `DialogService` class is as follows:

```
namespace MVVMBasedDialogs
{
   using System.Windows;
   public interface IDialogService
   {
       MessageBoxResult ShowMessageBox(string content,
           string title, MessageBoxButton buttons);
   }

   public class DialogService : IDialogService
   {
       public MessageBoxResult ShowMessageBox(string content,
           string title, MessageBoxButton buttons)
       {
           return MessageBox.Show(content, title, buttons);
       }
   }
}
```

In the preceding code, we saw how we can show `MessageBox` using `DialogService` so that view model is still unit testable. As we have seen before `internal` (C#) members be made visible to unit test assemblies. To unit testing this view model, the unit test code just needs to create a stub of the `IDialogService` interface and assign it to the internal `ApplicationDialogService`. Similar logic can be used to show similar types of dialogs including `OpenFileDialog`, `SaveFileDialog`, and `PrintDialog`. We just need to provide contract definition in the `IDialogService` interface and provide an implementation in `DialogService` class following the same pattern.

We might also want to be able to use a custom view to display messages to the users and style that is in accordance with application styles. Another thing to consider is that `MessageBox` is inherently modal. If we instead use a custom view then we can be more flexible and call `ShowDialog()` if we want to make a modal message box. We might want to set `Application.Current.MainWindow` as the owner of the custom dialog. Let's now take a look at an example of this approach.

Using DataTemplates with DialogService

DataTemplates can be used to map a view to a view model allowing our view models to not have to know about the views. In the section that follows, we are going to see how a view model can use `DialogService` to show another view by simply providing an instance of the desired view's associated view model to our dialog service. Obviously `DialogService` would be taking advantage of `DataTemplates` for this purpose but we are allowing our view models to be separated from that concern.

Let's consider a simple order entry form. Again we are creating the project as WPF `MVVMLight` project. The view just has a `ComboBox` for **Customer** selection. In order to minimize the noise let's just assume that there are some relevant order details at the bottom.

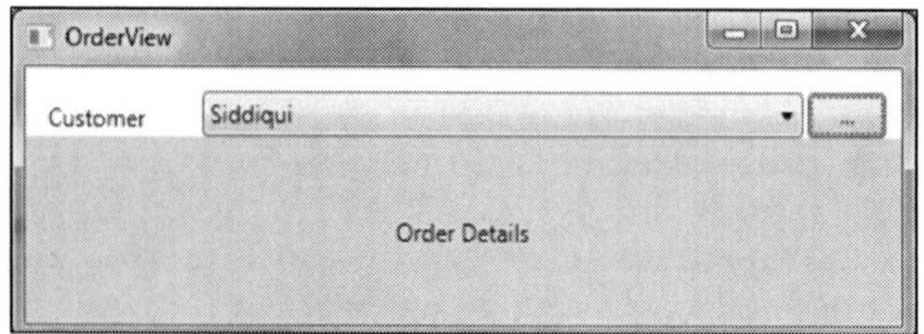

Let's see the XAML definition of `OrderView`:

```
<Window x:Class="MVVMBasedDialogs.OrderView"
        xmlns="http://schemas.microsoft.com/winfx/2006/xaml/
presentation"
        xmlns:x="http://schemas.microsoft.com/winfx/2006/xaml"
```

```
        xmlns:vm="clr-namespace:MVVMBasedDialogs.ViewModel"
        Title="OrderView" Height="300" Width="476">
    <Window.DataContext>
        <vm:OrderViewModel />
    </Window.DataContext>
    <Grid>
        <Grid.ColumnDefinitions>
            <ColumnDefinition Width="0.25*" />
            <ColumnDefinition Width="*" />
        </Grid.ColumnDefinitions>
        <Grid.RowDefinitions>
            <RowDefinition Height="auto" />
            <RowDefinition Height="*" />
        </Grid.RowDefinitions>
        <Label Content="Customer" Height="23"
HorizontalAlignment="Left"
               Margin="7,12,0,0" Name="lblCustomer"
VerticalAlignment="Top"
               Grid.Column="0" Grid.Row="0" Width="100" />
        <StackPanel Orientation="Horizontal" Grid.Column="1" Grid.
Row="0">
            <ComboBox Margin="2,12,0,0" Name="cmbCustomer"
                  DisplayMemberPath="LastName" Width="315"
                  ItemsSource="{Binding Customers}"
                  SelectedItem="{Binding SelectedCustomer}" />
            <Button Content="..."
                  Command="{Binding ShowCustomerDetailsCommand}"
                  Margin="2,12,0,0" Name="btnEditCustomer"
                  HorizontalAlignment="Right" Width="41" />
        </StackPanel>
        <Border BorderBrush="Silver" Grid.ColumnSpan="2"
                 Grid.Row="1" Background="LightGray">
            <TextBlock Text="Order Details"
HorizontalAlignment="Center"
                         VerticalAlignment="Center" />
        </Border>
    </Grid>
</Window>
```

The preceding view is using an instance of `OrderViewModel` as `DataContext`. It is constructing the instance with inline XAML and using it as `DataContext`. The view has some expectations from the view model. It should have a collection, called `Customers`, with its members having a `LastName` property. It should also have a `SelectedCustomer` property that should be the same type as the members of the `Customer` collection. It should provide an additional `ICommand` property `ShowCustomerDetailsCommand`. The definition of `OrderViewModel` is as follows:

```
namespace MVVMBasedDialogs.ViewModel
{
```

```
using GalaSoft.MvvmLight;
using System.Collections.ObjectModel;
using System.Windows.Input;
using GalaSoft.MvvmLight.Command;
class OrderViewModel : ViewModelBase
{
    ObservableCollection<CustomerViewModel> _customers =
        new ObservableCollection<CustomerViewModel>()
        {
            new CustomerViewModel() {
         FirstName = "Muhammad", LastName="Siddiqui"},
            new CustomerViewModel() {
         FirstName = "Ryan", LastName = "Vice"}
        };
    public ObservableCollection<CustomerViewModel> Customers
    {
        get
        {
            return _customers;
        }
    }
    CustomerViewModel _selectedCustomer;
    public CustomerViewModel SelectedCustomer
    {
        get
        {
            return _selectedCustomer;
        }
        set
        {
            _selectedCustomer = value;
            RaisePropertyChanged("SelectedCustomer");
        }
    }
    ICommand _showCustomerDetailsCommand;
    public ICommand ShowCustomerDetailsCommand
    {
        get
        {
            if (_showCustomerDetailsCommand == null)
            {
                _showCustomerDetailsCommand =
                    new RelayCommand(() =>
                        {
```

```
                                    DialogService.Instance
                                            .ShowDialog(SelectedCustomer);
                                },
                                () => SelectedCustomer != null);
                    }
                    return _showCustomerDetailsCommand;
                }
            }
        }
    }
```

Here we have used an updated definition of `DialogService` to show dialogs by specifying a view model as an argument. It is also implemented as an injectable singleton implementation to demonstrate another implementation you might consider.

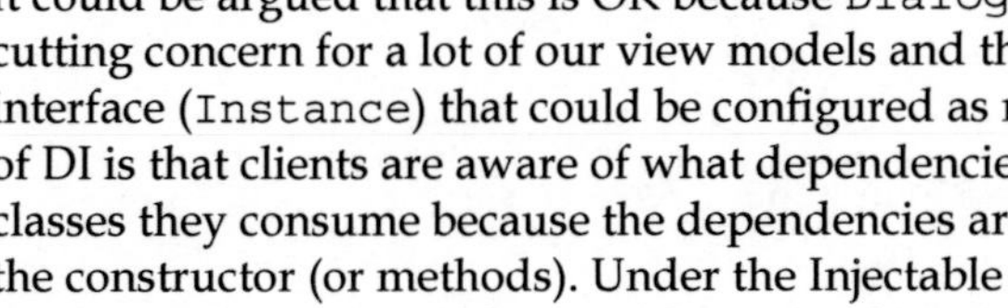

> Having `DialogService` implemented as an injectable singleton will allow for our code to be testable and provides good separation of concerns but is weaker in the area of dependency inversion as its dependencies are internalized and client code is not responsible for injecting them. It could be argued that this is OK because `DialogService` is a cross-cutting concern for a lot of our view models and that it is exposing an interface (`Instance`) that could be configured as needed. Another benefit of DI is that clients are aware of what dependencies are needed by the classes they consume because the dependencies are advertised from the constructor (or methods). Under the Injectable Singleton approach, the dependencies are obfuscated from the client arguably making our class harder to consume by clients. However, because `DialogService` represents a cross-cutting concern in our view models, it could be argued that the benefit of advertising dependencies is less as we would have this component configured and available at runtime in our view models. As with most things you should spend some time considering the various tradeoffs when architecting your project and pick the approach that fits your needs the best.

These dialogs would be modal to the whole application. We need to add a `ShowDialog()` method to `DialogService`. Since all our view models inherit from MVVM Light's `ViewModelBase`, we can use it as parameter type.

Here `CustomerViewModel` can be defined as follows:

```
namespace MVVMBasedDialogs.ViewModel
{
    using GalaSoft.MvvmLight;

    class CustomerViewModel : ViewModelBase
```

```
    {
        string _firstName;
        public string FirstName
        {
            get { return _firstName; }
            set
            {
                _firstName = value;
                RaisePropertyChanged("FirstName");
            }
        }

        string _lastName;
        public string LastName
        {
            get { return _lastName; }
            set
            {
                _lastName = value;
                RaisePropertyChanged("LastName");
            }
        }

        public override string ToString()
        {
            return string.Format("{0} {1}", FirstName, LastName);
        }
    }
}
```

The implementation of `IDialogService` would also need to be updated as follows:

```
namespace MVVMBasedDialogs
{
    using System.Windows;
    using GalaSoft.MvvmLight;
    public interface IDialogService
    {
        MessageBoxResult ShowMessageBox(string content,
            string title, MessageBoxButton buttons);
        void ShowDialog(ViewModelBase viewModel);
    }

    public class DialogService : IDialogService
    {
        static IDialogService _instance;
```

```
        public static IDialogService Instance
        {
            get
            {
                if (_instance == null)
                {
                    _instance = new DialogService();
                }
                return _instance;
            }
        internal set
        {
            _instance = value;
        }
        }
        public MessageBoxResult ShowMessageBox(string content,
string title, MessageBoxButton buttons)
        {
            return MessageBox.Show(content, title, buttons);
        }
        public void ShowDialog(ViewModelBase viewModel)
        {
            var dialog = new DialogView() { DataContext = viewModel };
            dialog.Owner = Application.Current.MainWindow;
            dialog.ShowInTaskbar = false;
            dialog.ShowDialog();
        }
    }
}
```

Now we can simply specify view model, passed as argument, to the `DataContext` of `DialogView` instance and shown the Dialog. It is the responsibility of `DialogView` to determine how to actually display this. Again, internal setter of `Instance` is just for unit testability of the code and is why we call it an Injectable Singleton. Let's see how simply we can define `DialogView`.

```
<Window x:Class="MVVMBasedDialogs.DialogView"
        xmlns="http://schemas.microsoft.com/winfx/2006/xaml/
presentation"
        xmlns:x="http://schemas.microsoft.com/winfx/2006/xaml"
        SizeToContent="WidthAndHeight">
    <StackPanel>
        <ContentControl Content="{Binding}" />
    </StackPanel>
</Window>
```

The definition of `DialogView` also seems very simple and so you might wonder how would the runtime render the dialog using our view and view model? First of all, if we run this application in the current state, it would just call `ToString()` on `DataContext` and show the result. If we had **Siddiqui** selected in the view then it would show **Muhammad Siddiqui**. This is because we have overriden `ToString()` on `CustomerViewModel`. As we need a more sophisticated display with WPF controls, we can define `DataTemplate` for this view model type. Now whenever the WPF runtime encounters a situation like this, it would use that `DataTemplate` to display an instance of this type. Let us define `DataTemplate` in `App.xaml` so that it is accessible throughout the application. Before adding the following code, you would need to add the namespaces of view model and dialogs with alias `vm` and `local`, respectively:

```
<DataTemplate DataType="{x:Type vm:CustomerViewModel}">
   <local:CustomerView />
</DataTemplate>
```

Here `CustomerView` is simply `UserControl` as follows:

```
<UserControl x:Class="MVVMBasedDialogs.CustomerView"
         xmlns="http://schemas.microsoft.com/winfx/2006/xaml/
presentation"
         xmlns:x="http://schemas.microsoft.com/winfx/2006/xaml"
         xmlns:mc="http://schemas.openxmlformats.org/markup-
compatibility/2006"
         xmlns:d="http://schemas.microsoft.com/expression/blend/2008"
         mc:Ignorable="d"
         Width="446" Height="300"
         d:DesignHeight="300" d:DesignWidth="446">
    <Grid>
        <Grid.ColumnDefinitions>
            <ColumnDefinition Width="111*" />
            <ColumnDefinition Width="331*" />
        </Grid.ColumnDefinitions>
        <Grid.RowDefinitions>
            <RowDefinition Height="auto" />
            <RowDefinition Height="auto" />
            <RowDefinition Height="*" />
        </Grid.RowDefinitions>
        <Label Content="First Name" Height="25"
HorizontalAlignment="Left"
```

```
                Grid.Column="0" Grid.Row="0"
                Margin="6,13,0,0" VerticalAlignment="Top" Width="103" />
        <TextBox Height="28" HorizontalAlignment="Left"
Margin="4,12,0,0"
                Grid.Row="0" Grid.Column="1"
                Text="{Binding FirstName, UpdateSourceTrigger=PropertyC
hanged}"
                Name="txtFirstName" VerticalAlignment="Top"
Width="318"/>
        <Label Content="Last Name" Height="25"
HorizontalAlignment="Left"
                Grid.Column="0" Grid.Row="1"
                Margin="6,6,0,0"  Width="103" />
        <TextBox Height="28" HorizontalAlignment="Left"
                 Grid.Row="1" Grid.Column="1" Margin="3,6,0,0"
                 Text="{Binding LastName, UpdateSourceTrigger=Property
Changed}"
                 Name="txtLastName" VerticalAlignment="Top" Width="318"
/>
    </Grid>
</UserControl>
```

Here we have used `UpdateSourceTrigger` as `PropertyChanged` just to keep the view definiton simple. As we make updates to **First Name** or **Last Name**, it would be reflected in the view model and hence if it is a change in **LastName**, it would be reflected in the **Customer** combobox in `OrderView` as it is the same view model instance.

Let's run the application and select **Siddiqui** from the **Customer** list. This would enable the button. Clicking on the button would open the customer dialog.

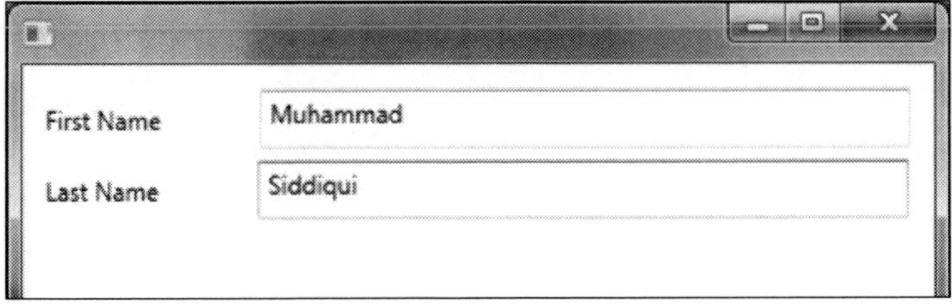

Now let's update **Last Name** to **Siddiqui** and close the dialog. You can see that the same change is reflected in `OrderView`. This is because we have passed the same collection member to be shown by `DialogService`. Updating `LastName` has resulted in the notification to the view to update itself via `INotifyPropertyChanged`.

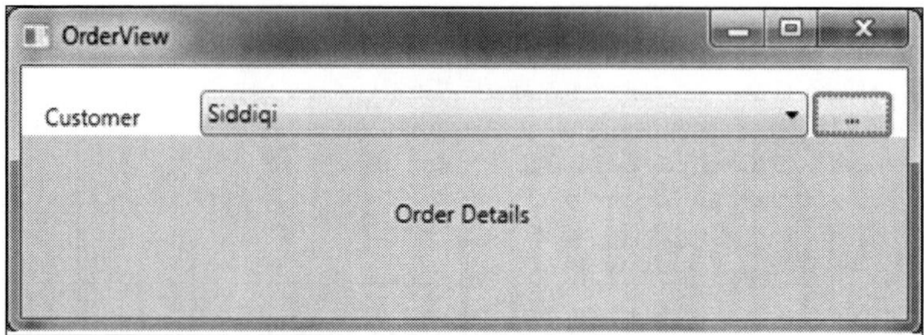

Convention over configuration

The preceding technique assumes that the framework has support for implicit `DataTemplate`. This is not always the case in Silverlight. Support for implicit data templates has been added to Silverlight 5 Beta but for earlier versions of Silverlight, we cannot use `ContentControl` directly. However, we can inherit from `ContentControl` and override it in a way that allows us to determine `DataTemplate` and apply our view model to it for display. The two possible techniques are to use convention or to use configuration for resolving data templates.

We can create a convention for naming our data templates, views, and view models, for example `CustomerTemplate`, `CustomerView`, and `CustomerViewModel`. Here if `DialogService` is requested to show a dialog with `CustomerViewModel` then it can easily determine that it should be using `CustomerTemplate` for this purpose, which can be implemented directly or can also be based on `UserControl` like `CustomerView`. Let's add this to `App.xaml`:

```
<DataTemplate x:Key="CustomerTemplate"
            DataType="{x:Type vm:CustomerViewModel}">
    <local:CustomerView />
</DataTemplate>
```

Here the namespace `vm` is defined as follows:

```
xmlns:vm="clr-namespace:MVVMBasedDialogs.ViewModel"
```

Let's specialize the `ContentControl` for this approach.

```
namespace MVVMBasedDialogs.Control
{
   using System.Windows.Controls;
   using System.Windows;

   class ConventionContentControl : ContentControl
   {
       protected override void OnContentChanged(object oldContent,
        object newContent)
       {
           base.OnContentChanged(oldContent, newContent);

           string viewModelName = newContent.GetType().Name;
           string templateName =
        string.Format("{0}Template",
                 viewModelName.Substring(0,
            viewModelName.IndexOf("ViewModel")));
           ContentTemplate =
               (DataTemplate)Application.Current.
Resources[templateName];
       }
   }
}
```

Now we can update the definition of `DialogView` to use `ConventionContentControl` instead.

```
<Window x:Class="MVVMBasedDialogs.DialogView"
       xmlns="http://schemas.microsoft.com/winfx/2006/xaml/
presentation"
       xmlns:x="http://schemas.microsoft.com/winfx/2006/xaml"
       xmlns:Controls="clr-namespace:MVVMBasedDialogs.Control"
       SizeToContent="WidthAndHeight">
   <StackPanel>
       <Controls:ConventionContentControl
Content="{Binding}" />
   </StackPanel>
</Window>
```

The preceding approach will behave exactly the way as implicit `DataTemplate` approach was working. Here we are checking the applied content. Based on convention, we are determining the template to use to display this content.

`DialogService` can also be configured to map between views and view models. This can be code based or XML based. In this case, it would just look at configuration to determine which view goes with particular view model. It then instantiates the view, assign view model instance as `DataContext`, and shows it. All the updates in the view model should be reflected on the caller `ViewModel` if it is keeping the instance of this view model.

It is also possible that the same view model is displayed by using different views for different contexts. `DialogService` has no automatic mechanism to determine the context. In this case, we can update `DialogService` to use tokens. Here different token can specify different context which can be used by `DialogService` to determine which view to display. Tokens can be used in both techniques, that is convention and configuration.

Using dialog service has made the view model unit testable but the code of `DialogService`, itself, is not unit testable as it contains view logic. Since this is considered as part of the View/UI layer, this is generally not a concern.

Mediators

Mediators are the implementation of Gang of Four's Mediator pattern. In MVVM-based applications, they can be used to connect different disconnected parts of the application. Mediators aren't available directly in WPF or Silverlight but most of the MVVM toolkits have provided a mediator implementation. PRISM and MVVM Light have the `EventAggregator` and `Messenger` respectively as mediators. They are implemented based on Publisher/Subscriber model. One party publishes a message and if any other part of the application has subscribed to that message then the mediator hands message over to them. If, however, there are no subscribers then the message is ignored. Mediators generally have no limitations on the number of subscriber for a particular message so it could also be used for broadcasting certain information like **Disconnected from Server** or **Logging off**. Messages are generally received by a subscriber on the same thread that it was published on. Some MVVM toolkits allow publishing message on UI thread so that the handler could update UI directly without using `Dispatcher`. In most toolkits, the mediators are built using weak references so that they won't cause memory leaks. Some implementations also support filtered messages. Event aggregator supports them by using `Predicates`. In addition to the message handler, the subscriber can also specify a predicate during subscription. The handler code would only be executed if the predicate condition is satisfied. This saves us from having various checks before doing the real work in the handler logic.

Let's first consider simple notification dialogs. These dialogs are generally displayed when user is to be notified about some useful information. They are generally displayed with just the **OK** button. Let's consider a simple view as shown in the screnshot in the *Dialog service* section.When user clicks on the **Show Dialog** button, a notification dialog should display with the message **Notification Message**. The dialog should have an **OK** button. Clicking on the button should close the dialog.

The design of the view may be as follows:

```
<Window x:Class="MVVMBasedDialogs.MainWindow"
        xmlns="http://schemas.microsoft.com/winfx/2006/xaml/
presentation"
        xmlns:x="http://schemas.microsoft.com/winfx/2006/xaml"
        xmlns:d="http://schemas.microsoft.com/expression/blend/2008"
        xmlns:mc="http://schemas.openxmlformats.org/markup-
compatibility/2006"
        mc:Ignorable="d"
        Height="300"
        Width="357"
        Title="MVVM Survival Guide"
        DataContext="{Binding Main, Source={StaticResource Locator}}">
    <Window.Resources>
        <ResourceDictionary>
            <ResourceDictionary.MergedDictionaries>
                <ResourceDictionary Source="Skins/MainSkin.xaml" />
            </ResourceDictionary.MergedDictionaries>
        </ResourceDictionary>
    </Window.Resources>
    <Grid x:Name="LayoutRoot">
        <Grid.RowDefinitions>
            <RowDefinition Height="*" />
            <RowDefinition Height="0.25*" />
        </Grid.RowDefinitions>
        <TextBlock FontSize="36" Grid.Row="0"
                   FontWeight="Bold"
                   Text="{Binding Welcome}"
                   VerticalAlignment="Center"
                   HorizontalAlignment="Center"
                   TextWrapping="Wrap" />
        <Button Grid.Row="1" Content="Show Dialog"
```

```
                Command="{Binding ShowDialogCommand}" />
    </Grid>
</Window>
```

As expected by the preceding view, `MainViewModel` should have a property `Welcome`. It should also have an ICommand `ShowDialogCommand`. The definition of `MainViewModel` is as follows:

```
namespace MVVMBasedDialogs.ViewModel
{
   using GalaSoft.MvvmLight;
   using System.Windows.Input;
   using GalaSoft.MvvmLight.Command;
   using GalaSoft.MvvmLight.Messaging;
   using System.Windows;
   public class MainViewModel : ViewModelBase
   {
       public string Welcome
       {
           get
           {
               return "Welcome to MVVM Light";
           }
       }

       ICommand _showDialogCommand;
       public ICommand ShowDialogCommand
       {
           get
           {
               if (_showDialogCommand == null)
               {
                   _showDialogCommand = new RelayCommand(
                       () =>
                       {
                           var message =
                new DialogMessage("Notification Message", null)
                           {
                               Caption = "test",
                               Button = MessageBoxButton.OK
                           };
                           Messenger.Default.Send(message);
                       }
                       );
               }
               return _showDialogCommand;
           }
       }
   }
}
```

The preceding view model uses MVVM Light's `Messenger` to send a `DialogMessage` with relevant information. It specifies that the dialog box should have content **Notification Message**, header as **test**. The dialog should just have an **OK** button. This code specifies enough information to display a dialog. This information is of no use unless used by interested recipient. Any interested recipient can register for this message and use it to display the dialog. Since all this information is specified by the view model, it is in complete control. The class hierarchy of MVVM Light's `DialogMessage` is as follows:

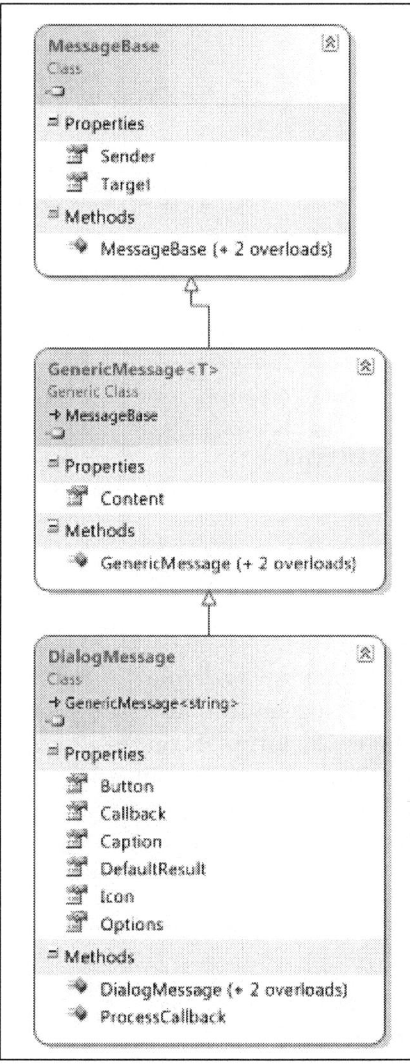

Now the main question is who should be listening to this message. Generally, the view itself registers for this message. When view receives this message, it utilizes the information specified to display the dialog. Let's see the code behind `MainWindow`:

```
namespace MVVMBasedDialogs
{
   using System.Windows;
   using MVVMBasedDialogs.ViewModel;
   using GalaSoft.MvvmLight.Messaging;
   public partial class MainWindow : Window
   {
       public MainWindow()
       {
           InitializeComponent();
           Closing += (s, e) => ViewModelLocator.Cleanup();
           Messenger.Default.Register<DialogMessage>(
               this,
               msg =>
               {
                   var result = MessageBox.Show(
                       msg.Content,
                       msg.Caption,
                       msg.Button);
                   // callback
                   msg.ProcessCallback(result);
               });
       }
   }
}
```

When we run the application, the view is displayed with a message and button. When we click on the **Show Dialog** button, the dialog is displayed with the **Notification Message** message. Clicking **OK** on the dialog closes it. The preceding code just displays the dialog. There are times when we need to use the user selections on these dialogs. Let's update the example so that the view model could use user selection on the dialog. These are **Are you sure?** kind of dialogs. We update the view model as follows:

```
namespace MVVMBasedDialogs.ViewModel
{
   using GalaSoft.MvvmLight;
   using System.Windows.Input;
   using GalaSoft.MvvmLight.Command;
   using GalaSoft.MvvmLight.Messaging;
   using System.Windows;
```

```
    public class MainViewModelWithCallBack : ViewModelBase
    {
        string _welcome = "Dialogs & MVVM";
        public string Welcome
        {
            get
            {
                return _welcome;
            }
            set
            {
                _welcome = value;
                RaisePropertyChanged("Welcome");
            }
        }
        ICommand _showDialogCommand;
        public ICommand ShowDialogCommand
        {
            get
            {
                if (_showDialogCommand == null)
                {
                    _showDialogCommand = new RelayCommand(
                        () =>
                        {
                            var message =
                 new DialogMessage("Are you sure?",
DialogMessageCallback)
                            {
                                Caption = "test",
                                Button = MessageBoxButton.YesNo
                             };
                            Messenger.Default.Send(message);
                        }
                        );
                }
                return _showDialogCommand;
            }
        }
        private void DialogMessageCallback(MessageBoxResult result)
        {
            if (result == MessageBoxResult.Yes)
            {
                Welcome = "Yes";
```

```
            }
            else
            {
                Welcome = "No";
            }
        }
    }
}
```

In the preceding code, we have modified the `Welcome` property to support the changed notification by raising the `PropertyChanged` event. The main update (from the previous example) is that we have changed the buttons to `YesNo` and introduced `Callback`. In the callback, we are updating the `Welcome` property based on user selection. The view already supports calling the callback. If you look at the view code, it is calling the callback.

```
Messenger.Default.Register<DialogMessage>(
    this,
    msg =>
    {
        var result = MessageBox.Show(
            msg.Content,
            msg.Caption,
            msg.Button);
        // Send callback
        msg.ProcessCallback(result);
    });
```

We need to update the code of `ViewModelLocator` as follows:

```
public ViewModelLocator()
{
    CreateMain();
    CreateMainWithCallBack();
}
private static MainViewModelWithCallBack _mainWithCallback;
public MainViewModelWithCallBack MainWithCallBack
{
    get
    {
        return MainWithCallBackStatic;
    }
}
public static MainViewModelWithCallBack MainWithCallBackStatic
{
```

```
        get
        {
            if (_mainWithCallback == null)
            {
                CreateMainWithCallBack();
            }
            return _mainWithCallback;
        }
    }
    public static void CreateMainWithCallBack()
    {
        if (_mainWithCallback == null)
        {
            _mainWithCallback = new MainViewModelWithCallBack();
        }
    }
    public static void ClearMainWithCallBack()
    {
        _mainWithCallback.Cleanup();
        _mainWithCallback = null;
    }
    public static void Cleanup()
    {
        ClearMain();
        ClearMainWithCallBack();
    }
```

We also need to update `MainWindow` so that it uses `MainWithCallback` from `ViewModelLocator` as its `DataContext`.

```
<Window x:Class="MVVMBasedDialogs.MainWindow"
        xmlns="http://schemas.microsoft.com/winfx/2006/xaml/
presentation"
        xmlns:x="http://schemas.microsoft.com/winfx/2006/xaml"
        xmlns:d="http://schemas.microsoft.com/expression/blend/2008"
        xmlns:mc="http://schemas.openxmlformats.org/markup-
compatibility/2006"
        mc:Ignorable="d"
        Height="300"
        Width="300"
        Title="MVVM Survival Guide"
        DataContext="{Binding MainWithCallBack, Source={StaticResource
Locator}}">
    <Window.Resources>
        <ResourceDictionary>
```

```
            <ResourceDictionary.MergedDictionaries>
                <ResourceDictionary Source="Skins/MainSkin.xaml" />
            </ResourceDictionary.MergedDictionaries>
        </ResourceDictionary>
    </Window.Resources>
    <Grid x:Name="LayoutRoot">
        <Grid.RowDefinitions>
            <RowDefinition Height="*" />
            <RowDefinition Height="0.25*" />
        </Grid.RowDefinitions>
        <TextBlock FontSize="36" Grid.Row="0"
                   FontWeight="Bold"
                   Text="{Binding Welcome}"
                   VerticalAlignment="Center"
                   HorizontalAlignment="Center"
                   TextWrapping="Wrap" />
        <Button Grid.Row="1" Content="Show Dialog"
                Command="{Binding ShowDialogCommand}" />
    </Grid>
</Window>
```

Now we run the application. The view appears as shown in the screenshot in the *Dialog service* section. When we click on the **Show Dialog** button, the following dialog is displayed:

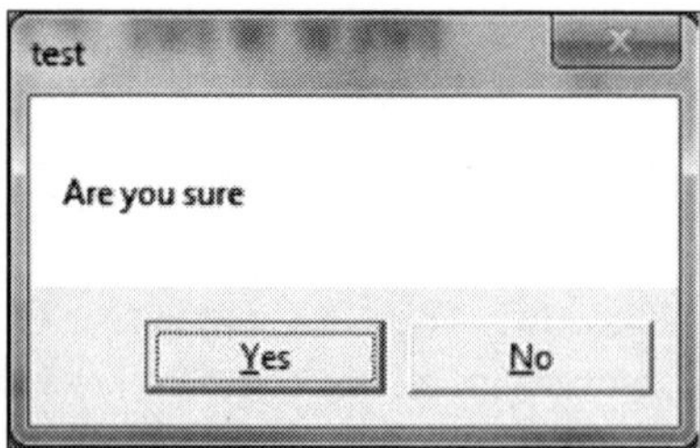

When we click on the **Yes** button, the view model sets the `Welcome` property as **Yes**. This is updated on the view as follows:

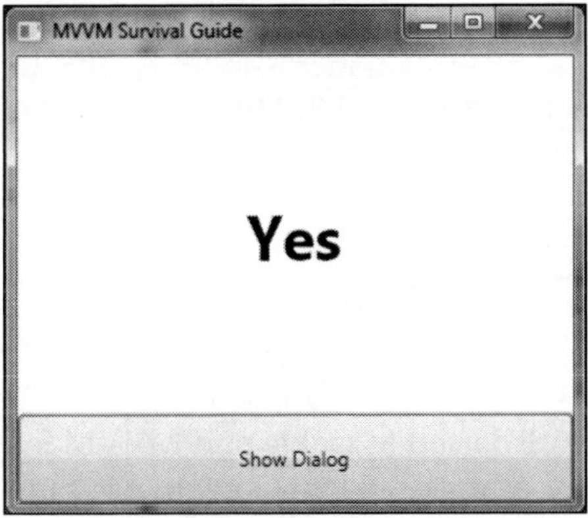

If we select **No** instead, then the view is updated as follows:

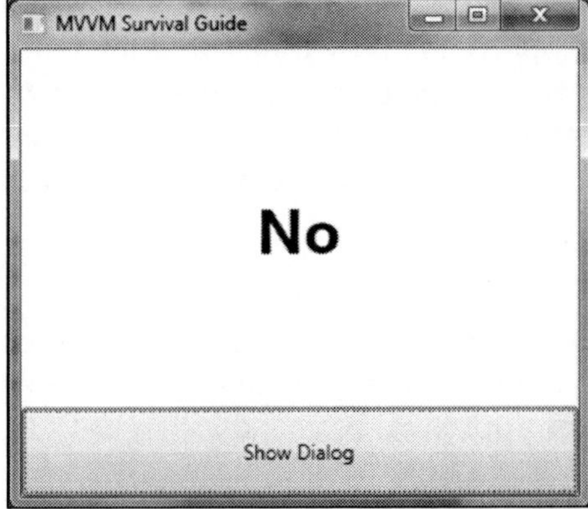

Still there are two issues:

- There is code-behind approach in `MainWindow` which is not recommended by the MVVM community. In order to avoid that we can subscribe to these simpleton messages by a separate service and use that to display these dialogs.
- Here we are showing simple `MessageBox` dialogs. Basically, in real world, we can show any types of dialogs. Both modal and modeless. If `DialogMessage` is registered somewhere else in the application then we also need to assign ownership of the dialog. We can assign `MainWindow` as the owner of the dialogs in such cases.

```
DialogBoxView.Owner = Application.Current.MainWindow
```

Based on the preceding observation, we can have a centralized manager to subscribe with `DialogMessage`. This `DialogManager` should be able to figure out which template to use to display the view model. This is a similar technique to the one explained in the *Dialog services* section.

Attached behaviors

Attached behaviors are generally used to cause some code to be executed on the view based on some property changes in the view model. They are phenomenal for this purpose. They are also used to tackle non-MVVM features of otherwise MVVM-based controls. For example, when using `Window` in WPF how can a view model cause it's associated window to be close? The only way to close a window is to directly call the `Window.Close()` method on the instance. Since we don't want our view models to hold references to our views, our view models cannot call `Close()` method directly. `Window` also does not have any `DependencyProperty` that could be bound to a view model property to allow for closing the window. One way to resolve this problem is using an attached behavior. Using this pattern, our view model sets a notification-based property and rest is taken care of by using the attached behavior approach shown next. For this technique, we need to use `INotifyPropertyChanged`, `Data Triggers`, and `Attached Properties`.

This is the same technique that we have used in the `NorthwindMVVM` project to display the `OrderWizard` dialog box. This technique can be combined with a mediator to allow for disconnected components. To display **Order Wizard Dialog**, we have used the Mediator approach.

Let's define an attached behavior to display our `OrderWizard` dialog. As with any attached behavior, this approach would involve defining an attached property. We will name our attached property `ShowOrderWizardProperty`. In the `PropertyChangedCallback` handler of this property's metadata, we will display the dialog box as shown in the following code:

```
namespace Northwind.UI.WPF.AttachedBehaviors
{
   using System.Windows;

   public static class MainWindowAttachedBehaviors
   {
       #region Show Order Wizard
       public static DependencyProperty ShowOrderWizardProperty =
           DependencyProperty.RegisterAttached("ShowOrderWizard",
typeof(bool),
             typeof(MainWindowAttachedBehaviors),
             new UIPropertyMetadata(false, OnShowOrderWizard));
```

```
        public static bool GetShowOrderWizard(DependencyObject obj)
        {
            return (bool)obj.GetValue(ShowOrderWizardProperty);
        }
        public static void SetShowOrderWizard(DependencyObject obj,
        bool value)
        {
            obj.SetValue(ShowOrderWizardProperty, value);
        }
        public static void OnShowOrderWizard(DependencyObject d,
            DependencyPropertyChangedEventArgs e)
        {
            if ((bool)e.NewValue)
            {
                Window wnd = (Window)d;
                OrderWizard orderWizard = new OrderWizard();
                orderWizard.Owner = wnd;
                orderWizard.ShowDialog();
            }
        }

        #endregion
    }
}
```

This attached property can be used in `MainWindow`. Like a classic attached behavior, we can set it in a `DataTrigger` action based on some property change in the `DataContext`.

```
<Window x:Class="Northwind.UI.WPF.MainWindow"
        xmlns="http://schemas.microsoft.com/winfx/2006/xaml/
presentation"
        xmlns:x="http://schemas.microsoft.com/winfx/2006/xaml"
        xmlns:ViewModel="clr-namespace:Northwind.
ViewModel;assembly=Northwind.ViewModel"
        xmlns:AttachedBehaviors="clr-namespace:Northwind.UI.WPF.
AttachedBehaviors"
        Title="{Binding Name}" Height="500" Width="700"
        DataContext="{Binding Source={x:Static
        ViewModel:ViewModelLocator.MainWindowViewModelBaseStatic}}">
    <Window.Style>
        <Style>
            <Style.Triggers>
                <DataTrigger Binding="{Binding IsShowOrderWizard}"
             Value="true">
```

```
                    <Setter
                        Property="AttachedBehaviors:MainWindowAttachedB
ehaviors.ShowOrderWizard"
                        Value="true" />
                </DataTrigger>
                <DataTrigger Binding="{Binding IsShowOrderWizard}"
              Value="false">
                    <Setter
                        Property="AttachedBehaviors:MainWindowAttachedB
ehaviors.ShowOrderWizard"
                        Value="false" />
                </DataTrigger>
            </Style.Triggers>
        </Style>
    </Window.Style>
    <!--Window Def.-->
</Window>
```

This expects the `IsShowOrderWizard` property in `DataContext`. The attached property in `MainWindowAttachedBehavior` would be assigned based on the value of `IsShowOrderWizard`.

```
RelayCommand _showOrderWizard;
public RelayCommand ShowOrderWizard
{
   get
   {
       if (_showOrderWizard == null)
       {
           _showOrderWizard = new RelayCommand(
               () => { IsShowOrderWizard = true; });
       }
       return _showOrderWizard;
   }
}
bool _isShowOrderWizard = false;
public bool IsShowOrderWizard
{
   get { return _isShowOrderWizard; }
   set
```

```
        {
            _isShowOrderWizard = value;
            RaisePropertyChanged("IsShowOrderWizard");
        }
    }
```

Here we are setting the `IsShowOrderWizard` property in the `Execute` method of `RelayCommand`. In `MainWindow` we have bound this `Command` with a `ContextMenu` item.

This is enough to display our dialog but would leave the value of `IsShowOrderWizard` property set to `true`. We need to reset `IsShowOrderWizard` to `false` so that we can display the dialog again. In the case of `OrderWizard`, we will use a messenger to notify to `MainWindowViewModel` that the dialog has been closed. Let's define a new message type.

```
namespace Northwind.ViewModel.Messeges
{
    class OrderWizardClosed
    {
    }
}
```

Now `OrderWizard` should send the following message when it is being closed:

```
public void FinishWizard()
{
    //Other stuff
    Messenger.Default.Send<OrderWizardClosed>(new OrderWizardClosed());
}
```

We can subscribe to this message in `MainWindowViewModel` and reset the `boolean` property when this message is received.

```
private void SubscribeMessages()
{
    //Other stuff
    Messenger.Default.Register<OrderWizardClosed>(this, (a) =>
        {
            IsShowOrderWizard = false;
        });
}
```

This works because `OrderWizard` is a modal dialog. If it were a modeless dialog, then would need to tweak the approach a bit as opening the dialog would need to set the `IsShowOrderWizard` property. Using the **Context Menu** to open another wizard would do nothing as it would attempt to set the `IsShowOrderWizard` property. Since this is already set, `DataTrigger` in `MainWindow` would not be triggered resulting in no new Order Wizard view. We can fix it by keeping `Dictionary<string, Boolean>`. Here we can keep the key as a unique identifier for each dialog. The values would serve the same purpose as the `boolean` property. We would also need to add one more message so that the Order Wizard could notify `MainWindow` about this identifier. When this message is received, `MainWindowViewModel` should add an entry to the dictionary with passed on identifier and `boolean` value. In that case, we would also need to update the message type `OrderWizardClosed` by adding the order details so that we could reset the appropriate property.

Summary

There are many different approaches for incorporating dialog boxes in MVVM-based applications. We discussed how to use dialog service, mediator, and attached behavior based approaches. The dialog service takes advantage of DataTemplates. For the technologies that don't have DataTemplates automatically, we looked at using convention or configuration to achieve the same results.

8
Workflow-based MVVM Applications

By Muhammad Shujaat Siddiqi

Windows WF was released as one of the three great features of .NET 3.0. The other two features were Windows Presentation Foundation and Windows Communication Foundation. Since then it's been used in various ways by different organizations in their product design but its industry penetration hasn't been that well. With .NET 4.0, it's been completely redesigned, with a lot of new features added along with support of state machine workflows in .NET 4.0 platform update 1. In this chapter, we will be discussing two different scenarios in which Windows WF can be a useful help developing MVVM-based application.WF has a natural application in the business rules execution, especially for long running processes. It can also be used to control the flow of execution of an application.

> In order to run the examples in this section, you need to install the following:
>
> Visual Studio 2010 Service Pack 1
>
> .NET Framework 4 Platform Update 1
>
> In addition, a basic understanding of Windows WF is assumed for the examples in this chapter.

WF for business rules execution

Defining business rules in workflow has several advantages. The first and foremost of which is improved communication between the different teams involved in a software project. Developers are just one part of a great software project. This includes people from various backgrounds including individuals involved from business side. It is generally difficult to communicate the way workflow works across these teams. Development teams have to present these workflows using some other tools. So there are two versions of these rules. One which is used for communication across different teams and another which is actually used by the software embedded in code. Many a times, they become out of sync. On the other hand, if WF is used then two versions of the workflows presentation are generally not required.

Defining business logic in workflows is also good for application performance and resource management. In a software product, different users might have visibility on different modules. Now if we have business logic divided intelligently in workflows for each modules then we can just load the rules for the respective module saving user extra memory. It is also possible that we create a big application but there are certain areas of our application which the user might need on a seldom basis but they are heavy. We can move that logic too with workflow objects loaded and used by model. When a model is done using them, it can unload them for hibernation until they are needed again. The application would also be light weight, which would definitely improve application responsiveness.

If we are using Unit of Work (UoW) [Fowler] for persistence then we can pass the whole session state to the workflow. The workflow would execute the business rules on each entity in the session state and return the validation result with some message that you can show to the user using the notification methods discussed in *Chapter 9, Validation*. Generally, we pass the model or a **Memento** [Gang of four] to the workflow logic. The workflow executes the business logic and returns the status of execution of business rules. This memento can also be used to save application state in case of application failures, which can be used for restoring the application state when application is restarted.

In an MVVM-based application, executing business rules is generally the responsibility of the model. It can use WF library to execute business rule and communicate with the layers above about execution results. Yes, WF supports both way communications. This is especially useful to pass the business objects to workflow and get the validation results back after WF executes the workflow.

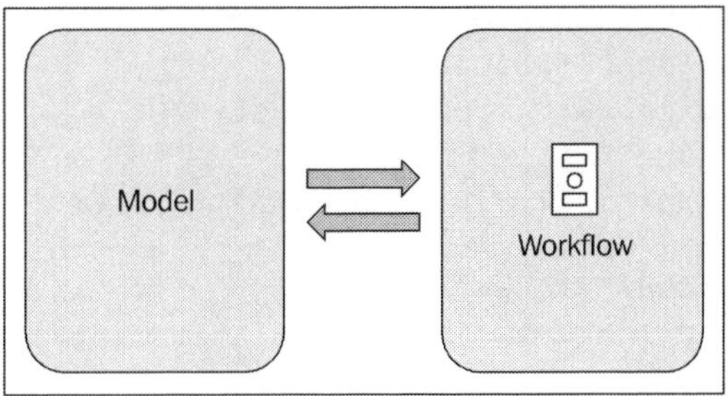

Let us create a simple order entry form. The system is interested in the customer name, the product being ordered, and its quantity. When a user submits the order, the system should validate the order. The system should notify the user about any validation issues.

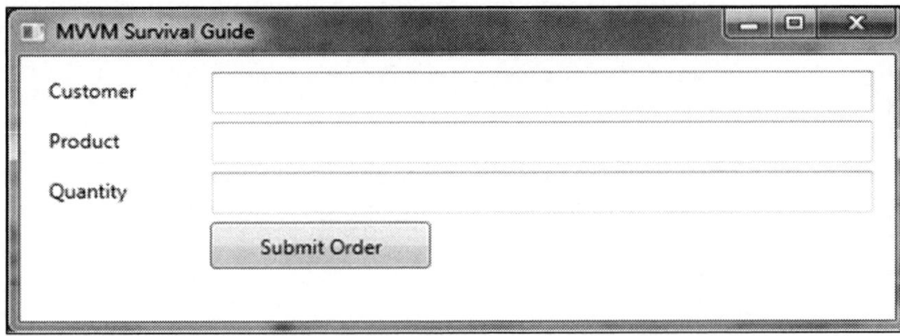

The XAML definition of the preceding view is as follows:

```
<Window x:Class="MVVMApp_WFBasedBusinessRules.OrderView"
    xmlns="http://schemas.microsoft.com/winfx/2006/xaml/presentation"
    xmlns:x="http://schemas.microsoft.com/winfx/2006/xaml"
    xmlns:local="clr-namespace:MVVMApp_WFBasedBusinessRules.ViewModel"
    Title="MVVM Survival Guide" Height="300" Width="531">
    <Window.DataContext>
        <local:OrderViewModel />
    </Window.DataContext>
    <Grid>
        <Grid.RowDefinitions>
            <RowDefinition Height="38*" />
            <RowDefinition Height="32*" />
            <RowDefinition Height="30*" />
            <RowDefinition Height="161*" />
        </Grid.RowDefinitions>
        <Grid.ColumnDefinitions>
            <ColumnDefinition Width="108*" />
```

```
            <ColumnDefinition Width="401*" />
        </Grid.ColumnDefinitions>
        <Label Content="Customer" Height="25"
HorizontalAlignment="Left"
               Margin="12,8,0,0" Name="lblCustomer"
VerticalAlignment="Top"
               Width="93" />
        <TextBox Height="26" HorizontalAlignment="Left"
Margin="3,10,0,0"
                 Name="txtCustomer" VerticalAlignment="Top"
Width="390"
                 Text="{Binding CustomerName}" Grid.Column="1" />
        <Label Content="Product" Height="25"
HorizontalAlignment="Left"
               Margin="12,1,0,0"
               Name="lblProduct" VerticalAlignment="Top" Width="93"
               Grid.Row="1" />
        <TextBox Height="26" HorizontalAlignment="Left"
Margin="3,3,0,0"
                 Name="txtProduct"
                 VerticalAlignment="Top" Width="390"
                 Text="{Binding ProductName}" Grid.Column="1" Grid.
Row="1" />
        <Label Content="Quantity" Height="25"
HorizontalAlignment="Left"
               Margin="12,0,0,0"
               Name="lblQuantity" VerticalAlignment="Top" Width="93"
               Grid.Row="2" />
        <TextBox Height="26" HorizontalAlignment="Left"
Margin="3,2,0,0"
                 Name="txtQuantity" VerticalAlignment="Top"
Width="390"
                 Text="{Binding ProductQuantity}" Grid.Column="1"
                 Grid.Row="2" />
        <GroupBox Header="Validation Errors" Height="111"
                  HorizontalAlignment="Left" Margin="3,38,0,0"
                  Name="grpBoxValidationSummary"
VerticalAlignment="Top"
                  Width="389" Grid.Column="1" Grid.Row="3">
            <GroupBox.Style>
                <Style TargetType="{x:Type GroupBox}">
                    <Setter Property="Visibility" Value="Collapsed" />
                    <Style.Triggers>
                        <DataTrigger Binding="{Binding IsValid}"
                                     Value="false">
```

```
                                <Setter Property="Visibility"
Value="Visible" />
                            </DataTrigger>
                            <DataTrigger Binding="{Binding IsValid}"
Value="true">
                                <Setter Property="Visibility"
Value="Collapsed" />
                            </DataTrigger>
                        </Style.Triggers>
                    </Style>
                </GroupBox.Style>
                <TextBlock Height="68" Name="tbValidationSummary"
                           Text="{Binding ValidationSummary}" Width="379"
/>
        </GroupBox>
        <Button Content="Submit Order" Height="29"
HorizontalAlignment="Left"
                Margin="2,3,0,0" Name="btnSubmitOrder"
VerticalAlignment="Top"
                Width="130" Grid.Row="3"
                Command="{Binding SubmitOrderCommand}" Grid.Column="1"
/>
    </Grid>
</Window>
```

The view is assigning an instance of `OrderViewModel` to its `DataContext`. `DataContext` should have the `CustomerName`, `ProductName`, and `ProductQuantity` properties. They are bound to the `Text` property of three `TextBox` in the preceding view. The view has `GroupBox`, `grpBoxValidationSummary`, to display the validation errors. It has a `DataTrigger` to set its visibility based on the `IsValid` property in the `DataContext`. The group box is only available when `IsValid` is set to `false`. The actual errors are displayed using the `TextBlock`, `tbValidationSummary`, which has a data binding with the `ValidationSummary` property from `DataContext`. The **Submit Order** button is using the `SubmitOrderCommand` property from `DataContext`. It should be an `ICommand` property in `DataContext`. Let's look at the definition of `OrderViewModel`.

```
namespace MVVMApp_WFBasedBusinessRules.ViewModel
{
   using GalaSoft.MvvmLight;
   using GalaSoft.MvvmLight.Command;
   using MVVMApp_WFBasedBusinessRules.Model;
   class OrderViewModel  : ViewModelBase
   {
       #region Private Fields
```

```
OrderModel _model = new OrderModel();
#endregion
#region Public Properties
string _customerName;
public string CustomerName
{
    get { return _customerName; }
    set
    {
        _customerName = value;
        RaisePropertyChanged("CustomerName");
    }
}
string _productName;
public string ProductName
{
    get { return _productName;}
    set
    {
        _productName = value;
        RaisePropertyChanged("ProductName");
    }
}
string _productQuantity;
public string ProductQuantity
{
    get { return _productQuantity; }
    set
    {
        _productQuantity = value;
        RaisePropertyChanged("ProductQuantity");
    }
}
string _validationSummary = string.Empty;
public string ValidationSummary
{
    get { return _validationSummary; }
    set
    {
        _validationSummary = value;
        this.RaisePropertyChanged("ValidationSummary");
    }
}
bool _isValid = true;
```

```
        public bool IsValid
        {
            get { return _isValid; }
            private set
            {
                _isValid = value;
                RaisePropertyChanged("IsValid");
            }
        }
        #endregion
        #region Commands
        RelayCommand _submitOrderCommand;
        public RelayCommand SubmitOrderCommand
        {
            get
            {
                if (_submitOrderCommand == null)
                {
                    _submitOrderCommand = new
RelayCommand(submitOrder);
                }
                return _submitOrderCommand;
            }
        }
        #endregion
        #region Private Methods
        private void submitOrder()
        {
            IsValid = true;
            _model.CustomerName = this.CustomerName;
            _model.ProductName = this.ProductName;
            _model.ProductQuantity = this.ProductQuantity;
            this.ValidationSummary = _model.Validate();
            if (this.ValidationSummary.Length > 0)
            {
                IsValid = false;
            }
        }
        #endregion
    }
}
```

`SubmitOrderCommand` is using the `Validate` method of `_model` for validation. This method returns validation errors in case of validation failures. It checks if there is any validation error returned, to set the `IsValid` property which would cause `DataTrigger` on the view to be triggered showing the validation message on the display. Now let's look how `OrderModel` uses WF-based workflow to validate the business rule.

```
namespace MVVMApp_WFBasedBusinessRules.Model
{
    using System.Collections.Generic;
    using Interfaces;
    using System.Activities;
    using BusinessRulesWF;

    class OrderModel : IOrder
    {
        public string CustomerName { get; set; }
        public string ProductName { get; set; }
        public string ProductQuantity { get; set; }

        public string Validate()
        {
            string validationSummary = string.Empty;

            OrderRuleService orderRuleService =
                new OrderRuleService();

            Dictionary<string, object> arguments =
                new Dictionary<string, object>() { { "Order", this }
};

            validationSummary =
                WorkflowInvoker.Invoke(orderRuleService, arguments)
                ["ValidationSummary"].ToString();

            return validationSummary;
        }
    }
}
```

This is a simple model with three properties `CustomerName`, `ProductName`, and `ProductQuantity`. The model is using `WorkflowInvoker` to execute the `OrderRuleService` workflow defined in a separate `BusinessRulesWF` assembly. The model implements the `IOrder` interface. Since we would need the same interface in the actual workflow which is defined in a separate assembly, let's create this interface in a separate assembly, which is referenced by both assemblies containing model and the actual workflow. This would avoid the circular reference. Both of them are added as class library projects.

```
namespace Interfaces
{
    public interface IOrder
    {
        string CustomerName { get; set; }
        string ProductName { get; set; }
        string ProductQuantity { get; set; }
    }
}
```

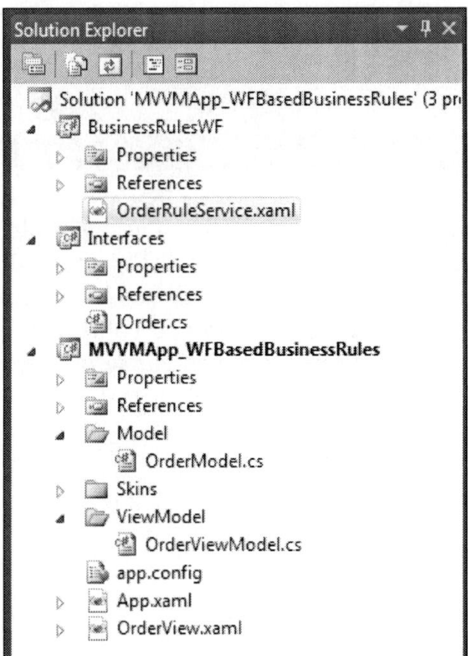

.NET 4.0 allows WF workflows to be executed using `WorkflowInvoker` and `WorkflowApplication`. `WorkflowInvoker` allows executing workflow synchronously on the calling thread. For more controlled execution of workflows `WorkflowApplication` is used. It executes workflow on a separate `ThreadPool` thread. It also provides certain events which can be used to get notified by calling code of the workflow execution.

As you can see in the definition of the `Validate` method of the model, the model is passing itself as an argument to the workflow. The workflow arguments are passed as `Dictionary<string, object>`. Each key/value pair would be specified with the name of argument and the actual value to be assigned to the argument. Based on this discussion, we can guess that the `OrderRuleService` workflow is expecting an `Order` parameter. After adding a reference of the `Interfaces` assembly, we can specify an input argument to the workflow. We also need to import the `Interfaces` namespace in the individual workflow.

In order to keep the example simple, let's create a very simple workflow. This just has one rule `ValidateLegitimateCustomer`, which is basically an `If` activity. This rule is checking if the name of the customer matches **Muhammad** or **Ryan**. If this is the case then it assigns the **You are not allowed** validation message to the return argument `ValidationSummary`. Please don't ask us why they don't want to do any business with us!

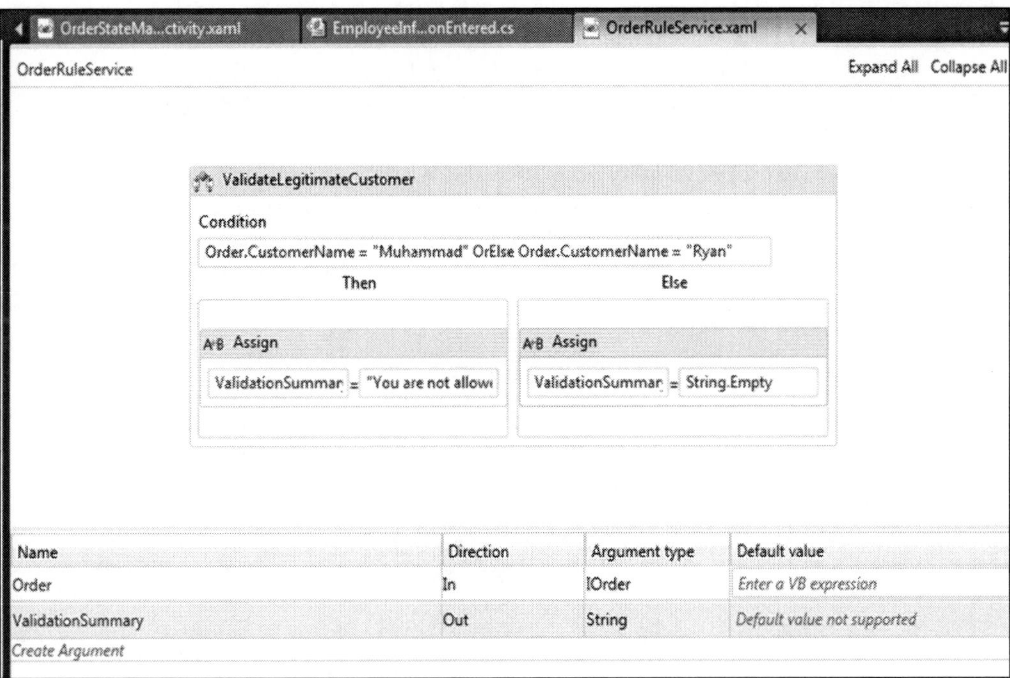

Add the reference of the `BusinessRulesWF` project and the `System.Activities` assembly to the `MVVMApp_WFBasedBusinessRules` project. Let's run this example. We enter the data by providing `Ryan` or `Muhammad` in the **Customer** field. The message **You are not allowed** is displayed in the view.

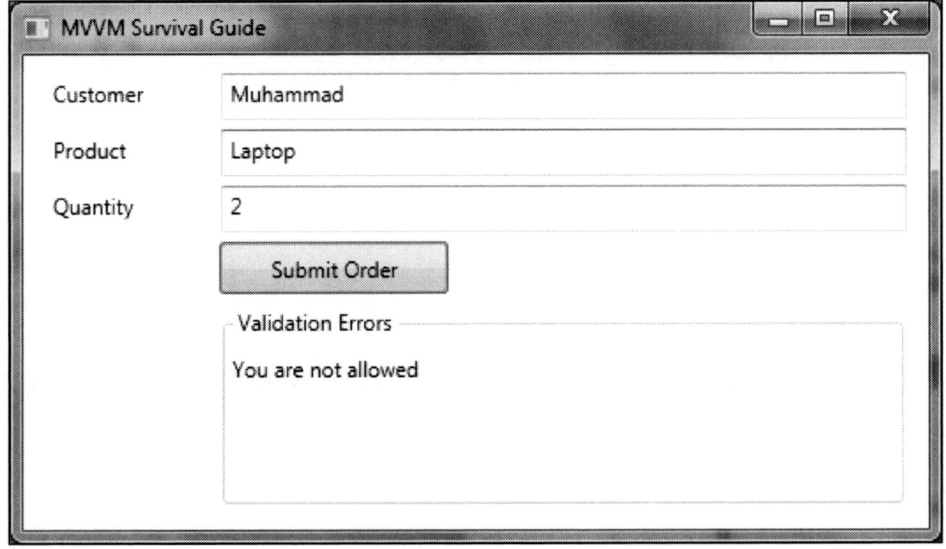

Handling delays in rules execution

The example discussed previously is very simple. It has the simplest workflow in the world. In a real enterprise application, this is generally not the case. The business rules will be complex and they will take a lot of time to execute. `WorkflowInvoke`, used previously, executes the workflow in the same thread as the calling thread. We, somehow, need to keep our application responsive even when the rules are being executed. We need to find ways that we could execute these workflows asynchronously so that we could keep the user interface responsive during this execution.

Using WorkflowInvoker in background thread

The natural solution to this problem is to execute the workflow in a different thread. However, before discussing that let's create a new activity, named `SlowOrderRuleService`, as follows:

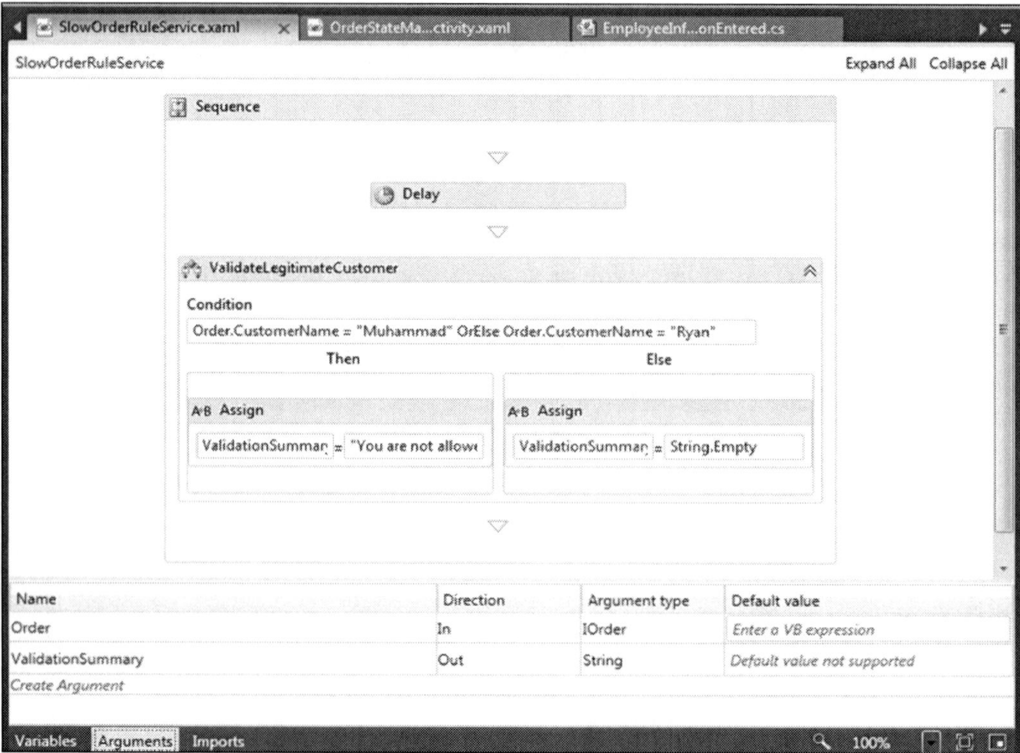

The preceding workflow is similar to the workflow in the previous example, except it has a delay activity before checking if this customer should be allowed or not. We can keep any arbitrary delay for this example (100 seconds for this example). This is to simulate the slow executing workflows.

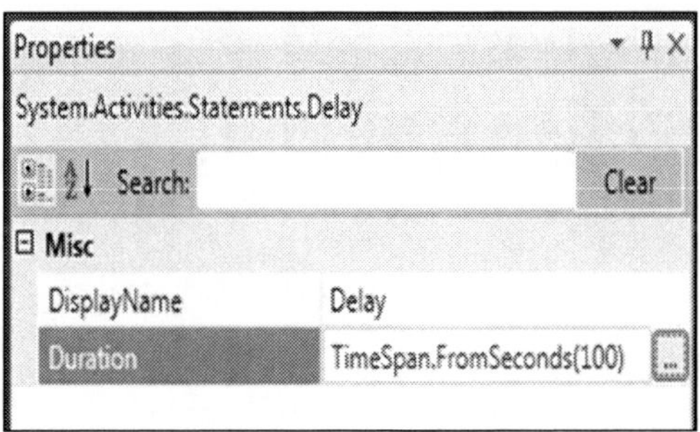

The workflow is still using an instance of a type which implements `IOrder` as an input argument. It has an output argument `ValidationSummary` of type string. Remember that we need to import the namespace of `IOrder` on the **Imports** tab in the workflow designer. The changes in the workflow would also need updates in the view model and model code, so that model could invoke this workflow asynchronously. After executing the workflow, model needs to notify the view model about results of execution of business rules. Let's see how we are updating the `OrderModel` code.

```
namespace MVVMApp_WFBasedBusinessRules.Model
{
    using System.Collections.Generic;
    using Interfaces;
    using System.Activities;
    using BusinessRulesWF;
    using System.Threading;
    using System.ComponentModel;

    class OrderModel : IOrder, INotifyPropertyChanged
    {
        public string CustomerName { get; set; }
        public string ProductName { get; set; }
        public string ProductQuantity { get; set; }
         string _validationSummary;
        public string ValidationSummary
        {
            get { return _validationSummary; }
            set
            {
```

```
                _validationSummary = value;
                RaisePropertyChanged("ValidationSummary");

            }
        }

        public void Validate()
        {
            ThreadPool.QueueUserWorkItem(
                new WaitCallback(RunValidationLogic));
        }

        public void RunValidationLogic(object stateInfo)
        {
            Dictionary<string, object> arguments =
                new Dictionary<string, object>()
                {
              { "Order", this }
                };

            ValidationSummary =
                WorkflowInvoker.Invoke(new SlowOrderRuleService(),
                arguments)["ValidationSummary"].ToString();
        }

        #region INotifyPropertyChanged implementation

        public event PropertyChangedEventHandler PropertyChanged
            = delegate { };

  private void RaisePropertyChanged(string propertyName)
        {
            PropertyChanged(this,
                new PropertyChangedEventArgs(propertyName));
        }

        #endregion

    }
}
```

The model now implements the `INotifyPropertyChanged` interface. It has a property `ValidationSummary` whose changes are notified to interested parties using the `PropertyChanged` event. Here we are using `WorkflowInvoker` on a `ThreadPool` thread. When the view model calls the `Validate` method of `OrderModel`, it pushes the execution of the `RunValidationLogic` method to a `ThreadPool` thread. In this way, the UI thread does not remain busy during the workflow execution, keeping the UI responsive.

Let's see what changes we need to make in `OrderViewModel` to use the updated definition of `OrderModel`. The first and foremost is using the `Validate` method of the model. Since it returns void now, so the validation summary assignment can be removed.

```
private void submitOrder()
{
    IsValid = true;

    _model.CustomerName = CustomerName;
    _model.ProductName = ProductName;
    _model.ProductQuantity = ProductQuantity;

    _model.Validate();

}
```

`OrderModel` implements `INotifyPropertyChanged`. We can subscribe to the `PropertyChanged` event of the model to handle the notification in its properties.

```
public OrderViewModel()
{
    _model.PropertyChanged +=
        new System.ComponentModel
            .PropertyChangedEventHandler(
                _model_PropertyChanged);
}
```

Since we are interested in only `ValidationSummary`, we can check if this is an update in the said property and update our values.

```
void _model_PropertyChanged(object sender,
    System.ComponentModel.PropertyChangedEventArgs e)
{
    if (e.PropertyName == "ValidationSummary")
    {
        ValidationSummary = _model.ValidationSummary;
        if (ValidationSummary.Length > 0)
        {
            IsValid = false;
        }
    }
}
```

When we run the application now and click on the **Submit** button, it is not blocked. The application keeps executing the workflow in the background. After the execution is finished, it notifies the validation results. If there is a validation failure (`ValidationSummary` assigned), then it is shown in the view.

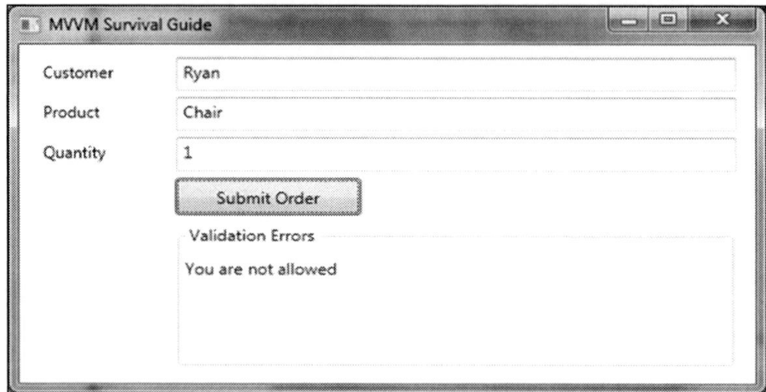

Using WorkflowApplication

`WorkflowApplication` allows the execution of workflow on a separate background thread. It also makes certain events available, which can be used to handle the lifetime of workflow execution. To use `WorkflowApplication`, we can use all the code from the previous example except that we need to update the definition of the `Validate` method of `OrderModel` to use `WorkflowApplication` instead.

```
public void Validate()
{
    Dictionary<string, object> arguments =
        new Dictionary<string, object>()
        {
            { "Order", this }
        };

    WorkflowApplication workflowApp =
        new WorkflowApplication(new SlowOrderRuleService(), arguments)
        {
            Completed = (e) => {
                ValidationSummary =
                    e.Outputs["ValidationSummary"].ToString();
            }
        };

    workflowApp.Run();
}
```

In the `Completed` event handler, `ValidationSummary` is updated with the value of `Output` variable of `SlowOrderRuleService`. This assignment would be notified to the view model and the error message, if invalid, would be displayed on the interface.

WF for controlling application flow

WF can also be used to control the flow of application execution. In this technique, the view model uses WF-based workflows to control the flow of application. This delegation results in better separation of concern by keeping the view model code more maintainable and testable. The following diagram uses workflow directly. It is preferable to introduce a service layer here between the view model and workflow. This would keep us from being over dependent on the Workflow technology. This also improves unit testability.

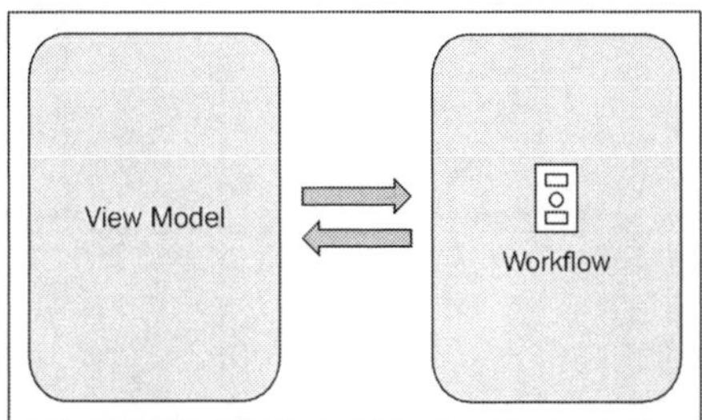

The latest platform update of .NET Framework 4.0 has included some features based on high public demand. State machine based workflow is one of them. In this section, we would use state machines to manage the flow of our views. It can even extend to control the flow of the whole application.

When we move to MVVM, we take many things out of view to view model. This includes the flow of application. The controls on the view just take user input and pass it to the view model. This has made our view models fat. They should rather be composite by using helpers for these operations. WF state machine might be such helper for determining the new state of the view based on user interaction with the application.

In the Northwind MVVM example project, we have created a simple Order Wizard using state machine workflows. In this example, an order is created in three steps. These steps are as follows:

1. Enter customer information.
2. Enter employee (sales rep) information.
3. Enter order details.

The user is allowed to go back and forth between these steps using the **Back** and **Next** buttons. A **Finish** button is provided at the last step to finish the order wizard. This flow can be represented in WF4.

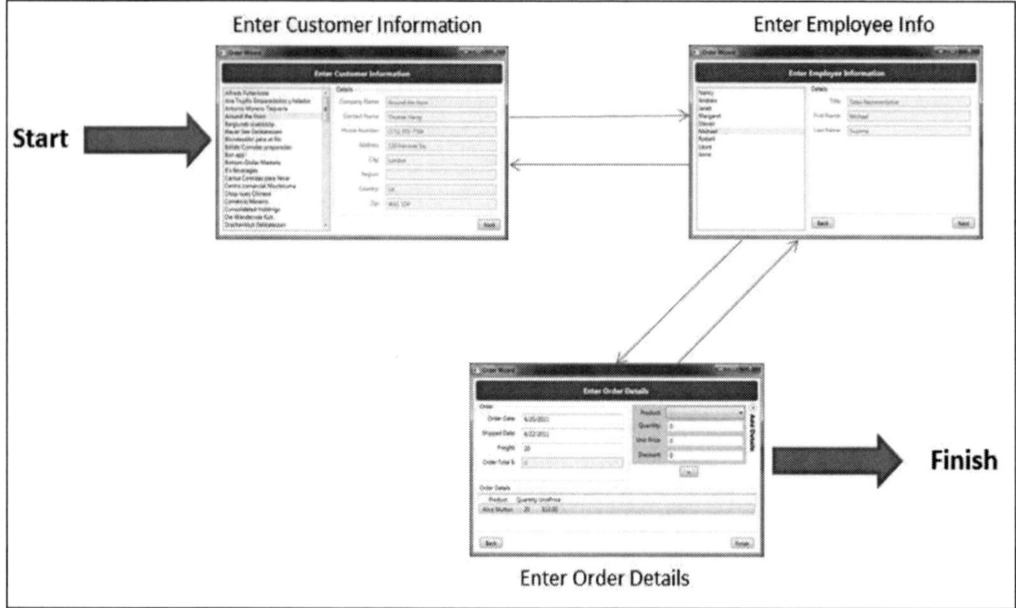

Let's create a workflow activity in the same project and name it `OrderWizardControlFlow.xaml`. We add a state machine workflow and update it as follows:

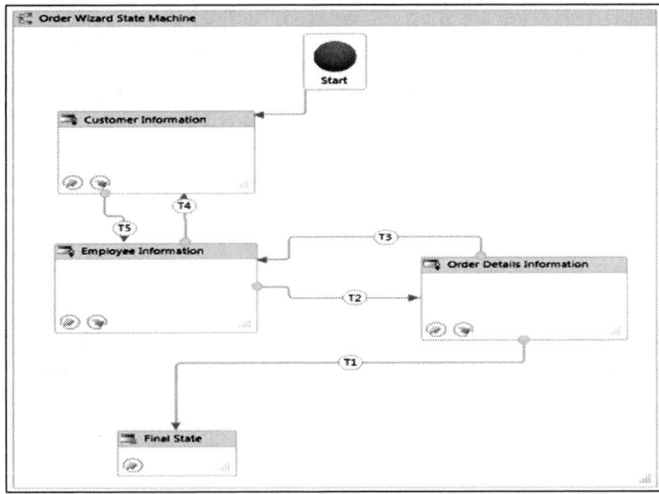

We are passing the view model as the argument and calling certain methods of the view model as Entry and Exit actions for these activities. For calling methods on the view model, we can use the `InvokeMethod` activity in WF. We also need to import relevant namespaces.

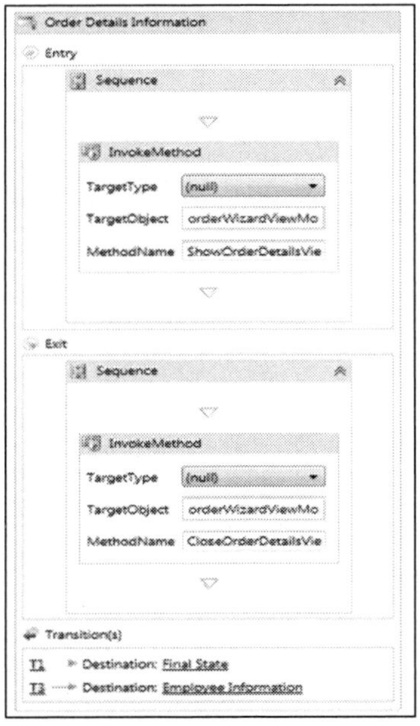

> We need to assign `SyncrhonizationContext` to `WorkflowApplication` if we need to update UI in these methods. This makes the correct dispatcher available.

State transitions can be controlled using bookmarks. Here we have used the following bookmarks for state transitions (`T1`, `T2`, `T3`, `T4`, and `T5`):

- `EnterCustomerInformation`
- `EnterEmployeeInformation`
- `EnterOrderDetailsInformation`
- `FinishOrderWizard`

In WF, a bookmark is basically a `NativeActivity`. A sample bookmark, used in the `NorthwindMVM` project (`EnterCustomerInformaiton`), is as follows:

```
namespace Northwind.ViewModel.Workflows.Bookmarks
{
    using System;
    using System.Collections.Generic;
    using System.Linq;
    using System.Text;
    using System.Activities;

    public class EnterCustomerInformation : NativeActivity<string>
    {
        protected override bool CanInduceIdle
        {
            get
            {
                return true;
            }
        }

        protected override void Execute(NativeActivityContext context)
        {
            context.CreateBookmark("EnterCustomerInformation");
        }
    }
}
```

The other bookmarks are defined similarly with their specified bookmark names. A bookmark can be used as a trigger for a state transition as follows:

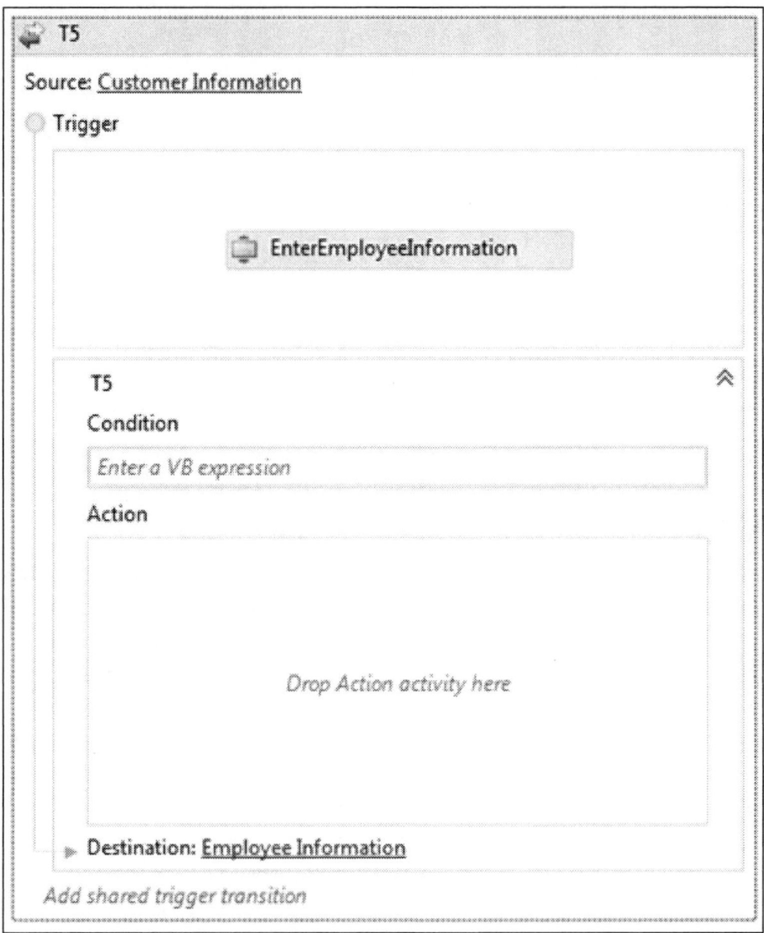

As soon as the workflow reaches the `Bookmark` activity, it executes its `Execute` method which creates a bookmark. Now the workflow just pauses here until there are instructions to move past this bookmark. These instructions can be provided using the `ResumeBookmark` method of `WorkflowApplication`.

```
ViewStateController.ResumeBookmark("FinishOrderWizard", null);
```

Here `ViewStateController` is a `WorkflowApplication` instance.

```
Dictionary<string, object> arguments =
    new Dictionary<string, object>()
    {
        { "orderWizardViewModel", this }
    };

ViewStateController =
    new WorkflowApplication(
        new OrderWizardControlFlow(),
        arguments);

ViewStateController.SynchronizationContext =
    DispatcherSynchronizationContext.Current;

ViewStateController.Run();
```

Summary

WF provides an extraordinary support for defining business rules. It is advisable to have a service layer between the workflow and the model. Application flow can also be defined using WF using the state machine workflows. A view can be considered as having different states; user actions cause transitioning between these states.

9
Validation

By Muhammad Shujaat Siddiqi

XAML technologies help us make rich applications for our customers in both web and desktop environments, allowing for better usability than the traditional applications. **Validation** is key to creating a good user experience, and having access to good validation tools is essential for being able to quickly create robust validations in an application. These tools should be generic enough to support various requirements and should not have a significant effect on application responsiveness. Validation tools should be flexible enough to allow validation issues to be communicated to users in the most elegant way, saving users the time and effort it would take to understand the issues with the data entered. **WPF** and **Silverlight** provide several tools to help us define the validation in our applications. There are so many tools available, and they have so much detail, that it is not possible to cover them all in a single chapter. However, we will be covering the validation techniques that are best aligned with MVVM.

Validations and dependency properties

`DependencyProperty` supports the validation of the value being assigned to it via a callback method. Whenever the property value is set, the WPF and Silverlight runtimes can call a callback to check if its value is valid. The callback method simply needs to return `true` for valid or `false` for invalid to take advantage of this feature. This feature is especially useful for custom controls and element adapters, which are implemented as `DependencyObject`. The callback is specified at the time that the dependency property is registered with the WPF runtime. The callback is passed as one of the parameters to the `Register` static method on the `DependencyProperty` class, as shown in the following code:

```
public static DependencyProperty Register(
  string name,
```

```
    Type propertyType,
    Type ownerType,
    PropertyMetadata typeMetadata,
    ValidateValueCallback validateValueCallback
)
```

Where `ValidateValueCallback` is as follows:

```
public delegate bool ValidateValueCallback(
    Object value
)
```

When the `dependency` property is set with an invalid value, `ValidateValueCallback` simply returns `false`. Whenever the WPF runtime gets the value `false` returned from a validation callback, `ArgumentException` will be raised. If `ValidatesOnException` is set as `true` when the control's property is bound, the control is set with an error template. The default error template highlights the bound control in red. The same result can be achieved by adding `ExceptionValidationRule` to binding validation rules.

Error templates

As we have discussed previously, we can notify the user of the error condition by highlighting the particular field that failed the validation in the view. By default, the element is highlighted with a red border. We can update this behavior by overriding the error template. Let's revisit the example in the previous chapter to demonstrate error templates. In that example, we had a simple order entry form where the user could submit an order by specifying a customer, a product, and its quantity. Let's now update `OrderViewModel`, as follows:

```
namespace MVVMApp_WFBasedBusinessRules.ViewModel
{
  using GalaSoft.MvvmLight;
  using GalaSoft.MvvmLight.Command;
  using MVVMApp_WFBasedBusinessRules.Model;

  class OrderViewModel : ViewModelBase
  {
    #region Constructors

      public OrderViewModel()
      {
        _model.PropertyChanged +=
        new System.ComponentModel
```

```
      .PropertyChangedEventHandler(
      _model_PropertyChanged);
    }


  #endregion Constructors

  #region Private Fields

    OrderModel _model = new OrderModel();

  #endregion

  #region Public Properties

    string _customerName;
    public string CustomerName
    {
      get { return _customerName; }
      set
      {
        _customerName = value;
        RaisePropertyChanged("CustomerName");
      }
    }

    string _productName;
    public string ProductName
    {
      get { return _productName; }
      set
      {
        _productName = value;
        RaisePropertyChanged("ProductName");
      }
    }

    int _productQuantity;
    public int ProductQuantity
    {
      get { return _productQuantity; }
      set
      {
        _productQuantity = value;
```

```
        RaisePropertyChanged("ProductQuantity");
      }
    }


    string _validationSummary = string.Empty;
    public string ValidationSummary
    {
      get { return _validationSummary; }
      set
      {
        _validationSummary = value;
        this.RaisePropertyChanged("ValidationSummary");
      }
    }

    bool _isValid = true;
    public bool IsValid
    {
      get { return _isValid; }
      private set
      {
        _isValid = value;
        RaisePropertyChanged("IsValid");
      }
    }

  #endregion

  #region Commands

    RelayCommand _submitOrderCommand;
    public RelayCommand SubmitOrderCommand
    {
      get
      {
        if (_submitOrderCommand == null)
        {
          _submitOrderCommand =
          new RelayCommand(submitOrder);
        }

        return _submitOrderCommand;
      }
```

```
        }

      #endregion

      #region Private Methods

        private void submitOrder()
        {
          IsValid = true;

          _model.CustomerName = CustomerName;
          _model.ProductName = ProductName;
          _model.ProductQuantity =
          string.Format("{0}", ProductQuantity);

          _model.Validate();

        }


      #endregion

      #region Event Handlers

        void _model_PropertyChanged(object sender,
        System.ComponentModel.PropertyChangedEventArgs e)
        {
          if (e.PropertyName == "ValidationSummary")
          {
            ValidationSummary = _model.ValidationSummary;
            if (ValidationSummary.Length > 0)
            {
              IsValid = false;
            }
          }
        }

      #endregion
    }
  }
```

As you can see, we have updated `Quantity` to `int`. We are binding this to a textbox in the view. Now, if a user enters something in the textbox that cannot be copied to the **Quantity** field, it results in a error and the same is displayed in the view. Now, we can run the application without any further changes and can enter the following information. The error is denoted by highlighting the **Quantity** textbox in red, as follows:

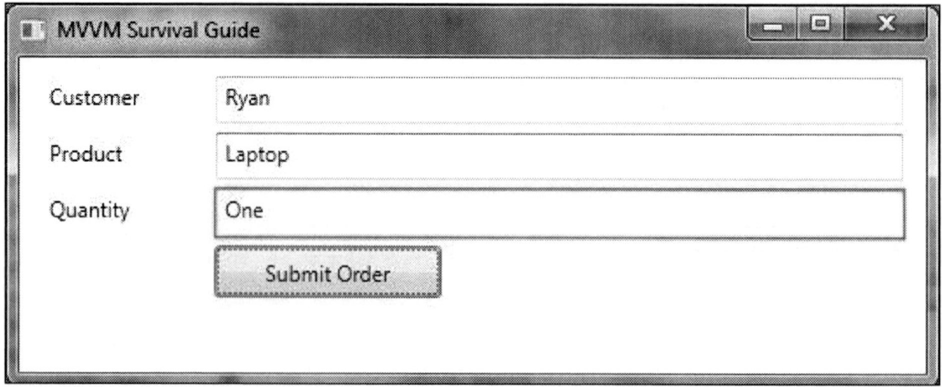

We can also change the error notification display of individual fields. In order to do that, we can define a control template to be used as the error template. We can do this by simply specifying the same error template for an element by using the `Validation.ErrorTemplate` attached property. In the control template, we use `AdornedElementPlaceHolder` to show the actual element in error. Let's update `OrderView`, as follows:

```
<Window x:Class="MVVMApp_WFBasedBusinessRules.OrderView"
  xmlns="http://schemas.microsoft.com/winfx/2006/xaml/presentation"
  xmlns:x="http://schemas.microsoft.com/winfx/2006/xaml"
  xmlns:local="clr-namespace:MVVMApp_WFBasedBusinessRules.ViewModel"
  Title="MVVM Survival Guide" Height="300" Width="531">
  <Window.Resources>
    <ControlTemplate x:Key="ValidationErrorTemplate">
      <Border BorderBrush="Blue" BorderThickness="2">
        <AdornedElementPlaceholder />
     </Border>
    </ControlTemplate>
  </Window.Resources>
  <Window.DataContext>
    <local:OrderViewModel />
  </Window.DataContext>
  <Grid>
    <Grid.RowDefinitions>
```

```
    <RowDefinition Height="38*" />
    <RowDefinition Height="32*" />
    <RowDefinition Height="30*" />
    <RowDefinition Height="161*" />
  </Grid.RowDefinitions>
  <Grid.ColumnDefinitions>
    <ColumnDefinition Width="108*" />
    <ColumnDefinition Width="401*" />
  </Grid.ColumnDefinitions>
  <Label Content="Customer" Height="25"
    HorizontalAlignment="Left"
    Margin="12,8,0,0" Name="lblCustomer" VerticalAlignment="Top"
    Width="93" />
  <TextBox Height="26"  HorizontalAlignment="Left"
    Margin="3,10,0,0"
    Name="txtCustomer" VerticalAlignment="Top" Width="390"
    Text="{Binding CustomerName}" Grid.Column="1" />
    <Label Content="Product" Height="25"
      HorizontalAlignment="Left"
      Margin="12,1,0,0"
      Name="lblProduct" VerticalAlignment="Top" Width="93"
      Grid.Row="1" />
    <TextBox Height="26" HorizontalAlignment="Left"
      Margin="3,3,0,0"
      Name="txtProduct"
      VerticalAlignment="Top" Width="390"
      Text="{Binding ProductName}" Grid.Column="1" Grid.Row="1"
    />
    <Label Content="Quantity" Height="25"
      HorizontalAlignment="Left"
      Margin="12,0,0,0"
      Name="lblQuantity" VerticalAlignment="Top" Width="93"
      Grid.Row="2" />
    <TextBox Height="26" HorizontalAlignment="Left"
      Margin="3,2,0,0"
      Name="txtQuantity" VerticalAlignment="Top" Width="390"
      Validation.ErrorTemplate="{StaticResource
      ValidationErrorTemplate}"
      Text="{Binding ProductQuantity}" Grid.Column="1"
      Grid.Row="2" />
    <GroupBox Header="Validation Errors" Height="111"
      HorizontalAlignment="Left" Margin="3,38,0,0"
      Name="grpBoxValidationSummary" VerticalAlignment="Top"
      Width="389" Grid.Column="1" Grid.Row="3">
      <GroupBox.Style>
```

```
            <Style TargetType="{x:Type GroupBox}">
              <Setter Property="Visibility" Value="Collapsed" />
              <Style.Triggers>
                <DataTrigger Binding="{Binding IsValid}"
                  Value="false">
                  <Setter Property="Visibility" Value="Visible" />
                </DataTrigger>
                <DataTrigger Binding="{Binding IsValid}" Value="true">
                  <Setter Property="Visibility" Value="Collapsed" />
                </DataTrigger>
              </Style.Triggers>
            </Style>
          </GroupBox.Style>
          <TextBlock Height="68" Name="tbValidationSummary"
            Text="{Binding ValidationSummary}" Width="379" />
        </GroupBox>
        <Button Content="Submit Order" Height="29"
          HorizontalAlignment="Left"
          Margin="2,3,0,0" Name="btnSubmitOrder"
          VerticalAlignment="Top"
          Width="130" Grid.Row="3"
          ="{Binding SubmitOrderCommand}" Grid.Column="1" />
    </Grid>
  </Window>
```

If we run the application, we can verify that we get a blue border around our control when validation fails, as shown in the image that follows. Here, we have specified the error template on an individual text box. This might be a reasonable approach if we use different error templates for different instances of the same element. If we have to use the same error template, we can specify `ValidationErrorTemplate` in a style in a more centralized scope than the individual elements. If we just remove the changes in the view from the previous XAML and update `App.xaml` as follows, we can achieve the same result. In the style, we have also added a trigger to show the first error message in the tool tip of the textbox, if there is any issue with the entered data.

```
<Application x:Class="MVVMApp_WFBasedBusinessRules.App"
  xmlns="http://schemas.microsoft.com/winfx/2006/xaml/presentation"
  xmlns:x="http://schemas.microsoft.com/winfx/2006/xaml"
  xmlns:d="http://schemas.microsoft.com/expression/blend/2008"
  xmlns:mc="http://schemas.openxmlformats.org/markup-
  compatibility/2006"
  xmlns:vm="clr-namespace:MVVMApp_WFBasedBusinessRules.ViewModel"
  StartupUri="OrderView.xaml"
  mc:Ignorable="d">
  <Application.Resources>
```

```
    <!--Global View Model Locator-->
    <vm:ViewModelLocator x:Key="Locator"
      d:IsDataSource="True"
    <ControlTemplate x:Key="ValidationErrorTemplate">
      <Border BorderBrush="Blue" BorderThickness="2">
        <AdornedElementPlaceholder />
      </Border>
    </ControlTemplate>
    <Style TargetType="TextBox">
      <Style.Setters>
        <Setter Property="Validation.ErrorTemplate"
          Value="{StaticResource ValidationErrorTemplate}" />
      </Style.Setters>
      <Style.Triggers>
        <Trigger Property="Validation.HasError" Value="true">
          <Setter Property="ToolTip">
            <Setter.Value>
              <Binding
                RelativeSource="{x:Static RelativeSource.Self}"
                Path="(Validation.Errors)[0].ErrorContent" />
            </Setter.Value>
          </Setter>
        </Trigger>
      </Style.Triggers>
    </Style>
  </Application.Resources>
</Application>
```

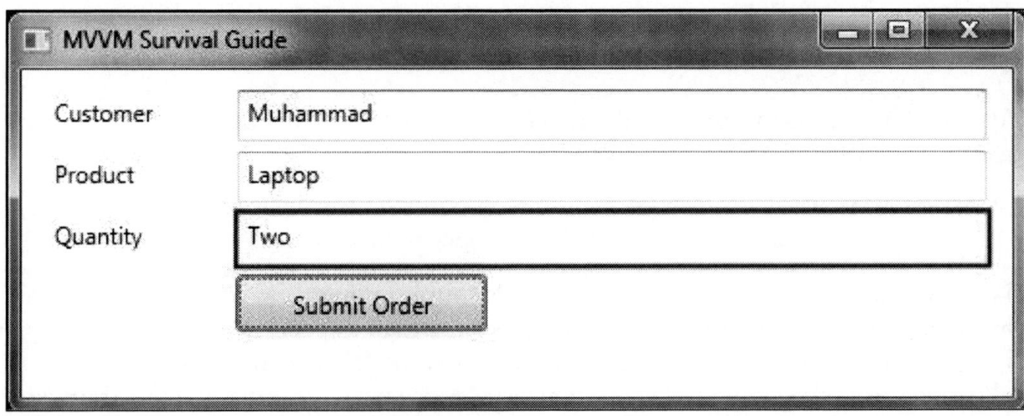

Validation in MVVM-based applications

As mentioned in the introduction to this chapter, we have a lot of validation options to choose from in XAML-based technologies. Let's now take a look at the options that are best suited for use in MVVM applications.

Validation rules

This is the simplest and most commonly used validation technique. A WPF binding can be associated with a number of custom validation rules, each subclassed from `ValidationRule`. There are only two validation rules provided as part of the library: `DataErrorValidationRule` and `ExceptionValidationRule`.

Using validation rules

We can define additional custom validation rules by inheriting from `ValidationRule`. We can add them to the `ValidationRules` collection for a binding, as follows:

```
<TextBox Height="26" HorizontalAlignment="Left"
         Margin="3,2,0,0"          VerticalAlignment="Top" Width="390"
         Grid.Column="1" Grid.Row="2" >
    <TextBox.Text>
        <Binding Path="ProductQuantity" >
            <Binding.ValidationRules>
                <validators:MaxDigitValidationRule />
            </Binding.ValidationRules>
        </Binding>
    </TextBox.Text>
</TextBox>
```

Here, `validators` is the alias for the namespace where we have defined the `MaxDigitValidationRule` class, as follows:

```
xmlns:validators=
        "clr-namespace:MVVMApp_WFBasedBusinessRules.ValidationRules"
```

The definition of `MaxDigitValidationRule` is simple enough, as we just need to validate that the data entered does not exceed more than a specified length (two digits), and that it doesn't start with a zero. If validation fails, we need to return validation errors specifying the validation issue. Since we have already defined the first error message that appears in the tool tip of the textbox, if the control shows an error, we can hover over the **Quantity** text box to get details about the validation issue.

```
namespace MVVMApp_WFBasedBusinessRules.ValidationRules
{
    using System.Windows.Controls;
    using System.Globalization;
    using System.Text.RegularExpressions;

    public class MaxDigitValidationRule : ValidationRule
    {
        public override ValidationResult
            Validate(object value, CultureInfo cultureInfo)
        {
            ValidationResult validationResult =
                ValidationResult.ValidResult;

            string val = string.Format("{0}", value);
            if (!Regex.IsMatch(val, "^[1-9]{1}[0-9]{0,1}$"))
            {
                validationResult =
                    new ValidationResult(false,
                        string.Format(
                        "Invalid Quantity : {0}", val));

            }

            return validationResult;
        }
    }
}
```

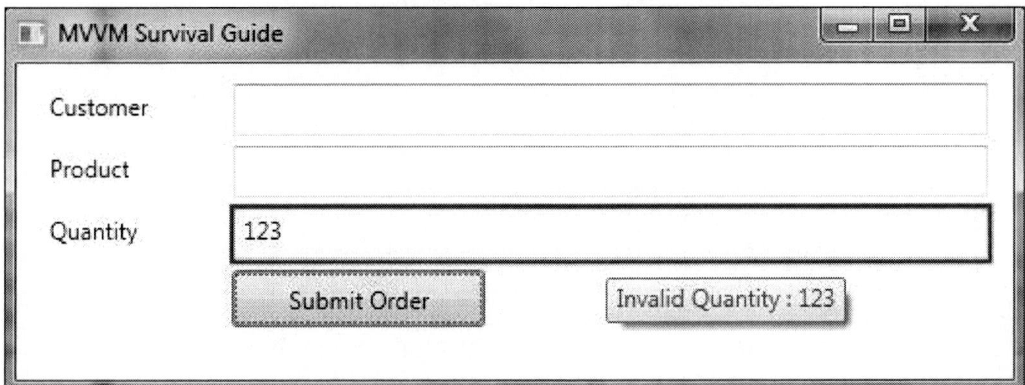

Specializing validation rules—supporting parameters

XAML technologies are quite flexible in passing parameters to converters and commands. Curious developers, like you, might be interested to know whether we can pass parameters to validation rules, allowing us to make the validation rules aware of the other fields. The answer is that we can, and we can even pass the whole data context as the parameter, if that makes sense for the scenario. This ability can help us to write more generic validation rules. In the previous example, we could write a generic rule to validate the number of digits specified by the parameter. Let's now take a look at how we can pass parameters to the validation rules.

`System.Windows.Controls.ValidationRule` is not a sealed class; on the contrary, it is an abstract class that we need to inherit from, to define validation rules. We do this by providing a definition for the `Validate` method. In our `ValidationRule` derived class, we can define other properties to use during validation processing. For example, in the following validation rule , we are adding the `MaxDigit` property and using it in the `Validate` method, to make our validation rule more generic:

```
namespace MVVMApp_WFBasedBusinessRules.ValidationRules
{
    using System.Windows.Controls;
    using System.Globalization;
    using System.Text.RegularExpressions;
    using System.Text;

    public class MaxDigitValidationRule : ValidationRule
    {
        public int MaxDigits { get; set; }

        public override ValidationResult
            Validate(object value, CultureInfo cultureInfo)
        {
            ValidationResult validationResult =
                ValidationResult.ValidResult;

            string val = string.Format("{0}", value);

            StringBuilder patternBuilder =
                new StringBuilder("^[1-9]{1}[0-9]{0,");
            patternBuilder.Append(MaxDigits - 1);
            patternBuilder.Append("}$");

            if (!Regex.IsMatch(val, patternBuilder.ToString()))
```

```
            {
                validationResult =
                    new ValidationResult(false,
                        string.Format(
                        "Invalid Quantity : {0}", val));

            }

            return validationResult;
        }
    }
}
```

Now, we can simply assign a value to our `MaxDigit` property in XAML to configure the behavior of `MaxDigitValidationRule`. The following definition would allow users to add up to three digits before seeing a validation error:

```
<TextBox Height="26" HorizontalAlignment="Left"
         Margin="3,2,0,0" Name="txtQuantity"
         VerticalAlignment="Top" Width="390"
         Grid.Column="1" Grid.Row="2" >
    <TextBox.Text>
        <Binding Path="ProductQuantity" >
            <Binding.ValidationRules>
                <validators:MaxDigitValidationRule MaxDigits="3" />
            </Binding.ValidationRules>
        </Binding>
    </TextBox.Text>
</TextBox>
```

In the previous example, `validators` is an alias for the namespace of our validation rules.

```
xmlns:validators=
    "clr-namespace:MVVMApp_WFBasedBusinessRules.ValidationRules"
```

Validation rules and converters

For the same field in the view, we can define both converter and validation rules. It is interesting to know the order in which each is applied, and it would be interesting to know how to control the order in which they are applied. The `ValidationStep` property of `ValidationRule` is used to exercise control over when the rule is applied.

The possible values of `ValidationStep` are as follows:

- `ConvertedProposedValue`
- `CommittedValue`
- `RawProposedValue`
- `UpdatedValue`

In the following code, we are assigning `ConvertedProposedValue` as a value to `ValidationStep`. This will result in our validation firing after any conversion that happens before the value is assigned to the binding source property.

```
<TextBox Height="26" HorizontalAlignment="Left"
         Margin="3,2,0,0" Name="txtQuantity"
         VerticalAlignment="Top" Width="390"
         Grid.Column="1" Grid.Row="2" >
    <TextBox.Text>
        <Binding Path="ProductQuantity"
                 Converter="{StaticResource productConverter}" >
            <Binding.ValidationRules>
                <validators:MaxDigitValidationRule
                    MaxDigits="3"
                    ValidationStep="ConvertedProposedValue" />
            </Binding.ValidationRules>
        </Binding>
    </TextBox.Text>
</TextBox>
```

Let's look at the definition of the converter.

```
namespace MVVMApp_WFBasedBusinessRules.Converters
{
    using System;
    using System.Windows.Data;

    public class ProductQuantityConverter : IValueConverter
    {
        public object Convert(object value, Type targetType,
            object parameter,
            System.Globalization.CultureInfo culture)
        {
            return value;
        }

        [System.Diagnostics.DebuggerStepThrough]
        public object ConvertBack(object value, Type targetType,
```

```
        object parameter,
        System.Globalization.CultureInfo culture)
    {
        string val = string.Format("{0}", value);

        int numValue = 0;
        if (!Int32.TryParse(val, out numValue))
        {
            val = val.ToUpper();

            switch (val)
            {
                case "ONE":
                    numValue = 1;
                    break;
                case "TWO":
                    numValue = 2;
                    break;
                case "THREE":
                    numValue = 3;
                    break;
                case "FOUR":
                    numValue = 4;
                    break;
                case "FIVE":
                    numValue = 5;
                    break;
                case "SIX":
                    numValue = 6;
                    break;
                case "SEVEN":
                    numValue = 7;
                    break;
                case "EIGHT":
                    numValue = 8;
                    break;
                case "NINE":
                    numValue = 9;
                    break;
                case "TEN":
                    numValue = 10;
                    break;
            }
        }
```

```
                return numValue == 0? value : numValue;
            }
        }
    }
```

Since the default value of `UpdateSourceTrigger` is `LostFocus`, as we move the focus away from the **Quantity** field, the converter and validation rule come into action. Since we have set `ConvertedProposedValue` as the value of the `ValidationStep` property, the converter is first used by the binding system converting `Eight` to `8`, and then `ValidationRule` is used to validated the converted value. In our case, the value passes the validation criterion and the field is not highlighted, allowing the form to show the converted value. The value is then copied to the binding source property.

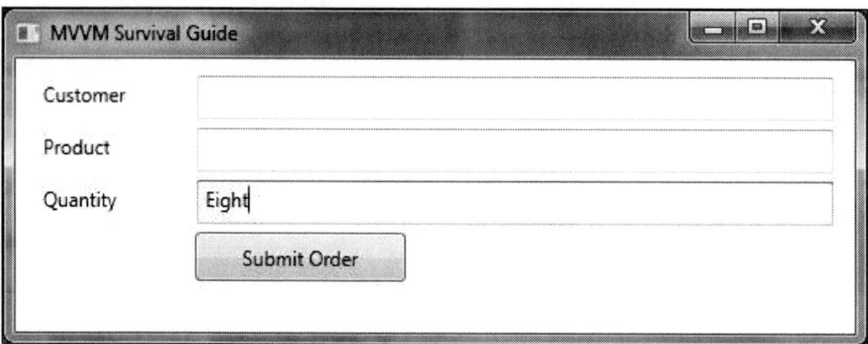

Since the binding source property is updated with the converted value, the same is updated on the binding target, that is, the `Text` property of the **Quantity** text box. The user should see the following view:

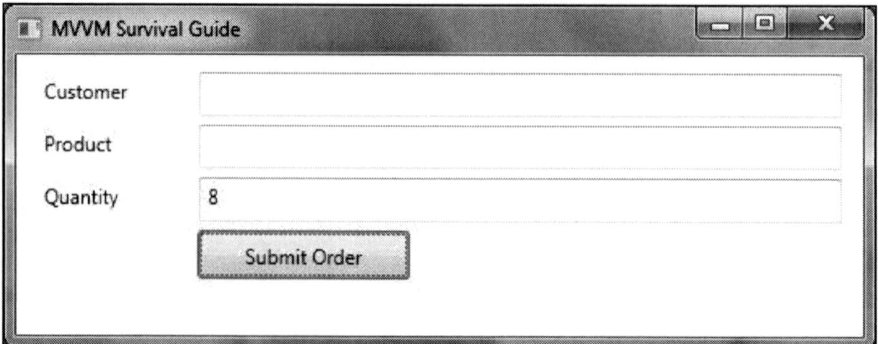

If the user enters an unexpected value, they will be notified that the value is invalid, with a blue border and tooltip, as follows:

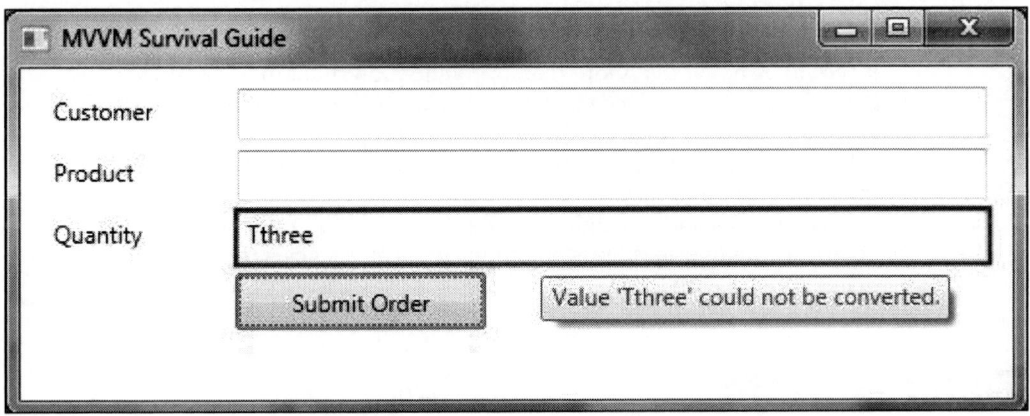

Here, we have used a scalar value with a parameter (`MaxDigit`) defined for `ValidationRule`. What if we want to pass a value from `DataContext`? Passing a value from `DataContent` is not an easy task. Since the target of our binding must be `DependencyProperty`, `MaxDigits` also needs `DependencyProperty`. However, `MaxDigitValidationRule` already inherits from `ValidationRule` and cannot inherit from `DependencyObject` to define `DependencyProperty`. We could get around this by using an attached behavior, but this would also require the instance of `ValidationRule` to be declared public, so that the attached behavior could pass on the updates from the binding source property to it. We could even pass `DataContext` to `ValidationRule` and use any property we desire for validation. However, the perceived gains from this approach can also be obtained from easier alternatives, so this should generally be avoided.

Validation mechanism in WPF and Silverlight

Validation logic is executed when the runtime copies values entered in the view to binding source properties. However, we have the flexibility to control this behavior. It can be controlled using the `UpdateSourceTriggers` property on the binding. The possible values are as follows:

- `LostFocus`: When the control loses focus.
- `PropertyChanged`: Any change in the property value is propagated to the bound property in the view model. This passes through the converter and validation rules before this.
- `Explicit`: When `UpdateSource` is called on binding.

Before a bound value is copied to the source property in the view model, the runtime runs all the validation rules for that binding. If any of the validation rules fails, we have an opportunity to notify the user.

It should be noted that more than one validation rule can be added to the `ValidationRules` collection of the binding and that the rules are executed based on their `ValidationStep` property. The validation rules, which have the same value for `ValidationStep`, are executed in the same order that they have been added to the collection. During this execution, if one of the validation rules fails, the binding sytem executes no further validation rules. Validation rules can also be added to a group of fields along with `BindingGroup`.

IDataErrorInfo

XAML technologies are a relatively a recent introduction to the enterprise toolbox. Companies have invested a lot of time in developing frameworks and toolkits to be used in their development environments, for validations, and it would be frustrating for them to have to throw all that code out. Because of this, Microsoft chose to leverage `IDataErrorInfo` in WPF and Silverlight, for validations. When using MVVM, our view models can implement `IDataErrorInfo` to validate their view state.

`IDataErrorInfo` was first introduced in .NET framework 1.x, in the `System.ComponentModel` namespace in the system assembly. Since then, many component writers have used it to provide validation support. By reusing this existing interface, these types can easily be integrated into XAML applications. In your scenario, you might find that your domain models already implement `IDataErrorInfo`. If this were the case, then both the model and the view model would implement `IDataErrorInfo`, and that is perfectly fine. This is similar to `INotifyPropertyChanged`, and as we have seen numerous times, it often makes sense to implement this interface in both the model and view model, especially when using the aggregated model approach.

The `IDataErrorInfo` declaration is as follows:

```
public interface IDataErrorInfo
{
  string this[string columnName] { get; }
  string Error { get; }
}
```

The indexer override takes a string argument, which is the name of the property to validate, and returns an error message if the validation fails. The `Error` property also returns an error message, but this error message is for the whole object's state and not a single property. Both can return an empty/null string to allow processing to continue, if there is no error. The indexer code is executed by the runtime for changes in each data-bound property. It is also accessed when this property is first displayed. Because of this validation, logic should be implemented in a way that allows the UI to remain responsive.

Validation rules are a great way to implement validation of the data entered by the user in simple scenarios. But, since validation rules only have access to the value entered by the system, they cannot be used beyond the simple data entry rules, such as checking for invalid characters and range validations. If we need to validate more complex rules that involve other property values from our data context, or want to delegate to a validation framework that utilizes other members of the session state, we will need to take advantage of `IDataErrorInfo`.

Let's see this in action now, by creating a new WPF MVVM light project—`MVVMAppIDataErrorInfo`.

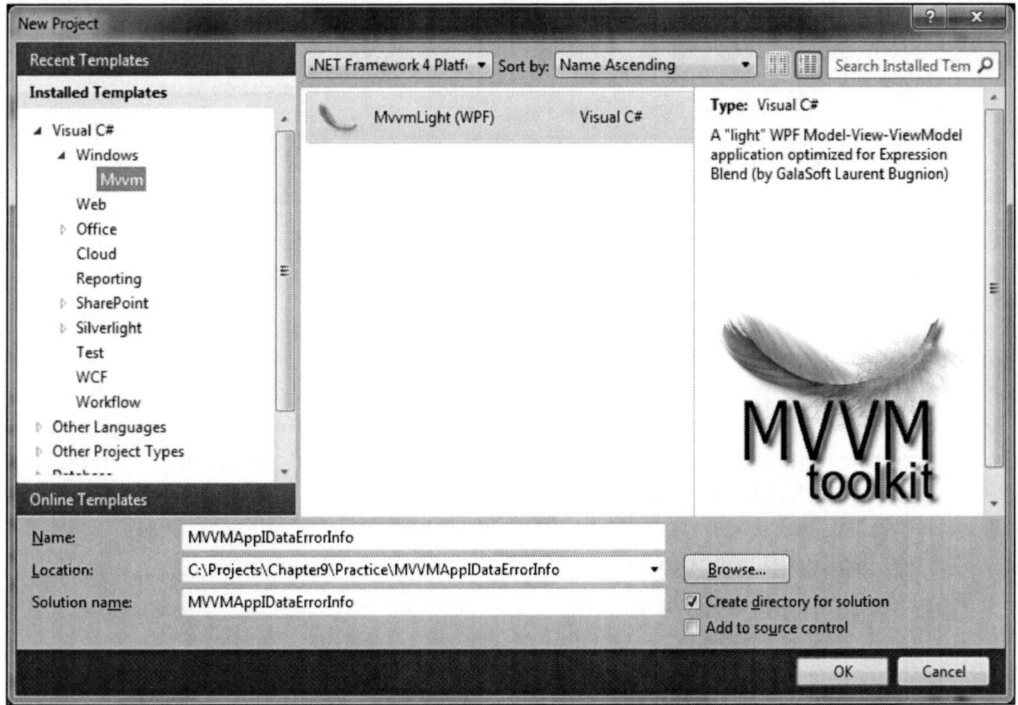

We will use the same error template to be used for text boxes in this application. This style highlights controls with blue borders when the `bound` property is considered invalid. It also shows the first error message in the tooltip if the bound data is in error. Add the following code snippet to `App.xaml`:

```
<ControlTemplate x:Key="ValidationErrorTemplate">
    <Border BorderBrush="Blue" BorderThickness="2">
        <AdornedElementPlaceholder />
    </Border>
</ControlTemplate>
<Style TargetType="TextBox">
    <Style.Setters>
        <Setter Property="Validation.ErrorTemplate"
                Value="{StaticResource ValidationErrorTemplate}" />
    </Style.Setters>
    <Style.Triggers>
        <Trigger Property="Validation.HasError" Value="true">
            <Setter Property="ToolTip">
                <Setter.Value>
                    <Binding
                        RelativeSource="{x:Static RelativeSource.
Self}"
                        Path="(Validation.Errors)[0].ErrorContent" />
                </Setter.Value>
            </Setter>

        </Trigger>
    </Style.Triggers>
</Style>
```

We are going to look at a sample view that allows entering information about the running hours of a piece of equipment. This plant maintenance system needs to record and execute a preventive maintenance schedule on the shop floor equipment. These schedules are due after a piece of equipment has run for a certain number of hours. The following view allows us to record the running hours. It's a contrived example and only tracks information about the equipment and number of hours it has been run for, but it allows us to explore these validation concepts. It also allows us to record the equipment operator's and shift supervisor's names.

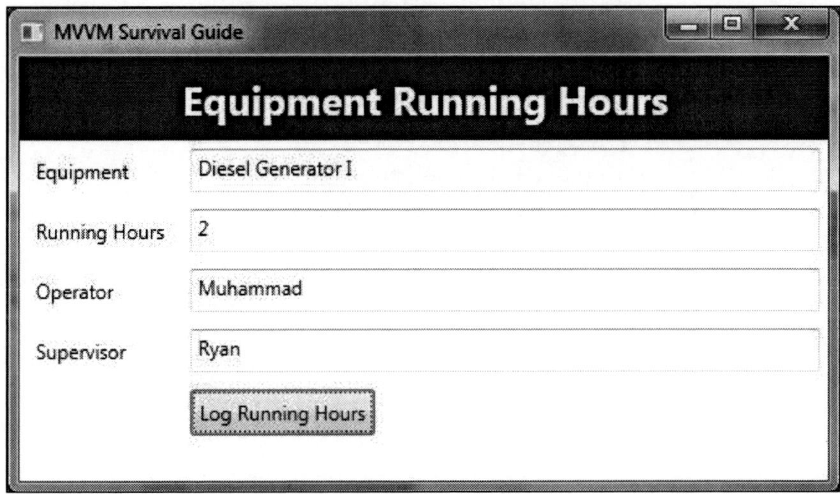

This view can be defined in XAML, as follows:

```
<Window
    x:Class="MVVMAppIDataErrorInfo.MainWindow"
    xmlns="http://schemas.microsoft.com/winfx/2006/xaml/presentation"
    xmlns:x="http://schemas.microsoft.com/winfx/2006/xaml"
    xmlns:d="http://schemas.microsoft.com/expression/blend/2008"
    xmlns:mc="http://schemas.openxmlformats.org/markup-
compatibility/2006"
    mc:Ignorable="d"
    Height="364"
    Width="515"
    Title="MVVM Survival Guide"
    DataContext="{Binding Main, Source={StaticResource Locator}}">

    <Window.Resources>
        <ResourceDictionary>
            <ResourceDictionary.MergedDictionaries>
                <ResourceDictionary Source="Skins/MainSkin.xaml" />
            </ResourceDictionary.MergedDictionaries>
        </ResourceDictionary>
    </Window.Resources>

    <Grid x:Name="LayoutRoot">
        <Grid.RowDefinitions>
            <RowDefinition Height="50" />
            <RowDefinition Height="auto" />
            <RowDefinition Height="*" />
```

```
        </Grid.RowDefinitions>
        <Grid Grid.Row="0" Background="Navy">
            <TextBlock FontSize="24"
                   FontWeight="Bold"
                   Foreground="White"
                   Text="Equipment Running Hours"
                   VerticalAlignment="Center"
                   HorizontalAlignment="Center"
                   TextWrapping="Wrap" />
        </Grid>
        <Grid Grid.Row="1">
            <Grid.ColumnDefinitions>
                <ColumnDefinition Width="0.25*" />
                <ColumnDefinition Width="*" />
            </Grid.ColumnDefinitions>
            <Grid.RowDefinitions>
                <RowDefinition Height="auto" />
                <RowDefinition Height="auto" />
                <RowDefinition Height="auto" />
                <RowDefinition Height="auto" />
                <RowDefinition Height="auto" />
            </Grid.RowDefinitions>
            <Label Content="Equipment" Grid.Column="0" Grid.Row="0"
                    Margin="5,5,5,5"/>
            <TextBox Text="{Binding Equipment,
ValidatesOnDataErrors=True}"
                     Margin="5,5,5,5" Grid.Column="1" Grid.Row="0" />
            <Label Content="Running Hours" Grid.Column="0" Grid.
Row="1"
                    Margin="5,5,5,5"/>
            <TextBox Margin="5,5,5,5" Grid.Column="1" Grid.Row="1">
                <TextBox.Text>
                    <Binding Path="RunningHours">
                        <Binding.ValidationRules>
                            <DataErrorValidationRule />
                        </Binding.ValidationRules>
                    </Binding>
                </TextBox.Text>
            </TextBox>
            <Label Content="Operator" Grid.Column="0" Grid.Row="2"
                    Margin="5,5,5,5"/>
            <TextBox
                Text="{Binding EquipmentOperator,
ValidatesOnDataErrors=True}"
```

```
                Margin="5,5,5,5" Grid.Column="1" Grid.Row="2" />
            <Label Content="Supervisor" Grid.Column="0" Grid.Row="3"
                    Margin="5,5,5,5"/>
            <TextBox
                Text="{Binding ShiftSupervisor,
ValidatesOnDataErrors=True}"
                Margin="5,5,5,5" Grid.Column="1" Grid.Row="3" />
            <Button Content="Log Running Hours" Grid.Row="4"
                    Margin="5,5,5,5" Grid.Column="1"
                    HorizontalAlignment="Left" Padding="4,4,4,4"
                    Command="{Binding LogRunningHoursCommand}"/>
        </Grid>
        <Grid Grid.Row="2" >
            <TextBlock Text="{Binding Error}"
                       Margin="5,5,5,5"
                       TextWrapping="Wrap"/>
        </Grid>
    </Grid>
</Window>
```

Like any MVVM light application, by default, the view model is constructed using the view model locator. As you can see from the bindings in this view, the view model needs to expose four properties:

- `Equipment`
- `RunningHours`
- `EquipmentOperator`
- `ShiftSupervisor`

The button's `Command` property is bound to the `LogRunningHoursCommand` property on the data context, which is a property based on `ICommand`. Also note the `ValidatesOnDataError` configuration of the binding. This is a short-cut method for specifying `DataErrorValidationRule`. You can also explicitly add `ValidationRules` to the bindings, as we did for `RunningHours`. Specifying `DataErrorValidationRule` is a way of asking the binding system to use the `IDataErrorInfo` implementation in data context, for validation.

```
namespace MVVMAppIDataErrorInfo.ViewModel
{
    using GalaSoft.MvvmLight;
    using System.ComponentModel;
    using GalaSoft.MvvmLight.Command;
    using System.Windows.Input;
```

```
public class MainViewModel
    : ViewModelBase, IDataErrorInfo
{
    #region Properties

    string _equipment = string.Empty;
    public string Equipment
    {
        get { return _equipment; }
        set
        {
            if (_equipment != value)
            {
                _equipment = value;
                RaisePropertyChanged("Equipment");
            }
        }
    }

    string _runningHours = string.Empty;
    public string RunningHours
    {
        get { return _runningHours; }
        set
        {
            if (_runningHours != value)
            {
                _runningHours = value;
                RaisePropertyChanged("RunningHours");
            }
        }
    }

    string _equipmentOperator = string.Empty;
    public string EquipmentOperator
    {
        get { return _equipmentOperator; }
        set
        {
            if (_equipmentOperator != value)
            {
                _equipmentOperator = value;
                RaisePropertyChanged("EquipmentOperator");
            }
```

```
        }
    }

    string _shiftSupervisor = string.Empty;
    public string ShiftSupervisor
    {
        get { return _shiftSupervisor; }
        set
        {
            if (_shiftSupervisor != value)
            {
                _shiftSupervisor = value;
                RaisePropertyChanged("ShiftSupervisor");
            }
        }
    }

    ICommand _logRunningHoursCommand = null;
    public ICommand LogRunningHoursCommand
    {
        get
        {
            if (_logRunningHoursCommand == null)
            {
                _logRunningHoursCommand =
                    new RelayCommand(
                        () =>
                        {
                            //Notify user if invalid
                            //otherwise submit the data
                            //entered by user
                        });
            }

            return _logRunningHoursCommand;
        }
    }
    #endregion

    #region IDataErrorInfo implementation

    public string Error
    {
        get { return null; }
    }

    public string this[string columnName]
```

```
        {
            get
            {
                string errorMessage = null;
                object propertyValue =
                    this.GetType()
                        .GetProperty(columnName)
                        .GetValue(this, null);

                if (propertyValue == null ||
                    propertyValue.ToString()
                                 .Trim()
                                 .Equals(string.Empty))
                {
                    errorMessage =
                        string.Format("{0} is required. ",
                        columnName);
                }

                return errorMessage;
            }
        }

        #endregion

    }
}
```

`MainViewModel` implements `IDataErrorInfo`, exposing the `Error` property and a string-based indexer. As we mentioned previously, the indexer will be called by the runtime, which will pass a property name as an argument to fire the validation logic and get any validation errors. The logic of the indexer will validate the property in the code block of the indexer's getter, allowing us to delegate to external validation libraries, if desired. After validation, a validation error message will be returned if the value fails our validation rules. In the previous view model, we take advantage of reflection to get the property of the view model with the property name being passed. As a validation rule for all the properties of the view model, we then check whether the value is either a null or an empty string. This allows us to invalidate our view, if any field is not populated with data. When we run our application and enter data in the fields, the indexer is called by the runtime, each time we change focus in our view. This is because, just as a regular validation rule, `IDataErrorInfo` depends on the `UpdateSourceTrigger` property of the binding. If you run the application, you will see that invalid entries in any of the fields will result in a blue border and a tooltip being displayed, as follows:

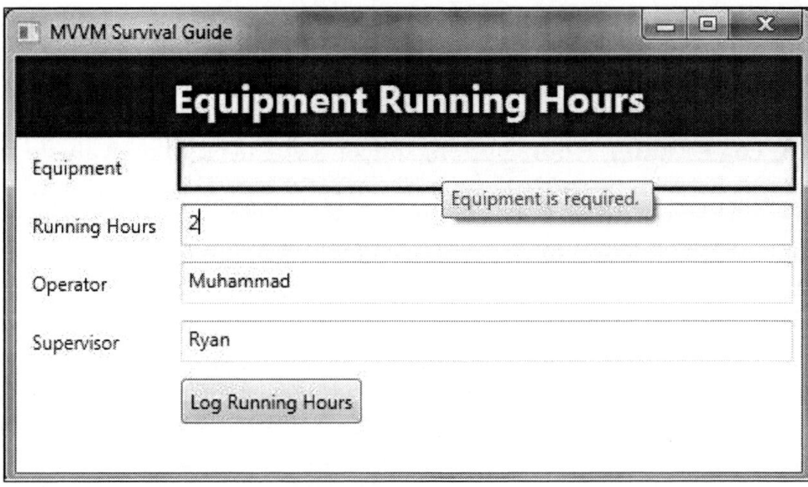

Validation states

If you have tried running this example, you might have noticed that the application is loaded with all the fields highlighted, showing all the fields in error when the view is first displayed. This would likely be irritating for our application users, and we'd want to be able to control this behavior. As we previously discussed, the indexer is accessed whenever a data-bound property is updated. Validation rules also fire when the view is first loaded, and that is why we see this behavior. Since the default view model property values are empty strings for all of our properties, they are considered invalid by our validation rules, and we get blue borders and tooltips as follows:

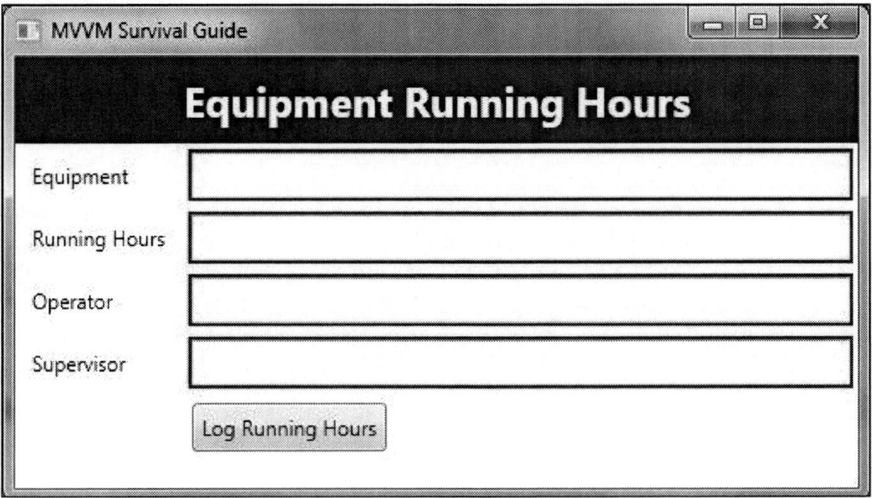

This issue can be mitigated by defining the different states of the view and applying different validation rules, depending on the current state. In this case, the empty values are definitely valid for the initial state when the form is loaded, but are invalid when the data is being committed. We can update our state when a user clicks on the **Log Running Hours** button, and since we need to re-evaluate the validation logic for each property value, we can raise the `PropertyChanged` event for each property. This will cause the indexer to be accessed for each property, resulting in re-evaluation of validation logic. Let's introduce an enumeration `StateOfView`, for this purpose, with two possible values: `Initial` and `Updated`.

> This concept can also used to define validation states based on the scenarios or user profiles. An enterprise application might need the same view under different scenarios, and the validation requirements can be different for these scenarios. Having alternatives to define validation based on the scenario or user profile can make life as an enterprise application architect a lot easier.

```
namespace MVVMAppIDataErrorInfo
{
    public enum StateOfView
    {
        Initial,
        Updated
    }
}
```

Let's add a field in the view model `_state` of the `StateOfView` enumeration type. We will also add a private method to update the value of `_state`. As the value is updated, the view needs to be notified to rerun the validation for all data-bound controls and this is why we will raise `PropertyChange` for all our properties, when `_state` changes. Add the following code to the view model.

> Another approach we could take would be to define a notification-based public property for state. We could then multi-bind each text box to its `data` property and also to the `State` property. For example, instead of binding the `Equipment` property to the `Text` property of the text box, we would multi-bind to both the `Equipment` and the `State` property. This would require us to also implement a converter. We are not going to cover the details here, but you can explore this option on your own, if the need arises.

```
#region Private Methods

private void RaisePropertyChanges()
{
    RaisePropertyChanged("Equipment");
    RaisePropertyChanged("RunningHours");
    RaisePropertyChanged("EquipmentOperator");
    RaisePropertyChanged("ShiftSupervisor");
}

private void UpdateState(StateOfView state)
{
    _state = state;
    RaisePropertyChanges();
}
#endregion

#region Private Fields

private StateOfView _state;

#endregion
```

Finally, let's update the code for the `Execute` method, to call the `UpdateState()` method. This would change the value of `_state` to `Updated` and call `PropertyChanged` for all data-bound properties. When the runtime receives a `PropertyChanged` event for a property, it uses the `IDataErrorInfo` indexer to validate the value, resulting in invalid controls being highlighted.

```
ICommand _logRunningHoursCommand = null;
public ICommand LogRunningHoursCommand
{
    get
    {
        if (_logRunningHoursCommand == null)
        {
            _logRunningHoursCommand = new RelayCommand(
                        () =>
                        {
                            UpdateState(StateOfView.Updated);
                        });
        }

        return _logRunningHoursCommand;
    }
}
```

We also need to update the indexer code, so that the empty values are just checked for the `Updated` state of the view.

```
public string this[string columnName]
{
    get
    {
        string errorMessage = null;

        if (_state == StateOfView.Updated)
        {
            object propertyValue =
            this.GetType()
                .GetProperty(columnName)
                .GetValue(this, null);

            if (propertyValue == null ||
                propertyValue.ToString()
                             .Trim()
                             .Equals(string.Empty))
            {
                errorMessage =
                    string.Format("{0} is required. ",
                    columnName);
            }
        }

        return errorMessage;
    }
}
```

Now when we run the application, the view is loaded without highlighting any controls, as follows:

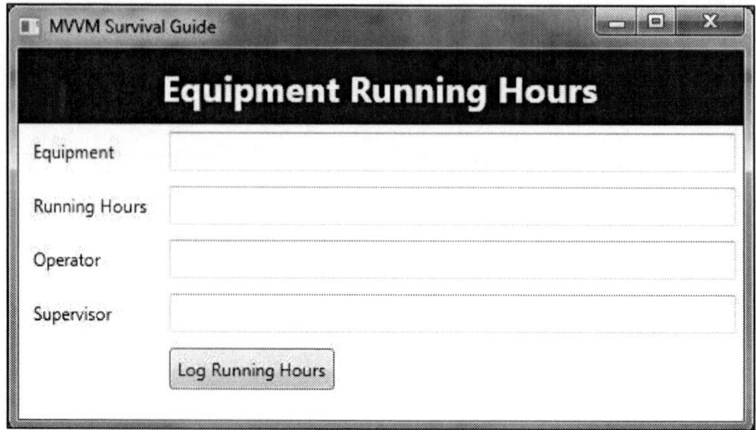

However, clicking on the **Log Running Hours** button will change the state in our view model, causing validation rules to fire and resulting in highlighted controls, as follows:

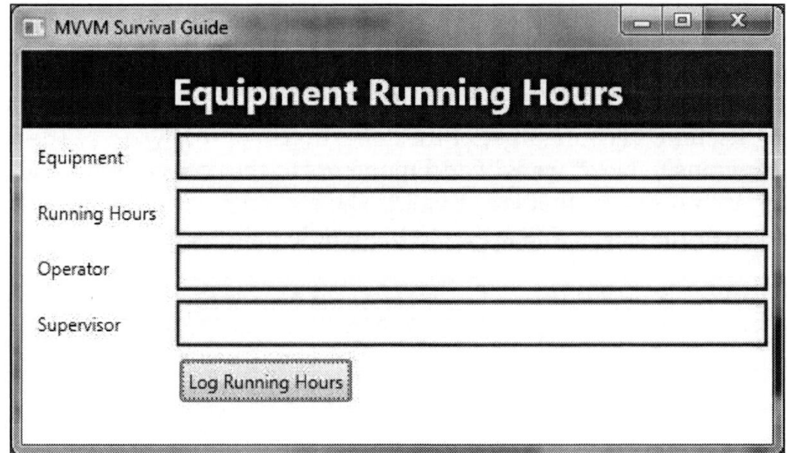

It would be better to disable the button until the form is valid, in a real-world application.

Providing a summary validation error

In the previous example, we have shown the error messages in the tooltip of the individual controls. Now, let's look at showing a consolidated error message to the user when they click on the **Log Running Hours** button. We can show the validation errors in a dialog box, have them inline in the view itself, or however else we want to. In the definition of the previous view, you may have noticed the declaration of a text block at the bottom. This text block is data-bound to the `Error` property of the data context. The implementation of getter for the `Error` property is a part of the contract of `IDataErrorInfo`, and if we don't need to show a consolidated error message, we can just return `null` in the getter, as we have been doing. However, let's now look at providing a consolidated error message.

Let's first add a new type to the project, to hold the information about error messages for each property in the view model. Let's name this type `ValidationError`. It has two properties—`PropertyName` and `ErrorMessage`. Both are strings and are defined to hold the property name and related error message, for each property in the view model.

```
    namespace MVVMAppIDataErrorInfo
{
     public class ValidationError
```

```
        {
            public string PropertyName { get; set; }
            public string ErrorMessage { get; set; }
        }
    }
```

Next, add a collection in the view model to hold the error messages for each individual property. Let's name this property `ValidationMessages` and make it an observable collection. Each member of the collection is of the type `ValidationError`, as defined previously. Next, we will add members to the collection to hold the error messages for each property that is not valid. The last item added to the collection will hold generic error messages that apply to the whole object.

```
ObservableCollection<ValidationError> _validationMessages;
ObservableCollection<ValidationError> ValidationMessages
{
    get
    {
        if (_validationMessages == null)
        {
            _validationMessages =
new ObservableCollection<ValidationError>()
                    {
                        new ValidationError()
                           {PropertyName = "Equipment"},
                        new ValidationError()
                            {PropertyName = "RunningHours"},
                        new ValidationError()
                            {PropertyName = "EquipmentOperator"},
                        new ValidationError()
                            {PropertyName = "ShiftSupervisor"},
                        new ValidationError()
                            {PropertyName = "Generic"},
                    };
        }

        return _validationMessages ;
    }
}
```

Now, we need to update the `IDataErrorInfo` indexer to update the corresponding member of our collection when the validation state of a property changes (also add the `System.Linq` namespace).

```
public string this[string columnName]
{
    get
    {
        string errorMessage = null;

        if (_state == StateOfView.Updated)
        {
            object propertyValue =
            this.GetType()
                .GetProperty(columnName)
                .GetValue(this, null);

            if (propertyValue == null ||
                propertyValue.ToString()
                             .Trim()
                             .Equals(string.Empty))
            {
                errorMessage =
                    string.Format("{0} is required. ",
                    columnName);
            }
        }

        ValidationMessages
           .Where<ValidationError>(e => e.PropertyName == columnName)
           .First<ValidationError>().ErrorMessage = errorMessage;

        return errorMessage;
    }
}
```

As discussed previously, the `IDataErrorInfo` definition only requires implementers to implement a getter for the `Error` property. However, if we are binding `Error` to the view, we need to notify the view about the updates in the `Error` properties values, and we must also define a setter. In the setter we will raise `PropertyChanged` notifications, so that our controls are updated to show the error message.

```
string _error = string.Empty;
public string Error
{
    get
    {
```

```
            return _error;
        }
        set
        {
            _error = value;
            RaisePropertyChanged("Error");
        }
    }
```

Next, we need to update `Error` when the user clicks on the **Log Running Hours** button. In order to do that, we will update the `Execute` method of the related `ICommand` property. If there are no error messages, we will go ahead and register the running hours of the equipment, otherwise the user will be shown a detailed error message with all the validation errors.

```
    public ICommand LogRunningHoursCommand
    {
        get
        {
            if (_logRunningHoursCommand == null)
            {
                _logRunningHoursCommand = new RelayCommand(
                            () =>
                            {
                                UpdateState(StateOfView.Updated);

                                Error = string.Join("",
                                    ValidationMessages
                                        .Select<ValidationError, string>
                                            (e => e.ErrorMessage)
                                        .ToArray<string>());

                                if (!string.IsNullOrEmpty(Error))
                                {
                                    //log running hours
                                }
                            });
            }

            return _logRunningHoursCommand;
        }
    }
```

Now, let's run the application. Since the view is in the initial state, there are no validation issues, and it is loaded as follows:

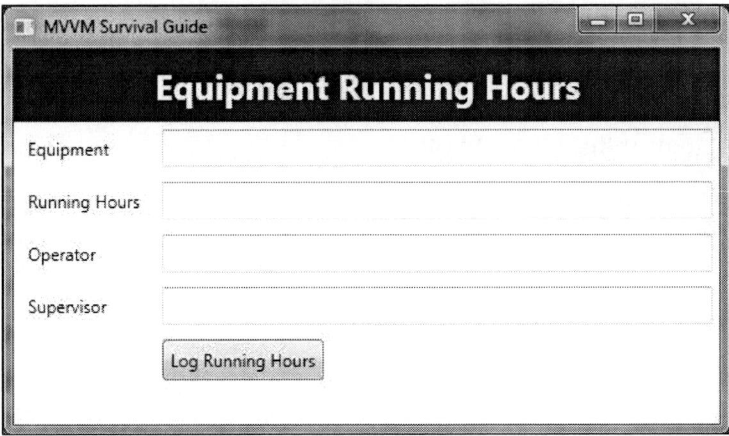

Clicking on the **Log Running Hours** button changes our state to `Updated`. This will generate change notifications for all the properties in the view model, causing validation logic to fire the indexer for each of the properties. Since all fields are empty, they are all considered invalid, and the control is marked as being in an invalid state. Next, the corresponding error message is set in the `ValidationMessages` collection. Now, in the `Execute` method, we are just consolidating the error messages for all the properties in the `Error` property. Since `Error` supports change notifications through the `PropertyChanged` event of `INotifyPropertyChanged`, the related text block is updated with the error message, as follows:

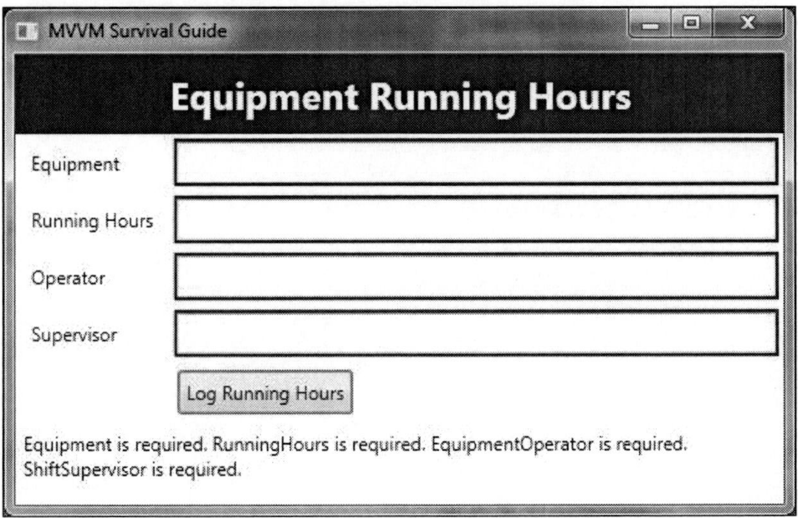

Unlike `ValidationRule`, since all the validations are defined in the scope of the view model body, we can make use of other properties in the view model to perform complex validations.

Let's examine this in more detail, by defining a new complex validation rule that requires further checking of the property in our view model. We will require that the operator and supervisor be different persons. In order to validate the value of either field, we must look at the value of both.

```
public string this[string columnName]
{
    get
    {
        string errorMessage = null;
        string propertyName = columnName;

        if (_state == StateOfView.Updated)
        {
            object propertyValue =
            this.GetType()
                .GetProperty(propertyName)
                .GetValue(this, null);

            if (propertyValue == null ||
                propertyValue.ToString()
                             .Trim()
                             .Equals(string.Empty))
            {
                errorMessage =
                    string.Format("{0} is required. ",
                    propertyName);
            }
        }

        switch (columnName)
        {
            case "EquipmentOperator":
            case "ShiftSupervisor":
             if (!EquipmentOperator.Equals(string.Empty) &&
                  EquipmentOperator.Equals(ShiftSupervisor))
             {
               errorMessage =
                "Equipment operator and Shift Supervisor must be
different. ";
             }
```

```
                propertyName = "Generic";

                break;
            }

            ValidationMessages
                .Where<ValidationError>(e => e.PropertyName ==
    propertyName)
                .First<ValidationError>().ErrorMessage = errorMessage;

            return errorMessage;
        }
    }
```

As you can see, this validation is not limited to the `Updated` state of the system. This would be executed for all the states. Since we are explicitly checking for the `null` value of the `EquipmentOperator` property, no related controls are considered invalid in the initial state of the system.

Let's run our application again and enter some invalid information to test our code. In the following screenshot, we have first entered `Muhammad` for the **Operator** followed by the same entry in the **Supervisor** field. Both are highlighted if we click on the button. Since the error message is copied to the `ValidationMessages` collection with `propertyName = "Generic"`, the error message is shown only once.

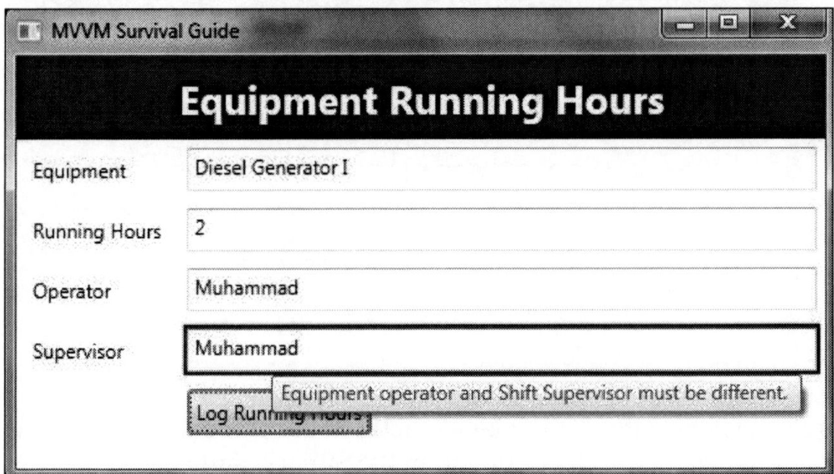

When we click on the **Log Running Hours** button, both fields are considered invalid and are highlighted.

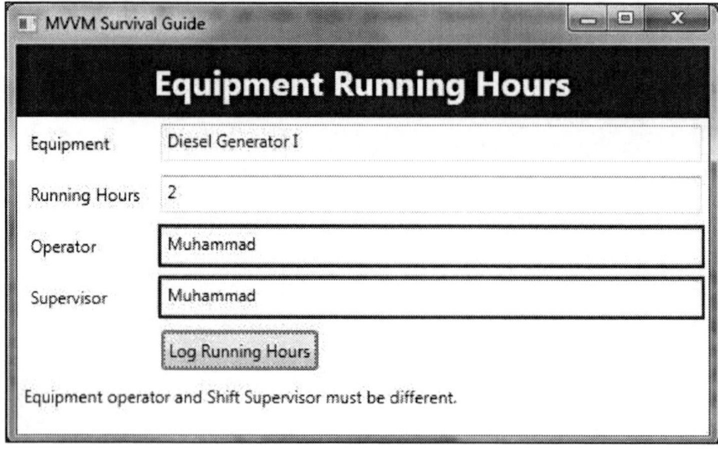

The validation logic determines that this is the same entry as in the **Operator** field, so it should consider the value entered in the **Supervisor** field as invalid. If we had entered the data first in the **Supervisor** field followed by the same entry in the **Operator** field, the latter would have been highlighted as follows:

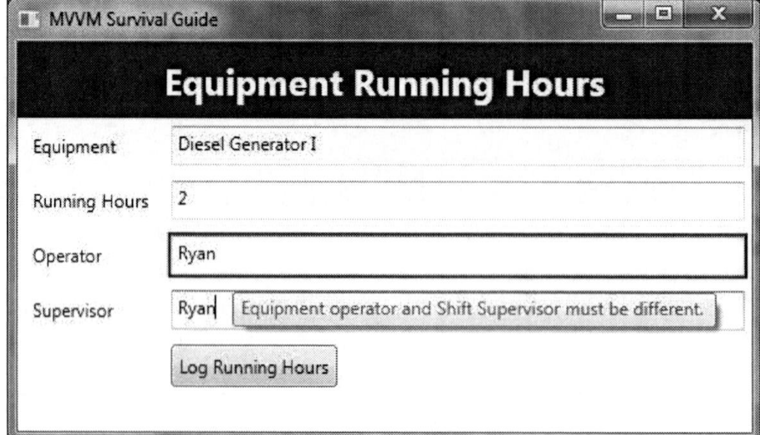

There is still one issue with this implementation. If the user enters the information and enters `Ryan` in both the **Operator** and in the **Supervisor** fields, as soon as the control leaves the **Supervisor** field, it is highlighted to indicate that it is in an invalid state. Now, if the user realizes that he/she actually wanted the employee to be `Muhammad` and then updates the **Operator** field correcting the mistake, the **Supervisor** field will still be shown invalid, as follows:

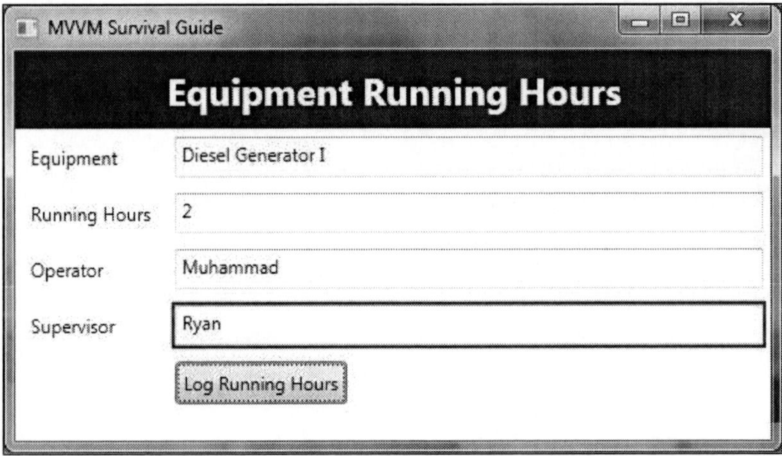

If the user clicks on the **Log Running Hours** button, the validation errors will be cleared, but this is awkward at best and is not desired.

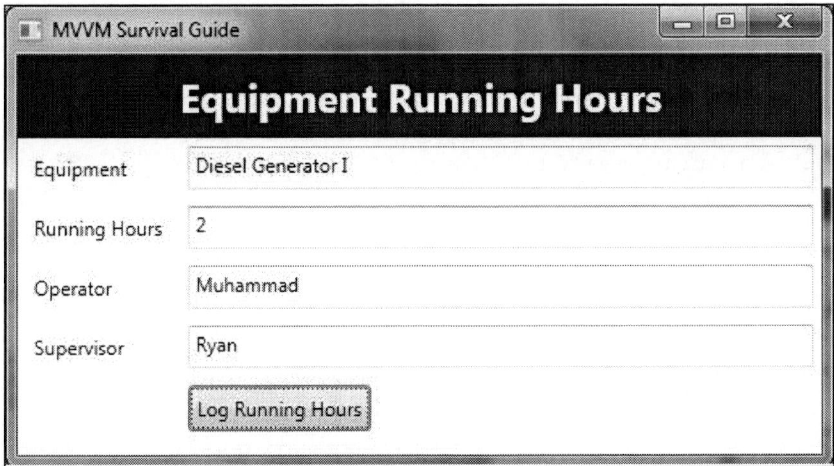

Invalidating multiple fields

Another thing that we might need to do is to highlight multiple, related fields when our form has invalid data. In the current example, we might need to highlight both the **Supervisor** and the **Operator** fields when their values match. This seems difficult as the runtime just calls the indexer for the field being updated, but it's actually an easy scenario to handle. Updating the data entered in the **Operator** field will execute the validation logic for the operator and add operator error messages to the `Error` property. But, the view won't get the notification to update the error state of the **Supervisor** field and will keep it highlighted.

In order to update the error state of the **Supervisor** field, we need to cause the indexer logic to be executed for the **Supervisor** field when this happens. We can easily do this by raising the `PropertyChanged` event for both the `EquipmentOperator` and the `ShiftSupervisor` properties when either is updated.

```
string _equipmentOperator = string.Empty;
public string EquipmentOperator
{
    get { return _equipmentOperator; }
    set
    {
        if (_equipmentOperator != value)
        {
            _equipmentOperator = value;
            RaisePropertyChanged("EquipmentOperator");
            RaisePropertyChanged("ShiftSupervisor");
        }
    }
}

string _shiftSupervisor = string.Empty;
public string ShiftSupervisor
{
    get { return _shiftSupervisor; }
    set
    {
        if (_shiftSupervisor != value)
        {
            _shiftSupervisor = value;
            RaisePropertyChanged("ShiftSupervisor");
            RaisePropertyChanged("EquipmentOperator");
        }
    }
}
```

Now, when we run the application and enter the same data for these two fields, both the fields will be highlighted and have their tooltip set to show an error message. Clicking on the **Log Running Hours** button will show the related error message in the view.

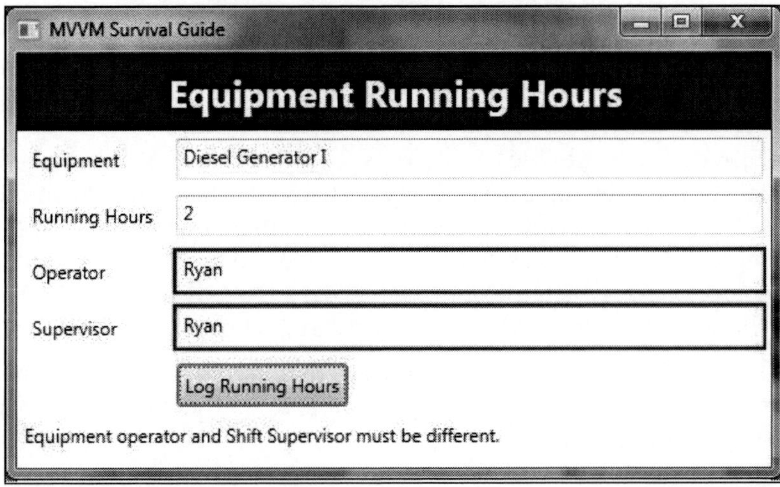

As soon as we update any of our fields and change the focus, both the fields will change their error state. Additionally, clicking on the **Log Running Hours** button will clear the error message in the view.

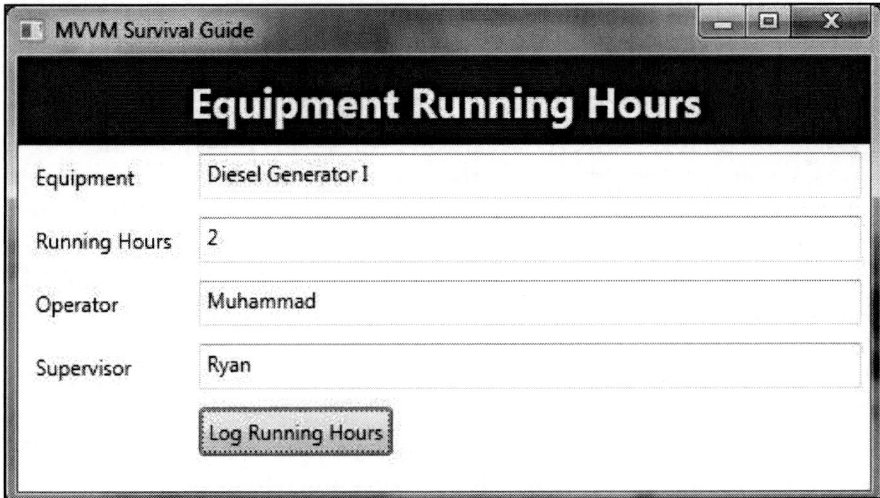

Limitations and gotchas

However, `IDataErrorInfo` has its own limitations and things that we need to consider when using it; the following list is worth keeping in mind:

- `IDataErrorInfo` provides an indexer for validation that is executed whenever the value of any property is changed. This happens on the UI thread, and so if the validation logic is slow, the UI will be unresponsive during validation processing. There is no way to fire `IDataErrorInfo` asynchronously, which makes `IDataErrorInfo` a difficult choice when we have long-running validation logic for various business rules.
- As we saw, for complex validation rules that involve more than one field, we must raise `PropertyChanged` to be able to notify the view that validation needs to be fired. This is less than ideal as our validation logic will be executed twice.
- The `Error` property of `IDataErrorInfo` and `indexer` allow for returning only a single error. If there is more than one validation issue, our best option is to build up a consolidated validation error and return it.
- As we discussed previously, in order to use the `IDataErrorInfo` support for executing the validation logic, we must use `DataErrorValidationRule` directly or set the `ValidationOnDataError` property to `true`. Since `DataErrorValidationRule` is a specialized validation rule, it seems tempting to use `ValidationStep` in order to get more control over the validation timing. However, this won't work. This is because the only way to access a field is through a property on our view model, and we can't access these values before they are passed through the converters. For this reason, we can't set `RawProposedValue` or `ConvertedProposedValue`; the default is `UpdatedValue`. We still can set it as `CommittedValue`, if we want all validation rules with `UpdatedValue` to finish execution before this.

INotifyDataErrorInfo

Silverlight introduced a new interface as an alternative to `IDataErrorInfo`. This interface is `INotifyDataErrorInfo`. It is available in the `System.ComponentModel` namespace in the `System.Windows` assembly. Backed by popular developer demand, this has also been included in .NET framework 4.5 Developers Preview.

```
public interface INotifyDataErrorInfo
{
        bool HasErrors { get; }
        event EventHandler<DataErrorsChangedEventArgs> ErrorsChanged;
        IEnumerable GetErrors(string propertyName);
}
```

Compared to `IDataErrorInfo`, this interface allows us to return more than one error message for a property. The framework calls `GetErrors` to get the validation errors associated with a property with the name passed as an argument. This is called by the framework when it handles the `ErrorChanged` event for the specified property. This makes it independent of the property change notifications. This also allows for asynchronous validation. When the `property` value is updated, we can start the validation in a background thread. Now, if the validation fails, we can raise the `ErrorsChanged` event for the property. Now, `GetErrors` should have access to those validation errors, so that they can be returned as `IEnumerable`. This asynchronous support improves the responsiveness of the application. This also keeps us from raising unnecessary `PropertyChanged` events when we just want to notify `FrameworkElement` about updates in the validation status of a property.

Let's create a new MVM Silverlight project named `MVVMAppNotifyDataErrorInfo`. Make sure that **Silverlight version 4** is selected for the project. This can be updated on the property page of a Silverlight project. Add a reference `System.Windows.Controls.Data.Input.dll` to the assembly. This is for the Label used in this example.

```
<UserControl
    x:Class="MVVMAppINotifyDataErrorInfo.MainPage"
    xmlns="http://schemas.microsoft.com/winfx/2006/xaml/presentation"
    xmlns:x="http://schemas.microsoft.com/winfx/2006/xaml"
    xmlns:d="http://schemas.microsoft.com/expression/blend/2008"
    xmlns:mc="http://schemas.openxmlformats.org/markup-
compatibility/2006"
    xmlns:sdk="http://schemas.microsoft.com/winfx/2006/xaml/
presentation/sdk"
    mc:Ignorable="d"
    Height="364" Width="515"
    DataContext="{Binding Main, Source={StaticResource Locator}}">

    <UserControl.Resources>
        <ResourceDictionary>
            <ResourceDictionary.MergedDictionaries>
                <ResourceDictionary Source="Skins/MainSkin.xaml" />
            </ResourceDictionary.MergedDictionaries>
        </ResourceDictionary>
    </UserControl.Resources>
    <Grid x:Name="LayoutRoot">
        <Grid.RowDefinitions>
            <RowDefinition Height="50" />
            <RowDefinition Height="auto" />
            <RowDefinition Height="*" />
        </Grid.RowDefinitions>
```

```
        <Grid Grid.Row="0" Background="Navy">
            <TextBlock FontSize="24"
                   FontWeight="Bold"
                   Foreground="White"
                   Text="Equipment Running Hours"
                   VerticalAlignment="Center"
                   HorizontalAlignment="Center"
                   TextWrapping="Wrap" />
        </Grid>

        <Grid Grid.Row="1">
            <Grid.ColumnDefinitions>
                <ColumnDefinition Width="0.25*" />
                <ColumnDefinition Width="*" />
            </Grid.ColumnDefinitions>
            <Grid.RowDefinitions>
                <RowDefinition Height="auto" />
                <RowDefinition Height="auto" />
                <RowDefinition Height="auto" />
                <RowDefinition Height="auto" />
                <RowDefinition Height="auto" />
            </Grid.RowDefinitions>
            <sdk:Label Content="Equipment" Grid.Column="0" Grid.
Row="0"
                    Margin="5,5,5,5"/>
            <TextBox
                Text="{Binding Equipment,
                ValidatesOnNotifyDataErrors=True,
                Mode=TwoWay}"
                Margin="5,5,5,5" Grid.Column="1" Grid.Row="0" />
            <sdk:Label Content="Running Hours" Grid.Column="0" Grid.
Row="1"
                    Margin="5,5,5,5"/>
            <TextBox Margin="5,5,5,5" Grid.Column="1" Grid.Row="1">
                <TextBox.Text>
                    <Binding Path="RunningHours"
                             ValidatesOnNotifyDataErrors="True"
                             Mode="TwoWay">
                    </Binding>
                </TextBox.Text>
            </TextBox>
            <sdk:Label Content="Operator" Grid.Column="0" Grid.Row="2"
                    Margin="5,5,5,5"/>
            <TextBox
```

```
                Text="{Binding EquipmentOperator,
                        ValidatesOnNotifyDataErrors=True,
                        Mode=TwoWay}"
                Margin="5,5,5,5" Grid.Column="1" Grid.Row="2" />
            <sdk:Label Content="Supervisor" Grid.Column="0" Grid.
Row="3"
                    Margin="5,5,5,5"/>
            <TextBox
                Text="{Binding ShiftSupervisor,
                        ValidatesOnNotifyDataErrors=True,
                        Mode=TwoWay}"
                Margin="5,5,5,5" Grid.Column="1" Grid.Row="3" />
            <Button Content="Log Running Hours" Grid.Row="4"
                    Margin="5,5,5,5" Grid.Column="1"
                    HorizontalAlignment="Left" Padding="4,4,4,4"
                    Command="{Binding LogRunningHoursCommand}"/>
        </Grid>
        <Grid Grid.Row="2" >
            <ListBox ItemsSource="{Binding Errors}"
                     DisplayMemberPath="ErrorMessage"
                     Margin="5,5,5,5" />
        </Grid>
    </Grid>
</UserControl>
```

Here, the default mode of binding is `OneWay`, so we need to explicitly specify `TwoWay` for the textbox binding mode. Please note the `ValidatesOnNotifyDataError` attribute of binding. This is to tell the binding system to use the features provided by the implementation of the interface. Let us define a base class for all view models, which would be based on this. Let's name it `ViewModelNotifyDataError`. Here, `ValidationError` is the same type as in the `MVVMAppIDataErrorInfo` namespace. You can add this to the `MVVMAppINotifyDataErrorInfo.ViewModel` namespace.

```
namespace MVVMAppINotifyDataErrorInfo.ViewModel
{
    using System;
    using GalaSoft.MvvmLight;
    using System.ComponentModel;
    using System.Collections;
    using System.Collections.Generic;
    using System.Threading;
    using System.Linq;
    using System.Collections.ObjectModel;

    public abstract class ViewModelNotifyDataError
```

```
        : ViewModelBase, INotifyDataErrorInfo
    {
        ObservableCollection<ValidationError> _errors;
        public ObservableCollection<ValidationError> Errors
        {
            get
            {
                if (_errors == null)
                {
                    _errors = new ObservableCollection<ValidationErr
or>();
                }
                return _errors;
            }
        }

        protected Dictionary<string, List<string>>
PropertyDependencies =
            new Dictionary<string, List<string>>();

        #region INotifyDataErrorInfo implementation

        public event EventHandler<DataErrorsChangedEventArgs>
                ErrorsChanged = delegate { };

        public virtual IEnumerable GetErrors(string propertyName)
        {
            IEnumerable<string> ret = null;

            ret = Errors
                    .Where<ValidationError>(e => e.PropertyName ==
propertyName)
                    .Select<ValidationError, string>(e =>
e.ErrorMessage);


            return ret;
        }

        public bool HasErrors
        {
            get { return false; }
        }

        #endregion
```

```
        #region Protected Methods

        protected void ValidateProperty(string propertyName)
        {
            this.VerifyPropertyName(propertyName);

            var worker = new BackgroundWorker();

            worker.DoWork +=
                (o, e) =>
                    {
                        Thread.Sleep(4000); //simulated validation
delay
                        e.Result = ValidatePropertySpecialized(proper
tyName);
                    };

            worker.RunWorkerCompleted +=
                (o, e) =>
                {
                    IEnumerable<string> messages =
                        e.Error == null ?
                            (IEnumerable<string>)e.Result :
                            Enumerable.Repeat<string>(e.Error.Message,
1);

                    UpdateErrors(propertyName, messages);

                };

            worker.RunWorkerAsync();
        }

        private void RaiseErrorsChanged(string propertyName)
        {
            ErrorsChanged(this, new DataErrorsChangedEventArgs(proper
tyName));

            if (PropertyDependencies.ContainsKey(propertyName))
            {
                foreach (string item in PropertyDependencies[property
Name])
                {
                    ValidateProperty(item);
```

```
                }
            }
        }

        protected abstract IEnumerable<string>
ValidatePropertySpecialized(string propertyName);

        protected virtual void UpdateErrors(string propertyName,
IEnumerable<string> errors)
        {
            Errors
                .Where<ValidationError>(e => e.PropertyName ==
propertyName)
                .ToList<ValidationError>()
                .ForEach((element) =>
                    {
                        Errors.Remove(element);
                    } );

            if (errors != null)
            {
                foreach (string item in errors)
                {
                    Errors.Add(new ValidationError()
{ PropertyName = propertyName, ErrorMessage = item });
                }
            }

            RaiseErrorsChanged(propertyName);
        }

        #endregion
    }
}
```

Since this view model implements `INotifyDataErrorInfo`, it needs to have a property `HasError` with a getter, an event `ErrorsChanged`, and a method that takes the property name as an argument and returns the errors in the form of `IEnumerable`. Since it is based on `INotifyDataErrorInfo`, we have the luxury of executing the validation workload in a separate thread. The same behavior is defined in the `ValidateProperty` method. We use `Backgroundworker` for this purpose. As we know that the `RunWorkerCompleted` event is raised on the same thread the worker thread was created on, it will be raised in the UI thread, so that we can just raise the `ErrorsChanged` event for any property. Before doing any validation, we verify the `name` of property using the `VerifyPropertyName` method from the `ViewModelBase` base class method available through MVVM Light framework. In the `RaiseErrorsChanged` method, we run the validations for all the dependent properties as maintained in the `PropertyDependencies` collection.

This class is an abstract class, so the child view model would need to provide the definition for the `ValidatePropertySpecialized` method. This method will not be executed in the UI thread, as it is being called by `Backgroundworker`. It should return the errors as `IEnumerable`. The same errors are passed to the `UpdateErrors` method by the `RunWorkerCompleted` handler. We have a default implementation of the `HasErrors` property. It always returns `false`. We can update that to use the `Errors` collection. We also have a primitive way to maintain property dependencies. This is a generic dictionary with its key as the dependee property. The value is a list of strings and should contain the names of all the properties that the key property is dependent on.

Now, let's look at the definition of `MainViewModel`. Since it inherits from `ViewModelNotifyDataError`, we are defining the `ValidatePropertySpecialized` method. The property name is passed in as argument. Here, we are performing the required field validation for all the fields. We can also perform other validations for individual properties in a `switch/case` block. In the constructor, we have defined the dependencies of the `EquipmentOperator` and `ShifSupervisor` fields. For bidirectional dependencies, we need to define dependencies for both properties. In real-world applications, we might need to implement a graph for all these dependencies, as efficient data structures. For more complex rules, we might need to include an inference-engine-based rule execution. Policy activity in Windows WF is inference-based.

```
using GalaSoft.MvvmLight;
using System.Windows.Input;
using GalaSoft.MvvmLight.Command;
using System.Collections;
using System.Linq;
using System.Collections.Generic;
using System.Collections.ObjectModel;

namespace MVVMAppINotifyDataErrorInfo.ViewModel
{
    public class MainViewModel : ViewModelNotifyDataError
    {
        #region Constructor

        public MainViewModel()
        {
```

```
            List<string> operatorDependencies = new List<string>();
            operatorDependencies.Add("ShiftSupervisor");

            PropertyDependencies.Add("EquipmentOperator",
operatorDependencies);

            List<string> supervisorDependencies = new List<string>();
            supervisorDependencies.Add("EquipmentOperator");
            PropertyDependencies.Add("ShiftSupervisor",
supervisorDependencies);
        }

        #endregion
        #region Properties

        string _equipment = string.Empty;
        public string Equipment
        {
            get { return _equipment; }
            set
            {
                if (_equipment != value)
                {
                    _equipment = value;
                    RaisePropertyChanged("Equipment");
                    ValidateProperty("Equipment");
                }
            }
        }

        string _runningHours = string.Empty;
        public string RunningHours
        {
            get { return _runningHours; }
            set
            {
                if (_runningHours != value)
                {
                    _runningHours = value;
                    RaisePropertyChanged("RunningHours");
                    ValidateProperty("RunningHours");
                }
            }
        }
```

```
string _equipmentOperator = string.Empty;
public string EquipmentOperator
{
    get { return _equipmentOperator; }
    set
    {
        if (_equipmentOperator != value)
        {
            _equipmentOperator = value;
            RaisePropertyChanged("EquipmentOperator");
            ValidateProperty("EquipmentOperator");
        }
    }
}

string _shiftSupervisor = string.Empty;
public string ShiftSupervisor
{
    get { return _shiftSupervisor; }
    set
    {
        if (_shiftSupervisor != value)
        {
            _shiftSupervisor = value;
            RaisePropertyChanged("ShiftSupervisor");
            ValidateProperty("ShiftSupervisor");
        }
    }
}

ICommand _logRunningHoursCommand = null;
public ICommand LogRunningHoursCommand
{
    get
    {
        if (_logRunningHoursCommand == null)
        {
            _logRunningHoursCommand = new RelayCommand(
                        () =>
                        {
                            ValidateAll();
                        });
        }
```

```
                return _logRunningHoursCommand;
            }
        }

        #endregion

        #region Overriden methods

        protected override IEnumerable<string>
ValidatePropertySpecialized(string propertyName)
        {
            List<string> errorMessages = new List<string>();
            //IEnumerable<string> ret = null;

            if (!string.IsNullOrEmpty(propertyName))
            {
                object propertyValue =
                    this.GetType()
                    .GetProperty(propertyName)
                    .GetValue(this, null);

                if (propertyValue == null ||
                    propertyValue.ToString()
                                 .Trim()
                                 .Equals(string.Empty))
                {
                    errorMessages.Add(string.Format("{0} is required.
",
propertyName));


                }
            }

            switch(propertyName)
            {
                case "RunningHours":
                    double runningHours;
                    double.TryParse(_runningHours, out runningHours);
                    if (runningHours == 0 && _runningHours.Length > 0)
                    {
                        string msg =
(_runningHours != null && _
```

```
runningHours.Equals("0")) ?
                                    "Zero not allowed for running
hours." :
                                    "Only numeric running hours are
allowed!";

                        errorMessages.Add(msg);
                    }
                    break;

                case "EquipmentOperator":
                case "ShiftSupervisor":
                    if (!string.IsNullOrEmpty(_equipmentOperator) &&
_equipmentOperator.Equals(_shiftSupervisor))
                    {
                        errorMessages.Add(
"EquipmentOperator and ShiftSupervisor must be different");
                    }
                    break;
                case "Equipment":
                    //some other validations
                    break;
                default:
                    //other validations if required
                    break;
            }

            return errorMessages.Count > 0 ?
errorMessages.AsEnumerable<string>() : null;
        }


        private void ValidateAll()
        {
            ValidateProperty("Equipment");
            ValidateProperty("RunningHours");
            ValidateProperty("EquipmentOperator");
            ValidateProperty("ShiftSupervisor");
        }

        #endregion
    }
}
```

Here, we have used `ListBox` to display all the error messages in a Silverlight page. This discussion would be incomplete without discussing the `ValidationSummary` control in Silverlight. It is used to get all the error messages from the controls. By default, it displays error messages from errors in the controls contained by the same parent. We can also specify a different target if needed. It can show not only both the property- and object-level error messages, but can also filter using the `Filter` property. We need to set `NotifyOnValidationErrors` for all the bindings whose errors are desired to be displayed by `ValidationSummary`.

```
<UserControl
    x:Class="MVVMAppINotifyDataErrorInfo.MainPage"
    xmlns="http://schemas.microsoft.com/winfx/2006/xaml/presentation"
    xmlns:x="http://schemas.microsoft.com/winfx/2006/xaml"
    xmlns:d="http://schemas.microsoft.com/expression/blend/2008"
    xmlns:mc="http://schemas.openxmlformats.org/markup-
compatibility/2006"
    xmlns:sdk="http://schemas.microsoft.com/winfx/2006/xaml/
presentation/sdk"
    mc:Ignorable="d"
    Height="364" Width="515"
    DataContext="{Binding Main, Source={StaticResource Locator}}">

    <UserControl.Resources>
        <ResourceDictionary>
            <ResourceDictionary.MergedDictionaries>
                <ResourceDictionary Source="Skins/MainSkin.xaml" />
            </ResourceDictionary.MergedDictionaries>
        </ResourceDictionary>
    </UserControl.Resources>
    <Grid x:Name="LayoutRoot">
        <Grid.RowDefinitions>
            <RowDefinition Height="50" />
            <RowDefinition Height="auto" />
            <RowDefinition Height="*" />
        </Grid.RowDefinitions>
        <Grid Grid.Row="0" Background="Navy">
            <TextBlock FontSize="24"
                   FontWeight="Bold"
                   Foreground="White"
                   Text="Equipment Running Hours"
                   VerticalAlignment="Center"
                   HorizontalAlignment="Center"
                   TextWrapping="Wrap" />
        </Grid>
```

```
        <Grid Grid.Row="1">
            <Grid.ColumnDefinitions>
                <ColumnDefinition Width="0.25*" />
                <ColumnDefinition Width="*" />
            </Grid.ColumnDefinitions>
            <Grid.RowDefinitions>
                <RowDefinition Height="auto" />
                <RowDefinition Height="auto" />
                <RowDefinition Height="auto" />
                <RowDefinition Height="auto" />
                <RowDefinition Height="auto" />
                <RowDefinition Height="auto" />
            </Grid.RowDefinitions>
            <sdk:Label Content="Equipment" Grid.Column="0" Grid.
Row="0"
                    Margin="5,5,5,5"/>
            <TextBox
                Text="{Binding Equipment,
                ValidatesOnNotifyDataErrors=True,
                NotifyOnValidationError=True,
                Mode=TwoWay}"
                Margin="5,5,5,5" Grid.Column="1" Grid.Row="0" />
            <sdk:Label Content="Running Hours" Grid.Column="0" Grid.
Row="1"
                    Margin="5,5,5,5"/>
            <TextBox Margin="5,5,5,5" Grid.Column="1" Grid.Row="1">
                <TextBox.Text>
                    <Binding Path="RunningHours"
                             ValidatesOnNotifyDataErrors="True"
                             NotifyOnValidationError="True"
                             Mode="TwoWay">
                    </Binding>
                </TextBox.Text>
            </TextBox>
            <sdk:Label Content="Operator" Grid.Column="0" Grid.Row="2"
                    Margin="5,5,5,5"/>
            <TextBox
                Text="{Binding EquipmentOperator,
                        ValidatesOnNotifyDataErrors=True,
                        NotifyOnValidationError=True,
                        Mode=TwoWay}"
                Margin="5,5,5,5" Grid.Column="1" Grid.Row="2" />
            <sdk:Label Content="Supervisor" Grid.Column="0" Grid.
```

```
Row="3"
                    Margin="5,5,5,5"/>
            <TextBox
                Text="{Binding ShiftSupervisor,
                        ValidatesOnNotifyDataErrors=True,
                        NotifyOnValidationError=True,
                        Mode=TwoWay}"
                Margin="5,5,5,5" Grid.Column="1" Grid.Row="3" />
            <Button Content="Log Running Hours" Grid.Row="4"
                    Margin="5,5,5,5" Grid.Column="1"
                    HorizontalAlignment="Left" Padding="4,4,4,4"
                    Command="{Binding LogRunningHoursCommand}"/>
            <sdk:ValidationSummary Margin="5,5,5,5"  Grid.Row="5"
                                   Grid.Column="0" Grid.
ColumnSpan="2"/>
        </Grid>
        <Grid Grid.Row="2" />
    </Grid>
</UserControl>
```

The following screenshot shows the default style in which `ValidationSummary` is displayed. We can update both the header and the content style. Here, property names are displayed as in the view model, which are obviously not the same as the labels shown for each field in the view. We can update that by using `DisplayAttribute` with properties in the view model.

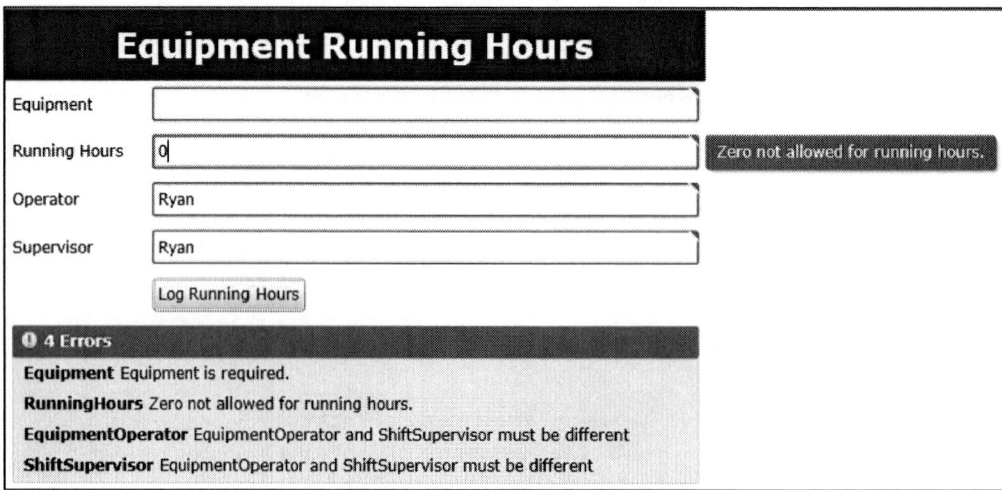

Enterprise library validation application block

Microsoft Enterprise library has a bunch of features, which makes development simpler. They call these features **Application Blocks**. They are generally used for developing cross-cutting concerns. They let the development teams focus on more important business features, relieving them from these base components. One of such application block is called **Validation Application Block**. In Enterprise Library 5.0, it added support for WPF. The Microsoft Patterns and Practices team has also released the Silverlight Integration pack for Enterprise library lately. In this section, we will briefly see how we can use the validation application block in MVVM-based applications.

The validation application block allows the defining of validation logic in different ways. It has the following options:

- Attributes
- Configuration
- Self validation

Now, let's see how we can use the validation application block to the simple order entry application we created in the discussion about validation rules. It just has three fields—**Customer name**, **Product**, and **Quantity**. We will see how the application block saves our lives.

This example requires Enterprise Library 5.0, which can be downloaded from Microsoft Download Center (`http://www.microsoft.com/download/en/details.aspx?displaylang=en&id=15104`).

Let's first see how we can define the rules in the attributes, and how the validation application block helps us in using those attributes in the view definition. These rules can be defined directly for the properties in the view model. Let's use the equipment running hours example. Let's create a WPF MVVM Light project named `MVVMAppEntLibraryValidationAppBlock`. We updated the view model as the view model in the previous example. Here, we have decorated the properties with some attributes. This includes the `TypeConversionValidatorAttribute` and `StringLengthValidator` attributes from the `Enterprise` library and `RequiredAttribute` from the `System.ComponentModel.DataAnnotations` library.

```
namespace MVVMAppEntLibraryValidationAppBlock.ViewModel
{
    using GalaSoft.MvvmLight;
    using System.Windows.Input;
    using GalaSoft.MvvmLight.Command;
```

```
using Microsoft.Practices.EnterpriseLibrary.Validation.Validators;
using System.ComponentModel.DataAnnotations;
using System.Collections.ObjectModel;

public class MainViewModel : ViewModelBase
{
    #region Properties

    string _equipment = string.Empty;

   [Required(ErrorMessage="Equipment is required")]
    public string Equipment
    {
        get { return _equipment; }
        set
        {
            if (_equipment != value)
            {
                _equipment = value;
                RaisePropertyChanged("Equipment");
            }
        }
    }

    string _runningHours = string.Empty;

    [TypeConversionValidator(typeof(double),
        MessageTemplate="Only numeric data allowed.",
        Ruleset="MainViewModelRuleSet")]
    public string RunningHours
    {
        get { return _runningHours; }
        set
        {
            if (_runningHours != value)
            {
                _runningHours = value;
                RaisePropertyChanged("RunningHours");
            }
        }
    }


    string _equipmentOperator = string.Empty;
```

```
        [StringLengthValidator(2, RangeBoundaryType.Inclusive, 10,
         RangeBoundaryType.Inclusive,
         MessageTemplate =
        "[EquipmentOperator] must be between {3} and {5}
characters.")]
        public string EquipmentOperator
        {
            get { return _equipmentOperator; }
            set
            {
                if (_equipmentOperator != value)
                {
                    _equipmentOperator = value;
                    RaisePropertyChanged("EquipmentOperator");
}
            }
        }

        string _shiftSupervisor = string.Empty;

        [StringLengthValidator(2, RangeBoundaryType.Inclusive, 10,
            RangeBoundaryType.Inclusive,
            MessageTemplate =
                "[ShiftSupervisor] must be between {3} and {5}
characters.")]
        public string ShiftSupervisor
        {
            get { return _shiftSupervisor; }
            set
            {
                if (_shiftSupervisor != value)
                {
                    _shiftSupervisor = value;
                    RaisePropertyChanged("ShiftSupervisor");
                }
            }
        }

        ICommand _logRunningHoursCommand = null;
        public ICommand LogRunningHoursCommand
        {
            get
            {
                if (_logRunningHoursCommand == null)
```

```
                {
                    _logRunningHoursCommand = new RelayCommand(
                                () =>
                                {
                                    Errors.Clear();

            //Get the Validation Block Error messages
            //from Validation.ValidateFromAttributes<MainViewModel>(this)
            //Get the DataAnnotations error message from TypeDescriptor
            //Add messages to Errors collection

                                });
                }

                return _logRunningHoursCommand;
            }
        }

        ObservableCollection<string> _errors;
        public ObservableCollection<string> Errors
        {
            get
            {
                if (_errors == null)
                {
                    _errors = new ObservableCollection<string>();
                }

                return _errors;
            }
        }

        #endregion

    }
}
```

The `Enterprise` library also supports the validation information, as a configuration. We can use the `Configuration` utility to provide the same feature. It is available as a start menu item and is also integrated with Visual Studio. It is available through a context menu item for `app.config`, as follows:

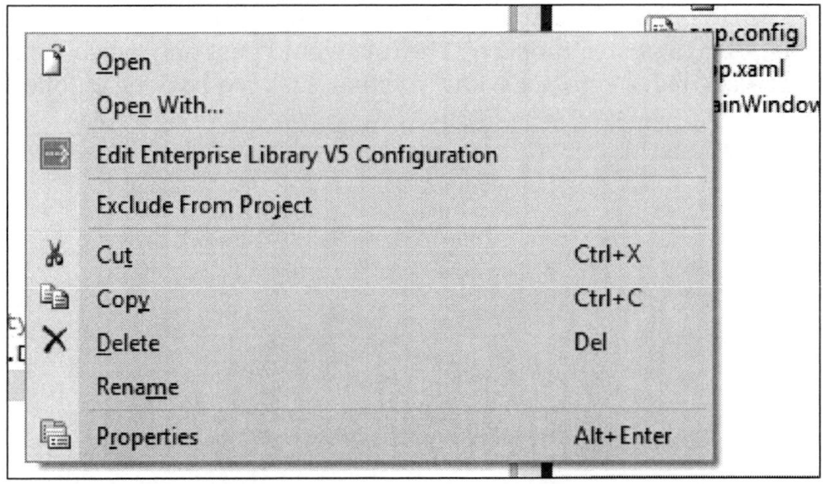

We need to specify the type for which the validations rules are supposed to be defined. For this purpose, we need to add the assembly to the tool. Then we can easily browse through the types within. Here, we have referenced the `MVVMAppEntLibraryValidationAppBlock` assembly and browsed the `MainViewModel` type.

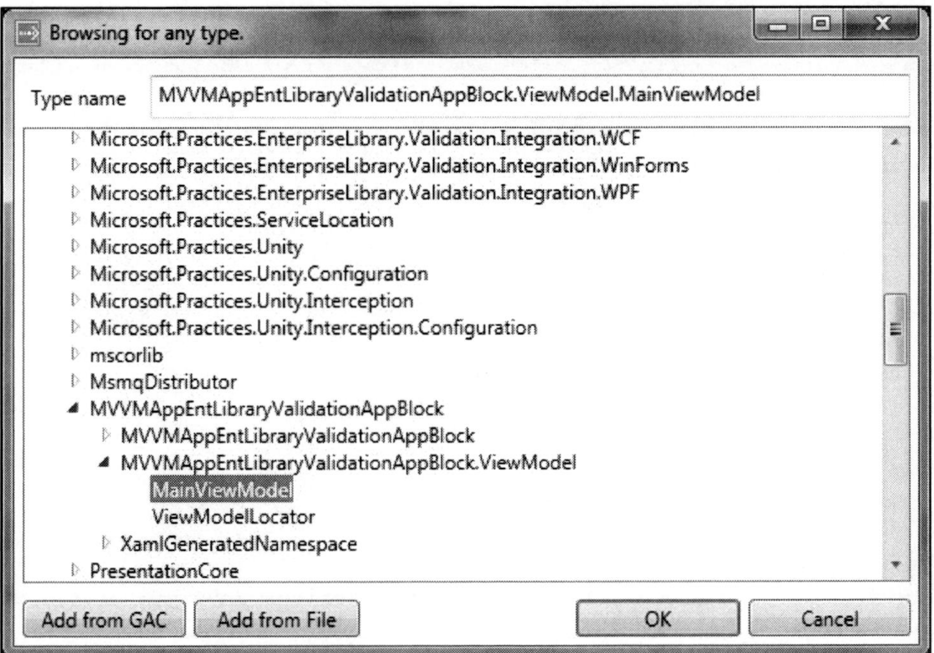

In order to keep the example simple, we are just defining one validation rule here. This is for the `RunningHours` property. The rule would pass only when the running hours neither start with a zero nor with a decimal. This can be done as follows:

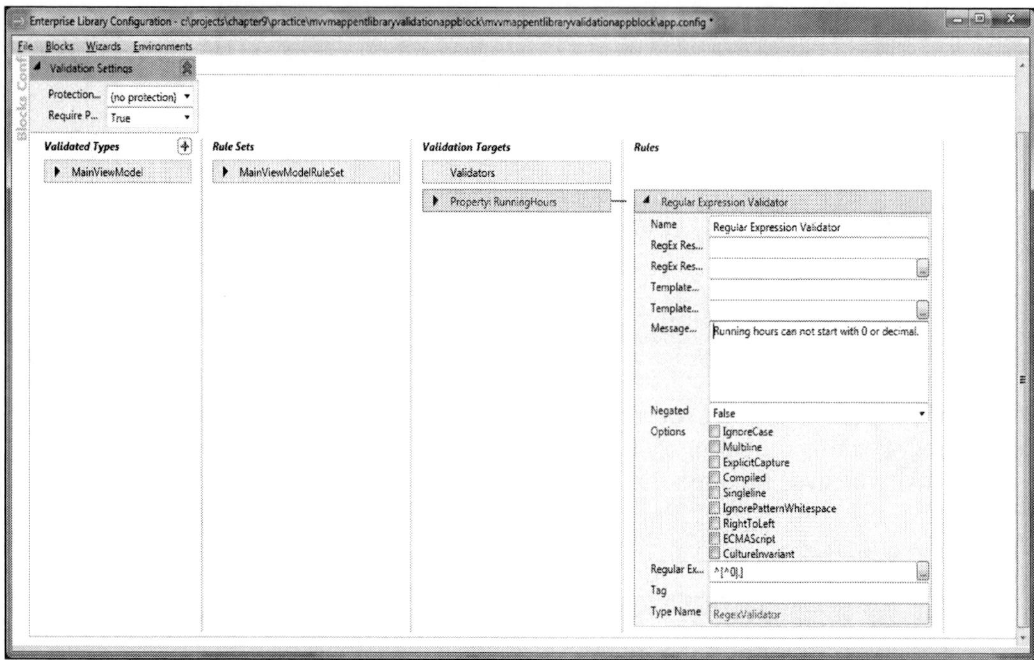

If we have started the tool through Visual Studio, it automatically adds the following configuration to `app.config`, when we save it in the preceding tool.

```
<validation>
    <type name="MVVMAppEntLibraryValidationAppBlock.ViewModel.
MainViewModel"
        assemblyName="MVVMAppEntLibraryValidationAppBlock,
Version=0.0.0.1,
                    Culture=neutral, PublicKeyToken=null">
        <ruleset name="MainViewModelRuleSet">
            <properties>
                <property name="RunningHours">
                    <validator
                        type="Microsoft.Practices.EnterpriseLibrary.
Validation.Validators.RegexValidator,
                            Microsoft.Practices.EnterpriseLibrary.
Validation,
                            Version=5.0.414.0, Culture=neutral,
                            PublicKeyToken=31bf3856ad364e35"
```

```
                      pattern="^[^0|.]"
patternResourceType=""
                           messageTemplate="Running hours can not start
with 0."
                           name="Regular Expression Validator" />
                     </property>
                 </properties>
             </ruleset>
         </type>
</validation>
```

Now, we update the view. There are a number of options to integrate the `Validation` block validations with the view. We can use `ValidatorRule`, as defined in the library, as we did for equipment. Here, we need to specify the source type and the actual property, which should be used to extract the validation information from its attribute. WPF integration of the library also supports the same shortcut that we have used for other properties. We just need to use the `Validate.BindingForProperty` attached property. It would automatically use the validation attributes from the source property of the binding for the particular property specified. We have used the same for running hours-, operator-, and supervisor-related fields. There is one more amazing thing. We can consolidate the validation rules from different sources. As you can see, we have a business rule for running hours in the view model. It should be convertible to a `double` type. In the configuration, we have stated that it should not start with a zero or a decimal. We want to consolidate these rules for validation purposes of the property. That is exactly what we have done here.

```
<Window
    x:Class="MVVMAppEntLibraryValidationAppBlock.MainWindow"
    xmlns="http://schemas.microsoft.com/winfx/2006/xaml/presentation"
    xmlns:x="http://schemas.microsoft.com/winfx/2006/xaml"
    xmlns:d="http://schemas.microsoft.com/expression/blend/2008"
    xmlns:mc="http://schemas.openxmlformats.org/markup-
compatibility/2006"
    xmlns:vab=
     "clr-namespace:Microsoft.Practices.EnterpriseLibrary.Validation.
Integration.WPF;assembly=Microsoft.Practices.EnterpriseLibrary.
Validation.Integration.WPF"
    xmlns:vm="clr-namespace:MVVMAppEntLibraryValidationAppBlock.
ViewModel"
    mc:Ignorable="d"
    Title="MVVM Survival Guide"
    Height="364" Width="515"
    DataContext="{Binding Main, Source={StaticResource Locator}}">
```

```
<Window.Resources>
    <ResourceDictionary>
        <ResourceDictionary.MergedDictionaries>
            <ResourceDictionary Source="Skins/MainSkin.xaml" />
        </ResourceDictionary.MergedDictionaries>
    </ResourceDictionary>
</Window.Resources>
<Grid x:Name="LayoutRoot">
    <Grid.RowDefinitions>
        <RowDefinition Height="50" />
        <RowDefinition Height="auto" />
        <RowDefinition Height="*" />
    </Grid.RowDefinitions>
    <Grid Grid.Row="0" Background="Navy">
        <TextBlock FontSize="24"
               FontWeight="Bold"
               Foreground="White"
               Text="Equipment Running Hours"
               VerticalAlignment="Center"
               HorizontalAlignment="Center"
               TextWrapping="Wrap" />
    </Grid>
    <Grid Grid.Row="1">
        <Grid.ColumnDefinitions>
            <ColumnDefinition Width="0.25*" />
            <ColumnDefinition Width="*" />
        </Grid.ColumnDefinitions>
        <Grid.RowDefinitions>
            <RowDefinition Height="auto" />
            <RowDefinition Height="auto" />
            <RowDefinition Height="auto" />
            <RowDefinition Height="auto" />
            <RowDefinition Height="auto" />
        </Grid.RowDefinitions>
        <Label Content="Equipment" Grid.Column="0" Grid.Row="0"
                Margin="5,5,5,5"/>
        <TextBox Margin="5,5,5,5" Grid.Column="1" Grid.Row="0"  >
            <TextBox.Text>
                <Binding Path="Equipment"
                         UpdateSourceTrigger="PropertyChanged" >
                    <Binding.ValidationRules>
                        <vab:ValidatorRule
                            SourceType="{x:Type vm:MainViewModel}"
                            SourcePropertyName="Equipment" />
```

```
                    </Binding.ValidationRules>
                </Binding>
            </TextBox.Text>
        </TextBox>
        <Label Content="Running Hours" Grid.Column="0"
               Grid.Row="1" Margin="5,5,5,5"/>
        <TextBox Text="{Binding RunningHours,
                                UpdateSourceTrigger=PropertyChang
ed}"
            vab:Validate.UsingRulesetName="MainViewModelRuleSet"
            vab:Validate.UsingSource="All"
            vab:Validate.BindingForProperty="Text"
            Margin="5,5,5,5" Grid.Column="1" Grid.Row="1" />
        <Label Content="Operator" Grid.Column="0" Grid.Row="2"
                Margin="5,5,5,5"/>
        <TextBox
            Text="{Binding EquipmentOperator,
                           UpdateSourceTrigger=PropertyChanged}"
         vab:Validate.BindingForProperty="Text"
            Margin="5,5,5,5" Grid.Column="1" Grid.Row="2" />
        <Label Content="Supervisor" Grid.Column="0" Grid.Row="3"
               Margin="5,5,5,5"/>
        <TextBox
            Text="{Binding ShiftSupervisor,
                           UpdateSourceTrigger=PropertyChanged}"
            vab:Validate.BindingForProperty="Text"
            Margin="5,5,5,5" Grid.Column="1" Grid.Row="3" />
        <Button Content="Log Running Hours" Grid.Row="4"
                Margin="5,5,5,5" Grid.Column="1"
                HorizontalAlignment="Left" Padding="4,4,4,4"
                Command="{Binding LogRunningHoursCommand}"/>
    </Grid>
    <Grid Grid.Row="2">
        <ListBox ItemsSource="{Binding Errors}"
                 DisplayMemberPath="ErrorMessage"
                 Margin="5,5,5,5" />
    </Grid>
  </Grid>
</Window>
```

> There are a lot of limitations in the validation application block integration provided by Microsoft. For example, if we wanted to validate the value of one property, based on the current value of any other property, the validation application block supports this by providing `PropertyComparisonValidator`. This is currently not supported for direct use by WPF. Yet, whatever it already supports definitely deserves a lot of appreciation. Hopefully, these limitations will be addressed in a later version of the toolkit.
>
> Silverlight developers can use the Silverlight Integration pack for Enterprise Library. The validation application block is a part of the installation.

Complex business rules

We have already discussed how we can use Windows WF to define complex business rules. Please see the first section of the previous chapter for details on how to do this.

Error notifications

Error notifications inform users that a particular action will not be performed and inform the user if they need to take any action in order to make it work.

Error message box

Message boxes are the oldest way to present error messages to the user. Whenever there are any issues in the data entered by users, we can notify them by just popping the dialog box. This can be modal or modeless, depending on the area of the application the message is about. This can also have different icons, such as `X` for error message and `!` for information messages. We have seen them and used them, and if they appear we are not surprised.

UX designers tell us that we need to reduce the number of clicks to accomplish a use case by the user. These dialog messages require us to try to submit by clicking on the **Submit** button first. Then, we need to close these dialogs by clicking on another button. These clicks affect the usability of our applications causing irritations to the end user.

Error message texts in the message box might be very big. They might not be clear enough to guide the user to fix the data in the actual fields. I think most of you have seen these error messages and scratched your head saying, "OK! Something is wrong, but what is it?". That is not acceptable!

There might be more than one issue with the data entry. Generally, these error messages are consolidated to be shown in a single message box. Now, the user hits the **Submit** button, and we show the error message to fix a number of fields. The messages are clear enough to understand. The user does understand it and closes the dialog. Now, he fixes one issue and the next, but he has to remember all these issues. When was the last time that you took a screenshot of the error message dialog, so that you could fix everything in a single attempt and avoid another message box? It was not very long ago for me.

We are living in the age of dashboard applications. When the user logs in, he sees everything on a single screen. There are different areas of the screen showing different "things of interest" to the user. There are specialized toolkits and frameworks, such as PRISM, in order to provide ease in developing these applications. They let us develop these areas as separate modules. These modules use different data sources. While loading the application, the framework discovers them and loads them in the special area of the screen as requested by the module. These modules are generally developed by different teams. Showing a dialog for some issue with data entry in a part of window is basically going outside the boundary of your team. No team should be allowed to hijack the whole application by showing a dialog that has nothing to do with data in any other module.

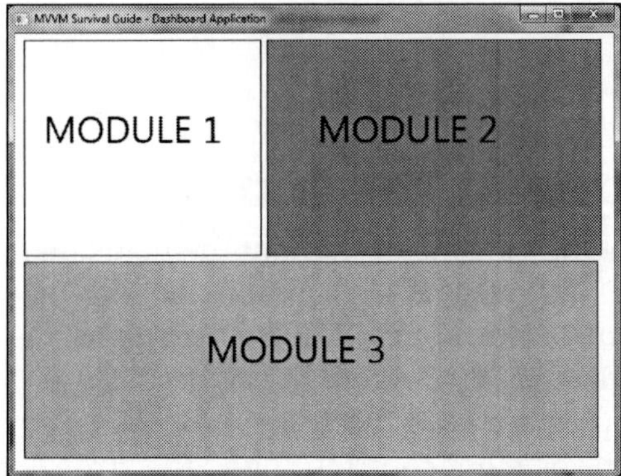

You can still find some instances in which you still need to show some urgent information to the end user. For example, if you may want to show that he is disconnected from the server or that there is a newer version of the application available, just hit the button to download. These messages are not module-specific and deserve the immediate attention of the user. Generally, decisions about showing the dialog should be taken by the architecture team, and the individual should be given clear advice to avoid these decisions. This is what we think. Now, if we were to show an error message from our view models directly, we would be sacrificing unit testability of the code. Please see *Chapter 7, Dialogs and MVVM*, to understand how we can show dialog in MVVM, so that the code is still testable.

Highlighting fields

XAML technologies highlight fields, if there is failure in validation. This might be an exception during copying the value to the source field. This can also be caused by an error result from the validation rule.

The good thing about WPF/Silverlight is that every feature is lookless—you can use it as it is provided. If you do not like the look and feel, change it. The framework would still support the same functionality. This has never been achieved before, and can be repeated with this feature. The fields are highlighted with a red border, by default. In this chapter, we have already discussed how we can override it. If you don't like it, we can even override the template with `null` and there would be no highlight.

```
<TextBox Height="37" HorizontalAlignment="Left"
         Margin="399,380,0,0" Name="textBoxAge"
         VerticalAlignment="Top" Width="217"
         Validation.ErrorTemplate="{x:Null}"
         >
    <TextBox.Text>
        <Binding Path="Age"
                 UpdateSourceTrigger="PropertyChanged" />
    </TextBox.Text>
</TextBox>
```

Error messages in the tooltip

Highlighting the control informs the user about the fields that need to be updated in order to fix the problem. But, what is the actual issue with the data in those fields? Just highlighting the control wouldn't guide the user about the actual issue. He needs to see the error message. By default, the error message is not displayed by WPF. Earlier in this chapter, we have discussed how we can update the validation error template, so that the element contributing to the error would show the error message in a tool tip, if the control is erroneous. Generally, we need the same error to be displayed for each type of control, so that we can define them in a **resource** dictionary and merge that in `App.xaml`. All the controls would automatically apply their error behavior.

Error messages beside the control

Winform developers must remember the property extenders to show the error messages. Having error messages beside the control is based on the same idea. We can update the error template so that an error message can be shown beside the actual control in the error. Obviously, there is limited space available to show this text, so we cannot provide enough information to the user. This brevity could be dangerous as it does not communicate the expectation of the system to the end users.

```
<ControlTemplate x:Key="ValidationErrorTemplate">
    <DockPanel>
        <Border BorderBrush="Blue" BorderThickness="2">
            <AdornedElementPlaceholder x:Name="controlInError" />
        </Border>
        <TextBlock DockPanel.Dock="Right" Foreground="Red">
            <TextBlock.Text>
                <Binding
                    Path="AdornedElement.(Validation.Errors)[0].
ErrorContent">                  <Binding.RelativeSource>
                        <RelativeSource Mode="FindAncestor"
                                        AncestorType="{x:Type
Adorner}" />
                    </Binding.RelativeSource>
                </Binding>
            </TextBlock.Text>
        </TextBlock>
    </DockPanel>
</ControlTemplate>
```

Validation summary pane

We have used this technique in a few examples in this chapter. In this technique, we set aside some space assigned to display error messages. This technique is especially suitable when real estate is not a problem on the view.

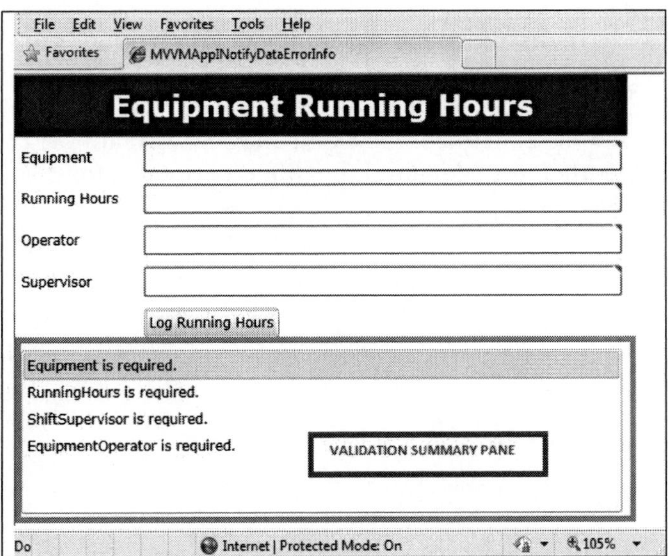

The validation summary pane can also be added to an expander. It can be expanded to show the error message. Now, a user can expand it, if he wants to peek at the message again. The visibility can be set in such a way that the control becomes invisible to the user when there are no error messages.

Flip controls

This is the latest technique to display such error messages. WPF 3D hasn't been adopted a lot in business applications, except in charting applications and controls. The idea is to develop a control that has two faces: front and back. All the content is laid out in the same way as in the regular view on the front side of the control. When the user submits, we run the validation logic in the same way as in the regular view. In case there is an error, the control is flipped and user is shown with the validation error messages. After reading the messages, the user can flip it back to the front view and update the fields accordingly. Ideally, this will highlight the fields in error, and the user will be allowed to go back and forth between the front and back sides of the control.

Although no commercial flip controls are available yet, some open source controls can be found on the internet. They seem to have a lot of issues with the available control libraries, so test them before you decide to use them in a commercial application. This area is interesting for further study, and hopefully many amazing controls will be seen in the future.

Summary

In this chapter, we have discussed the different validation options in WPF and Silverlight. We have outlined how these validation techniques can work together with MVVM. These techniques include the `Enterprise` library validation application block and the `IDataErorInfo` and `INoityfyDataErrorInfo` validation rules. In the end, we tried to understand the different options for displaying validation results.

10

Using Non-MVVM Third-party Controls

By Muhammad Shujaat Siddiqi

The development community has been slow in adopting MVVM and as a result there are many third-party libraries and controls on the market that don't follow the pattern. One of the most common challenges faced when adopting MVVM is how to use non-MVVM libraries and controls in MVVM architecture. The good news is that we will review several techniques which will allow you to minimize the impact of the non-MVVM code in your design and maximize the testability of your codebase.

As an example, we are going to use the WPF **WebBrowser** control. This is complex enough example to explain all the different available techniques and yet simple enough to be covered in a single chapter. The `WebBrowser` control is just a WPF wrapper around same old `WebBrowser` ActiveX control from the Win32/MFC days. Like many Silverlight and WPF controls on the market, the `WebBroswer` control wasn't built using the MVVM approach and instead has forms, controllers, and code behind design.

Let's start by looking at a simple example by following these steps:

1. Create a new WPF MVVMLight project called `UsingNonMVVMElements`.
2. Update `MainWindow.xaml` as shown in the following code. Here we have set the `Source` statically to `http://www.google.com`.

```
<Window x:Class="UsingNonMVVMElements.MainWindow"
        xmlns="http://schemas.microsoft.com/winfx/2006/xaml/
presentation"
        xmlns:x="http://schemas.microsoft.com/winfx/2006/xaml"
        xmlns:d="http://schemas.microsoft.com/expression/
blend/2008"
        xmlns:mc="http://schemas.openxmlformats.org/markup-
```

```
compatibility/2006"
        mc:Ignorable="d"
        Height="481" Width="688"
        Title="MVVM Survival Guide">
    <Grid x:Name="LayoutRoot">
        <WebBrowser Source="http://www.google.com" />
    </Grid>
</Window>
```

3. When we run the preceding code, it loads a window with Google's home page displayed. Now let's introduce a `ViewModel` class used as `DataContext` of preceding `Window` as shown in the following code:

```
namespace UsingNonMVVMElements.ViewModel
{
    using GalaSoft.MvvmLight;

    public class MainWindowViewModel : ViewModelBase
    {
        string _sourcePage = "http://www.google.com";
        public string SourcePage
        {
            get { return _sourcePage; }
            set
            {
                _sourcePage = value;
                RaisePropertyChanged("SourcePage");
            }
        }
    }
}
```

4. Next we need to wire up the `MainWindowViewModel.SourcePage` property to the `WebBrowser.Source` property of `MainWindow`. To do this, let's update the definition of `MainWindow` as follows:

```
<Window x:Class="UsingNonMVVMElements.MainWindow"
        xmlns="http://schemas.microsoft.com/winfx/2006/xaml/
presentation"
        xmlns:x="http://schemas.microsoft.com/winfx/2006/xaml"
        xmlns:d="http://schemas.microsoft.com/expression/
blend/2008"
        xmlns:mc="http://schemas.openxmlformats.org/markup-
compatibility/2006"
        mc:Ignorable="d"
        Height="481" Width="688"
```

```
        xmlns:local="clr-namespace:UsingNonMVVMElements.ViewModel"
        Title="MVVM Light Application">
    <Window.DataContext>
        <local:MainWindowViewModel />
    </Window.DataContext>
    <Grid x:Name="LayoutRoot">
        <WebBrowser Source="{Binding SourcePage}" />
    </Grid>
</Window>
```

It seems like this would work as we are binding the `Source` property of a `WebBrowser` instance to `SourcePage` of `DataContext`. However, when we run the application we get the exception as shown in the following screenshot:

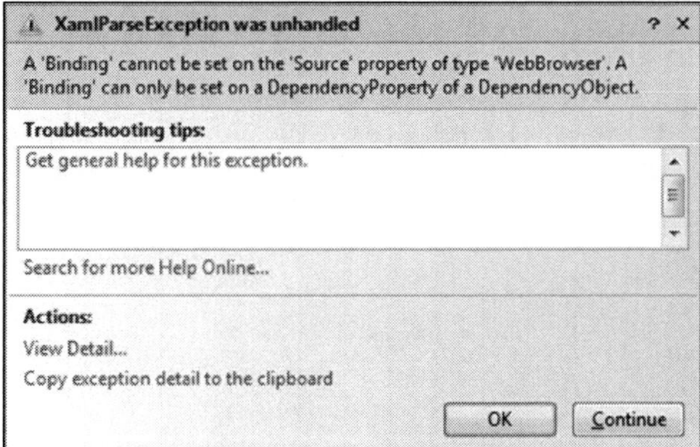

One of the requirements of data binding is that the binding target must be a `DependencyProperty`. Here we are using `Source` property of the `WebBrowser` control as the `Binding` target, which is not `DependencyProperty` and hence the exception.

We will now look at several techniques that will allow us to use the `WebBrowser` control in an MVVM-friendly way.

Using attached behaviors

We can resolve the `Binding` issue of controls exposing non-dependency properties by using attached behaviors. This technique is a simple matter of registering an attached property, which is implemented as dependency properties in WPF. We can use the attached property as a binding target and whenever the source value changes, we can pass the updated value to the non-bindable property.

To do this, add a new class called `WebBrowserAttachedBehavior` and define it as follows:

```
namespace UsingNonMVVMElements.AttachedBehaviors
{
    using System.Windows;
    using System.Windows.Controls;

    public class WebBrowserAttachedBehavior
    {
        public static DependencyProperty SourcePageProperty =
            DependencyProperty.RegisterAttached("SourcePage",
                typeof(string), typeof(WebBrowserAttachedBehavior),
                new PropertyMetadata("",
OnSourcePagePropertyChanged));

        public static string GetSourcePage(DependencyObject obj)
        {
            return (string)obj.GetValue(SourcePageProperty);
        }

        public static void SetSourcePage(DependencyObject obj, string
value)
        {
            obj.SetValue(SourcePageProperty, value);
        }

        public static void OnSourcePagePropertyChanged(DependencyObje
ct browser,
            DependencyPropertyChangedEventArgs args)
        {
            if (args.NewValue != null && browser is WebBrowser)
            {
                WebBrowser webBrowser = (WebBrowser)browser;
                webBrowser.Source = new System.Uri(args.NewValue.
ToString());
            }
        }
    }
}
```

As discussed previously, we are just using the `PropertyChanged` event of the `Dependency` property, and using it to pass on the updates to the underlying non-bindable property. Attached properties are implemented by following a pattern, which creates a set of static methods, as shown in the preceding code. Once defined, an instance of an attached property can be attached to an instance of a different class. When we created the attached property previously, we associated the `OnSourcePagePropertyChanged()` method with the property's `Changed` event, which will be called each time the property value changes. When this method is called, it will be passed as a reference to the instance that the attached property is attached to. This allows us to easily update values on the instance. This is how we will be able to pass through updates from our view model to our non-bindable property using the the attach behavior pattern as we will see next.

Next, let's update the definition of `MainWindow` as follows:

```
<Window x:Class="UsingNonMVVMElements.MainWindow"
        xmlns="http://schemas.microsoft.com/winfx/2006/xaml/
presentation"
        xmlns:x="http://schemas.microsoft.com/winfx/2006/xaml"
        xmlns:d="http://schemas.microsoft.com/expression/blend/2008"
        xmlns:mc="http://schemas.openxmlformats.org/markup-
compatibility/2006"
        mc:Ignorable="d"
        Height="481" Width="688"
        xmlns:local="clr-namespace:UsingNonMVVMElements.ViewModel"
        xmlns:AttachedBehaviors =
            "clr-namespace:UsingNonMVVMElements.AttachedBehaviors"
        Title="MVVM Survival Guide">
    <Window.DataContext>
        <local:MainWindowViewModel />
    </Window.DataContext>
    <Grid x:Name="LayoutRoot">
        <WebBrowser
            AttachedBehaviors:WebBrowserAttachedBehavior.SourcePage=
                "{Binding SourcePage}" />
    </Grid>
</Window>
```

Now run the preceding code and you will see that a window is shown with the `WebBrowser` control displaying the **Google** home page as shown in the following screenshot:

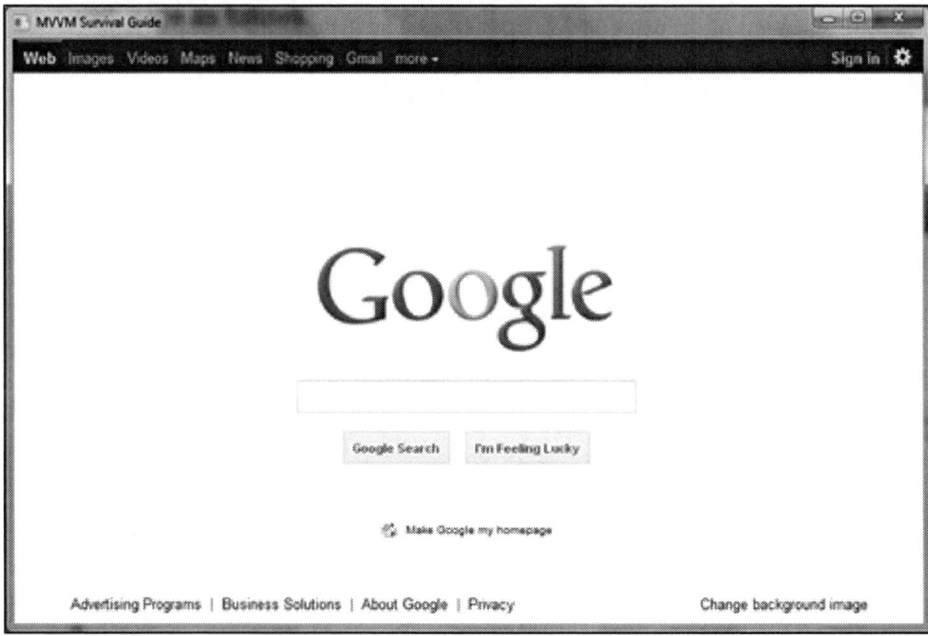

We can use the attached behavior approach to bind all non-dependency properties to the properties in view models and let the binding system take care of updates.

Let's update the code to allow users to have control over which page they want to browse to. We just need `TextBox` and a button to fulfill this requirement. `TextBox` is bound to the `SuggestedSourcePage` string property in the view model while button's `Command` property is bound to the `NavigateUriCommand` property in `DataContext` as shown in the following code:

```
<Window x:Class="UsingNonMVVMElements.MainWindow"
        xmlns="http://schemas.microsoft.com/winfx/2006/xaml/
presentation"
        xmlns:x="http://schemas.microsoft.com/winfx/2006/xaml"
        xmlns:d="http://schemas.microsoft.com/expression/blend/2008"
        xmlns:mc="http://schemas.openxmlformats.org/markup-
compatibility/2006"
        mc:Ignorable="d"
        Height="481" Width="688"
        xmlns:local="clr-namespace:UsingNonMVVMElements.ViewModel"
        xmlns:AttachedBehaviors ="clr-namespace:UsingNonMVVMElements.
```

```
AttachedBehaviors"
        Title="MVVM Survival Guide">
    <Window.DataContext>
        <local:MainWindowViewModel />
    </Window.DataContext>
    <Grid x:Name="LayoutRoot">
        <TextBox Height="27" HorizontalAlignment="Left"
Margin="2,1,0,0"
                 Name="textBoxUrl" VerticalAlignment="Top" Width="611"
                 Text="{Binding UserSuggestedSourcePage}" />
        <Button Content="Go" Height="27" HorizontalAlignment="Left"
                Margin="615,1,0,0" Name="btnGo"
VerticalAlignment="Top"
                Width="39" IsDefault="True"
                Command="{Binding NavigateUrlCommand}" />
        <WebBrowser
            AttachedBehaviors:WebBrowserAttachedBehavior.
SourcePage="{Binding SourcePage}"
            Margin="0,34,0,0" />
    </Grid>
</Window>
```

We need to update the view model for the preceding changes in the view. The following view model provides the `SuggestedSourcePage` property and also provides an `ICommand` property called `NavigateUriCommand`. We are using MVVMLight's `RelayCommand` here. In the `Execute` method of this command, we are just copying the value of this property to the `SourcePage` property. Remember that this is the same property that the previously defined attached behavior is using to copy to the `Source` property of the `WebBrowser` control.

```
namespace UsingNonMVVMElements.ViewModel
{
    using GalaSoft.MvvmLight;
    using GalaSoft.MvvmLight.Command;
    using System;

    public class MainWindowViewModel : ViewModelBase
    {
        #region Public Properties

        string _sourcePage = "http://www.google.com";
        public string SourcePage
        {
            get { return _sourcePage; }
            set
```

```
        {
            _sourcePage = value;
            RaisePropertyChanged("SourcePage");
        }
    }

    string _userSuggestedSourcePage = "http://www.google.com";
    public string UserSuggestedSourcePage
    {
        get { return _userSuggestedSourcePage; }
        set
        {
            _userSuggestedSourcePage = value;
            RaisePropertyChanged("UserSuggestedSourcePage");
        }
    }

    #endregion

    #region Commands

    RelayCommand _navigateUrlCommand;
    public RelayCommand NavigateUrlCommand
    {
        get
        {
            if (_navigateUrlCommand == null)
            {
                _navigateUrlCommand = new RelayCommand(
                    () =>
                    {
                        if (Uri.IsWellFormedUriString(
                            _userSuggestedSourcePage,
                            UriKind.Absolute))
                        {
                            this.SourcePage =
                                this.UserSuggestedSourcePage;
                        }
                    });
            }

            return _navigateUrlCommand;
        }
    }
```

```
        #endregion

    }
}
```

Now when the form is shown, the `Browser` control is loaded with the Google page. As the user types some other `Url` and clicks on the **Go** button, the browser navigates to the specified `Url` as shown in the following screenshot:

Using binding reflector

Although attached behaviors seem to solve the limitation of binding to a binding target that isn't a dependency property, the approach can be less appealing if there are a large number of properties that we need to bind to. If we are using attached behaviors then we need to define an attached behavior for each property for each type of control we are using in our application. This can end up being a lot of work if we are using a lot of third-party controls and it would be nice if there was a simpler approach that required less coding and hence less maintenance. Fortunately, the binding reflector technique can come to our rescue.

We know the requirement that a binding target has to be `DependencyProperty` but the requirements for binding source are not so strict. A binding source can simply be a Plain Old CLR property. In the binding reflector technique, we capitalize on this flexibility. Using this approach, binding reflector is `FrameworkElement` that is not available for the display of the user. It is similar to a hidden field in HTML that is added to a web page for data reasons and not display. It works just like a reflecting surface and that is why the name was chosen. As the binding reflector is notified about changes in the `Source` property, it simply reflects those changes to the `Target` property. Since the `Target` property cannot listen to the changes in the `Source` property, the binding reflector does the listening for changes in the `Source` property and then passes those changes on to the `Target` property as shown in the following diagram:

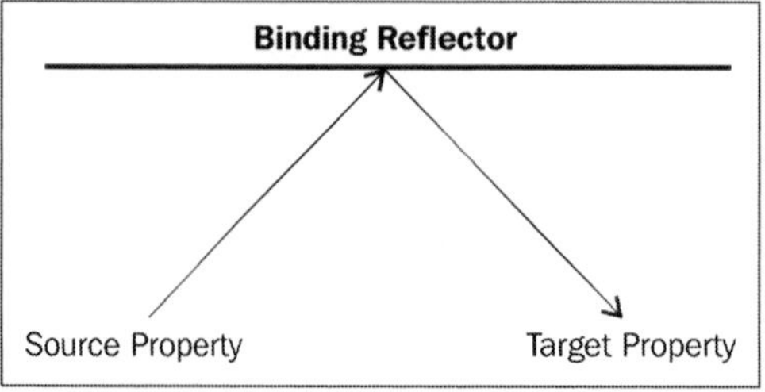

We can define a binding reflector as follows:

```
namespace UsingNonMVVMElements.Core
{
    using System.Windows;
    using System.Windows.Data;
    using System;

    class BindingReflector : FrameworkElement
    {
        public static DependencyProperty SourceProperty =
            DependencyProperty.Register("Source", typeof(object),
            typeof(BindingReflector),
            new FrameworkPropertyMetadata()
            {
                DefaultUpdateSourceTrigger =
                    UpdateSourceTrigger.PropertyChanged,
                BindsTwoWayByDefault = false,
                PropertyChangedCallback = OnSourceChanged
            });

        public object Source
```

```
        {
            get { return GetValue(SourceProperty); }
            set { SetValue(SourceProperty, value); }
        }

        public static DependencyProperty TargetProperty =
            DependencyProperty.Register("Target",
            typeof(object), typeof(BindingReflector),
            new FrameworkPropertyMetadata() {
                BindsTwoWayByDefault = false,
                DefaultUpdateSourceTrigger =
                    UpdateSourceTrigger.PropertyChanged
            });

        public object Target
        {
            get { return GetValue(TargetProperty); }
            set { SetValue(TargetProperty, value); }
        }

        private static void OnSourceChanged(DependencyObject d,
            DependencyPropertyChangedEventArgs e)
        {
            var reflector = (BindingReflector)d;
            if (reflector.Source != reflector.Target)
            {
                reflector.Target = reflector.Source;
            }
        }
    }
}
```

Now let's look at how we can use `BindingReflector`. Let's start by creating a new window and keep the view model the same as introduced in the previous example.

```
<Window x:Class="UsingNonMVVMElements.MainWindowBindingReflectorView"
        xmlns="http://schemas.microsoft.com/winfx/2006/xaml/
presentation"
        xmlns:x="http://schemas.microsoft.com/winfx/2006/xaml"
        Height="481" Width="688"
        xmlns:vm="clr-namespace:UsingNonMVVMElements.ViewModel"
        xmlns:converter="clr-namespace:UsingNonMVVMElements.Converter"
        xmlns:core="clr-namespace:UsingNonMVVMElements.Core"
        Title="MVVM Survival Guide - Binding Reflector">
    <Window.DataContext>
```

```
            <vm:MainWindowViewModel />
        </Window.DataContext>
        <Window.Resources>
            <converter:UriConverter x:Key="uriConverter" />
        </Window.Resources>
        <Grid x:Name="LayoutRoot">
            <TextBox Height="27" HorizontalAlignment="Left"
Margin="2,1,0,0"
                     Name="textBoxUrl" VerticalAlignment="Top" Width="611"
                     Text="{Binding UserSuggestedSourcePage}" />
            <Button Content="Go" Height="27" HorizontalAlignment="Left"
                    Margin="615,1,0,0" Name="btnGo"
VerticalAlignment="Top"
                    Width="39" IsDefault="True"
                    Command="{Binding NavigateUrlCommand}" />
            <WebBrowser x:Name="webBrowser" Margin="0,34,0,0" />
            <core:BindingReflector
                x:Name="sourceReflector">
                <core:BindingReflector.Target>
                    <Binding ElementName="webBrowser"
                             Path="Source" Mode="OneWayToSource" />
                </core:BindingReflector.Target>
                <core:BindingReflector.Source>
                    <Binding Path="SourcePage" Mode="OneWay"
                             Converter="{StaticResource
                                 uriConverter}"/>
                </core:BindingReflector.Source>
            </core:BindingReflector>
        </Grid>
</Window>
```

We have to create an instance of `BindngReflector` for each non-bindable property.

As you can see in the preceding code, we simply bound the `Source` property directly to the view model's `SourcePage` property and then we bound `Target` to the `WebBrowser.Source` property. Now we can let the WPF binding system take care of the updates.

Binding reflector can also be used on any `StaticResource` or `DynamicResource` property.

The following is the definition for `UriConverter`:

```
namespace UsingNonMVVMElements.Converter
{
    using System;
    using System.Windows.Data;

    public class UriConverter : IValueConverter
    {
        public object Convert(object value,
            System.Type targetType, object parameter,
            System.Globalization.CultureInfo culture)
        {
        return value;
        }

        public object ConvertBack(object value,
            System.Type targetType, object parameter,
            System.Globalization.CultureInfo culture)
        {
            string uri;
            if (value == null ||
                value.ToString().Trim() == string.Empty)
            {
                uri = "http://www.microsoft.com";
            }
            else
            {
                uri = value.ToString();
            }

            return new Uri(uri);
        }
    }
}
```

When we run the application, Google's web page is loaded in the browser. Now if we enter a different URL, for example Microsoft's URL and click on the **Go** button, then Microsoft's home page is loaded. This shows that binding reflector is successfully reflecting the updates of its `Source` property to the `WebBrowser.Source` property.

readonly CLR properties (with no change notification support)

The `WebBrowser` control also has `readonly` CLR properties like `CanGoBack`. When we get the value of this property, the control looks at its navigation list and determines if there are any pages in the list and returns `true` if there are some navigable pages or `false` otherwise. Like any other web browser, our web browser needs to support backward navigation, if possible. For this purpose, we want to include a **Back** button on the interface. It seems like this would be easy to implement using the `CanGoBack` property. We could use this property in `CanExecute` of `ICommand` and use an instance of the command for this button. The only issue is that `CanGoBack` is `readonly` and does not support change notifications.

```
namespace UsingNonMVVMElements.Command
{
    using System;
    using System.Windows.Input;
    using System.Windows.Controls;

    class GoBackCommand : ICommand
    {
        public bool CanExecute(object parameter)
        {
            bool ret = true;

            if (parameter != null && parameter is bool)
            {
                ret = (bool)parameter;
            }

            return ret;
        }

        public event EventHandler CanExecuteChanged
        {
            add { CommandManager.RequerySuggested += value; }
            remove { CommandManager.RequerySuggested -= value; }
        }
```

```
            public void Execute(object parameter)
            {
          //execution logic
            }
        }
    }
```

The command is expecting a `boolean` parameter. If there is one then `CanExecute` returns the value of the parameter. If there is no parameter then `CanExecute` always returns `true`. Now let's discuss how we can use this `ICommand` in the view.

```
<Window x:Class="UsingNonMVVMElements.
MainWindowBindingReadOnlyProperties"
        xmlns="http://schemas.microsoft.com/winfx/2006/xaml/
presentation"
        xmlns:x="http://schemas.microsoft.com/winfx/2006/xaml"
        Height="481" Width="688"
        xmlns:vm="clr-namespace:UsingNonMVVMElements.ViewModel"
        xmlns:converter="clr-namespace:UsingNonMVVMElements.Converter"
        xmlns:core="clr-namespace:UsingNonMVVMElements.Core"
        xmlns:command="clr-namespace:UsingNonMVVMElements.Command"
        Title="MVVM Light Application">
    <Window.DataContext>
        <vm:MainWindowViewModel />
    </Window.DataContext>
    <Window.Resources>
        <converter:UriConverter x:Key="uriConverter" />
        <command:GoBackCommand x:Key="goBackCommand" />
    </Window.Resources>
    <Grid x:Name="LayoutRoot">
        <TextBox Height="27" HorizontalAlignment="Left"
Margin="2,1,0,0"
                 Name="textBoxUrl" VerticalAlignment="Top" Width="611"
                 Text="{Binding UserSuggestedSourcePage}" />
        <Button Content="Go" Height="27" HorizontalAlignment="Left"
                Margin="615,1,0,0" Name="btnGo"
VerticalAlignment="Top"
                Width="39" IsDefault="True"
                Command="{Binding NavigateUrlCommand}" />
        <WebBrowser x:Name="webBrowser" Margin="0,59,0,0" />
        <core:BindingReflector
            x:Name="sourceReflector">
            <core:BindingReflector.Target>
```

```
                <Binding ElementName="webBrowser"
                         Path="Source" Mode="OneWayToSource" />
            </core:BindingReflector.Target>
            <core:BindingReflector.Source>
                <Binding Path="SourcePage" Mode="OneWay"
                         Converter="{StaticResource uriConverter}"/>
            </core:BindingReflector.Source>
        </core:BindingReflector>
        <Button Content="Back" Height="26"
            HorizontalAlignment="Left"
           Command="{Binding
               Source={StaticResource goBackCommand}}"
CommandParameter="{Binding
              ElementName=webBrowser, Path=CanGoBack}"
           Margin="2,30,0,0" Name="btnBack"
           VerticalAlignment="Top"
           Width="67" />
    </Grid>
</Window>
```

This seems like a perfectly reasonable approach but it doesn't work. When you run the application, the **Back** button is always disabled no matter how many pages you browse. So what's the problem? When we request the value of `CanGoBack` directly, it goes through the navigation list and returns accordingly. However, it doesn't notify all observers through any mechanism of change notification when `CanGoBack` has changed. Because of this, the view always holds on to the initial value of `CanGoBack`, which is `false` and therefore our button is always disabled.

So what are our options for resolving this issue? One thing we could try is polling but fortunately we have better options available. The best choice might be to update the property to somehow support change notification but since the control is from a third-party vendor that is not even an option.

Let's define a new implementation of `ICommand` as follows:

```
namespace UsingNonMVVMElements.Command
{
    using System;
    using System.Windows.Input;
    using System.Windows.Controls;

    class GoBackWithWebBrowserParameterCommand : ICommand
    {
        public bool CanExecute(object parameter)
```

```
        {
            bool ret = true;

            if (parameter is WebBrowser)
            {
                WebBrowser browser = (WebBrowser)parameter;
                ret = browser.CanGoBack;
            }

            return ret;
        }

        public event EventHandler CanExecuteChanged
        {
            add { CommandManager.RequerySuggested += value; }
            remove { CommandManager.RequerySuggested -= value; }
        }


        public void Execute(object parameter)
        {
            if (parameter is WebBrowser)
            {
                WebBrowser browser = (WebBrowser)parameter;
                browser.GoBack();
            }
        }
    }
}
```

In the preceding code, whenever a command re-evaluation is required, `CanGoBack` property of `WebBrowser` will be checked to see if this is possible. If `true`, then it would return `true`, which enables the button. We have also included the code to navigate backwards if user actually clicks on the button. The WebBrowser's `GoBack()` causes the browser to navigate back.

The preceding code gets the job done but I'd suspect a few eyebrows might be raised when looking at the code. We are using the `WebBrowser` control directly for the parameter of `Command`. One of the main goals of MVVM is to avoid having presentation controls in our code and so we have clearly failed with this approach. This should be alright as this is not in the view model but this is definitely not easily unit testable and definitely seems to be an MVVM code smell. Well, we will see later how we can improve this situation and avoid the need for controls in our code.

Let's now look at how we can use `Converter` in the updated view as shown in the following code:

```
<Window
  x:Class="UsingNonMVVMElements.
MainWindowBindingReadOnlyPropertiesWithWebBrowserCommandParameter"
  xmlns="http://schemas.microsoft.com/winfx/2006/xaml/presentation"
  xmlns:x="http://schemas.microsoft.com/winfx/2006/xaml"
  Height="481" Width="688"
  xmlns:vm="clr-namespace:UsingNonMVVMElements.ViewModel"
  xmlns:converter="clr-namespace:UsingNonMVVMElements.Converter"
  xmlns:core="clr-namespace:UsingNonMVVMElements.Core"
  xmlns:command="clr-namespace:UsingNonMVVMElements.Command"
  Title="MVVM Survival Guide">
    <Window.DataContext>
        <vm:MainWindowViewModel />
    </Window.DataContext>
    <Window.Resources>
        <command:GoBackWithWebBrowserParameterCommand
            x:Key="goBackCommand" />
        <converter:UriConverter x:Key="uriConverter" />
    </Window.Resources>
    <Grid x:Name="LayoutRoot">
        <TextBox Height="27" HorizontalAlignment="Left"
Margin="2,1,0,0"
                 Name="textBoxUrl" VerticalAlignment="Top" Width="611"
                 Text="{Binding UserSuggestedSourcePage}" />
        <Button Content="Go" Height="27" HorizontalAlignment="Left"
                Margin="615,1,0,0"  Name="btnGo"
VerticalAlignment="Top"
                Width="39" IsDefault="True"
                Command="{Binding NavigateUrlCommand}" />
        <WebBrowser x:Name="webBrowser" Margin="0,59,0,0" />
        <core:BindingReflector
            x:Name="sourceReflector">
            <core:BindingReflector.Target>
                <Binding ElementName="webBrowser"
                         Path="Source" Mode="OneWayToSource" />
            </core:BindingReflector.Target>
            <core:BindingReflector.Source>
                <Binding Path="SourcePage" Mode="OneWay"
                         Converter="{StaticResource uriConverter}"/>
            </core:BindingReflector.Source>
        </core:BindingReflector>
```

```
        <Button Content="Back" Height="26" HorizontalAlignment="Left"
                Command="{Binding
                    Source={StaticResource goBackCommand}}"
                CommandParameter="{Binding
                    ElementName=webBrowser}"
                Margin="2,30,0,0" Name="btnBack"
VerticalAlignment="Top"
                Width="67" />
    </Grid>
</Window>
```

Change `App.xaml` so that this view is set as startup page and then run the application. The browser is again shown with Google's main page. Navigate to any other page by typing the URL in the address bar. Now you will see that the **Back** button is enabled. This is what we wanted. If you click on the **Back** button, it will successfully browse back. Although we have directly used the `WebBrowser` type in `Converter`, we have avoided the code behind it by keeping it in a separate `ICommand`. Keeping it in separate `ICommand` instead of using `RelayCommand` in view model has also kept the view model clean.

Using .NET 4.0 dynamic

Using `WebBrowser` or any other GUI controls in code is not the ideal approach when implementing MVVM because it has poor testability and poor separation of concerns. We will now look at how we can improve this situation by making our design testable using the new `dynamic` feature from .NET 4.0. Let's update `Command` as follows:

```
namespace UsingNonMVVMElements.Command
{
    using System;
    using System.Windows.Input;

    internal class GoBackWithWebBrowserDynamicParameterCommand
        : ICommand
    {
        public bool CanExecute(object parameter)
        {
            bool ret = true;

            if (parameter != null)
            {
                dynamic browser = parameter;
                ret = browser.CanGoBack;
```

```
            }

            return ret;
        }

        public event EventHandler CanExecuteChanged
        {
            add { CommandManager.RequerySuggested += value; }
            remove { CommandManager.RequerySuggested -= value; }
        }


        public void Execute(object parameter)
        {
            if (parameter != null)
            {
                dynamic browser = parameter;
                browser.GoBack();
            }
        }
    }

}
```

As you can see that in the preceding `ICommand` code, we have used the `dynamic` keyword instead of directly using the `WebBrowser` reference. This would help us in testing this. Let's use this in the view as follows:

```
<Window
     x:Class="UsingNonMVVMElements
     .MainWindowBindingReadOnlyPropertiesWithDynamicParameter"
     xmlns="http://schemas.microsoft.com/winfx/2006/xaml/presentation"
     xmlns:x="http://schemas.microsoft.com/winfx/2006/xaml"
     Height="481" Width="688"
     xmlns:vm="clr-namespace:UsingNonMVVMElements.ViewModel"
     xmlns:converter="clr-namespace:UsingNonMVVMElements.Converter"
     xmlns:core="clr-namespace:UsingNonMVVMElements.Core"
     xmlns:command="clr-namespace:UsingNonMVVMElements.Command"
     Title="MVVM Light Application">
    <Window.DataContext>
        <vm:MainWindowViewModel />
    </Window.DataContext>
    <Window.Resources>
```

```
        <command:GoBackWithWebBrowserDynamicParameterCommand
            x:Key="goBackCommand" />
        <converter:UriConverter x:Key="uriConverter" />
    </Window.Resources>
    <Grid x:Name="LayoutRoot">
        <TextBox Height="27" HorizontalAlignment="Left"
Margin="2,1,0,0"
                 Name="textBoxUrl" VerticalAlignment="Top" Width="611"
                 Text="{Binding UserSuggestedSourcePage}" />
        <Button Content="Go" Height="27" HorizontalAlignment="Left"
                Margin="615,1,0,0" Name="btnGo"
VerticalAlignment="Top"
                Width="39" IsDefault="True"
                Command="{Binding NavigateUrlCommand}" />
        <WebBrowser x:Name="webBrowser" Margin="0,59,0,0" />
        <core:BindingReflector
            x:Name="sourceReflector">
            <core:BindingReflector.Target>
                <Binding ElementName="webBrowser"
                         Path="Source" Mode="OneWayToSource" />
            </core:BindingReflector.Target>
            <core:BindingReflector.Source>
                <Binding Path="SourcePage" Mode="OneWay"
                         Converter="{StaticResource uriConverter}"/>
            </core:BindingReflector.Source>
        </core:BindingReflector>
        <Button Content="Back" Height="26" HorizontalAlignment="Left"
                Command="{Binding Source={StaticResource
goBackCommand}}"
                CommandParameter="{Binding ElementName=webBrowser}"
                Margin="2,30,0,0" Name="btnBack"
VerticalAlignment="Top"
                Width="67" />
    </Grid>
</Window>
```

Now let's look at testability of this design. The first thing we need to do is create a stub that will work with our dynamic solution. Let's start by creating a new test project `UsingNonMVVMElements.Test`. Now update the access modifier of the `Command` class to be internal and introduce this attribute in `AssemblyInfo.cs` from the `System.Runtime.CompilerServices` namespace:

```
[assembly: InternalsVisibleTo("UsingNonMVVMElements.Test")]
```

Let's add a new interface `IWebBrowser` as follows:

```
namespace UsingNonMVVMElements
{
    public interface IWebBrowser
    {
        bool CanGoBack { get; set; }
        void GoBack();
    }
}
```

We will be using **Rhino Mocks 3.5** here to create stubs based on the `IWebBrowser` interface. Now add Rhino Mocks and the `PresentationCore` assemblies to test project and add the following test:

```
namespace UsingNonMVVMElements.Test
{
    using Microsoft.VisualStudio.TestTools.UnitTesting;
    using UsingNonMVVMElements.Command;
    using Rhino.Mocks;

    [TestClass]
    public class GoBackWithWebBrowserDynamicParameterCommandTest
    {

        [TestMethod]
        public void CanExecuteTestWhenNavigationPossible()
        {
            GoBackWithWebBrowserDynamicParameterCommand target =
                new GoBackWithWebBrowserDynamicParameterCommand();

            IWebBrowser browser = MockRepository.
GenerateStub<IWebBrowser>();
            browser.CanGoBack = true;

            Assert.IsTrue(target.CanExecute(browser));
        }
```

```
        [TestMethod]
        public void CanExecuteTestWhenNavigationNotPossible()
        {
            GoBackWithWebBrowserDynamicParameterCommand target =
                new GoBackWithWebBrowserDynamicParameterCommand();

            IWebBrowser browser = MockRepository.
GenerateStub<IWebBrowser>();
            browser.CanGoBack = false;

            Assert.IsFalse(target.CanExecute(browser));
        }

        [TestMethod]
        public void CanExecuteTestWhenNullParameter()
        {
            GoBackWithWebBrowserDynamicParameterCommand target =
                new GoBackWithWebBrowserDynamicParameterCommand();

            Assert.IsTrue(target.CanExecute(null));
        }
    }
}
```

Now let's run all tests and verify that they all pass. The dynamic feature of .NET 4.0 allows us to inject a stub from an entirely different class without the two having to share an interface! This is a powerful technique as you can declare an interface that implements only the contract that is needed and nothing more and then at runtime the dynamic will work with the real object as long as it finds the methods and properties that are needed.

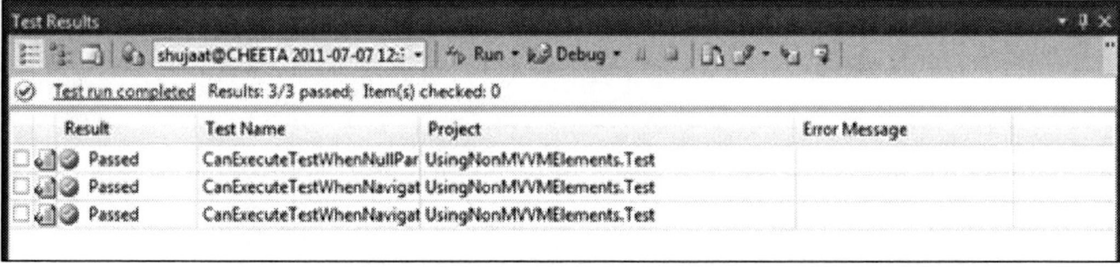

Using MVVM adapters

Using this approach, we will create an MVVM adapter around the non-MVVM control.

The adapter pattern is a Gang of Four [GOF] pattern that involves adding a layer of abstraction over a class to change its interface. There are two approaches that can be taken when implementing the adapter pattern—inheritance based or aggregation based. In the inheritance version, you simply create a subclass of the class that needs to be adapted and then expose a new interface while the aggregation version involves aggregating the class and then making pass through calls from the adapter to the adaptee as needed.

We have to make a decision about whether we should implement an aggregation adapter or an inheritance adapter. Here, we can implement an aggregation-based adapter. This obviously needs more work than their inheritance counterparts for pass-through calls to the aggregated object. However, it's common to find that third-party libraries' types are `sealed` for inheritance (like `WebBrowser` in our case). On the contrary, inheritance-based adapter just requires adding the extra functionality to the sub-type with no pass-through calls, generally used when there is no restriction of target type and more focus on the required functionality.

Let us assume that we need simple `WebBrowser` and we just need to bind the `Source` property to a property in `DataContext`. The contract for the adapter will be as follows:

```
namespace UsingNonMVVMElements
{
    public interface IWebBrowserAdapter
    {
        string Source { get; set; }
    }
}
```

Let's simply use `UserControl` as adapter of the `WebBrowser` control:

```
<UserControl x:Class="UsingNonMVVMElements.WebBrowserAdapter"
        xmlns="http://schemas.microsoft.com/winfx/2006/xaml/
presentation"
        xmlns:x="http://schemas.microsoft.com/winfx/2006/xaml"
        xmlns:mc="http://schemas.openxmlformats.org/markup-
compatibility/2006"
        xmlns:d="http://schemas.microsoft.com/expression/blend/2008"
        mc:Ignorable="d"
```

```
        d:DesignHeight="300" d:DesignWidth="300">
    <WebBrowser x:Name="webBrowser" />
</UserControl>
```

The code behind the user control is as follows:

```
namespace UsingNonMVVMElements
{
    using System;
    using System.Windows;
    using System.Windows.Controls;

    /// <summary>
    /// Interaction logic for WebBrowserAdapter.xaml
    /// </summary>
    public partial class WebBrowserAdapter
        : UserControl, IWebBrowserAdapter
    {
        public WebBrowserAdapter()
        {
            InitializeComponent();
        }

        #region Dependency Properties

        public static DependencyProperty SourceProperty =
            DependencyProperty.Register(
            "Source", typeof(string), typeof(WebBrowserAdapter),
            new PropertyMetadata(string.Empty));

        public string Source
        {
            get { return (string)GetValue(SourceProperty); }
            set { SetValue(SourceProperty, value); }
        }

        #endregion

        #region Overriden methods

        protected override void OnPropertyChanged(
            DependencyPropertyChangedEventArgs e)
        {
            base.OnPropertyChanged(e);
```

```
                if (e.Property == SourceProperty &&
                    e.NewValue != null &&
                    !string.Equals(webBrowser.Source, e.NewValue))
                {
                    webBrowser.Source =
                        new Uri(e.NewValue.ToString());
                }
            }

            #endregion

        }
    }
```

The user control implements the `IWebBrowserAdapter` interface. We are adding the `Source` dependency property to the user control. We will be using the same property for `Binding`. Also, take notice of the overridden method `OnPropertyChanged`. When `SourceProperty` is updated, we are propagating the same change to the adaptee (`WebBrowser`). Now let's consume this adapter in a window similar to that in the first example discussed in this chapter:

```
<Window x:Class="UsingNonMVVMElements.MainWindowWebBrowserAdapter"
        xmlns="http://schemas.microsoft.com/winfx/2006/xaml/
presentation"
        xmlns:x="http://schemas.microsoft.com/winfx/2006/xaml"
        Height="481" Width="688"
        xmlns:vm="clr-namespace:UsingNonMVVMElements.ViewModel"
        xmlns:local="clr-namespace:UsingNonMVVMElements"
        Title="MVVM Survival Guide">
    <Window.DataContext>
        <vm:MainWindowViewModel />
    </Window.DataContext>
    <Grid x:Name="LayoutRoot">
        <TextBox Height="27" HorizontalAlignment="Left"
Margin="2,1,0,0"
                 Name="textBoxUrl" VerticalAlignment="Top" Width="611"
                 Text="{Binding UserSuggestedSourcePage}" />
        <Button Content="Go" Height="27" HorizontalAlignment="Left"
                Margin="615,1,0,0" Name="btnGo"
VerticalAlignment="Top"
                Width="39" IsDefault="True"
                Command="{Binding NavigateUrlCommand}" />
        <local:WebBrowserAdapter Source="{Binding SourcePage}"
                    Margin="0,34,0,0" />
    </Grid>
</Window>
```

Let's update `App.xaml` so that `Window` in the preceding code is the startup window. Run the application. It should load up as shown in the screenshot in the *Using attached behaviors* section.

Now enter some other URL, say `http://www.microsoft.com`, in the address bar and click on the **Go** button. The user control passes this update through overridden `OnPropertyChanged` to the `WebBrowser` control. `WebBrowser` then successfully updates the page to Microsoft's main page.

Aggregation-based adapters hide the actual adaptee and provide an interface to execute only certain operations on them. However there are scenarios, like this one, when we just need to provide extra implementation and, otherwise, the adapter should behave exactly as the adaptee would have. This adapter is more like a decorator. We can achieve that using `DynamicObject` from .NET 4.0. We need to inherit the adapter from `DynamicObject` and override the `TryGetMember`, `TrySetMember`, and `TryInvoke` methods. In the implementation of these methods, we can simply pass the request to the adaptee. However, `UserControl` is not `DynamicObject`, and we need the features of both `UserControl` and `DynamicObject`. Here the limitation is unavailability of multiple inheritance for the adapter. We should keep in mind that we have not run out of options yet as we can have the adapter implement `IDynamicMetaObjectProvider` and provide a similar implementation to that of a `DynamicObject`. In this way, we can achieve the same effect but since it would be diving unnecessarily into the .NET Framework 4.0 features, we will leave it up to the reader to look into this further.

Summary

In this chapter, we discussed how we can use non-MVVM based controls in a MVVM based application. We discussed various techniques including attached properties, binding reflector, .NET 4.0 Dynamic, and MVVM adapters.

11
MVVM and Application Performance

By Muhammad Shujaat Siddiqi

In this chapter, we will look at some advanced techniques that can be used to help with application performance. Application performance is a vast subject, and we cannot discuss everything in a single chapter. The main focus of this chapter will be to utilize the framework features for improving application performance, with a focus on MVVM.

Asynchronous binding

`Binding.IsAsync` allows loading the binding source asynchronously, without blocking the application UI. When using `Binding.IsAsync`, WPF will use a `ThreadPool` thread to resolve the binding asynchronously. When the data is available from the binding source, it is copied to the `Target` property.

1. Let us create a small WPF application with just a `TextBlock` that displays the message of the day.

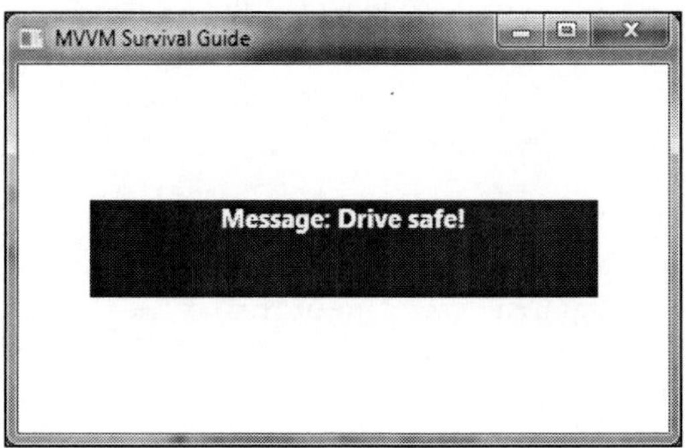

The previous view can be defined in XAML, as follows:

```
<Window x:Class="MVVMAppPerformanceimprovement.MainWindow"
      xmlns="http://schemas.microsoft.com/winfx/2006/xaml/
presentation"
        xmlns:x="http://schemas.microsoft.com/winfx/2006/xaml"
        xmlns:local="clr-namespace:MVVMAppPerformanceimprovement"
        Title="MVVM Survival Guide" Height="250" Width="400">
    <Window.DataContext>
        <local:MainWindowViewModel />
    </Window.DataContext>
    <Grid>
        <TextBlock  Width="300" Height="56" Foreground="White"
                    HorizontalAlignment="Center" FontSize="15"
                    VerticalAlignment="Center"  FontWeight="Bold"
                    TextAlignment="Center" Background="Navy" >
            <TextBlock.Text>
                <Binding Path="Message"
                         StringFormat="Message: {0}" />
            </TextBlock.Text>
        </TextBlock>
    </Grid>
</Window>
```

2. Here, we are using `MainWindowViewModel` as the `DataContext` property of the view. We are binding the `Message` property from the View Model to the `Text` property of the `TextBlock` property.
3. The definition of the View Model might be as follows:

```
namespace MVVMAppPerformanceimprovement
{
    using System.ComponentModel;

    class MainWindowViewModel : INotifyPropertyChanged
    {
        MessageOfTheDay _messageOfTheDay =
                            new MessageOfTheDay();

        public string Message
        {
            get
            {
                return _messageOfTheDay.Message;
            }
            set
```

```
            {
                _messageOfTheDay.Message = value;
                OnPropertyChanged("Message");
            }
        }

        #region INotifyPropertyChanged

        public event PropertyChangedEventHandler PropertyChanged;

        private void OnPropertyChanged(string propertyName)
        {
            if (PropertyChanged != null)
            {
                PropertyChanged(this,
                    new PropertyChangedEventArgs(propertyName));
            }
        }

        #endregion

    }
}
```

As you can see, `Message` is defined as a proxy property over a property with the same name from the `MessageOfTheDay` class. Here, the `MessageOfTheDay` class is used as the model. Additionally, the View Model implements the `INotifyPropertyChanged` interface. Now let's look at the definition of the `MessageOfTheDay` class. The `Message` property has a delay in the getter, since the view accesses the property in the UI thread. This would cause the whole application to become idle during this time. The delay is achieved by simply calling `Thread.Sleep` with a duration of 10 seconds.

```
namespace MVVMAppPerformanceimprovement
{
    using System.Threading;

    class MessageOfTheDay
    {
        string _message;
        public string Message
        {
            get
            {
                //imaginary delay
```

```
                Thread.Sleep(10000);
                return _message ;
            }
            set
            { _message = value; }
        }

        public MessageOfTheDay()
        {
            _message = "Drive safe!";
        }
    }
}
```

4. Now, let's run the application. After we hit *F5*, at the least there is a 10-second delay before the application is successfully shown on the screen. The delay is caused because one of the properties in some model is slow at giving responses. Now, imagine an enterprise application with a number of such properties. It would be a nightmare just to launch the application, as the application responsiveness would be extremely choppy and sluggish.

   One obvious solution is to make the WPF property system get the binding source value in a separate thread. Once the binding system is able to obtain a value from the binding source, the value is dispatched back to the UI thread, automatically. As we mentioned earlier, the binding system supports this kind of asynchronous behaviour through the `Binding.IsAsync` property.

5. Let's take a look at this by updating our view, as follows:

```
<Window x:Class="MVVMAppPerformanceimprovement.MainWindow"
        xmlns="http://schemas.microsoft.com/winfx/2006/xaml/
presentation"
        xmlns:x="http://schemas.microsoft.com/winfx/2006/xaml"
        xmlns:local="clr-namespace:MVVMAppPerformanceimprovement"
        Title="MVVM Survival Guide" Height="250" Width="400">
    <Window.DataContext>
        <local:MainWindowViewModel />
    </Window.DataContext>
    <Grid>
        <TextBlock  Width="300" Height="56" Foreground="White"
                    HorizontalAlignment="Center" FontSize="15"
                    VerticalAlignment="Center"  FontWeight="Bold"
                    TextAlignment="Center" Background="Navy" >
            <TextBlock.Text>
                <Binding Path="Message"
                         StringFormat="Message: {0}"
```

```
                                IsAsync="true"
                                FallbackValue="Loading..." />
                </TextBlock.Text>
            </TextBlock>
        </Grid>
</Window>
```

6. Now, the property system will access the source property asynchronously, without blocking the current UI thread. The view will show the `FallbackValue` property defined for binding until the actual property is available that is **Loading...**, as shown in the following screenshot:

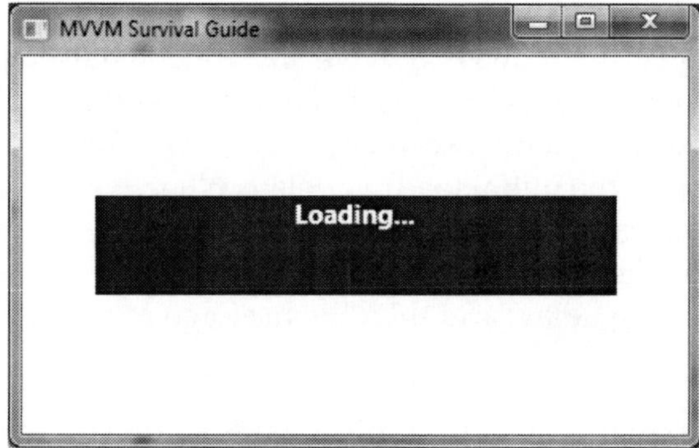

After the property value becomes available, the view is updated with the actual value, **Drive Safe**, as shown previously.

Asynchronous View Model construction

We can improve the productivity of our designers using MVVM, by making design-time data available either directly in our View Models or by using an **IoC** (**Inversion of Control**) to swap in stubbed View Models in the designer. Doing this allows designers to have working sample data at design-time to help them create sophisticated views for our users. This is a productive working style, as designers don't have to access anything (such as the database or web services) and it provides a separation between designers and developers that allows them to work in parallel without blocking each other. However, when the real application is run outside of the designer, all of the dependencies will be live, and loading this data can slow things down when it comes to loading our views. We need to improve the application responsiveness as much as we can, so that the application doesn't become idle when data is being read.

We can illustrate the previous scenario by introducing a delay in a View Model's construction. Since we are creating the View Model inline, the view becomes idle until the View Model is constructed. Let's introduce a delay in the constructor of `MessageofTheDay`. Since this is happening in the constructor of our View Model, the view will be unresponsive while it waits for the constructor call to complete.

```
public MessageOfTheDay()
{
    Thread.Sleep(10000);
    _message = "Drive safe!";
}
```

You might wonder whether `Binding.IsAsync` has any effect in preventing this delay, and the answer is *NO*, it does not have any effect whatsoever.The `Binding.IsAsync` property provides asynchronous behavior in bindings. If there is any delay before the binding code is actually executed, as is the case here, having asynchronous bindings won't help with the initial loading delay. When we run our application, the application first has a delay of at least 10 seconds to load the View to account for our constructor. After that, there will be a **Loading...** message on the screen for at least 10 seconds for the binding delay, and then the message of the day will be shown on the screen.

Now, how can we make sure that our application is loaded on the screen in a responsive way, preventing the user from dealing with a frustrating experience when launching our application? We can do this by constructing our View Model asynchronously. Using the asynchronous approach, the View can be loaded with default values for its Binding Targets, and then once the View Model is loaded, the Binding Targets will be updated via the binding system's change notification mechanism. We can accomplish this by using the `ObjectDataProvider` property for our View Model construction, which has built-in support for loading its object asynchronously.

Let's update the `DataContext` section of the view, as follows:

```
<Window.DataContext>
    <ObjectDataProvider
        ObjectType="{x:Type local:MainWindowViewModel}"
        IsAsynchronous="True"  />
</Window.DataContext>
```

Now, when we run the application, the window is immediately launched on the screen. Since the object assigned to the `DataContext` property is not available yet, the `TextBlock` shows **Loading...**, during this time. After the View Model becomes available, there is another delay of 10 seconds to access the `Message` property. So, the view would continuously show the **Loading...** message, and then finally, the message of the day.

Priority binding

Binding supports the `FallbackValue` property, if the desired source property is not available. This is good, but we might want to show the user some other useful information until the actual binding source is available. We might even want a list of bindings, applied in the order of their configured priority. We'd want the property system to attempt to pick up the available binding source with the highest priority for us. If a lower priority binding source is bound and a higher priority binding source becomes available, we'd want the property system to use the newly available binding source. And finally, we would want to be able to use a static fall-back value, if no binding source is available.

Basically, WPF Priority Binding is here to support just this scenario. We can define a list of bindings in the order of their priorities. The property system picks up the available property with the highest priority, and if a binding source is available with a higher priority, it updates itself. It also supports `FallbackValue`.

Let's update `MainWindowViewModel` so that it has two properties—`Message1` and `Message2`. The getter of `Message1` has a delay of seven seconds, while that of `Message2` has three seconds.

```
namespace MVVMAppPerformanceimprovement
{
    using System.ComponentModel;
    using System.Threading;

    class MainWindowViewModel : INotifyPropertyChanged
    {
        string _message1 = "Message1";
        public string Message1
        {
            get
            {
                Thread.Sleep(7000);
                return _message1;
            }
            set
            {
                _message1 = value;
                OnPropertyChanged("Message1");
            }
        }

        string _message2 = "Message2";
        public string Message2
```

```
            {
                get
                {
                    Thread.Sleep(3000);
                    return _message2;
                }
                set
                {
                    _message2 = value;
                    OnPropertyChanged("Message2");
                }
            }

            #region INotifyPropertyChanged

            public event PropertyChangedEventHandler PropertyChanged;

            private void OnPropertyChanged(string propertyName)
            {
                if (PropertyChanged != null)
                {
                    PropertyChanged(this,
                        new PropertyChangedEventArgs(propertyName));
                }
            }

            #endregion

        }
    }
```

It is important that we use `IsAsync` for each binding to make sure that the access to the property takes place on a separate thread. Otherwise, it will just block the UI thread, causing the application to become idle. Now, let's discuss how we can use these two properties with `PriorityBinding`. We update the view as follows:

```
<Window x:Class="MVVMAppPerformanceimprovement.MainWindow"
        xmlns="http://schemas.microsoft.com/winfx/2006/xaml/
presentation"
        xmlns:x="http://schemas.microsoft.com/winfx/2006/xaml"
        xmlns:local="clr-namespace:MVVMAppPerformanceimprovement"
        Title="MVVM Survival Guide" Height="250" Width="400">
    <Window.DataContext>
        <ObjectDataProvider
            ObjectType="{x:Type local:MainWindowViewModel}"
```

```
                IsAsynchronous="True"  />
        </Window.DataContext>
        <Grid>
            <TextBlock  Width="300" Height="56" Foreground="White"
                        HorizontalAlignment="Center" FontSize="15"
                        VerticalAlignment="Center"  FontWeight="Bold"
                        TextAlignment="Center" Background="Navy" >
                <TextBlock.Text>
                    <PriorityBinding FallbackValue="Loading...">
                        <Binding Path="Message1" IsAsync="True" />
                        <Binding Path="Message2" IsAsync="True" />
    </PriorityBinding>
                </TextBlock.Text>
            </TextBlock>
        </Grid>
    </Window>
```

Let's run it now. The application is now initially loaded with the **Loading...** message in the `TextBlock`. This is because none of the binding sources are available initially, and the binding is using the configured `FallbackValue` property.

After three seconds, `Message2` becomes available as the binding source from the priority binding list. Since it is the highest priority binding available at the current time, it is used by the target property.

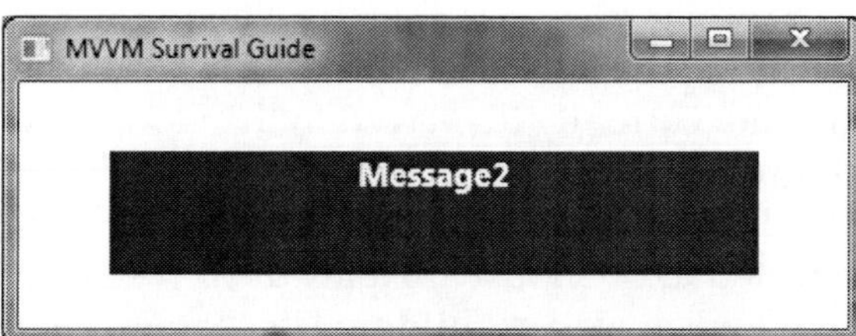

Finally, after a few seconds, `Message1` becomes available and the view is updated as follows:

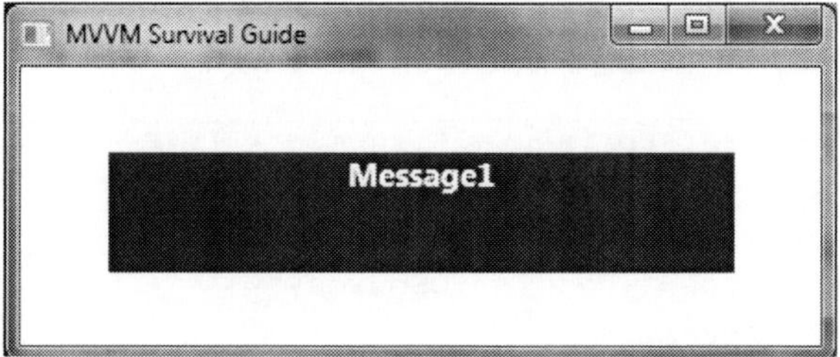

Virtualization and paging

In enterprise applications, we have to deal with data in different formats and sizes. We need to find ways to display and collect this data in the most user-friendly and performance-efficient way. Nobody likes an application that has all the beautiful controls and features but that takes a lot of time to run basic operations. So, performance and responsiveness are an implicit requirement for enterprise applications. I'd argue that it makes more sense to make it an explicit requirement, so that it can be properly planned for and managed.

Virtualization and paging are common techniques that are used when we need to deal with more data than it makes sense to load into memory at one time. With data virtualization and data paging techniques, we load just the data from the repository that is currently displayed on the screen, and we dynamically load more data as needed. Based on the idea of spatial locality of reference, we could also load some extra data to create a fast buffer to help improve responsiveness and performance. The special data for a page can be specified in LINQ, using `Take` and `Skip` operators, making it the responsibility of a LINQ provider to translate it into the actual query code.

This data selected using data virtualization techniques can be specified as the data source of an `ItemsControl` and is displayed to the user with a scrollbar to scroll through the list. With WPF/Silverlight, we can further improve this by using UI virtualization. Basically, `ItemsControl` are based on `ItemsPanel`. Most of the `ItemsControl` are based on the `VirtualizingStackPanel`, which supports UI virtualization. `VirtualizingStackPanel` creates the needed controls for the data and for the controls that are currently displayed in the view. As we scroll through data, it creates new controls to display the currently visible data. We can even enable recycling, so that instead of creating new controls, `VirtualizingStackPanel` recycles the controls created to previously display data. We always want to keep this functionality in mind when we are building UIs that use controls derived from `ItemSource`.

In the following example, we are simply overriding the `ItemsPanel` property of a `ComboBox` to use the `VirtualizingStackPanel`. The `ItemsSource` of the `ComboBox` has been specified as the `DSource` property from the current `DataContext`. This property would ideally be an `ObservableCollection`.

```
<ComboBox Height="22" HorizontalAlignment="Left"
          Margin="40,61,0,0" Name="comboBox1"
          VerticalAlignment="Top" Width="378"
          ItemsSource="{Binding DSource}" >
    <ComboBox.ItemsPanel>
        <ItemsPanelTemplate>
```

```
            <VirtualizingStackPanel />
        </ItemsPanelTemplate>
    </ComboBox.ItemsPanel>
</ComboBox>
```

When profiling the memory footprint of an application using this technique, you will generally see a significant decrease in the memory footprint after applying this technique.

Using BackgroundWorker

As we have seen, desktop applications have to be multi-threaded to be responsive. When multi-threading our applications, we spawn a new thread (or use the `ThreadPool`) and then when the background thread finishes executing, the background thread might need to notify the other threads (especially the UI thread). There are signalling constructs available in .NET, such as `EventWaitHandle` for thread synchronization, that we can use. We also frequently need to show the progress of execution of certain tasks to the user, using something like a progress bar or status bar. The .NET framework makes all of this possible, but it requires a lot of understanding of multithreading and code that is difficult to develop and maintain.

`BackgroundWorker` is an easier alternative to accomplishing the goals listed previously. It executes the operations on a background thread using the `ThreadPool`. `BackgroundWorker` also makes progress reporting to the UI thread easier, by providing a `ProgressChanged` event. Additionally, `BackgroundWorker` provides a `WorkCompleted` event that is raised when the background operation is completed. These events are dispatched to the thread which initiated the work on the `BackgroundWorker` using the `SynchronizationContext`. Both WinForms and WPF store the UI thread in the default `SynchronizationContext`, and this is why we can use `BackgroundWorker` in both technologies.

The other benefit of `BackgroundWorker` is that it simplifies error handling. When an unhandled exception occurs on a background thread, the .NET runtime will close the application, and it takes a decent amount of effort to marshal exceptions back to the UI thread for more graceful processing. When an unhandled exception occurs on a background thread, the `BackgroundWorker` simplifies things for us a great deal. It provides error details in the `WorkCompleted` event. The application will not crash, and the client code can subscribe to the `WorkCompleted` event to get the exception details. Using `BackgroundWorker` just requires handling a few events.

To see an example of this technique, see www.RyanVice.net.

Targeting system configuration

Although we want to develop the best application that will run fast on all machines in all circumstances, we know that, practically speaking, this isn't possible. It is best to develop a minimum system requirement standard early in our development cycle, to allow us to manage application performance appropriately during development.

One other option is to enable/disable features based on machine capabilities. This way, if a user has less than minimum configuration, we can disable features such as those that require higher CPU/memory consumption, as needed. We can notify the user about the disabled features list at application startup, so that they are aware that they are not getting the full-blown application performance.

Alternatively, we can define different modes of our system. We can determine the machine configuration and use the appropriate mode suitable for the configuration of that machine. For less powerful machines, there could be modes with lesser graphics-processing requirements.

We can easily determine the details about the machine's configuration using **Windows Management Instrumentation (WMI)**. It allows us to write WQL-based queries. The queries are a lot like SQL queries.

```
Select * from win32_ComputerSystem
```

Event Throttling

No enterprise application works in isolation, as they all have dependencies of some kind. They have to work with other applications in the enterprise ecosystem to add value to organizational processes. These applications can be built using completely different technology stacks and they might have been developed in different programming languages and they might support data in different formats. If we need to communicate with these systems, we might need to define some sort of enterprise messaging framework. A common approach for this is messaging through a database or messaging system (**MSMQ**, **NServiceBus**, and so on). In a client-server application developed using Microsoft's APIs, we might use sockets for messaging, or other techniques such as named pipes. The most modern of all in our times is message queuing. It is based on the publisher/subscriber model. There are different message queuing systems available in the market. Microsoft also has its own product, called **MSMQ**. The idea is that the messaging system runs as a separate process maintaining several queues. Any two applications that want to communicate can use one of its queues. The publisher keeps pushing data to the queue. The queuing system keeps data until it is de-queued or the message expires. The message can be peaked or de-queued by another application that it uses for carrying out its operations.

As these messages are consumed by the subscribers, the user is also notified about them or the subscriber can do certain computations and update its state. Now the user interface needs to be updated based on the current session state. Let's assume we receive a number of these messages per second. First of all, these messages should be handled in some threads other than the UI thread, so that the interface is not idle when we are processing these messages. But after computation, we need to update the UI, which has to be done on the UI thread. Since we are receiving many of these messages per second, the UI will continuously be updated, tying up the UI thread and affecting the responsiveness of the application.

One way to avoid this situation is to use event throttling. When using the event throttling technique, we throttle these messages, so that only a few events are read over a certain interval of time in the UI, no matter how many source events are published. **Reactive Extensions** (**Rx**) is a research project at Microsoft that has in-built support for event throttling. You can find it on Microsoft's download centre and download it.

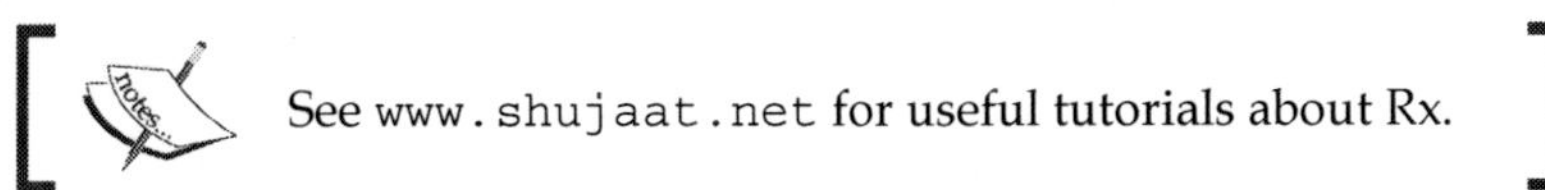

See `www.shujaat.net` for useful tutorials about Rx.

Lazy Initialization

During development, we will frequently use types that are resource-intensive for construction in terms of memory or computation time. So we might want to delay the construction of these types until we actually need them. This can be achieved by a new feature introduced in .NET framework 4.0, called **Lazy Initialization**. We can use this feature to improve the performance of our applications by delaying the instance construction of types.

Let's look at a sample window which is part of a contrived medical application. Let's create a **WPF MVVM Light** project, called `MVVMAppLazyInitialization`, in .NET Framework 4. In this sample, patients are selected and loaded, as shown in the following screenshot, so that their information can be viewed. As shown, some of their information can be viewed and edited. If we start loading everything in a single pass, it would take a lot of time for the window to show up, as data is fetched from persistence stores.

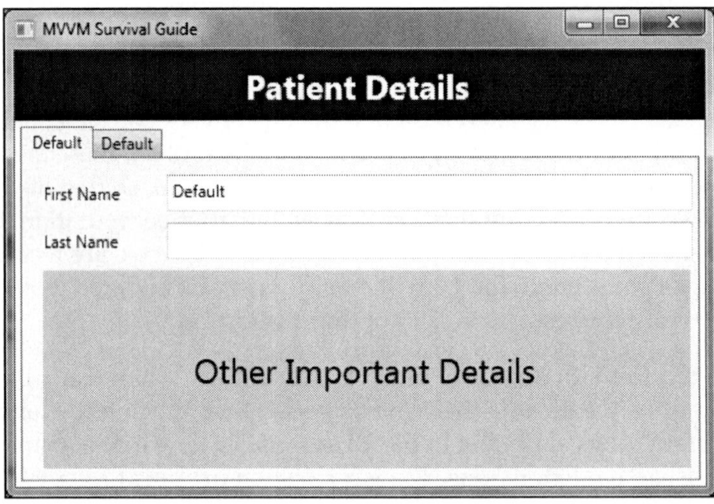

A patient's data might come from different sources. We can load this data into the `Patient` class, as shown in the following code . Here, we will simulate the delay using `Thread.Sleep()`.

```
namespace MVVMAppLazyInitialization.Model
{
    using System.Threading;

    class Patient
    {
        public string PatientFirstName { get; set; }
        public string PatientLastName { get; set; }

        public Patient()
        {
            //Loading other useful information
            Thread.Sleep(3000);
        }
    }
}
```

If we select 10 customers, this would cause a delay of 30 seconds at least. We can improve the performance and responsiveness of the application by using lazy initialization. We can delay the instantiation of our patient instances until the user tries to modify a field.

```
namespace MVVMAppLazyInitialization.ViewModel
{
    using GalaSoft.MvvmLight;
    using System;
    using MVVMAppLazyInitialization.Model;

    public class PatientViewModel : ViewModelBase
    {
        #region Fields

        Lazy<Patient> _model = new Lazy<Patient>();

        #endregion

        #region Constructor

        public PatientViewModel()
        {
            _patientFirstName = "Default";
        }

        #endregion

        #region Properties

        string _patientFirstName;
        public string PatientFirstName
        {
            get { return _patientFirstName; }
            set
            {
                if (_patientFirstName != value)
                {
                    _patientFirstName = value;
                    _model.Value.PatientFirstName = value;
                    RaisePropertyChanged("PatientFirstName");
                }
            }
        }
```

```
        string _patientLastName;
        public string PatientLastName
        {

            get { return _patientLastName; }
            set
            {
                if (_patientLastName != value)
                {
                    _patientLastName = value;
                    _model.Value.PatientLastName = value;
                    RaisePropertyChanged("PatientLastName");
                }
            }
        }

        #endregion
    }
}
```

In the preceding code, `_model.Value` will instantiate a patient instance, if one hasn't been created. Now, we need another View Model to hold the collection of instances of `PatientViewModel` for all patients selected for editing. The same View Model can be used as the DataContext for the Window. Let's name this `MainWindowViewModel`.

```
namespace MVVMAppLazyInitialization.ViewModel
{
    using GalaSoft.MvvmLight;
    using System.Collections.ObjectModel;
    using System.ComponentModel;

    public class MainViewModel  : ViewModelBase
    {
        ObservableCollection<PatientViewModel> _patientViewModels;

        public ObservableCollection<PatientViewModel>
PatientViewModels
        {
            get
            {
                if (_patientViewModels == null)
                {
                    _patientViewModels =
                        new ObservableCollection<PatientViewModel>();
```

```
                    _patientViewModels.Add(new PatientViewModel());
                    _patientViewModels.Add(new PatientViewModel());
                }
                return _patientViewModels;
            }
        }

    }
}
```

We would need to update the XAML definition of `MainWindow`, as shown in the following code:

```
<Window x:Class="MVVMAppLazyInitialization.MainWindow"
    xmlns="http://schemas.microsoft.com/winfx/2006/xaml/presentation"
    xmlns:x="http://schemas.microsoft.com/winfx/2006/xaml"
    xmlns:local="clr-namespace:MVVMAppLazyInitialization"
    Title="MVVM Survival Guide" Height="350" Width="525">

    <Window.DataContext>
        <local:MainWindowViewModel />
    </Window.DataContext>
    <Grid>
        <Grid.RowDefinitions>
            <RowDefinition Height="50" />
            <RowDefinition Height="*" />
        </Grid.RowDefinitions>
        <Border Background="Navy" Grid.Row="0">
            <TextBlock Foreground="White" FontWeight="Bold"
                       FontSize="24"
                       HorizontalAlignment="Center"
                       VerticalAlignment="Center"
                       Text="Patient Details" />
        </Border>
        <TabControl Margin="4,4,4,4" Grid.Row="1"
                    ItemsSource="{Binding PatientViewModels}" >
            <TabControl.ItemTemplate>
                <DataTemplate>
                    <TextBlock Text="{Binding PatientFirstName}" />
                </DataTemplate>
            </TabControl.ItemTemplate>
            <TabControl.ContentTemplate>
                <DataTemplate>
                    <Grid Margin="8,8,0,0">
                        <Grid.RowDefinitions>
```

```
                            <RowDefinition Height="auto" />
                            <RowDefinition Height="8" />
                            <RowDefinition Height="auto" />
                            <RowDefinition Height="*" />
                        </Grid.RowDefinitions>
                        <Grid.ColumnDefinitions>
                            <ColumnDefinition Width="0.25*" />
                            <ColumnDefinition Width="*" />
                        </Grid.ColumnDefinitions>
                        <Label Content="First Name" Grid.Row="0"
                               Grid.Column="0"/>
                        <TextBox Text="{Binding
Path=PatientFirstName}"
                                 Grid.Row="0" Grid.Column="1" />
                        <Label Content="Last Name"
                               Grid.Row="2" Grid.Column="0"/>
                        <TextBox Text ="{Binding PatientLastName}"
                                 Grid.Row="2" Grid.Column="1"/>
                        <Border Grid.Row="3" Grid.Column="0"
                                Margin="4,8,2,4"
Background="lightGray"
                                Grid.ColumnSpan="2" >
                            <TextBlock Text="Other Important Details"
                                       VerticalAlignment="Center"
                                       HorizontalAlignment="Center"
                                       FontSize="24"/>
                        </Border>
                    </Grid>
                </DataTemplate>
            </TabControl.ContentTemplate>
        </TabControl>
    </Grid>
</Window>
```

Now, our view will only create patients on an on-demand basis.

Summary

In this chapter, we looked at several techniques that you can use to improve application performance and responsiveness. We saw how asynchronous bindings will allow us to create asynchronous behaviour directly in XAML. We saw how to construct our View Models asynchronously, using the `ObjectDataProvider`. We looked at how we can use priority binding to allow for best-case binding, where you display the best available binding source dynamically. We looked at built-in support for virtualization and paging when using an `ItemSource` control and `VirtualizingStackPanel`. We saw how we could take advantage of the `BackgroundWorker` to greatly simplify asynchronous programming. And we finished off by talking about the idea of system requirements followed by looking at the new **Lazy** keyword in .NET 4.0.

We went through great efforts when writing this book. We tried very hard to make it a comprehensive guide that would allow developers to build enterprise solutions that take advantage of MVVM's benefits without experiencing all the difficulties that are so common when taking on MVVM. We are hopeful to see the support for MVVM improve in the future releases of WPF and Silverlight, so that there will be fewer frameworks and special techniques needed, and most importantly, shorter books!

Good luck on your MVVM adventures!

MVVM Frameworks

By Muhammad Shujaat Siddiqi

The XAML community has been blessed with extraordinary developers who are always willing to volunteer their time. There are a myriad of MVVM frameworks available and it is a tough decision which one to choose from. This is because it is such a core architectural decision that it is nearly impossible to change the underlying framework in later stages of development without extreme risks. Here, MVVM Light Toolkit is our personal favorite.

Name	Author	License
MVVM Light Toolkit	Laurent Bugnion	MIT
Prism	Microsoft Patterns and Practices Team	Microsoft Patterns and Practices License (Custom)
Calcium	Daniel Vaughan	BSD
Caliburn	Rob Eisenberg	MIT
Cinch	Sacha Barber	MS-PL
Catel	Geert Van Horrik	MS-PL

As a guideline, we should be looking at how any particular framework will help us in incorporating MVVM in our design without sacrificing other enterprise architecture design requirements. We should also look at how loosely coupled it is with its own features. If a framework supports all these features but it forces you to use a particular Dependency Injection mechanism then you would definitely have to think about it. This would also help us in picking and choosing different features from different frameworks. It would be easier if they allow such choices. The base feature set to look for is as follows:

- INotifyPropertyChanged Implmementation (for base view model)
- ICommand Implementation

- Messenger (Mediator)
- Dialog support
- Validation (for base view model)
- Supported platforms (WPF, SL, WP, WinRT)
- Project templates and quick starts
- Documentation and active online community

In addition to the preceding features , these frameworks have also been incorporating other features (for example, logging) in order to be a complete enterprise application framework. You can also use those features when comparing these frameworks but since they are not particularly related to MVVM, we haven't discussed them here.

B

Binding at a Glance

By Muhammad Shujaat Siddiqi

Basics

- Binding is a markup extension.
- Binding target must be a dependency property.
- Binding source must be public property.
- Binding Target: Where Binding is defined `[Petzold]`.
- Use `MultiBinding` for multiple Binding sources for the same target. Changes in any of them cause target to be updated
- If an entire object is used as a binding source then binding can use the implicit/explicit `DataTemplate` defined for the type, otherwise, it uses the `ToString()` method for the type.
- In a partial trust environment, we cannot bind to dynamic object property or CLR property of a non-public class.

Validation

ValidationRules

- Inherit `ValidationRule` and override `Validate()`.
- Instantiate and add to the `Binding.ValidationRules` collection.
- Use the `ValidationStep` property to control when it should be applied. The possible values are `ConvertedProposedValue`, `CommittedValue`, `RawProposedValue`, and `UpdatedValue`.

IDataErrorInfo

- Used for sync validation where only single validation result suffices. Implemented by View Model. Apply `ValidatesOnDataErrors` or `DataErrorValidationRule` for binding.

INotifyDataErrorInfo [.net 4.5]

- Used for sync/async validation when more than one validation result is available. Implemented by View Model. Apply `ValidatesOnNotifyDataErrors` or `NotifyDataErrorValidationRule` for binding.

Enterprise Library 5.0 Validation Application Block

- Supports defining validation rules by using attributes, configuration, and self-validation which can also be consolidated

Windows WF

- Used for more complex sync/async business rules validations

Validation.ErrorTemplate

- Used to specify the template when control value fails validation

Static properties/fields

- A markup extension, to bind to the static field/properties of a class.

  `{x:Static Member=prefix:typeName.staticMemberName}`

Executing code in DataContext

- Introduce an ICommand-based property in the DataContext and bind it to the `Command` property of button-based controls. Third-party frameworks also support binding them to element's events.
- Support parameters which support data binding.
- Commands can be bound to key and mouse gestures.

Binding to DataContext[DC]

- A DependencyProperty defined in FrameworkElement which supports containment inheritance in the visual hierarchy
- For `ItemsControl` bound to a collection source, individual element's DC is automatically set as single item of collection

```
{Binding}: binds directly to DC.
{Binding Path="P1"}: binds to property P1 in the DC.
{Binding Path="P2.P1"}: binds to P1 property of P2 in DC
```

Resources

- Identified by unique key, implicit or explicit `[x:Key directive]`.
- Can be created/overwritten in the `Resources` section for a FrameworkElement/FrameworkContentElement or Application. Can also be defined in Resource Dictionaries and merged with Application resources.
- Recommended creation at the minimum level possible.
- `Binding.Source` uses them with `StaticResource` or `DynamicResource`.

Types with default constructor

- Can be instantiated directly in the `Resources` section. Their public properties can be set in XAML which can also be a source for binding

XmlDataProvider

- Enables declarative access to XML node tree from the inline XML data, XML data file, or `XmlDocument`. It is the slower among the two data providers

ObjectDataProvider

- Allows instantiation using specific constructor. Can also use any method of the type for data with specific parameters. The parameters can also be used as a binding source.
- `Binding.BindsDirectlyToSource`: When true, specifies that the binding path is relative to the `Data` property.

Binding to resource

- Use Binding's `Source` property to bind resources.

Static resource

`{Binding Source="{StaticResource resourceKey}"}`

- A markup extension, uses load-time resource for the key
- Not suggested for forward reference of resources
- Doesn't update when target resource changes for the key
- Suggested when target resource can't change at runtime

Dynamic resource

`{Binding Source="{DynamicResource resourceKey}"}`

- A markup extension, uses runtime resource for the key
- Suggested for forward reference of resources
- Updates when target resource changes for the key
- Suggested when target resource can change at runtime

Updating source

Binding.UpdateSourceTrigger

- `PropertyChanged`: Updates immediately
- `LostFocus`: Updates when focus target element loses focus
- `Explicit`: Update when `UpdateSource()` is called
- `Default`: Uses the default value for binding target

Binding.Delay: [.net 4.5] [Binding.Mode:TwoWay / OneWayToSource]

- Milliseconds to wait before source is updated

Mode [Binding.Mode] [T:Target, S:Source]

- `TwoWay`: Updates other when either changes
- `OneWay`: Updates `[T]` when source changes
- `OneTime`: Updates `[T]` when source changes/view is loaded.
- `OneWayToSource`: Updates `[S]` when `[T]` changes
- `Default`: Uses default from the `[T]` dependency property

Binding to other elements in the view

ElementName

`{Binding ElementName = "elementName" }`

- `ElementName` is the source of binding another element in the view (defined with the `x:Name` directive or the `Name` property)

RelativeSource

`{Binding RelativeSource=…}`

- Binds to an element in the containment hierarchy of the target element. The source can be an ancestor of the element or its templated parent. Can also be used to bind to `Self`.

Conversion

Binding.StringFormat [SF]

- Use `Binding.StringFormat` for formatting source data for display when the target dependency property is of type string

Converter [C]

- Use `IValueConverter` for single binding source.
- Use `IMultiValueConverter` for multiple binding sources.
- Instantiate in the `Resources` section. Use with `StaticResource`.
- `Convert()` from source to target and `ConvertBack()` for otherwise.
- Use `Binding.ConverterParameter` for parameter to methods.
- If both `[SF]` and `[C]` are used, `[SF]` is applied after `[C]` for target update.

Performance

Async binding

```
{Binding IsAsync="true"}
```

- Causes async value to be updated for slow source property get accessor
- Binding can use `FallbackValue` for the default value of the target `DependencyProperty` until the value becomes available

ObjectDataProvider.IsAsynchronous

- Allows instantiation in worker thread

PriorityBinding

- Allows multiple binding sources for a single target applied in the order of their priority and availability

Index

Symbols

A

B

C

D

E

F

G

N

O

P

R

S

T

U

V

W

X

Thank you for buying

MVVM Survival Guide for Enterprise Architectures in Silverlight and WPF

About Packt Publishing

Packt, pronounced 'packed', published its first book "Mastering phpMyAdmin for Effective MySQL Management" in April 2004 and subsequently continued to specialize in publishing highly focused books on specific technologies and solutions.

Our books and publications share the experiences of your fellow IT professionals in adapting and customizing today's systems, applications, and frameworks. Our solution based books give you the knowledge and power to customize the software and technologies you're using to get the job done. Packt books are more specific and less general than the IT books you have seen in the past. Our unique business model allows us to bring you more focused information, giving you more of what you need to know, and less of what you don't.

Packt is a modern, yet unique publishing company, which focuses on producing quality, cutting-edge books for communities of developers, administrators, and newbies alike. For more information, please visit our website: `www.packtpub.com`.

About Packt Enterprise

In 2010, Packt launched two new brands, Packt Enterprise and Packt Open Source, in order to continue its focus on specialization. This book is part of the Packt Enterprise brand, home to books published on enterprise software – software created by major vendors, including (but not limited to) IBM, Microsoft and Oracle, often for use in other corporations. Its titles will offer information relevant to a range of users of this software, including administrators, developers, architects, and end users.

Writing for Packt

We welcome all inquiries from people who are interested in authoring. Book proposals should be sent to author@packtpub.com. If your book idea is still at an early stage and you would like to discuss it first before writing a formal book proposal, contact us; one of our commissioning editors will get in touch with you.

We're not just looking for published authors; if you have strong technical skills but no writing experience, our experienced editors can help you develop a writing career, or simply get some additional reward for your expertise.

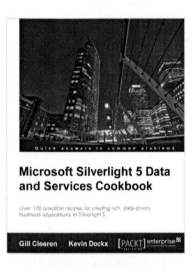

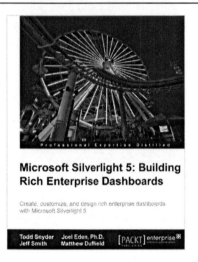